# Free and Open Source Enterprise Resource Planning:

## Systems and Strategies

Rogerio Atem de Carvalho
*Instituto Federal Fluminense, Brazil*

Björn Johansson
*Lund University, Sweden*

| | |
|---|---|
| Managing Director: | Lindsay Johnston |
| Senior Editorial Director: | Heather Probst |
| Book Production Manager: | Sean Woznicki |
| Development Manager: | Joel Gamon |
| Development Editor: | Myla Harty |
| Acquisitions Editor: | Erika Gallagher |
| Typesetter: | Christopher Shearer |
| Print Coordinator: | Jamie Snavely |
| Cover Design: | Nick Newcomer |

Published in the United States of America by
Business Science Reference (an imprint of IGI Global)
701 E. Chocolate Avenue
Hershey PA 17033
Tel: 717-533-8845
Fax: 717-533-8661
E-mail: cust@igi-global.com
Web site: http://www.igi-global.com

Library of Congress Cataloging-in-Publication Data

Free and open source enterprise planning: systems and strategies / Rogerio Atem de Carvalho and Bjorn Johansson, editors.
   p. cm.
Includes bibliographical references and index.
   ISBN 978-1-61350-486-4 (hardcover) -- ISBN 978-1-61350-487-1 (ebook) -- ISBN 978-1-61350-488-8 (print & perpetual access) 1. Management information systems. 2. Business planning. 3. Open source software. 4. Small business--Management. I. Carvalho, Rogerio Atem de. II. Johansson, Bjorn, 1963-
   HD30.213.F74 2012
   658.4'01--dc23
                    2011035561

British Cataloguing in Publication Data
A Cataloguing in Publication record for this book is available from the British Library.

All work contributed to this book is new, previously-unpublished material. The views expressed in this book are those of the authors, but not necessarily of the publisher.

# Table of Contents

# Detailed Table of Contents

**Chapter 1**
*Rogerio Atem de Carvalho, Instituto Federal Fluminense, Brazil*
*Björn Johansson, Lund University, Sweden*

This chapter introduces basic differences between Free/Open Source Enterprise Resources Planning systems (FOS-ERP) and Proprietary ERP (P-ERP), revisiting the previous work of Carvalho (2008). Taking into account that some years has passed and the economic downturn came, it updates key aspects of FOS-ERP under both vendor and adopter perspectives. Like its predecessor, this chapter contributes to broaden the discussion around FOS-ERP, showing that its differences from its proprietary counterpart go beyond the cost factor.

**Chapter 2**
*Marcelo Monsores, Federal University of the Rio de Janeiro State, Brazil*
*Asterio Tanaka, Federal University of the Rio de Janeiro State, Brazil*

With the growing complexity and dynamics of modern organizations, ERP systems contribute to the management of business processes and allow strategic decisions to be taken more quickly and more safely, through a systemic, integrated view of the corporation. Free/Open Source software has consolidated as an increasingly viable alternative for this kind of systems, through the flexibility provided by its business and development model and the consequent possibility of total cost reduction. The objective of this chapter is to present a comparative survey of the main free/open source ERP systems currently available in the marketplace, their features focused in Brazilian companies and a general overview on its potential market.

**Chapter 3**
*Nasimul Huq, Jönköping University, Sweden*
*Syed Mushtaq Ali Shah, Jönköping University, Sweden*
*Daniela Mihailescu, Jönköping University, Sweden*

This chapter introduces the key factors that motivate Small and Medium Sized Enterprises (SMEs) to select Open Source ERP (OS ERP) over the proprietary ERP. The chapter starts with the related previous research works by stating the basic concepts of OS ERP selection. The goal of this chapter is to empirically identify the most important factors that may motivate the Small and Medium Sized Enterprises (SMEs) to select this category of enterprise systems. Therefore this chapter proposes a Theoretical Model for Open Source ERP selection by SMEs and later on conducts an empirical study based on that theoretical model. The chapter tries to broaden the discussion around the important selection factors by including the perspective of the suppliers along with the perspective of OS ERP implementer SMEs.

*Carmen de Pablos Heredero, Rey Juan Carlos University, Spain*
*David López Berzosa, IE Business School, Spain*
*Andres Seco, Caja Guadalajara, Spain*

Caja Guadalajara has succeeded in the migration from privative to open source systems. In this book chapter we describe the process of open source software implementation in Caja Guadalajara and the main motives for the success achieved. The case we present can mean an inspiration for the implementation of further open source ERP systems in this company of other ones. The size of the company, the absence of organizational conflicts, the clearness of objectives on information and communication technology possibilities, the training and knowledge in private and open source possibilities, the belief and motivation towards open source solutions and the trust of the top management on the technical areas have become relevant factors for achieving success in this project.

*Swanand J. Deodhar, Management Development Institute, India*
*Kulbhushan C. Saxena, Management Development Institute, India*
*Rajen Gupta, Management Development Institute, India*
*Mikko Ruohonen, University of Tampere, Finland*

Open source approach to software development has been used to develop the so-called 'horizontal infrastructure' software such as databases and application servers. However, there is an increasing acceptance of open source approach for developing business applications like enterprise resource planning (ERP) software. Indeed, organizations are building business models around ERP and similar business application developed using open source. In this chapter, we analyze the business model of one such open source ERP and explain increasing importance of software licensing and partner networks in FOS-ERP business models.

*Torben Tambo, Aarhus University, Denmark*
*Christian Koch, Aarhus University, Denmark*

With the proliferation of commercial Packaged ERP (P-ERP) systems in today's enterprises, many reasons exist to look for alternatives in the quest for innovation, business development, cost, agility and dependency. P-ERP provides a solid and proven business support, an ecosystem of consultancies and integrators, senior management having gained confidence over the last 20 years, and commercially based support and development. This leaves companies with still more expensive P-ERP costs, still less flexibility, a still harder push to lose possibilities for differentiation, still more homogenised business processes, and absence of flexibility to change suppliers and systems. FOS-ERP offers an answer to most of these questions, but is facing issues in market penetration. In this chapter, barriers of FOS-ERP are reviewed; proposals are made on how to manage barriers. An approach managing co-existence of P-ERP and FOS-ERP is suggested. Concluding, FOS-ERP is seen as a strong option for enterprises in the future, but a clear understanding and distinction must be the offset, barriers needs to be managed, and optimal co-existence will in most cases be the realistic scenario.

Whilst there are numerous benefits for a business from procuring a ERP on the basis of FOS licensing terms, there are a number of legal risks which need to be considered. These legal risks include: (a) assuming all FOS licences are the same; (b) uncertainty as to the enforceability of FOS licences; (c) lack of clarity in relation to the legal characterisation of FOS licences; (d) risk of poor performance; (e) risk of IPR infringement claim; (f) issues arsing from reciprocity; (g) legal challenges to FOS licences; and (h) the issues arising from the missing contractual provisions. The chapter outlines these legal risks and provides recommendations as to how to mange such risks.

# Chapter 8

Free/Open Source software (FOSS) has made Enterprise Resource Planning (ERP) systems more accessible for Small and Medium Enterprises (SMEs) including overseas subsidiaries of large companies. However, the consulting required to configure an ERP to meet the specific needs of an organization remains a major financial and organizational burden for SMEs. Automatic ERP package configuration based on knowledge engineering, machine learning and data mining could be a solution to lessen the burden of the implementation process. This chapter presents two approaches to an automation of selected configuration options of the FOS-ERP package ERP5. These approaches are based on knowledge engineering with decision trees and machine learning with classifiers. The design of the ERP5 Artificial intelligence Toolkit (EAT) aims at the integration of these approaches into ERP5. The chapter also shows how FOS-ERP can boost Information System (IS) research. The investigation of the automation approaches was only possible because the free source code and technical documentation of ERP5 was accessible for TU Dresden researchers.

# Chapter 9

Free/Open Source Enterprise Resource Planning (FOS-ERP) software is an emerging phenomenon having the potential to revolutionize the ERP market worldwide. This chapter focuses on the FOS-ERP market for Small and Medium-sized Enterprises (SMEs) and aims at informing managers, scholars, students and researchers of the opportunities and the related risks for SMEs wishing to adopt and implement a FOS-ERP solution. It is widely accepted that SMEs, which have limited capital and other resources, are among the organizations to be benefited by the existence of FOS-ERP by acquiring a system similar to that used by large enterprises. At the same time there are certain risks in adopting a FOS-ERP solution such as security issues and hidden costs. Guidelines for SMEs to eliminate these risks are provided. In order to define the backdrop of FOS-ERP systems, Web 2.0, cloud computing and Open Source Software (OSS) are also discussed.

## Chapter 10

*Kris Ven, University of Antwerp, Belgium*
*Dieter Van Nuffel, University of Antwerp, Belgium*

Notwithstanding the increasing interest in open source ERP (OS-ERP) products in the past few years, their adoption by Belgian organizations is still very limited. To gain more insight into this phenomenon, we performed an exploratory investigation of which barriers inhibit the adoption of OS-ERP by Belgian SMEs. Based upon our previous research, we identified two main barriers, namely a lack of functionality and a lack of support. Next, we performed a screening of the Belgian OS-ERP market to investigate the functionality and support offered by various OS-ERP products. This allowed us to determine how the perceptions of organizations compare to the actual market for OS-ERP in Belgium. Our results provide more insight into the barriers to the adoption of OS-ERP by Belgian SMEs and provide various avenues for future research.

## Chapter 11

*Mirjana Stojanovic, University of Belgrade, Serbia*
*Vladanka Acimovic-Raspopovic, University of Belgrade, Serbia*
*Slavica Bostjancic Rakas, University of Belgrade, Serbia*

This chapter aims to provide a critical evaluation of security issues and potential solutions related to the use of free and open enterprise resource planning (FOS ERP) systems in highly dynamic and heterogeneous next generation networks (NGN). We first present a brief state of the art with respect to technologies, features and applicability of the existing security solutions for ERP systems. Second, we address security issues in FOS ERP systems. Further, we consider research directions concerning NGN infrastructure security, with a particular focus to the importance of building advanced security management systems. Properly defined service level agreement between the customer and the provider represents a starting point for provisioning of secure services with the required quality. We also propose policy-based security management architecture, in a wider context of quality of service management system.

# Preface

## INTRODUCTION

Enterprise information systems are designed to integrate all of an organization's information system computing. They increase the speed with which information flows through a company. They can lead to reduced inventories, shortened cycle times, lower costs, and improved supply chain management practices. Enterprise information systems:

- create value through integrating networks across a firm or firms (Metcalfe's Law),
- implement of best practices for each business process,
- standardize processes within organizations,
- provide one-source data resulting in less confusion and error, and
- can give on-line access to information.

All of these features facilitate better organizational planning, communication, and collaboration.

The enterprise system market has seen a great deal of evolution in the 21$^{st}$ Century. We have seen a great deal of change in this market, as Oracle has acquired PeopleSoft and J.D. Edwards, and BAAN has been acquired by another software firm. SAP and Oracle continue to dominate the high end of the lucrative enterprise system market, joined by Microsoft. While SAP claims in its television ads that it also serves small businesses, Microsoft has made great inroads in the enterprise system market by offering its products to medium enterprises that are more affordable than the prices needed for SAP or Oracle.

## OPEN SOURCE SOFTWARE

OSS has become a viable means of software creation. Sun Microsystems long viewed OSS as a means to develop long-range market strength (Babcock, 2009), although this effort was insufficient to avoid short-term takeover by Oracle. Other firms, however, have been able to make OSS work, to include Dell computers (Conry-Murray, 2009).

Open source technology makes possible cooperative development of information technology tools, in turn making it possible to use small bits of functionality developed by others and tested by the market rather than having to develop everything yourself. With OSS, developers and users are free to utilize and modify OSS by accessing open code. Web 2.0 provides a cooperative development environment allowing widespread participation. Products such as the Web server Apache, the database query engine MySQL, and the cash management system GNU Cash have been highly successful (Jaisingh et al., 2008-9). Hossain and Zhu (2009) attribute open source software development as being faster and more responsive, leading to more robust and secure software. Open source products have been developed for financial applications (Kane and Masters, 2009), marketing applications (Fleisher, 2008), and many other fields.

While products in the Free Open Source Enterprise Resource Planning (FOS-ERP) domain are developed by proprietary firms, there is a related open source ERP business model for distribution.

## Open Source ERP

There is a demand for less expensive systems by many organizations. Hauge et al. (2006) cited evidence that few SMEs in Eastern Europe have implemented ERP systems, due to lack of needed financial and human resources. Recently, ERP vendors have realized that open source systems (OSS) have robust capabilities, both as a source of content for vendors as well as a threat to the proprietary enterprise system market share from competitors based on OSS development or delivery (Grewal et al., 2006). Open source ERP systems are used by firms such as Home Depot, Toyota, and Fidelity (Weber, 2005). Web delivery has been selected as a means to distribute a number of interesting enterprise system software, led by Compiere and Nexedi from France. Compiere (and many similar products) are open in the sense that they are downloadable for free. The business model is based on collecting fees for service and support.

Olsen and Saetre (2007) reported that in-house development of ERP was feasible and cost effective due to the availability of modern development tools. Open source ERP products can provide similar flexibility, and we would expect that to be at even lower cost. Three potential benefits in using OSS ERPs are increased adaptability, decreased reliance on a single supplier, and reduced costs.

## ERP Support to Small Organizations

Open source ERP systems have appeared as a viable alternative for small businesses. The business driver has been lower costs, but the ability to customize has also been important. Barriers to successful implementation include database migration, synchronization of software to company workflow, developing user interfaces and user support, and integrating third-party software. This volume provides valuable insights into the potential and risks involved in FOS-ERP.

## VOLUME CONTENTS

The volume is opened by Carvalho and Johansson with a discussion of what is different about Free/ Open Source (FOS-ERP) and Proprietary ERP systems. They emphasize the cost benefits of FOS-ERP, comparing that with what they offer their adopters. Balancing this cost advantage are issues in specific software business model evaluation, software selection, customization, and maintenance. Challenges and opportunities are discussed. There are different ways in which a small organization can adopt an ERP. Offering a product in the FOS-ERP market is relatively easy, but that creates a dynamic market with easy entry for new competitors. Furthermore, lower cost comes with lower service levels. Carvalho and Johansson cite new developments in the form of improved training materials in the FOS-ERP industry, as well as a changing market where Proprietary ERP vendors have responded by offering cheaper versions of their software in software-as-a-service mode. The need for certification and consulting processes to match the quality of Proprietary ERP vendor networks was raised. This chapter provides a strong basis to describe the field of FOS-ERP.

Monsores and Tanaka survey the primary FOS-ERP systems available on the market, focusing on Brazil. A survey of SourceForge.net was the basis for this research. They draw upon their prior research to establish that FOS-ERP projects are maturing, and that there has been a significant increase in such projects in 2010 over 2009. Monsores and Tanaka also reviewed seven FOS-ERP projects (Adempiere, Openbravo, PostBooks, WebERP, Compiere, OFBiz, and ERP5) based on SourceForge.net as well as information gathered from vendor Web sites. Each system was qualitatively evaluated, concluding with report of market presence in Brazil. Their analysis concludes that FOS-ERP has a very promising market in that rapidly growing economy.

Huq, Shah and Mihailescu evaluate key factors motivating small organizations to adopt FOS-ERP. Reported reasons for ERP system selection were reviewed, along with critical success factors. Huq et al. then develop a theoretical framework based upon results from a purposive sample of nine international small business ERP installations and one organization classified as of medium size. The sample was generated from a list of FOS-ERP users, querying them concerning motivations for their selection decision. Ten consultants and vendors were also sampled on the same questions. Differences in rankings were analyzed, along with expert judgment (obtained from one of the editors of this volume). The article is a source of factors that were found to be most important in FOS-ERP adoption by small businesses.

Heredero, Berzosa and Seco give a case description of FOS-ERP implementation for a Spanish financial company. The processes of selection and implementation were described with the intent of demonstrating decision making processes, inferring critical success factors, and identifying relative advantages obtained from FOS-ERP. The characteristics of successful implementation project leadership were inferred based upon the experience. A specific technical factor found to be critical to success was the importance of software testers.

Deodhar, Saxena, Gupta and Ruohonen analyze business models of open source ERP, emphasizing the importance of software licensing and partner networks. Business models are defined in terms of product strategy, revenue logic, distribution model, and delivery of maintenance and service. Concepts are demonstrated through a case of implementation of an OpenBravo ERP system in Spain. The approach these authors give emphasizes viewing FOS-ERP benefits and risks from both vendor and user perspectives.

Tambo and Koch review the expenses involved in proprietorial ERP systems. FOS-ERP offers a way to obtain needed computing system support at lower costs. But barriers to FOS-ERP adoption exist. These barriers are reviewed through desk study, and means of managing them outlined. The potential of software-as-a-service and other rapid developments in the ERP market give FOS-ERP relative advantages over proprietary ERP. But while there are cost advantages, risks are more uncertain. Tambo and Koch emphasize the need to view FOS-ERP adoption as risk taking, balancing opportunities with threats.

De Silva examine legal risks of FOS-ERP with respect to England and Wales. The developing nature of this legal domain was recognized. The need for licensing was argued, and copyright restrictions listed. Twenty open source licensing systems were measured by popularity. Risks included enforceability and the distinction between copyright and contract. Key legal challenges to date were reviewed.

Wölfel and Smets discuss the role of consulting support available to aid small and medium enterprises (SMEs) in selecting FOS-ERP. Smets is associated with Nexedi, the provider of ERP5, and thus this chapter gives valuable advice concerning tailoring FOS-ERP. The research questions addressed are: (1) which tailoring options are most suitable for automation in general, and specifically for ERP5; and (2)

How can ERP5 tailoring options be automated? A design science paradigm consisting of expert interviews, desk research, and an example was used to answer these questions. The development of ERP5 was reviewed, with a presentation of tailoring options. The problem of automatic system configuration (tailoring) was discussed from the perspectives of knowledge engineering and artificial intelligence. The ERP5 AI Toolkit was described. Wölfel and Smets show how ERP5 category configuration can be automated. Prototypes and initial validations were found to be promising, yielding decision trees that worked well. Further research needed for more complex configurations was outlined.

Stefanou provides a chapter elaborating on opportunities and risks for smaller organizations in adopting FOS-ERP. Because they have revolutionized the way in which business software is developed and distributed, Web 2.0, cloud computing, and open source software are reviewed to frame these opportunities and risks. The primary risks considered are security and hidden costs. Stefanou offers guidelines to eliminate such risks. He also reviews small organization characteristics favorable to either FOS-ERP or Proprietary ERP. Given the importance of risk management in today's world, this chapter is a very good source for potential adopters in their initial evaluation of FOS-ERP.

Ven and Van Nuffel describe adoption of an open source ERP in Belgium. Barriers to adoption identified from prior research included lack of functionality and lack of support. Literature reporting ERP selection criteria of SMEs was reviewed, as were specific criteria used by Belgian SMEs. Ven and Van Nuffel went to SourceForge.net and Freshmeat.net to obtain information about open source ERP adoption in Belgium. Functionality of 36 open source ERP products was compared. Ven and Van Nuffel then selected ten of these products (those demonstrating the most comprehensive functionality) and analyzed the network of consultant support available for each, categorized by areas of Belgium, its neighbors, the European Union, and the world. The study concluded that lack of open source ERP functionality is not an issue, but that lack of support continues to be a problem.

Stojanovic, Acimovic-Raspopovic and Bostjancic Rakas focused on the issue of security in FOS-ERP. FOS-ERP system security can be vulnerable to external threats. The state of current technology was reviewed, along with a listing of security issues. Means to secure network infrastructure are given. These authors identified properly defined service level agreements as a starting point to assure required security, and proposed a security management architecture to fit within a service management quality system. This chapter gives excellent advice in designing a more secure FOS-ERP.

## THE POTENTIAL FOR OSS ERP

As demonstrated by the chapters in this volume, many ERP products have been developed to serve smaller organizations (Business, non-profit, government). The open source approach can be applied to any type of product development. However, since the code is freely distributed, the business model is complicated. Revenues can be generated through a variety of strategies, to include sale of complementary products and services.

This volume brings together an outstanding selection of papers describing FOS-ERP, comparing differences with proprietorial ERP products, and demonstrating key research factors. It includes cases demonstrating how small enterprises have benefited from FOS-ERP in Spain and in Belgium, along with difficulties encountered and solutions developed. It addresses key issues such as security and legal risks. There are excellent discussions of challenges and opportunities, along with barriers to adoption.

This edited edition should serve as an excellent resource to researchers in the field of enterprise information systems.

*David L. Olson*
*University of Nebraska, USA*

## REFERENCES

Babcock, C. (2009) Open source will pay dividends in the cloud, *informationweek.com*, 30 March, p. 18.

Conry-Murray, A. (2009) Can enterprise social networking pay off? *Informationweek.com*, 23 March, pp. 23-29.

Fleisher, C. S. (2008). Using open source data in developing competitive and marketing intelligence. *European Journal of Marketing, 42*(7/8), 852–866. doi:10.1108/03090560810877196

Grewal, R., Lilien, G. L., & Mallapragada, G. (2006). Location, location, location: How network embeddedness affects project success in open source systems. *Management Science, 52*(7), 1043–1056. doi:10.1287/mnsc.1060.0550

Hauge, J. B., Imtiaz, A., Auerbach, M., Eschenbächer, J., & Seifert, M. (2006) Enhancements in performance through virtual collaboration among SMEs: Potentials, needs, and research challenges, *IFIP International Federation for Information Processing, Vol. 224, Network-Centric Collaboration and Supporting Frameworks*, eds. Camarinha-Matos, L., Afsarmanesh, H., Ollus, M. (Boston: Springer) pp. 255-264.

Hossain, L., & Zhu, D. (2009). Social networks and coordination performance of distributed software development teams. *The Journal of High Technology Management Research, 20*, 52–61. doi:10.1016/j.hitech.2009.02.007

Jaisingh, J., See-To, E. W. K., & Tam, K. Y. (2008/9) The impact of open source software on the strategic choices of firms developing proprietary software. *Journal of Management Information Systems, 25*(3), 241–275. doi:10.2753/MIS0742-1222250307

Kane, D., & Masters, J. D. (2009). Open source finance. *Journal of Investing, 18*(1), 92–96. doi:10.3905/JOI.2009.18.1.092

Olsen, K. A., & Saetre, P. (2007). ERP for SMEs – Is proprietary software an alternative? *Business Process Management Journal, 13*(3), 379–389. doi:10.1108/14637150710752290

Weber, S. (2005). *The Success of Open Source*. Cambridge, MA: Harvard University Press.

# Chapter 1
# Key Aspects of Free and Open Source Enterprise Resource Planning Systems

**Rogerio Atem de Carvalho**
*Instituto Federal Fluminense, Brazil*

**Björn Johansson**
*Lund University, Sweden*

## ABSTRACT

*This chapter introduces basic differences between Free/Open Source Enterprise Resources Planning systems (FOS-ERP) and Proprietary ERP (P-ERP), revisiting the previous work of Carvalho (2008). Taking into account that some years has passed and the economic downturn came, it updates key aspects of FOS-ERP under both vendor and adopter perspectives. Like its predecessor, this chapter contributes to broaden the discussion around FOS-ERP, showing that its differences from its proprietary counterpart go beyond the cost factor.*

## INTRODUCTION

Enterprise resource planning (ERPs) systems experienced an implementation peak during the pre- and post-Y2K periods, when most of the high-end adopters take their chance of substituting legacy systems implementing integrated management, in search for achieving competitive edge in their business areas (Church, 2008;

DOI: 10.4018/978-1-61350-486-4.ch001

Hendricks, Singhal & Stratman, 2007). After that period, the ERP market segment started to saturate and major ERP vendors started to seek for new business opportunities, in special towards small and medium-sized enterprises (SMEs) (Kim & Boldyreff, 2005).

At the same time it is also the case that Free/ Open Source[1] ERP (FOS-ERP) systems are gaining a growing acceptance and consequently improving their market share. In a market study, LeClaire (2006) reported that FOS-ERP related services were expected to hit about US$ 36 billion by 2008. If on one hand this is still unclear, given the difficulties of evaluating a market where many deployments are of a do-it-yourself fashion, or done by small consultancy companies, other effects can now be reported.

Robb (2011), states that FOS-ERP, together with the economic downturn is currently putting a pressure on P-ERP licenses, given that an "One IDC survey found high usage of open source enterprise applications; 9 percent of respondents already had an open source back office application deployed, while 7 percent of respondents were running an open source CRM application." In a market where big players hold approximately 10 percent of market share the open source phenomena is certainly helping to put P-ERP prices down, in special on the Small and Medium Enterprise segment. Robb (2011) goes further, affirming that open source "is the vanguard of a new wave of innovation. Consequently, many companies are looking for next-generation ERP solutions that have new capabilities and are easy to use and deploy.", confirming the key innovative aspect of FOS-ERP highlighted by Carvalho (2008). The reason for that is that most mature FOS-ERP projects, such as Compiere and ERP5, are less than one decade and a half old, meaning that they are based on more recent technologies and therefore don't need to provide backward compatibility to the old ones.

A controversial point is the way SME are adopting ERP. While Robb (2011), Carvalho and Johansson (2010), and Kimberling (2010) states that they tend to use Software as a Service (SaaS) solutions, in Harmon's (2010) opinion, SME "are not ramping SaaS as fast as large enterprises and are taking greater advantage of open source software." Apparently, besides the vendor lock-in problem, many SME are reporting that SaaS fees tend to rise after the first year of use (Lilly, 2010). Maybe the solution for this problem lives on business models such as the one used by the FOS-ERP ERP5 "Tio Live" version: it is a SaaS

solution that is free for basic use (inventory control, sales, human resources, CRM etc). If the adopter needs customization and/or personalized support, it has to pay, however, at any moment, the contract can be resigned, and the adopter organization can download all its code and data. Whether other FOS-ERP will follow this model is still an open question.

Given this increase on FOS-ERP importance, this chapter will highlight differences between FOS-ERP and P-ERP in terms of business models, selection, customization and maintenance, and identify the challenges and opportunities that they offer to stakeholders and developer communities.

## WHAT IS KNOWN ABOUT FOS-ERP

The fact that only a small percentage of academic papers treat FOS-ERP specifically, as stated by Carvalho (2008) and Carvalho (2006), is still a reality. Although simply searching Google Scholar[2] cannot be considered as strict "scientific" results, the relation is that only approximately 0,7% of articles on ERP refer specifically to the term "open source ERP", when searching for articles published from 2009 onwards. By comparing this number with the ones presented by Robb (2011) and refered in the previous topic, a rough approximation if 10 to 1 can be found between the adoption level and the treatment by academics.

Again, these findings are not a result of a strict method for counting hits, however, it gives a notion of the distance between the practice and the research on FOS-ERP. A possible reason for this can also be the fact that FOS-ERP is a recent phenomena[3], and therefore deployments of this type of enterprise software are also recent, thus hardening the obtainment of data on them. This seems to be confirmed by doing the same search on IEEE and ACM digital libraries, which returns a dozen articles dealing specifically with this subject[4].

In other words, we can still say that "research on FOS-ERP software is rather deficient, and, therefore, a series of relevant aspects of FOS-ERP, which differentiate them from P-ERP, are still not well understood." (Carvalho, 2008). These facts show how FOS-ERP is a young research area, with relatively little academic effort put on it until now.

However, some good work on related topics, which can be related to FOS-ERP can be found. An in-depth analysis of economic impact of Free/Open Source Software (FOSS) in enterprise systems is reported by Dreiling et al. (2005), with findings that are still actual. They argue that "standards that supposedly open development by ensuring interoperability tend to be interpreted by enterprise systems global players according to their interest". The authors follow this reasoning showing the deeper consequences of this: "[global players interests] might be incongruent with the interests of the software industry at large, those of users organizations, and may also have effects on local and national economies." And more: "despite control of interfaces and standards by few software developers, even integration of the information infrastructure of one single company with one brand of enterprise system cannot be consolidated over time [citing many other authors]." On the open standards subject, they conclude, "software engineering principles and open standards are necessary but not sufficient condition for enterprise software development becoming less constrained by the politics of global players, responsive to user interests, and for ensuring a healthy software industry that can cater for regional market."

On the innovation side, Dreiling et al. (2005) state that many economists agree to the point of dominant companies – like the ERP global players – are less disposed to respond to articulated customer requirements, and monopolies as well oligopolies tend to stifle product and service innovation. Furthermore, "controlling architectures by means of proprietary software and open standards in the enterprise application industry appears to actually preclude innovation that could be of

benefit for many users of enterprise systems", which includes less developed economies. On the other hand, it is important to remark that the small number of suppliers for mature FOS-ERP can maybe reduce the vendor lock-in advantage.

If on one hand FOS-ERP can foster innovation and give more power to adopters, on the other some important questions are yet to be answered, given that this type of FOSS is still considered a newcomer to the enterprise systems landscape. Even some enthusiasts recognize that FOS-ERP vendors service level have much to improve and gain experience, while in contrast, P-ERP have a mature network of consulting partners and a long history of success and failures (Serrano & Sarrieri, 2006). In fact, evaluating FOS-ERP for adoption is a matter that still needs more attention. In that direction, Herzog (2006) presents a very comprehensive approach that identifies three different methods for implementing a FOS-ERP solution – select a package, develop one by itself, and integrate best of breed solutions – and five criteria for evaluating alternatives: functional fit, flexibility, support, continuity, and maturity. This method introduces the interesting theoretical possibility of integrating solutions from different vendors through Enterprise Application Integration (EAI) techniques. Although a successful case study on mixing P-ERP solutions is described by Alshawi et al. (2004), the literature lacks examples on doing the same with FOS-ERP.

Also in the FOS-ERP evaluation arena, De Carvalho (2006) presents the PIRCS method, which holds some similarity with Herzog's[5], however stressing more on risk evaluation, by recognizing the strategic nature of ERP. In fact, according to Caulliraux et al. (2000) ERP is strategic, given that "it is a major commitment of money, and thus with long range implications even if only from a financial point of view", and ERP systems are also important not only as a tangible asset, but "as a catalyst through their implementation in the formation of intangible assets and the company's self-knowledge." Aiming to include risk considerations, the PIRCS method seeks to identify weaknesses in the FOS-ERP's development environment during its evaluation process phases. These phases name the process, and are summarized as Prepare the evaluation process, Identify the alternatives, Rate alternatives' attributes, Compare alternatives' results, and Select the one that best fits the adopter needs.

Many other subjects related to open software in general that affect FOS-ERP could be addressed to better understand their dynamics. Crowston and Howison (2006) assess the health of Open Source communities as a way of helping checking if an FOSS is suitable for the adopter or contributor needs – this kind of assessment can be one of the tools to check a specific FOS-ERP project maturity. Assessing FOS-ERP communities means understanding other organizations' behavior towards the project: since ERP in general are not for individual use, contributors most of times are companies' employees, not free-lancers. Hence, to understand the differences between this and other types of open software, it is necessary to understand how commercially sponsored and community built FOSS projects behave. According to West and O'Mahony (2005), one of the key moments of commercial FOSS is the start-up phase: when the project code is opened, "an infant community is presented with a large complex system that may be harder to decipher", thus the FOS-ERP creator may have to wait until contributions from other firms become viable and also advantageous - the main economic incentive for firm participation is the emancipation from the price and license conditions imposed by large software companies (Wang and Chen, 2005), but the potential for doing such substitution must be only latent in the project. The same type of incentive is identified by Riehle (2007), who states that solution providers can take advantage from open source software "because they increase profits through direct costs savings and the ability to reach more customers through improved pricing flexibility". Other aspect on

the vendor side identified by these authors is that opening the code can reduce the costs on software testing as well as research and development tasks. Bruce, Robson, and Spaven (2006) describe the usage of open source in business applications as the third wave of open source adoption. The first wave being the adoption of open source as operating systems, the second wave adoption of open source as infrastructure systems (middleware, browsers, and databases). Furthermore, Goth (2005) affirms that the open software market is on the "third wave" towards enterprise software, and that FOSS business models are finally ready for facing this new market challenge. These two last references points to a general improvement on the relation between FOSS communities and enterprise systems users.

Despite the differences, FOS-ERP and P-ERP certainly have one thing in common: both have a company behind their deployment activities. Although there exists FOS-ERP maintained almost solely by communities formed basically by individuals, it seems that only company-sponsored FOS-ERP, such as Compiere, ERP5, OpenMFG, and SQL Ledger, are really successful. In other words, FOS-ERP are typically of the *commercial open source* kind, which "a for-profit entity owns and develops", according to Riehle (2007) classification. The next sections show how FOS-ERP differs from P-ERP, present opportunities and challenges that this kind of software offer to developers and adopters, and finally drawn some conclusions on the subject.

## DIFFERENCES BETWEEN FOS-ERP AND P-ERP

The exposition of code promoted by FOS-ERP forces vendors and adopters processes to accommodate the fact that customization and maintenance can be done by other organization than the vendor. This fact means that the adopter is free to choose the participation level of the vendor in the different phases of the ERP life cycle – meaning that, to some extent, vendor participation can be also customized.

Therefore, it is interesting to introduce the concept of *adopter positioning* in relation to the FOS-ERP customization and development. The adopter can behave as a simple *consumer*, only getting the solution from the vendor, or become a *prosumer* (Xu, 2003), by mixing passively purchasing commodity parts of the system with actively developing or customizing strategic ones by itself. Of course, choosing how to behave is not a simple decision in these cases, since it involves a series of demands like expertise on the FOS-ERP platform and architecture, dealing with the developer community – which can mean managing demands of disparate stakeholders (West & O'Mahony, 2005), and allocating resources for development. It is a question of weighting the direct and indirect gains of developing parts of the system with the shortcomings of doing so.

In spite of the adopter positioning, analyzing differences between open source and proprietary ERP has to be done from the perspective of from what side of the commercial relation the organization resides. In other words if the ones involved is an adopter or a vendor, therefore this section discuss differences for adopters and for vendors, respectively.

## Differences for Adopters

Selecting an ERP for adoption is a complex process, because, besides the size of the task, it is an important enterprise component that impacts the adopter organization in financial and in self-knowledge terms. Therefore, it is important to use a framework to understand how open source alternatives can impact this kind of project.

The Generalized Enterprise Reference Architecture and Methodology (GERAM) is a well-known standard that provides a description of all elements recommended in enterprise engineering

and a collection of tools and methods to perform enterprise design and change with success (IFIP – IFAC, 1999), providing a template life cycle to analyze FOS-ERP selection, deployment, and evolution. GERAM defines seven life-cycle phases for any enterprise entity that are pertinent during its life. These phases, presented on Figure 1, can be summarized as follows:

a.  Identification: identifies the particular enterprise entity in terms of its domain and environment.
b.  Concept: conceptualizes an entity's mission, vision, values, strategies, and objectives.
c.  Requirements: comprise a set of human, process, and technology oriented aspects and activities needed to describe the operational requirements of the enterprise.
d.  Design: models the enterprise entity and helps to understand the system functionalities.
e.  Implementation: the design is transformed into real components. After tested and approved the system is released into operation.
f.  Operation: is the actual use of the system, and includes user feedback that can drive to a new entity life cycle.

*Figure 1. GERAM life cycle phases. The design phase is subdivided into preliminary and detailed design.*

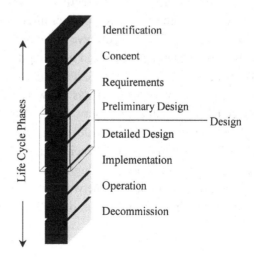

g. Decommission: represents the disposal of parts of the whole entity, after its successful use.

Except for *decommission* and *identification*, which are not influenced by licensing models, these phases can be used to better understand how FOS-ERP differs from P-ERP, providing key aspects for evaluating alternatives and successively refining objectives, requirements and models, as next subsections address.

## Concept

During this phase, high-level objectives are established, such as the acquisition strategy, preliminary time and cost baselines, and the expected impact of ERP adoption. In the case of FOS-ERP, the level of involvement of the adopter in development can be established. In other words, at this point the adopter can start considering the possibility of actively contributing to an open source project, becoming a *prosumer*. Of course, this decision will be possible only during the more advanced phases, when the adopter better knows the solution requisites and the decision alternatives.

For P-ERP, the involvement comes in another shape, since they are often delivered under a partnership model (Johansson & Newman, 2010). This means that the adopters are not directly involved in customization tasks, but indirectly involved by cooperation with the specific partner hired to deploy the system. Therefore, the level of involvement is limited to choose between adopting the "old" partnership model, such as SAP/R3, and the "new" way of delivering P-ERPs as software as a service (SaaS), such as Workday. In the SaaS model the adopter engagement in development of the P-ERP is lower than in the partnership model, since the partnership model to a higher extent is built through closer cooperation between adopters and partners during the adjustment of the ERP.

## Requirements and Preliminary Design

Taking as a principle that most software development (and customization) today is done through interactive and incremental life cycles, it can be considered that there is no clear borderline between the requirements and preliminary design phases and between the detailed design and implementation phases, thus they are considered together in this analysis.

The requirements phase deals with system's functional and non-functional requirements. The adopter may model some business processes – part of the Preliminary Design – as a way to check how the alternatives fit to them. At this point FOS-ERP starts to differ more from P-ERP. Evaluating P-ERP involves comparing alternatives under the light of functionality, Total Cost of Ownership (TCO), and technological criteria. For FOS-ERP these criteria and others related specifically to FOSS in general, such as the maturity level of the project, its survivability, and its partner network strength, must be taken into account – remembering that even if the implementation represents a smaller financial impact, in terms of a company's self-knowledge it can assume a much bigger importance, since it holds not only a inventory of records and procedures, but also how those records and procedures are realized in technological form – through source code (Carvalho, 2007).

At this point the core matter of the so-called "best practice" becomes more visible. A best practice can be defined as the most efficient and effective way of accomplishing a given business process, based on repeatable procedures that have proven themselves over time for large numbers of organizations. However, given that organizations differ from each other, adopters first need to find the solution that fits better to their business, and then either reconfigure existing business processes or reconfigure the software, so that the software and the business processes fits each other. In the case of P-ERP, best practices are built on top of many years of experience of the global players, making these practices well tested and experimented, allowing a safer implementation on the adopter side. On the other hand, if FOS-ERP, being relatively younger software projects, offer less experimented practices, an adopter can use the ones based on standardized procedures - such as payroll - as is and for free; and then expend its resources on adapting solutions related to more strategic tasks. This adaptation can be done by the adopter – demanding more knowledge on the solution, or by someone from the FOS-ERP partner network, like in P-ERP.

From this standpoint, the strategic positioning of an adopter in relation to a FOS-ERP seems to be of greatest importance, given the possibility of deriving competitive advantage from the source code. Therefore, the adopter must decide to behave as a simple consumer, only getting the solution from the vendor, or become a prosumer. Thus it is clear that when an adopter considers FOS-ERP as an alternative, it should also consider developing parts of it to fit its requirements – taking into account that, as said before, this kind of positioning involves allocating managerial and technical resources for development tasks in a FOSS environment.

In other words, a FOS-ERP can have a smaller financial impact but a much bigger knowledge and innovation impact. Although P-ERP are also highly parameterized, and adaptable through APIs and/or dedicated programming languages, the access to the source code in FOS-ERP can drive much better exploration of the ERP's capabilities, thus allowing a better implementation of differentiated solutions (Carvalho, 2008).

However, as stated above, this demands a higher level of knowledge about the ERP's technology and framework, and if adopters do not have this they have to trust on other sources for having that knowledge. This dependency can become a problem since in some countries the number of FOS-ERP experts is limited, possibly raising costs for hiring them.

## Detailed Design and Implementation

The detailed design phase focus on refining models, and is associated with business process modeling and parameter identification and value definition. The implementation phase concentrates on validating, integrating modules, and releasing its modules for initial use.

If adopters decide to participate actively in the selected FOS-ERP project, deeper design decisions are involved, such as creating entire new modules or extending the basic framework. A consequence of assuming a more active role is to invest more human and financial resources for learning the FOS-ERP platform and framework, developing and maintaining parts of it, and managing the relationship with the project community. In that case, customization and maintenance contracts must define responsibilities of each part on the deployment process. For instance, what the vendor should do if the adopter finds a bug in the original code, written by the first, which is being adapted by the second. It could be asked what the priority is that the vendor must follow for correcting this bug. Actually, it could be questioned if the vendor is responsible for correcting that bug, since for this part the adopter decided to take advantage of the solution's free license, therefore exempting vendors' responsibility of the bug.

The adopter has the option of assuming different grades of involvement for each part of the system. For ordinary modules, like payroll, the adopter can let the vendor do the work – or use them *as is*. However, for strategic modules, where the adopter holds competitive advantage in the underlying business processes, it can take an active role from detailed design to implementation and maintenance, to be sure that the business knowledge, or at least the more precious details that keep the competitive advantage, will be kept in the adopter company. In that situation the vendor is limited to act as a kind of advisor to the adopter. One can think that it is possible to keep secrecy on parts of the system by properly contracting a P-ERP vendor, which is true, but the adopter will become dependent of the vendor in a strategic part of the system. Becoming dependent means to wait for other vendor's priorities or pay high fees to become *the* priority when changes are necessary. Even if the P-ERP adopter decides to develop these strategic parts, it will have to deal with licensing costs anyway.

A very interesting point is the openness of parts customized for and sponsored by a specific adopter. Maybe the adopter doesn't want to become a developer at all – which is most likely to happen, but it still wants to keep some tailored parts of the system in secret. In these cases, the vendor must adapt the licensing terms for its solution, so that general openness of the code is guaranteed, while some client-sponsored customized parts can be kept closed[6].

In the P-ERP case, the development of new features takes a different path, usually in the form of add-ons. A solution partner often develops these add-ons for a specific vendor's product, which can be customer specific, but most often can be used by several adopters. If the adopter decides to develop add-ons, it has to consider that it could be problematic in the future when new versions of the core product are released. The case is that software vendors do not take responsibility for that the new version is interoperable with the customers developed and implemented add-ons.

## Operation

During the operation phase the resources of the entity are managed and controlled so as to carry out the processes necessary for the entity to fulfill its mission. Deviations from goals and objectives or feedbacks from the environment may lead to requests for change; therefore during this phase system maintenance and evolution occur. During operation the adopter can decide at any moment, unless contractual clauses hinders, to shift to another vendor or to assume the system's

maintenance by itself. Minor changes can also be conducted by the own adopter or even by community individuals that may help on specific matters.

In the P-ERP case the adopter exchanges independence on the software vendor for a high grade of support, depending on if the adopter chose to sign a service contract or not. The service agreement is nothing that is forced on the adopter, but if the adopter chose that, it has access to a service organization that helps it on software problems. In the case of FOS-ERP, prospective adopters must be aware of the type of FOSS project the ERP is, since in sponsoring terms there are two kinds of free/open source projects, which are the community and the commercially sponsored projects (West & O'Mahony, 2005). In the first case, the adopter will become more or less dependent on voluntarism or in others words, uncertain schedules and priorities. Only the commercially sponsored FOS-ERP normally offers a partner network in a similar mode of P-ERP.

As a conclusive remark on the differences of FOS-ERP on the adopter side, experience has shown that most of the times the adopter will not get involved on customization or even maintenance tasks. Still, FOS-ERP can be a good choice, since it reduces vendor dependency. Moreover, the openness of code on FOS-ERP also makes adapting it to specific needs easier, thus reducing costs in customization and further evolution of the software. In other words, the central points to consider are cost reduction and freedom of choice. Last but not least, as a general rule, FOS-ERP also relies on other open source technologies, such as office suites, databases and operational systems – thus reducing licensing costs on ERP supportive software too.

## Differences for Vendors

The FOS-ERP vendor business models are a consequence of the customer's freedom of choice and of the general open source market characteristics. Like in other types of FOSS, if on one hand vendors benefit from the community improvements and testing work, on the other hand they face the competition of this community when dealing with deployment and maintenance. In fact, as previously shown, even an adopter can become a competitor, at some extent of course. It is important to note that there are three types of vendor: the original system creator, its partners, and free-lance vendors. In the case of partners, a formal, most of times contractual, agreement is set between them and the system creator. This agreement involves some responsibilities to the partner, in special, following creator's deployment practices, communicating new business generated by the system, opening the source code of new and improved parts of the system, and helping in

development tasks managed by the creator. Free-lance vendors are free of these obligations, and as a consequence, have no special treatment by the creator, that expects that the free-lancer at least open the code of its own system improvements, following the general FOSS code of ethics[7].

Following the common reasoning about FOSS pricing, FOS-ERP vendors can take advantage from open source software because, according to Riehle (2007), FOSS "increase profits through direct costs savings and the ability to reach more customers through improved pricing flexibility", as shown on Figure 2.

Figure 2 shows a situation that maybe is more applicable to partners and free-lance vendors of FOS-ERP, that can switch from more expensive proprietary software to less expensive open source

*Figure 2. Sales margins and number of customers. (a) The lower price limit determines the customers the system integrator takes on. (b) Switching from closed source software to open source software can result in more customers and higher profits (Source: Riehle, 2007, with permission).*

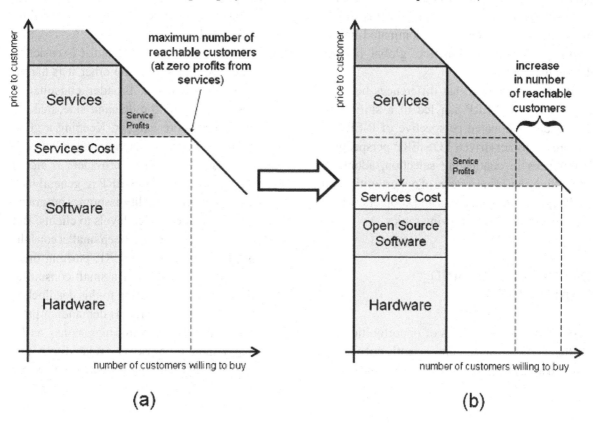

software, thus potentially increasing their profit margin. The creator organization must know how to manage the community around the project, finding prospective partners, hiring individuals that become highly productive on the project whenever possible, and even trying to transform free-lancers into partners. Like their proprietary counterparts, FOS-ERP needs a network of partners that can help on deployment projects where the creator has no conditions to be the main contractor, and finding new markets and customers for the system. However, gathering contributors for starting and keeping a FOS-ERP project can be a hard task. As said before, ERP users are organizations[8], not individuals, and therefore the creator must learn how to attract partner firms that are willing to contribute to the project without becoming competitors. This means that FOS-ERP vendors must work hard to both form a community around the project and to retain customers. This seems to be a big difference between open and proprietary licensing models, since the risk of losing a client after deployment is almost inexistent in the current P-ERP dominated market landscape, where, in practice, global players dictate market rules.

It can be assumed that differences between FOS-ERP and P-ERP can led to a shift from the vendor-dominated perspective of P-ERP to a more customer-driven FOS-ERP perspective. Differences in conducting selection, adoption, and selling also bring a series of opportunities and challenges for both vendors and adopters, which are addressed in the following topics.

## OPPORTUNITIES AND CHALLENGES

FOS-ERP exposes a series of opportunities and challenges for actors that are currently out of, or ill inserted into, the ERP market, as explained below.

## For Smaller Consulting Firms:

a. *Opportunities:* P-ERP vendors generally impose a rigid set of rules for firms that desire to enter their partner network, raising the costs for smaller companies to become players in this market. In contrast, smaller consulting firms can enter the FOS-ERP market in an incremental way, by increasing their commitment to a project as new business opportunities appear and bring more financial income. In other words, firms can start contributing with small improvements to the project as a way of gaining knowledge on the system platform and framework, and, as customers to the solution appears, more money can be invested on a growing commitment to the project. Additionally, with the raising of venture capitalism investment on FOSS startups, a smaller firm can even get financed in a way that would be very unlikely to happen if it worked on top of a P-ERP solution, given the restrictions imposed by the global players.

b. *Challenges*: If on one hand it is easier to enter the market, on the other it is harder to retain clients: a broader consultancy basis empowers the demand side, making customers more exigent. Keeping a good quality level in a heterogeneous network of consulting services providers is also a major challenge. FOS-ERP in general lack certification and quality assurance programs that guarantee service levels to clients. But exactly those programs keep smaller consulting firms way from P-ERP, pushing them towards FOS-ERP. For a small consulting firm, a possible solution to this deadlock is to start with smaller, less demanding projects, and then go towards bigger ones, as the deployment processes and related activities gain maturity. This maturity will become the competitive advantage of the firm on a high competitive FOS-ERP market. Nevertheless,

FOS-ERP skeptics argue that relatively few reliable consulting firms have experience on implementing them.

## For Smaller Adopters:

a. *Opportunities:* lower costs open new opportunities for small firms to become ERP adopters. With globalization, small firms suffer more and more with competition, and when they try to modernize their processes, they hit the wall of global players' high costs, or have to adopt smaller off-the-shelf (and also proprietary) solutions that ties them to a single supplier that normally doesn't have a partner network. In contrast, FOS-ERP is less expensive and support can be found in different ways, including individuals and other firms. This is also true for local governments and countries in development in general. FOS-ERP can reduce costs technological dependency from global players. In fact, FOSS in general is an opportunity for countries in development to shift from buyers to players in the software industry (Ouédraogo, 2005).

b. *Challenges*: lower costs can also mean that adopters have to deal with lower service levels, then stressing the necessity of carefully evaluating FOS-ERP alternatives, in special the maturity of their supportive services. Actually, as said before, consulting certification is yet on the early stages for FOS-ERP, thus quality of service must be carefully addressed during contract negotiation.

## For Researchers:

a. *Opportunities:* One of the authors has been contributing to a FOS-ERP project[9] since its conception. During this time it was possible to know deeply, and sometimes take part of, all the process that compose an ERP solution, from conception and development,

to business models, deployment, operation and maintenance, and evolution. This is a really good opportunity, since most research papers on ERP are related to deployment and operation, given that P-ERP companies do not usually open their projects' internals for outsiders. Smaller research groups can find their way in this area by getting associated with a FOS-ERP project, and contributing to specific parts of it, in the same way smaller companies can do.

b. *Challenges[10]*: If on one hand the openness of FOS-ERP may give researchers more information on their internal features and development processes, on the other hand it is harder to get information from a distributed set of partners that sometimes carry informal agreements. Social and economical aspects, like reward structures, must be taken into account to understand the dynamics of FOS-ERP, like in every FOSS, bringing more components to be analyzed.

## For Individuals

a. *Opportunities:* FOS-ERP represent an unique opportunity for an individual to install an ERP framework and understand its internals. It is the chance of participating in a big software development project without being an employee of a big company (Spinellis, 2006). Also, the developer can incrementally gain knowledge of the system, and get free support from the community, without the necessary investment on the P-ERP costly training and certification programs. In that way, an individual can improve his/her employability without investing too much money on courses, books and certifications. These advantages can make more free-lance developers enter FOS-ERP communities, currently formed mostly by companies' employees.

b. *Challenges*: learning the internals of a FOSS in general means to spend considerable time in understanding system architecture, design decisions, and specific features. Although FOS-ERP projects are improving their documentation and training material, many times the individual developer must count on Web sites, mailing lists, discussion forums, and the good will of community members to acquire deeper knowledge on the framework.

## CONCLUSION

The basic differences between open source and proprietary ERP found by Carvalho (2008) are still valid nowadays, however, in two points things have changed in the FOS-ERP scenario. The first is related to the training material available for users, consultants, and developers of the main projects, which improved a lot during the last few years. The second is that the growing in acceptance by small and medium enterprises is probably smaller than expected, given the fact that P-ERP vendors started to offer cheaper versions of their software in SaaS mode, which, approximated them of the FOS-ERP in terms of adoption advantages and disadvantages. This is specially true to small companies, which will almost never enter a development process, given the lack of resources (Carvalho and Johansson, 2010).

It is important to note that FOS-ERP inherits all advantages and shortcomings of open source software in general and have some more of both. As a matter of fact, in FOS-ERP two main advantages are directly related to FOSS: lower TCO given the reduced or non-existent licensing costs - including of supportive software, like spreadsheets, databases, networking and operational systems; and the possibility of having direct access to the source code whenever is needed.

A movement that is growing in both types of ERP is the offering of basic sets of modules for free, such as Microsoft's small ERP system Office Accounting (in US and UK), and ERP5's TioLive version. However, lower costs can also mean that adopters have to deal with lower service levels, then stressing the necessity of carefully evaluating service levels and pricing. In the case of FOS-ERP, consulting certification is yet on the early stages, thus quality of service must be carefully addressed during contract negotiation. On the other hand, although SMEs can change their business processes faster than bigger companies, cheaper but restrictive P-ERP support contracts can make the software change slower than the real business.

Continuing on the economic side, following the common reasoning about FOSS pricing, FOS-ERP vendors can take advantage from other open source software because, according to Riehle (2007), open source systems "increase profits through direct costs savings and the ability to reach more customers through improved pricing flexibility", allowing partners and free-lance vendors switch from more expensive proprietary software to less expensive open source software, since, as a general rule, FOS-ERP relies on other open source technologies.

Another economic factor is that P-ERP vendors generally impose high costs and a rigid set of rules for companies that desire to enter their partner network, raising the difficulties for smaller firms to become players in this market. In contrast, smaller consulting firms can enter the FOS-ERP market in an incremental way, increasing their commitment to a project as new business opportunities appear and bring more financial income. In other words, firms can start contributing with small improvements to the project as a way of gaining knowledge on the system platform and framework, and, as contracts to the solution appears, more money can be invested on a growing commitment to the project. With more partners entering the market, consulting costs can be reduced, help shifting the market from the vendor perspective to the adopter perspective. On the other hand, the P-ERP partner networks rely on more mature consulting processes and experiences of global ERP players. In that sense, FOS-ERP must learn on how to create certification and consulting processes that are at the same time high quality products, like the P-ERP ones, and cheaper than those, to survive on the market.

On the development and customization arena, the free access to the source code does not mean that the adopter will get involved in development tasks. In fact, the experience has shown that most of the times the adopter will not get involved in customization or even maintenance tasks. Still, FOS-ERP can be a good choice, since it reduces vendor dependency. Moreover, its code openness also makes adapting it to specific needs easier, thus reducing costs in customization and further evolution of the software.

However, an interesting finding is that FOS-ERP and P-ERP development become more and more similar. P-ERP developers work more and more with open source in their products and they also to a higher degree start to make the source code available, while FOS-ERP development is mostly carried by professionals who are paid by software vendors – the so-called Sponsored Open Source (West & O'Mahony, 2005). When thinking of customizing the ERP by itself, a critical question for an adopter is if it has the resources needed for implementing ERPs. In both FOS-ERP and P-ERP cases it is very unlikely that a small firm will have the resources and the knowledge for making the necessary modifications by itself. This situation is forcing a shift to the SaaS business model, which indicates that in the future SaaS as delivery model will be the most common option, regardless the licensing terms (open or proprietary). As examples on the evolution of SaaS delivered ERPs is ERP5 TioLive[11], on the open source side, and Fortnox on the proprietary side. For medium enterprises, which have more IT resources, it could be easier to adopt a FOS-ERP and take part in its customization, as occurred in some cases.

The question is then what the new delivery models mean when it comes to differences between support in the open source case and the proprietary case. One possible outcome is that only the solutions that have a high level of relevant services connected to the solution will survive. It also means that FOS-ERPs and P-ERPs will become closer to each other and this movement maybe, to some extent, makes it harder for the adopting organization to decide on which kind of ERP it should select.

Independent if it is FOS-ERPs or P-ERPs that are discussed, another interesting observation is the fact that empirical evidence (Hendricks, Singhal & Stratman, 2007) shows that it is not the software as such that provides an organization with competitive advantage, instead it can be claimed that it is the usage of the software, in the form of internal capabilities (Fosser, Leister, Moe & Newman, 2008; Mata, Fuerst, & Barney, 1995), that influences whether an organization is competitive or not. This then implies that even if two organizations working in the same industry adopts the same ERP they could have different performance. The question is then if this depends on that the inherited business process in the software are so generic that it supports only the very basic needs. It could be the fact that to be able to gain competitive advantage from adoption of ERPs, the system needs to be highly adjustable, but, also that the adopters could adjust the software by itself in a convenient way.

Nevertheless, despite the growing interest on this subject, it still has many topics to be explored by researchers and practitioners, given the short period of time that passed since this kind of software appeared in the market and the relatively small number of users, which indicates that the list of opportunities and challenges aforesaid is a reflection of current tendencies that must be confirmed and better scrutinized as new deployments occur. For instance, currently there are no research on FOS-ERP success rates. In other words, in this arena, it is necessary that more data on deployment, customization, operation, and evolution become available so that *tendencies* may be confirmed and can become *facts* and *figures*.

Hence, as a relatively new kind of software, FOS-ERP has a potential to be realized, but many questions about it are yet to be answered. Nevertheless, their growing commercial acceptance is a fact, and their lower costs, easier adaptation, and potentially more competitive supplier market can slowly force a shift in the ERP market from the current vendor perspective to a customer perspective.

## REFERENCES

Alshawi, S., Themistocleous, M., Almadani, R. (2004). Integrating diverse ERP systems: a case study. *The Journal of Enterprise Information Management*, Volume 17, Number 6,. Emerald Group Publishing Limited, pp.454-462.

Bruce, G., Robson, P., & Spaven, R. (2006). OSS opportunities in open source software — CRM and OSS standards. *BT Technology Journal*, *24*(1), 127–140. doi:10.1007/s10550-006-0028-9

Carvalho, R. A. (2006). *Issues on Evaluating Free/Open Source ERP Systems. Research and Practical Issues of Enterprise Information Systems* (pp. 667–676). Springer-Verlag. doi:10.1007/0-387-34456-X_72

Carvalho, R. A. (2007). Issues on evaluating Free/open source ERP systems, *Research and Practical Issues of Enterprise Information Systems* 667-676. New York: Springer Verlag New York Inc.

Carvalho, R. A. (2008). *(Org.). Handbook of Research on Enterprise Systems. Information Science Reference* (pp. 32–44). Hershey, USA: Free and Open Source Enterprise Resources Planning. In Jatinder N. D. Gupta, Mohammad Abdur Rashid, Sushil K. Sharma.

Carvalho, R. A., & Johansson, B. (2010). *ERP Licensing Perspectives on Adoption of ERPs in Small and Medium-sized Enterprises*. In The Fourth IFIP International Conference on Research and Practical Issues of Enterprise Information Systems, Natal, Brazil.

Caulliraux, H. M. Proença, A. & Prado, C. A. S. (2000). ERP Systems from a Strategic Perspective. *Sixth International Conference on Industrial Engineering and Operations Management*, Niteroi, Brazil.

Church, Z. (2008) SAP ERP on-demand challenge lofty, but not impossible. p. Available from: http://searchcio-midmarket.techtarget.com/news/article/0,289142,sid183_gci1301840,00.html.

Crowston, K., & Howison, J. (2006). Assessing the Health of Open Source Communities. *IEEE Computer*, May, pp. 89-91.

Dreiling, A. Klaus, H. Rosemann, M. & Wyssusek, B. (2005). Open Source Enterprise Systems: Towards a Viable Alternative. *38th Annual Hawaii International Conference on System Sciences*, Hawaii.

Fosser, E., Leister, O. H., Moe, C. E., & Newman, M. (2008). Organisations and vanilla software: What do we know about ERP systems and competitive advantage? *16th European Conference on Information Systems*. Galway, Ireland.

Goth, G. (2005). Open Source Business Models: Ready for Prime Time. *IEEE Software*, (November/December): 98–100. doi:10.1109/MS.2005.157

Harmon, T. (November, 01, 2010). *Forrester Research: Making IT work in small and mid sized firms*. Available from: http://www.computerweekly.com/Articles/2010/11/01/243612/Forrester-Research-Making-IT-work-in-small-and-mid-sized.htm

Hendricks, K. B., Singhal, V. R., & Stratman, J. K. (2007). The impact of enterprise systems on corporate performance: A study of ERP, SCM, and CRM system implementations. *Journal of Operations Management, 25*(1), 65–82. doi:10.1016/j.jom.2006.02.002

Herzog, T. (2006). *A Comparison of Open Source ERP Systems*. Master thesis, Vienna University of Economics and Business Administration, Vienna, Austria.

IFIP – IFAC Task Force on Architectures for Enterprise Integration. (1999). GERAM: Generalized Enterprise Reference Architecture and Methodology, 31p.

Johansson, B., & Newman, M. (2010). Competitive advantage in the ERP system's value-chain and its influence on future development. *Enterprise Information Systems, 4*(1), 79–93. doi:10.1080/17517570903040196

Kim, H., & Boldyreff, C. C. (2005). Open Source ERP for SME. *Third International Conference on Manufacturing Research*, Cranfield, U.K.

Kimberling, E. (November, 15, 2010). *Top Ten ERP Software Predictions for 2011*. Available from: http://panorama-consulting.com/top-ten-erp-software-predictions-for-2011

LeClaire, J. (December 30, 2006). *Open Source, BI and ERP: The Perfect Match?* http://www.linuxinsider.com/story/LjdZlB0x0j04cM/Open-Source-BI-and-ERP-The-Perfect-Match.xhtml

Lilly, N. (November, 03, 2010). *Not Sweet*. Available from: http://www.erpgraveyard.com/2010/11/not-sweet.html

Mata, F. J., Fuerst, W. L., & Barney, J. B. (1995). Information technology and sustained competitive advantage: A resource-based analysis. *Management Information Systems Quarterly, 19*(4), 487–505. doi:10.2307/249630

Ouédraogo, L.-D. (2005). *Policies of United Nations System Organizations Towards the Use of Open Source Software (OSS) in the Secretariats*. Geneva, 43p.

Riehle, D. (2007). The Economic Motivation of Open Source Software: Stakeholder Perspectives. *IEEE Computer, 40*(4), 25–32.

Robb, D. (January, 26, 2011). *Ten More ERP Trends: Open Source and Pricing Pressures*. Available from: http://www.ecrmguide.com/article.php/3922361/ten-more-erp-trends-open-source-and-pricing-pressures.htm

Serrano, N., & Sarrieri, J. M. (2006). Open Source ERPs: A New Alternative for an Old Need. *IEEE Software*, (May/June): 94–97. doi:10.1109/MS.2006.78

Smets-Solanes, J., & De Carvalho, R. A. (2003). ERP5: A Next-Generation, Open-Source ERP Architecture. *IEEE IT Professional, 5*(4), 38–44. doi:10.1109/MITP.2003.1216231

Spinellis, D. (2006). Open Source and Professional Advancement. *IEEE Software*, (September/October): 70–71. doi:10.1109/MS.2006.136

Wang, F.-R. He, D. & Chen, J. (2005). Motivations of Individuals and Firms Participating in Open Source Communities. *Fourth International Conference on Machine Learning and Cybernetics*, p309-314.

West, J., & O'Mahony, S. (2005). Contrasting Community Building in Sponsored and Community Founded Open Source Projects. *38th Annual Hawaii International Conference on System Sciences*, Hawaii.

Xu, N. (2003). An Exploratory Study of Open Source Software Based on Public Archives. Master Thesis, John Molson School of Business, Concordia University, Montreal, Canada.

## KEY TERMS AND DEFINITIONS

**ERP:** Enterprise Resources Planning, a type of Enterprise Information System which main goal is to integrate the business processes of a given organization data and processes of an organization into a unified system.

**ERP Business Model:** Broad range of informal and formal methods used by a vendor to make profit from an ERP system deployment, customization, and maintenance.

**ERP Evaluation:** Process of selecting an ERP package, by evaluating alternatives' compliance to the adopter's business processes and strategic requirements, as well as technological and budgetary aspects.

**Free Software:** According to the Free Software Foundation, is a Software that gives to the user the freedom to run the program for any purpose, study how the program works and adapt it to his/her needs, redistribute copies, improve the program, and release his/her improvements to the public, so that the whole community benefits.

**Free/Open Source ERP:** ERP systems that are released as Free Software or as Open Source Software.

**Free/Open Source Software Adopter Types:** Software users can be classified in accordance to its positioning in relation to a given FOSS: *Consumer:* a passive role where the adopter will just use the software as it is, with no intention or capability of modifying or distributing the codes. *Prosumer:* an active role where the adopter will report bugs, submit feature requests, post messages to lists. A more capable Prosumer will also provide bug fixes, patches, and new features. *Profitor:* a passive role where the adopter will not participate in the development process but simply will use the software as a source of profits. *Partner:* an active role where the adopter will actively participate in the whole open source development process for the purpose of earning profits.

**Open Source Software:** According to the Open Source Initiative (OSI), an open source software must be licensed under the following ten conditions: 1) The software can be freely given away or sold. 2) The source code must either be included or freely obtainable. 3) Redistribution of modifications must be allowed. 4) Licenses may require that modifications be redistributed only as patches. 5) No Discrimination Against Persons or Groups. 6) No Discrimination Against Fields of Endeavor. 7) The rights attached to the program must apply to all to whom the program is redistributed without the need for execution of an additional license by those parties. 8) The program cannot be licensed only as part of a larger distribution. 9) The license cannot insist that any other software it is distributed with must also be open source. 10) License Must Be Technology-Neutral. The official definition of Open Source Software is very close to the definition of Free Software, however, it allows in practice more restrictive licenses, creating a category of "semi-free" software.

## ENDNOTES

[1]    The precise definitions of Free Software and Open Source Software are on the chapter's Key Terms list. Although there are differences between them – the Free Software Movement has also some political connotations for instance - for the goals of this work the two terms will be treated as synonyms.

[2]    A search done in February, 21, 2011 found 90 hits for "open source erp" and 13,400 for "ERP", considering the period from 2009 onwards.

[3]    The first academic papers on this specific subject were Smets-Solanes and De Carvalho (2003) describing Open Source ERP and De Carvalho (2006) on evaluating FOS-ERP

[4] If it is considered articles that treats open source for enterprises in general, this numbers raises to aproximatelly a hundred hits.

[5] Despite the fact that these methods hold some similarities, they were developed without having knowledge of each other and were published in a very close range of time: Carvalho's method was published in April and Herzog's in June, 2006.

[6] Although this seems to be nonsense in FOSS terms, it is a common real life situation in FOS-ERP. In fact, the authors know a case where an adopter company sponsored the whole development of an FOS-ERP during a three-year period, without becoming a *prosumer*, and keeping only a specific algorithm, related to its product pricing schedule, in secret. The original license had to be changed to fit this customer demand.

[7] In practice, this return from free-lancers doesn't happen all the times.

[8] Although "personal ERP" are already appearing in the landscape, it is too early to get feedback from individuals experiences.

[9] ERP5 http://www.erp5.com

[10] The authors consider that these challenges represent, in fact, new research opportunities.

[11] TioLive has an innovative business model, in use for five years, which allows the adopter to download all code and data and deploy it locally, at any moment, regardless the level of customization that was applied to the adopter's instance.

# Chapter 2

# An Analytical Survey of Free/Open Source ERP Systems and their Potential Marketplace in Brazil

**Marcelo Monsores**
*Federal University of the Rio de Janeiro State, Brazil*

**Asterio Tanaka**
*Federal University of the Rio de Janeiro State, Brazil*

## ABSTRACT

*With the growing complexity and dynamics of modern organizations, ERP systems contribute to the management of business processes and allow strategic decisions to be taken more quickly and more safely, through a systemic, integrated view of the corporation. Free/Open Source software has consolidated as an increasingly viable alternative for this kind of systems, through the flexibility provided by its business and development model and the consequent possibility of total cost reduction. The objective of this chapter is to present a comparative survey of the main free/open source ERP systems currently available in the marketplace, their features focused in Brazilian companies and a general overview on its potential market.*

## INTRODUCTION

In a general perspective, software products can be distinguished between the so called "off-the-shelf software" products, like text editors and spreadsheets, internet browsers, e-mail clients and multimedia players, and "customized software" products, which are those that, in addition to being acquired, also require aggregated services in order to be used according to the particular needs of each company. ERP systems fit into this second category.

DOI: 10.4018/978-1-61350-486-4.ch002

As there are not two identical companies, besides installation, the ERP system will need parameterization and, probably, will also need customization. It is important that the ERP system holds the possibility of being functionally adapted to the company's business processes with few modifications, permitting the customization costs and the deployment time to be reduced. For this to occur optimally, flexibility is a mainstay. More than customization, this flexibility should also provide consistent interfaces for the development of additional modules. From this point of view, the unrestricted access to the source code, allied with the possibility of analysis and modification, makes Free/Open Source software model a viable alternative for ERP systems.

The aim of this paper is to present the results of an analytical survey conducted in 2009 and updated in 2010 on development projects of free/open source solutions for ERP systems, the major alternatives and their features focused in Brazilian companies and their potential market. From this point on, the free/open source and proprietary ERP systems will also be referenced using the nomenclature proposed by de Carvalho (2006): respectively FOS-ERP and P-ERP.

Until recently, packages of integrated management systems provided by a single supplier were not the preferred kind of solution by small companies, which normally would opt for the internal development of their own systems or even the manual control of their operations (FIESP, 2004; Bigaton, 2005), through simpler applications like electronic spreadsheets. According to Bigaton, the Integrated Management Systems propagation between the companies of this size is hampered by their financial situation, since the investment needed for deployment of the systems available today almost always exceeds values available in their budgets (Bigaton, 2005). In this regard, the FOS-ERP tend to get a bigger slice of market acceptance of this, once they make possible for companies to reduce costs with features like

software licensing and stimulation of competition. Obviously, the costs reduction of this kind of software opens new possibilities for small and medium companies to adopt them (de Carvalho & Johansson, 2009).

The remainder of this paper presents an overview of the marketplace for FOS-ERP systems from a survey of registered projects in the Sourceforge repository and a comparison of seven major FOS-ERP systems. After it there is also an overview about future researches related to this topic and a conclusion with the final considerations.

## BACKGROUND

There are different criteria in the market that can be used to rank organizations by its size, according to the context in which the analysis is done. Mercosul, NAFTA and The European Union, for example, adopt their own official classifications, different from each other. Some commonly used criteria are: (Longenecker et al., 1997):

- Number of employees
- Sales amount
- Financial status
- Assets value
- Workforce insurance
- Warehouse volumes

The increasingly strained competition and the consequent increase in market requirements have brought to small and medium enterprises needs of organization and control in levels previously required only by large companies. On the other side, the trend of higher costs withdraws small and medium enterprises from the major P-ERP systems. Since they have less favorable credit terms than large companies and therefore are more sensitive to economic cycles, this inhibits their efforts with technological improvements (la Rovere, 2001).

Nothing prevents FOS-ERP systems to be used also in large enterprises, but even in P-ERP the market focus has been SME (Small and Medium Enterprises) (Teixeira Jr., 2006; Herzog, 2006; Abboud, 2007; Panorama, 2008; de Carvalho & Johansson, 2009), since the majority of the large companies already have implemented their chosen ERP systems and the effort and costs involved in the replacement of a ERP system are bigger than those involved in implementing it in companies that do not already have one (ABBOUD, 2007).

Even in P- ERP, the value of software licenses is just part of the total cost of deployment, which is composed mainly by the services involved. In a FOS-ERP system, the services are still there and being charged, eliminating only the cost of licensing. However, not only free/open source software products, but also proprietary ones, are increasingly shifting their business focus to services sales. Hajjar and Moura (Hajjar & Moura, 2009) suggest that this is the case of the SaaS (Software as a Service) business model that, according to them, aims to generate products with aggressive policies of innovation and price, competing for opportunities to acquire new customers which are moving from large IT integrators, targeting costs savings. The authors also claim that SaaS is an excellent way of commercialization, with major financial benefits for the customer, allowing the purchase to be set to cash flow and regarded as an expense.

Currently, the largest international repository for Free/Open Source software projects is Sourceforge. Through a survey conducted in this repository in June 2009, it was possible to identify the existence of 654 registered projects in the 'ERP' subcategory under the 'Corporate' category. In July 2010, when this research was performed again, the number of projects with the same categorization had risen to 731, representing an increase of 11.8%. The analysis of samples from both lists revealed that many projects are not FOS-ERP projects themselves, but other kinds of projects such as:

- Instantiation of FOS-ERP systems for specific business areas;
- Locale projects of the main FOS-ERP for specific countries;
- Additional modules for other ERP systems;
- Specific CRM, accounting, human resources e project management systems, among others.

In 2009, only 213 (32.6%) among 654 projects had already left the conceptual stage and provided some kind of downloadable file. In 2010, this number increased to 253 (34.6%) among 731 projects.

## FOS-ERP PROJECTS SURVEY

In order to get a market overview about the number of FOS-ERP available to be used, the Sourceforge projects under the classification "Corporate / ERP" were taken as a basis. The following topics segregate and filter these subsets according to several criteria, in order to obtain the number of ERP systems which can actually be considered Free/Open Source software and offer conditions for real use.

### FOS-ERP Characterization

To identify and guarantee that only really independent FOS-ERP projects would be analyzed, a basic individual verification of each of these projects was done. The following criteria were formulated for this filtering:

1. The project cannot be just an instantiation of an existing ERP for specific business areas;
2. The project cannot be just a locale project of an existing ERP;
3. Even being a new system, the project can not be restricted to few countries and/or business areas;

4.  The proposed system must provide at least the basic modules for inventory management, purchasing, sales, financial and accounting.

After the verification of these criteria, for 2009 the resulting amount was 38 projects, equivalent to 17.8% of 213 projects in 'Corporate / ERP' category with files available for download, while for the 2010 there was an increase of 26.3%, resulting in 49 projects, equivalent to 19.4% of 253 projects with the same situation.

## Lifetime

Although the structure behind Free/Open Source software is not a new concept, it has just started to be considered an economically viable business model. Moreover, its application to ERP systems occurred late in comparison to other types of softwares, such as operating systems and web servers, for example. Table 1 segregates these projects over their lifetimes, considering the date they were registered at Sourceforge.

In (Monsores, 2009) three hypotheses were proposed, based on two premises, by observing the results of the survey, reproduced in Table 2:

From the analysis of Table 1, it was possible to infer two important new features:

*   FOS-ERP projects in general are maturing. While the amount of projects with less than 3 years of existence remained practically stable (16 in 2009 against 17 in 2010), projects with 3 years or more achieved a considerable increase (22 in 2009 against 32 in 2010);
*   In 2010, there was a remarkable increase in the amount of new projects: in the 12 preceding months of the research, 5 new projects were created, while at the same interval prior to the 2009 survey, only one had been created.

*Table 1. Project segmentation according to lifetime*

| Lifetime | 2009 | | 2010 | | Evolution |
|---|---|---|---|---|---|
| | Amount | % | Amount | % | |
| < 1 year | 1 | 2.6% | 5 | 10.2% | +400.0% |
| >= 1 year e < 3 years | 15 | 39.5% | 12 | 24.5% | -20.0% |
| >= 3 years e < 5 years | 17 | 44.7% | 19 | 38.8% | +11.8% |
| >= 5 years | 5 | 13.2% | 13 | 26.5% | +160.0% |

*Table 2. Hypothesis for the low quantity of new projects (Monsores, 2009)*

| Premises | Hypothesis |
|---|---|
| Only projects with available downloads were analyzed | H1 - One year is not enough time for the projects to be sufficiently developed to the point of making downloads available. When they reach the range of "1-3 years", they will have the same quantity (or greater) than those which are in this range today. |
| The activity level of the major projects keeps constantly high, placing some of them consistently among the 10 most active among 79 000+ ones with files already available. | H2 - New collaborators are still entering the area of FOS-ERP projects, but they choose to take part in one of the available projects instead of creating a new one. |
| | H3 - The projects are still being kept by the teams formed earlier and now FOS-ERP has been unable to attract new collaborators, neither to create new projects nor to collaborate with the existing ones |

## Maturity Level

At Sourceforge, hosted projects are also qualified according to the maturity level of their development. Table 3 shows the distribution of the projects among the seven existing levels. As Sourceforge permits simultaneous assignment of more than one level of maturity, in the projects where this happens, only the most advanced level was considered.

Due to the involved risks, the adoption of softwares which are still at "Beta" or earlier development phases is not a common behavior of organizations in general. Thus, only systems in "Production / Stable" and "Mature" development levels were considered "ready to use". In the 2009 research, there were 19 projects at these maturity levels, representing 50% of those really identified as FOS-ERP or only 2.9% of the projects defined as ERP at Sourceforge. In 2010, there was a small variation, changing these percentages respectively to 53.1% and 3.6%, referring to the 26 remaining projects.

## MAJOR FOS-ERP PROJECTS

For the purpose of comparison, four FOS-ERP projects were selected among the 10 most active in the weekly rankings released by Sourceforge over the past 24 months. This classification (re-produced in "Rating" row at Table 4) is done by assigning a grade depending on the amount of traffic of the project, its frequency of contributions on the source code and the volume of communication through forums and other resources. It directly reflects the probability of continuation and rapid deployment of fixes and improvements in these systems.

Besides these projects, the survey also includes three of the oldest FOS-ERP systems, which are not hosted at Sourceforge but played a crucial role in the creation and planning of several others, as well in the characterization of this new market share and in convincing the first-time users. Table 4 lists the main features of these seven FOS-ERP. The first four are ordered according to their ranking at Sourceforge, with the worst and best rating discarded.

The following information was obtained from the projects official websites and their entries on Wikipedia and Sourceforge (for the systems hosted on it). The positive and negative highlights of each system were formulated after a basic review of their on line demo versions and the features presented in their official websites.

## Compiere

Compiere is considered, in the FOS-ERP community, a precursor of the Free/Open Source model applied to ERP systems. Its development initiated

*Table 3. Projects segmentation according to the maturity level*

| Stage | 2009 | | 2010 | | Evolution |
|---|---|---|---|---|---|
| | Amount | % | Amount | % | |
| Planning | 2 | 5.3% | 3 | 6.1% | +50.0% |
| Pre-alpha | 3 | 7.9% | 2 | 4.1% | -33.3% |
| Alpha | 5 | 13.2% | 10 | 20.4% | +100.0% |
| Beta | 9 | 23.7% | 8 | 16.3% | -11.10% |
| Production/Stable | 16 | 42.1% | 21 | 42.9% | +31.3% |
| Mature | 3 | 7.9% | 4 | 8.2% | +33.3% |
| Inactive | 0 | 0.0% | 1 | 2.0% | --- |

*Table 4. Comparative list of the major FOS-ERP projects*

| | | Adempiere | Openbravo | PostBooks | WebERP | Compiere | OFBiz | ERP5 |
|---|---|---|---|---|---|---|---|---|
| **General Characteristics** | | | | | | | | |
| Rating[1] | Best | 1 | 1 | 1 | 8 | --- | --- | --- |
| | Worst | 5 | 20 | 17 | 199 | --- | --- | --- |
| | Average | 2,8 | 3,8 | 5,5 | 28,6 | --- | --- | --- |
| Focus | | NA | SME | SME | SME | NA | NA | NA |
| Creation year | | 2006 | 2006 | 2007 | 2003 | 1999 | 2001 | 2002 |
| Downloads (x1000) | | 425 | 1020 | 260 | 250 | NA | NA | NA |
| Languages | | 21 | 12 | 8 | 23 | 21 | 39 | 9 |
| Programming language | | Java | Java | C++ | PHP | Java | Java | Python |
| Maturity | | Stable | Stable | Stable | Mature | NA | NA | NA |
| Web interface | | yes | yes | no | yes | yes | yes | yes |
| Client/Server interface | | yes | no | yes | no | yes | no | no |
| Databases | | Oracle, PostgreSQL | Oracle, PostgreSQL | PostgreSQL | MySQL | Oracle | MySQL | Todos |
| **Modules** | | | | | | | | |
| Inventory | | yes | yes | yes | yes | yes | yes | yes |
| Logistics | | yes | yes | yes | no | yes | no | yes |
| Manufacturing | | yes | yes | no | yes | yes | no | yes |
| Financial | | yes | yes | yes | yes | yes | yes | yes |
| Purchasing | | yes | yes | yes | yes | yes | yes | yes |
| Sales | | yes | yes | yes | yes | yes | yes | yes |
| Accounting | | yes | yes | yes | yes | yes | yes | yes |
| Project Management | | yes | yes | no | no | yes | no | yes |
| CRM | | yes | yes | yes | yes | yes | yes | yes |
| PoS | | yes | yes | no | no | yes | yes | no |
| Human Resources | | yes | no | no | no | yes | no | yes |
| **Other Resources** | | | | | | | | |
| Workflow | | yes | no | no | no | yes | no | yes |
| SOA | | no | no | no | no | no | yes | no |
| multi-currency | | yes | yes | yes | yes | yes | yes | yes |
| multi-organization | | yes | yes | no | no | yes | yes | yes |
| **Commercial Features** | | | | | | | | |
| Sponsored by a company | | no | yes | yes | no | yes | yes | yes |
| Offers "Premium Versions" | | no | no | yes | no | yes | no | no |
| On line demo | | yes | yes | yes | yes | yes | yes | no |

NA: Not Available

SME: Small and Medium Enterprises

in 1999 under the sponsorship of "Goodyear Tire & Rubber Company" in Germany, where it was implemented during the following year and later was made available on the Internet under the banner of Free/Open Source software. Today the project is managed by a company created for this purpose, called Compiere Inc.

The project is targeted to the global market, supporting multiple currencies, taxes, costs, accounts and organizations. These features permit flexibility in the analysis of the same information under various aspects, being helpful to companies which have operations in more than one country. One of the most interesting aspects of Compiere is a robust and flexible application dictionary used to store software metadata and rules. This dictionary contains data entity definitions (types, validations, etc.), exhibition definitions (screen tags and reports, presentation order, position relative to other fields, etc.), exhibition rules, security rules, access control and relationships between these elements.

Compiere Inc. position is frequently contested by the Free/Open Source Software contributor communities, since the inclusion of new features and suggestions on the direction of the project is restricted to company's licensed partners, a status obtained only through the payment of fees. Some of its components, as the web interface, are not Free/Open Source software. Despite being fairly complete, this ERP complete documentation is not available for free download, being necessary to pay for it.

In Brazil, Compiere has only one official partner, which developed a Brazilian locale module and has a list in its website with ten clients where the system is implemented. One of these clients is the state-owned company CEAGESP (São Paulo State Food Supply Company) (Arima, 2009). In 2003, FINEP, a funding agency of the Ministry of Science and Technology, released a program to fund projects related to Free/Open Source Software. Conceptia Consulting company, in partnership with UNICAMP (State University of Campinas), obtained funding for a project to adapt Compiere to PostgreSQL, but this contribution was not incorporated to the main project, once Conceptia was not an official Compiere Inc. partner.

## OFBiz

OFBiz or "Open for Business" is one of the oldest FOS-ERP. Its development begun in 2001 and some years later was incorporated to the Apache Software Foundation projects group, where it became one of the major software since 2006. Today, OFBiz is presented by its collaborators more as a framework for the development of integrated management systems than as a ready-to-use ERP system.

Its data model is based on a research about industry practices for data modeling done by Len Silverston and published in the books "The Data Model Resource Book, Revised Edition", volumes 1 and 2. The development of the central framework is clearly segregated between data, business and presentation layers. The first layer deals exclusively with data persistence and retrieval while the third layer provides these data to the users, concentrating all the process logic in the second layer. The use of SOA architecture makes the integration with other applications and resources very flexible. Differently from companies involved in other FOS-ERP, Apache Software Foundation just supports OFBiz development, without interfering on its direction or aiming straight financial returns from its use.

The web interface still needs improvements in the aesthetic point of view. The nonexistence of a desktop client to be installed at the workstations restricts the integration with other softwares and devices and hinders the provision for more sophisticated usability features. The excessive concern in presenting OFBiz only as a development framework infers a false impression that, unlike other systems, it is not a ready-to-use ERP for organizations with fewer particularities in their business processes.

There is a list at the OFBiz main website with various users of the system, however none from Brazil. Its collaborators listing contains Brazilian partners, though no sales representatives. OFBiz is translated to Brazilian Portuguese but does not have a Brazilian locale module.

## ERP5

ERP5 project was created in 2002, when a French company called Coramy decided to migrate its own ERP to a new Free/Open Source model. Nexedi was created as an independent company, with the tasks of developing, deploying and disseminating ERP5 technology.

ERP5 architecture is conceptualized through an abstraction layer for business management, based on five generic classes used by all modules: resource, node, movement, item, and path. This model, known as "ERP5 Universal Business Model", facilitates code reuse through abstraction from specific domains and the encapsulation of the relationships and actions that are common to many business processes. The official website is www.erp5.com, but this ERP system also has a community portal for developers and collaborators under www.erp5.org, which has many documentation and general information about the project.

In spite of its good usability ensured through useful resources such as the possibility of accessing all the functionalities from any screen, the web interface still needs improvements in the aesthetic point of view. The inexistence of a desktop client to be installed at the workstations restricts the integration with other softwares and devices and hinders the provision of more sophisticated usability features. Python language is simpler, but still has fewer developers than other languages like Java and PHP. Currently, the choice of this language by ERP5 can be an inhibitor for the ingression of new collaborators to the project.

In Brazil, the activities related to ERP5 are coordinated by the Research Group on Information Systems from the Fluminense Federal Institute for Education, Science and Technology (IFF), in collaboration with the Department of Industrial Engineering from São Paulo State University of Bauru (UNESP-Bauru). The ERP still doesn't have a Brazilian locale module available for use, but this feature was under development during the writing of this chapter.

ERP5 has two related projects that deserve attention. One of them is TioLive (www.tiolive.com), which delivers pre-configured ERP5 instances to Small and Medium Enterprises (SMEs) through the SaaS business model. The other is the O.S.O.E. project (www.osoe-project.org), which stands for "One Student One ERP". It is an educative platform to teach business processes based on the ERP5 model through TioLive.

## Adempiere

The project was created in 2006 as a fork from Compiere, after a long period of divergence between Compiere Inc. and its community of collaborators, in relation to the commercial restrictions imposed by the company for the collaboration over the project.

Besides the typical functions of an ERP package, Adempiere also has resources for PoS, CRM, SCM, BI, project management and human resources management. Some of these modules were developed as independent projects to complement the functionalities of Compiere and were embedded into the Adempiere main project after its creation. All the transactions can be accessed through two kinds of web interfaces (Java servlets or HTML/Ajax) or through a desktop client software installed in the workstation. The amount of resources and interfaces is due, in part, to the high level of project activity according to the Sourceforge statistics, where the project appears among the most active ones since its creation.

The main points for improvement are the graphical interfaces and the user documentation. Despite its functionality and user-friendliness, the interfaces have yet to evolve under the aesthetic point of view. The project documentation is distributed into two sites: www.adempiere.com and www.adempiere.org. The first one is targeted on developers and contains development guides and general documentation. The second one, targeted on users, does not have sufficient information about the available features and enough documentation about the parameterization process.

Nowadays, this is the only FOS-ERP with an open project of Brazilian locale ready to be used, created in 2007. The official website lists a total of 27 deployments already made in Brazil through four different companies. However, through a quick Google search it was possible to identify at least five other companies working with this ERP system.

## OpenBravo

OpenBravo was initiated in 2006 by professionals from the University of Navaja, Spain. Its design is based on the main architectural concepts of Compiere. Its development is directed and coordinated by the company Openbravo Inc.

As it was designed exclusively for the web environment since the beginning, OpenBravo did not need to direct efforts towards the difficulties faced by other ERP systems to provide further functionality in this kind of environment. Its official websites are www.openbravo.org and www.openbravo.com, which currently lead to the same content, where it is possible to easily find relevant information to end users. This content also has a section published under the Wiki format with a very complete and organized documentation, both for users and for developers and configurators. Like Adempiere, OpenbBravo is historically ranked among the most active projects at Sourceforge.

Despite the functional and user-friendly web interface, the absence of a desktop client to be installed on workstations restricts the integration with other softwares and devices and hampers the provision of more sophisticated usability features.

OpenBravo currently has two official partners in Brazil and through Google it was possible to identify three other companies. A free/open source Brazilian locale project is under planning, but it was not initiated yet. There is already a fully functional project which adapts OpenBravo to the Brazilian legislation, but it is a proprietary solution of one of its sales representatives.

## PostBooks

The OpenMFG project was created in 2000 as a "shared source" system, to which only companies that had acquired licenses could have access. However, in 2007, the company of the same name was renamed xTuple and released PostBooks as a free/open source version of OpenMFG, making his code publicly available. Both of them are focused on accounting and financial modules, but while PostBooks is intentioned to small and medium enterprises, OpenMFG is aimed at manufacturing and is indicated by xTuple also for large companies.

The development in a compiled language (C++), instead of interpreted languages as used by the majority of the other FOS-ERP systems, is a different proposal and brings up performance increase as its main advantage. Furthermore, this makes it unnecessary to install intermediate virtual machines, such as those necessary to the execution of systems developed with Java and .Net. The main website for end users is www.xtuple.com, which presents complete information about PostBooks and OpenMFG, offering also a comparison between different versions. Meanwhile, the website for developers and contributors is www.xtuple.org, which also has extensive documentation. The project also lays constantly among the ten most active at Sourceforge

For the client application to be as light as possible, many features were developed embedded at the PostgreSQL database, using resources as triggers e stored procedures. Although contributing positively to the software performance, this makes it impossible to use other database servers without adapting pieces of this embedded source code. The unavailability of a web interface prevents the system to be accessed without the desktop client software installed on the workstation.

This ERP system is partially translated to Brazilian Portuguese and does not have a Brazilian locale project. The list of collaborators and users of the website has 30 registered Brazilians, but no representatives or business users were found in Brazil.

## WebERP

One of the oldest projects, WebERP is another system targeted to small and medium companies, but aims to provide adequate performance through a light web interface without relying on broadband connections. To achieve this goal, it makes use of a lean structure for the server, based on LAMP (Linux operating system, Apache web server, MySQL database server e PHP programming language).

Performance is certainly the major positive aspect of this ERP system. The use through a common and light structure as LAMP allows companies to easily host their ERP system in an external web service provider, without having to handle hardware and maintenance themselves specifically for this purpose. The information about this ERP system is at www.weberp.org, where it is possible to find appropriate documentation for end users, developers and other collaborators.

The objectives highly centered in performance and simplicity imposes some limitations to this ERP system. The web interface, although functional, has no enhanced graphic resources and more complex features. The inexistence of a desktop client to be installed directly in workstations restricts the integration with other softwares and devices and hinders he availability of more sophisticated usability features.

WebERP does not have a Brazilian locale project, but it has Brazilians in its collaborators list and is fully translated to Brazilian Portuguese. No representatives or user companies were found in Brazil.

## FUTURE RESEARCH DIRECTIONS

In 2009, having only the results of the first research, Monsores highlighted that it would only be possible to properly discard or confirm the hypotheses of Table 2 (reproduced in this paper) by monitoring the evolution of the projects over a period of at least 24 months (Monsores, 2009). However, the new features identified in the 2010 survey permitted to assume some hypotheses about these trends:

- **H1:** Five new projects created in the 12 months preceding the 2010 survey have made available files for download, indicating that this time may be sufficient to make project versions available (even rudimentary). However, one more year is still necessary to evaluate this hypothesis properly, since all projects classified in the range of "1-3 years" in 2009 will have migrated to the range of "3-5 years";
- **H2:** Between the dates of the two surveys, the structure of the Sourceforge site was completely reformulated. As of the date of the survey in 2010, there were no resources available in the new interface for measuring the amount of collaborators of the projects. Despite the impossibility of verifying the size of the teams, the creation of new projects (especially those not originated from forks) indicates that new collaborators may be taking part in the development of FOS-ERP projects, even that it was not possible to guarantee this regarding their participation in existing projects.

To confirm or refute the hypotheses reported in Table 2 and also the new two above, it will be necessary to repeat this research some years more, especially in intervals of 24 months. This attendance is suggested due to the average subdivision in slices of two years in Table 1. In these intervals, all projects without exception will necessarily have changed the subgroup they were reported before, making clear the tendencies of evolution.

With the consolidation of FOS-ERP solutions, in some years it will also be necessary to compare the systems of this kind between themselves, but also against P-ERP. This comparison will allow a better understanding of the scenarios where FOS-ERP systems are really viable and competitive.

One of the biggest problems for Free / Open Source researchers in general is to have the actual amount of companies which use solutions of this kind. In one hand, there is not a company controlling the sales of the solutions and in the other, a single download doesn't necessarily mean that the system will be used in production. This is will be among the hardest challenges for these future researches, because without this data it is not possible to know the real size of the market and which systems are being mostly used. This also impedes a real market share comparison with P-ERP.

Leaving aside the comparisons and market surveys, as FOS-ERP is a relatively new solution it still have many possibilities of integration with other kinds of solutions. Therefore, researches with the aim of adding value to this type of system through interacting with new technologies will be a strong mainstay.

## CONCLUSION

It is important to highlight that, as with Free/Open Source Software against Proprietary Software in general, the objective of the ERP systems which adopt the first model is not to be the only option in every scenario or under every condition, but to present itself as a viable alternative to be evaluated by organizations, according to their needs, goals and structures.

Especially in this type of software, where the licensing costs are proportionally lower compared to the cost of the services involved in its implementation, customization and maintenance, it is important to consider not only the influence of Free/Open Source Software over the acquisition value, but also over the costs of the entire ERP lifecycle, without neglecting the flexibility proposed by this model as well.

It is also important to note that it is increasingly common to find projects under the tutelage of companies which sustain themselves exclusively with these systems and share the development between their own teams and the Free/Open Source Software community. Some of the projects structured under this format provide more complete or closed versions with support and training services as value aggregation.

Although the size of the companies where a FOS-ERP system can be used is not restricted, it is notorious that these are especially suitable for Small and Medium enterprises. This is mainly due to the direction that the market of ERP systems as a whole is taking, since the majority of the larger companies already has or is implementing ERP packages they have already chosen. Another factor influencing this focus is the size of the service providers involved with FOS-ERP systems. Most of them still do not have the infrastructure and resources necessary to serve large enterprises, especially when dealing with the replacement of systems currently in use. Despite only three of the seven systems evaluated (Openbravo, Postbooks and WebERP) explicitly stated their focus on SME (small and medium enterprises), it is clear at the websites and discussion lists that almost all of its representatives aim mainly customers of this size.

The Brazilian economy and specially its micro and small enterprises are undergoing a good time. According to the Brazilian Institute of Geography and Statistics, in 2006 there were 6.72 million companies formally registered in Brazil, 94.1% of which (6.32 million) were micro enterprises and 4.9% (332.2 thousand) were small enterprises. In quantitative terms, between 2003 and 2006 there was an expansion of 9.53% for micro enterprises and 18.5% for small enterprises, while for the economy as a whole this expansion was approximately 10%. During this period, industrial companies represented 12% of the micro enterprises and 16% of the small enterprises, while commercial and services companies represented 82.8% of the micro enterprises and 78.5% of the small enterprises (SEBRAE, 2007). The junction of the current brazilian economy status with the direction taken by FOS-ERP service providers creates a well suitable potential market in Brazil for FOS-ERP adoption.

As a conclusion, the analytical survey presented in this chapter serves as a subsidy of great usefulness for ERP system selection. The highlighted gap between the needs of appropriate information and the financial capacity of small and medium enterprises, as a limiting factor for the acquisition of an ERP system, opens a new market niche to be explored. In addition, due to the direction that the marketplace and the economy have been taking as a whole, it is possible to conclude that the FOS-ERP solution is particularly appropriate to this new market niche.

# REFERENCES

Abboud, L. (2007). *SAP's New Model: Think Smaller*. The Wall Street Journal On Line, USA: 2007, available at http://online.wsj.com/article/SB119016383913731920.html, Retrieved in 2009, July.

Arima, K. (2009). *O ERP Agora é Open Source. Info Exame Magazine, 2009* (pp. 94–95). June, Brazil: Editora Abril. (in Portuguese)

Bigaton, A. L. W. (2005). *Gestão Estratégica da Informação nas Pequenas Empresas: Estudo Comparativo de Casos em Empresas do Setor Industrial de São José do Rio Preto – SP*. Unpublished Master Degree Dissertation, University of São Paulo, São Carlos, Brazil, 2005. (in Portuguese)

de Carvalho, R. A. (2006). Issues on Evaluating Free/Open Source ERP Systems. In Tjoa, A. M., Xu, L., Chaudhry, S., (eds). *IFIP International Federation for Information Processing, Volume 205, Research and Practical Issues of Enterprise Information Systems*, p.667-675. Boston: Springer.

de Carvalho, R. A., & Johansson, B. (2009). Enterprise Resource Planning Systems for Small and Medium Enterprises. In Ramachandran, M., & de Carvalho, R. A. (Eds.), *Handbook of Research on Software Engineering and Productivity Technologies: Implications of Globalisation* (pp. 373–381). Hershey, PA: IGI Global. doi:10.4018/978-1-60566-731-7.ch024

FIESP. (2004). *Perfil da Empresa Digital 2003/2004*. Sao Paulo State Federation of Industries, Retrieved from http://www.idigital.fea.usp.br/iDigital/Repositorio/0/Documentos/iDigital2004.pdf, Retrieved in 2009, July. (in Portuguese)

Hajjar, D., & Moura, R. (2009). *Acabaram as fusões no mercado de ERP?* Reseller Web, 2009, Retrieved from http://www.resellerweb.com.br/noticias/index.asp?cod=58588, Retrieved in 2009, May. (in Portuguese)

Herzog, T. (2006). *A Comparison of Open Source ERP Systems*. Unpublished Master Degree Dissertation, Vienna University of Economics and Business Administration, Austria: 2006.

la Rovere, R. L. (2001). *Perspectivas das micro, pequenas e médias empresas no Brasil. Journal of Contemporary Economy, Special Edition Economy Institute*. Brazil: UFRJ. (in Portuguese)

Longenecker, J. G., Moore, C. W., & Petty, J. W. (1997). *Administração de Pequenas Empresas: Ênfase na Gerência Empresarial*. São Paulo, CA: Makron Books.

Monsores, M. (2009). *Software Livre e Sistemas ERP: Levantamento Analítico e Proposta de Metodologia de Pré-Implantação*. Unpublished Master Degree Dissertation, Federal University of the Rio de Janeiro State, Rio de Janeiro, 2009. (in Portuguese)

Panorama Consulting Group. (2008). *2008 ERP Report*, USA, Denver, 2009.

SEBRAE. (2007). *Relatório de Gestão Estratégica do Sistema SEBRAE. Brazilian Service of Micro and Small Enterprises Supporting*. Brazil: SEBRAE. (in Portuguese)

Teixeira, S., Jr. (2006). *A Busca Pelos Pequenos*. Available at http://portalexame.abril.com.br/revista/exame/edicoes/0859/negocios/m0080278.html, Retrieved in 2009, August. (in Portuguese)

## ADDITIONAL READING

Bernroider, E., & Koch, S. (2001). ERP selection process in midsize and large organizations. *Business Process Management Journal, 7*(3), 251–257. doi:10.1108/14637150110392746

Botta-Genoulaz, V., Millet, P. A., & Grabot, B. A. (2005). Survey on the recent research literature on ERP systems. *Computers in Industry, 56*(6), 510–522. doi:10.1016/j.compind.2005.02.004

Caldeira, M. M., & Ward, J. M. (2002). Understanding the successful adoption and use of IS/IT in SME's: an explanation from Portuguese manufacturing industries. *Information Systems Journal, 12*(2), 121–152. doi:10.1046/j.1365-2575.2002.00119.x

Cereola, S. (2008). *The performance effects of latent factors on assimilation of commercial open-source ERP software on small-medium enterprises*. Unpublished Ph.D. dissertation. Virginia Commonwealth University, USA: 2008. Available at http://digarchive.library.vcu.edu/handle/10156/2295. Retrieved in 2010, November.

Davis, A. (2008), Enterprise resource planning under open source software. In C. Ferran, R. K. Salim, *Enterprise Resource Planning for Global Economies: Managerial issues and challenges*. Hershey, PA: Information Science Reference, 2008. p. 56–76.

de Carvalho, R. A. (2009). Free and Open Source Enterprise Resources Planning. In Gupta, J. N. D., Sharma, S., & Rashid, M. A. (Eds.), *Handbook of Research on Enterprise Systems* (pp. 32–44). Hershey, PA: IGI Global. doi:10.4018/978-1-59904-859-8.ch003

Feller, J., Fitzgerald, B., Hissam, S. A., & Lakhani, K. R. (2005). *Perspectives on Free and Open Source Software*. England: MIT Press.

Fitzgerald, B. (2006). The Transformation of Open Source Software. *Management Information Systems Quarterly, 30*(3), 587–598.

Frick, N., & Schubert, P. (2009), *Future Requirements of ERP Software From the Vendors Point of View*. Available at http://3gerp.iwvi.uni-koblenz.de/docs/2009-ECIS-ERP-Study-Paper.pdf, Retrieved in 2011, January.

Johansson, B. (2007). Developing a ´Better´ ERP system: The Risk of Loosing Competitive Advantage, In *CONFENIS2007, the IFIP TC8 International Conference on Research and Practical Issues of Enterprise Information Systems, vol. 2*, p. 1169-1178.

Johansson, B., & Carvalho, R. A. (2009). *Management of Requirements in ERP development: A Comparison between Proprietary and Open Source ERP*. Available at http://3gerp.iwvi. uni-koblenz.de/docs/Managing_of_Requirements_in_ERP.pdf. Retrieved in 2010, January.

Johansson, B., & Sudzina, F. (2008). *ERP systems and open source: an initial review and some implications for SMEs*. Available at http://3gerp.iwvi. uni-koblenz.de/docs/JEIM_paper_Johansson_Sudzina_2008.pdf. Retrieved in 2010, January.

Johansson, B., & Sudzina, F. (2008b). *ERP Systems Implementation: Factors Influencing Selection of a Specific Approach?* Available at http://3gerp. iwvi.uni-koblenz.de/docs/johansson-sudzina-selection-factors.pdf. Retrieved in 2010, January.

Johansson, B., & Sudzina, F. (2009). *Choosing open source ERP systems: What reasons are there for doing so?* Available at http://3gerp.iwvi.uni-koblenz.de/docs/OSS2009paper.pdf. Retrieved in 2010, January.

Lima, A. D. A. (2003). *Implantação de Pacote de Gestão Empresarial em Pequenas e Médias Empresas*. Brazil: KMPress.Available at http://www.kmpress.com.br/portal/artigos/preview. asp?id=147. Retrieved in 2009, September. (in Portuguese)

Mendes, J. V., & Filho, E. E. (2003). Sistemas Integrados de Gestão (ERP) em Pequenas e Médias Empresas: Um Confronto entre a Teoria e a Prática Empresarial. In Souza, C. A. & Saccol, A. Z. *Sistemas ERP no Brasil – Teoria e Casos*, Brazil: Editora Atlas, 2003. p.243-265 (in Portuguese)

Saccol, A. Z., Macadar, M. A., & Soares, R. O. (2003). Mudanças Organizacionais e Sistemas ERP. In Souza, C. A., & Saccol, A. Z. (Eds.), *Sistemas ERP no Brasil – Teoria e Casos* (pp. 173–190). Brazil: Editora Atlas. (in Portuguese)

Serrano, N., & Sarriegi, J. M. (2006). Open source software ERPs: A new alternative for an old need. *IEEE Software*, *23*(3), 94–97. doi:10.1109/MS.2006.78

Sudzina, F., Pucihar, A., & Lenart, G. (2008), *ERP System Selection: Criteria Sensitivity*, 31[th] IRIS Proceedings. Available at http://www.iris31.se/papers/IRIS31-067.pdf. Retrieved in 2011, January.

Wheeler, D. A. (2010). *How to evaluate open source software / free software (OSS/FS) programs*. Available at http://www.dwheeler.com/oss_fs_eval.html. Retrieved in 2011, January.

Wikipedia. (2007). *List of ERP software packages*. Available at http://en.wikipedia.org/wiki/List_of_ERP_software_packages. Retrieved in 2011, January.

## KEY TERMS AND DEFINITIONS

**Business Intelligence (BI):** Software or software modules for gathering, storing, analyzing, and providing access to enterprise data in an improved way, in order to help users making better business decisions.

**Customer Relationship Management (CRM):** Software and general procedures and resources that help an enterprise to manage customer relationships in an optimized way.

**Free/Open Source Software Collaborators:** People who contribute not only development, but also other important activities, such as planning, testing and documentation of free/open source softwares.

**Point of Sales (PoS):** A software or software module to be used in sales operations, normally to end customers without purchase orders or purchase contracts.

**Software as a Service (SaaS):** Software commercialization model in which applications are hosted by a vendor or service provider and distributed to customers through a broadband a network, typically the Internet.

**Software Customization:** Tuning software for the needs of an enterprise through development (source coding) of smaller pieces or even whole modules.

**Software Parameterization:** Tuning software for the needs of an enterprise through the configuration of its predefined options (parameters).

**Supply Chain Management (SCM):** Coordination and integration of the material, financial and information flows from supplier to consumer, through manufacturer, wholesaler, retailer and other intermediate actors.

**Wiki:** A server interface which allows users to collaborate in forming the content of a Web site, editing contents contents, including other users' contributions, using a regular Web browser.

## ENDNOTE

[1] When this research was repeated in 2010, the projects historical ranking was no longer available in Sourceforge. Therefore, this classification considers the data for the period of June 2008 to July 2009.

# Chapter 3
# Why Select an Open Source ERP over Proprietary ERP?
## A Focus on SMEs and Supplier's Perspective

**Nasimul Huq**
*Jönköping University, Sweden*

**Syed Mushtaq Ali Shah**
*Jönköping University, Sweden*

**Daniela Mihailescu**
*Jönköping University, Sweden*

## ABSTRACT

*This chapter introduces the key factors that motivate Small and Medium Sized Enterprises (SMEs) to select Open Source ERP (OS ERP) over the proprietary ERP. The chapter starts with the related previous research works by stating the basic concepts of OS ERP selection. The goal of this chapter is to empirically identify the most important factors that may motivate the Small and Medium Sized Enterprises (SMEs) to select this category of enterprise systems. Therefore this chapter proposes a Theoretical Model for Open Source ERP selection by SMEs and later on conducts an empirical study based on that theoretical model. The chapter tries to broaden the discussion around the important selection factors by including the perspective of the suppliers along with the perspective of OS ERP implementer SMEs.*

## INTRODUCTION

The global ERP market is growing at a fast rate and continues to grow due to an increased demand for integrated solutions. The ERP systems have rapidly become the de facto industry standard for

DOI: 10.4018/978-1-61350-486-4.ch003

replacement of legacy systems (Parr & Shanks, 2000). As long as Open Source has become matured, it gained more reliability. Open Source has become strong in business applications areas like ERP, CRM, content management and Business Intelligence (Bruce et al., 2006). Open Source ERP is considered as a viable alternative of proprietary ERP paradigm (Dreiling et al., 2005). These categories of enterprise systems are getting more and more acceptance (de Carvalho, 2009). ERPs are complex and costly systems. For SMEs it is difficult to deploy such costly systems. Smets-Solanes and de Carvalho (2003) cited in Johansson and Sudzina (2008) points the elevated cost to be the major factor that prevent SMEs to implement ERPs. Only the large firms have been able to enjoy the benefits of ERP systems (Cereola, 2000). According to Johansson and Sudzina (2008), it is SMEs that downloads open source ERPs and use them as a source of supply. Serrano and Sarreiegi (2006) argue that 12 SMEs successfully implemented Open Source ERP after evaluating proprietary ERPs and the interesting fact is that the adopting SMEs were not interested in Open Source license (cited in Johansson & Sudzina, 2008). There might be some other motivating factors than cost involved in the selection process when organizations make a decision on adoption of Open Source ERP (Johansson & Sudzina, 2008). But in the academic sector those factors were not empirically explored and there have not been enough research work done about different issues of Open Source ERP (de Carvalho, 2009).

This chapter aims to identify empirically the most important factors that may motivate the Small and Medium Sized Enterprises (SMEs) to select OS ERP. For this, perspective of Users (SMEs) and Suppliers (Vendors/Consultants) of OS ERP as well as the potential difference between their perspectives is analyzed in this chapter. Finally mutually most important factors are represented. The basic question discussed in the chapter is: *what are the most important factors from the perspective of users (SMEs) and Suppliers in Open Source ERP selection?*

## BACKGROUND

Open Source ERP is defined in the context of 'Open Source' and 'ERP'. Literature review reveals that Open Source ERP got acceptance because may be organizations were confronted with problems while using Proprietary ERP systems or Open Source phenomenon got maturity (Johansson & Sudzina, 2008). Valkov (2008) discusses problems of traditional ERP systems and illustrate that current commercial ERP software models are too complex, hard to extend or update which leads to high costs, big development efforts, and redundant data structures. The author further argues that the integration and implementation are too complicated, sluggish, costly and unable to meet the needs of clients in most of the cases.

Johansson (2008) explains that vendors of Proprietary ERPs face various challenges, which they should tackle of if they want to remain in business market in upcoming times. The authors illustrate that the question, whether or not Open Source software can serve as a useful input to manage future challenges engender by current proprietary ERP systems. Kim and Boldyreff (2005) explain that Open Source is still in its infancy but the Open Source Software community has started to move into ERP sector. The authors further discuss that because of the complexity associated with large corporations of their business processes, Open Source ERP might never be suitable for them, while SMEs are more suitable candidates for it as they can more easily adapt themselves to ever changing business environments.

Dreiling et al. (2005) argue that dissatisfaction with Proprietary Enterprise Systems can be explained by the relation between developers and users, which is in favor of developers and the proprietary nature of software licensed to organizations is a significant cornerstone for that. With various successful Open Source development initiatives the Open Source software development provides a viable alternative to proprietary development of Enterprise Systems. Soh et al. (2000) describe that problem of 'misfit' persists in adopting software package, which means that there is a gap between the functionality offered by the package and the functionality required by adopting organization. This gap can be trounced by the Open Source phenomenon. Valkov (2008) emphasizes the importance of the concept of Open Source ERP system and refers to it as an innovative business platform which is based on global collaboration. Herzog (2006) illustrates that Open Source ERP has less than 5 percent of the business software market. Although there is opportunity for expansion of this kind of software, most of the Open Source solutions are too small and there target groups includes mostly SMEs.

According to Johansson and Sudzina (2008), observing the number of downloads of the Open Source ERP software's in recent years, reveals increased interest of organizations in this sort of software. The authors acknowledge that although the number of downloads does not give any confirmation of the adoption of the Open Source ERP by organizations, it might be assumed that the rate of adoption will increase with the increment of downloads. According to them, examination of number of downloads of six different Open Source ERP solutions indicates that at this moment the SMEs are more interested in using these Open Source ERPs.

## FACTORS THAT MOTIVATE SMES TO SELECT OPEN SOURCE ERP

As the purpose of this chapter is to identify the factors that may motivate SMEs to select Open Source ERP systems, all the factors are selected considering its effect on organizational size and Openness of the ERP Systems. From the review of these factors in the literature a model is proposed. In the light of that model the empirical investigation is conducted.

Deploying an Enterprise Resource Planning (ERP) system is a significant decision for the company that affects the future performance of the company (Wei et al., 2005) and it has effect on the strategic position of the company (Stefanou, 2001). Due to the complexity in the business environment and variety of ERP offerings, the

selection process of ERP systems is somehow tedious and time consuming (Wei et al., 2005). ERP systems architecture is not appropriate for the entire business requirement (Sarkis & Sundarraj, 2000; Teltumbde, 2000; Hong & Kim, 2002; Wei et al., 2005). Therefore it is very important for the companies to choose a flexible ERP systems and a cooperative vendor that in turn can be responsive to the customer needs (Wei et al., 2005). SMEs are evident to be different than the large organizations in their practices. There are also differences between large organization and SMEs in terms of the selection process of an ERP system (Bernroider & Koch, 2001). These different organizational practices and unique business processes of SMEs cause them prioritizing different factors while selecting an Open Source ERP (Baki & Cakar, 2005). The factors that affect the selection process of an OS ERP by the SMEs can be categorized in to three categories. Factors that are critical for successful ERP Implementation, Factors related to organizational size, and Factors related to openness of the ERP software.

## Factors that are Critical for Successful ERP Implementation

ERP systems automate core activities of the organization by re-engineering core business activities or by making adjustment in the software according to organizations requirement (Holland & Light, 1999). The successful implementation of ERP system promises huge benefits but the disastrous effect of it is also built-in it (Vidyaranya & Cydnee, 2005). Hence selection of appropriate ERP systems is really important for the organization. Among the previous literatures on the Critical Success Factors (CSF's) of successful ERP implementation one of the main CSF's is the 'Selection of the Right ERP Package' itself matching organizational needs and implementation partner (Nah et al., 2001). Somers & Nelson (2001) in their study proposed careful package selection to be one of the most important critical success factors of successful ERP implementation. A closer look on to the literature identified more factors that are directly related to the 'Selection of the Right ERP Package'.

Al-Mashari et al. (2003) grouped the critical success factors in three phases. In the implementation phase ERP Package selection itself is an important factor and 'Training and Education' is another important factor. The implementing organizations think about 'Training and Education' from the vendors/consultants before deciding to implement a particular ERP solution, because a particular challenge of ERP implementation is selecting an appropriate plan for Education and training for end user (Al-Mashari et al., 2003). Sia (2008) argues that the SMEs are evident to fail to achieve the benefits from the ERP project because of the lack of staff with appropriate education and training on technology related to the ERP systems. Hence it is an important that the implementing organization evaluates whether the vendors or Suppliers of ERP solutions provide enough training and education. Johansson and Sudzina (2009) also identified that it is an important selection criteria of Open Source ERP Selection.

Motwani et al. (2005) have described CSFs in three different steps pre-implementation, Implementation and Post-implementation throughout the lifecycle of ERP system. Among the CSFs they included 'ERP Package selection that best fits with current business procedures' and 'Exhaustive analysis of current business processes'. Everdingen et al. (2000) in their study found best fit with current business procedures to be most important factor to be evaluated before the selection of the certain ERP Solution. As they mentioned, fit with current business process is the most important selection criteria for a new system. Johansson & Sudzina (2009) also identified it as an important selection criterion of Open Source ERP Selection.

'Exhaustive analysis of current business processes' in the Implementation step that allow the organization to identify if certain system fits with the current business processes or not and is also

related to the 'Business Process Reengineering (BPR) and minimum customization' which is also one important Critical Success Factors of ERP implementation (Loh & Koh, 2004). Al-Mashari et al. (2003) mention that taking full advantages from ERP implementation requires Business Process Reengineering (BPR) and it is achieved through 'Exhaustive Analysis of Current Business Processes'. It helps to identify potential changes in the Business Processes to avoid customization of the software.

Loh and Koh (2004) found several Critical Success Factors of ERP implementation in the SMEs based on four implementation phases. Among those factors 'Business Process Reengineering (BPR) and minimum customization' needs to be evaluated before selecting a solution. 'Exhaustive Analysis of Current Business Processes' is also related to it as mentioned by Al-Mashari et al. (2003). 'Business Process Reengineering (BPR) and minimum customization' is more critical than having a business plan and vision (Loh & Koh, 2004). 'Vendor Support' is also one of the most important critical factors mentioned by Somers & Nelson (2001). Johansson & Sudzina (2009) in their study found it to be one of the most important selection criteria in selecting an Open Source ERP system. It is also evident to be importantly related to organizational size as Sia (2008) mention 'Vendor Support' to be important to the smaller organizations as they lack educated and trained staffs. Based on the literature review following critical success factors have been identified:

**Training and education:** Training from Suppliers (vendors/consultant). Type and amount of training depends on the ERP solution that the implementing organization is going to implement. For training organizations depend on Suppliers (vendors/consultant) but in terms of Open Source ERP this service can be found from community as well (Johansson & Sudzina, 2009).

**ERP Package selection that best fits with current business procedures:** While selecting the ERP solution for the organization it is important to select one that best fit with organizational current business processes because it is not easy to change in the software and it seems problematical for both Open Source and proprietary ERP (Johansson & Sudzina, 2009).

**Exhaustive analysis of current business processes:** The organization should thoroughly analyze the current business processes as it provides them with information that which ERP solution fits Processes of the organization and what business process needs to be re-engineered (Al-Mashari et al., 2003).

**Business Process Reengineering (BPR) and minimum customization:** It is an important factor because the organization's business processes need to fit with the new system in order to get maximum benefits and it is critical to align business process with the system implementation (Nah et al., 2001).

**Vendor support:** Vendor Support should be taken in to account while selecting the ERP Solution (Nah et al., 2001). In proprietary ERP customers are locked with single vendors or Suppliers for support.

## Factors Related to Organizational Size and Openness of the ERP System

The criteria for the selection of a particular ERP systems show different priorities related to the organization size (Baki & Cakar, 2005). Bernroider and Koch (2001) studied the selection criteria of the ERP systems among SME and large organization. Total 29 different ERP selection criteria were used but only 12 criteria were evident to have strong association with organizational size (Bernroider & Koch, 2001). Their study indicates that only two factors are important for the smaller organizations

and those two are 'Short Implementation time' and 'Adaptability and flexibility of software'. While increasing organizational flexibility, process improvement, internationality and additional organizational ties with customers are evident to be less important to the SMEs (Bernroider & Koch, 2001).

Johansson and Sudzina (2009) describe a common set of selection criteria and compared these criteria with respect to Open Source and Proprietary ERP Systems. According to them these criteria show obvious difference between Open Source ERP and proprietary ERP and hence needed to be studied further in order to determine specific Open Source ERP selection criteria.

Price of the software as one of the most important selection criterion as mentioned by Johansson and Sudzina (2009). Wei et al. (2004) describe the Total Cost of ERP to consist of: price of the software, maintenance cost, consultant expenses, infrastructure cost, and mentioned 'Implementation Time' as a separate selection criteria. According to (Bernroider & Koch, 2001), a short implementation time results in lower cost. And since implementation time is related to cost it might be an important issue to the implementing organization to be examined no matter the ERP is OS or proprietary. Johansson and Sudzina (2009) expressed implementation time as 'Ease/speed of implementation' and mentioned 'Ease/speed of implementation' as most important selection criteria of Open Source ERP solution.

Rao (2000) proposes that SMEs should focus on the 'Affordability' of the software including the attractive price and support. Johansson and Sudzina (2009) also mentioned OS ERPs to be affordable due to less licensing fees.

Rao (2000) also proposed 'Domain Knowledge of the Suppliers' and 'Local Support' from Suppliers in terms of IT expertise and do-main knowledge as the criteria for the SMEs to focus on while selecting ERP system. Johansson and Sudzina (2009) also mentioned 'Vendor Support' as one of the most important to factor which was also mentioned as critical success factor in the previous section.

Free Open Source Software represent a viable alternative to proprietary systems from a software quality and reliability point of view (Tawileh, Rana, Ivins & McIntosh, 2006).

'Ease of use' and 'Functionality' are also mentioned to be important by Johansson and Sudzina (2009) and Everdingen et al. (2000).

Free Open Source Software represents a viable alternative to proprietary systems from a software quality and reliability point of view (Tawileh, Rana, Ivins & McIntosh, 2006). Beside software quality and reliability high flexibility and adaptability of Open Source ERP can also be an influential reason for selecting Open Source ERP (Raymond, 2005cited in Johansson & Sudzina, 2008). 'Customization' is also important factor mentioned in Johansson and Sudzina (2009). It is an important issue to the organizations who need to adjust the system. While openness of the code increases the adaptability which is also important (Johansson & Sudzina, 2008). According to Serrano & Sarriegi (2006), Greater benefits can be obtained by deploying Open Source ERP than other Open Source software systems mainly due to three reasons: 'Increased adaptability', 'Decreased reliance on a single supplier' and 'reduced cost' (cited in Johansson & Sudzina, 2008). 'Reliance on large Community' is one of the most important factors that can make the OS ERP more appealing (in Johansson & Sudzina, 2008). Apart from these factors Johansson and Sudzina(2009) mentioned 'Integration', 'Vendor Reputation' and 'Upgrades' as common ERP Selection criteria which might have been important in OS ERP selection.

Accordingly the factors related to the organizational size and openness of the ERP systems identified in the literature:

**Short implementation time/Speed of implementation:** ERP Implementation is costly and company-wide project (Baki & Cakar, 2005).

Implementation time is directly connected to strategy being followed and implementation scope, while more customization needs more time and cost as described by Baki and Cakar (2005). It refers to the required time to implement ERP systems. It also refers to how fast and easily ERP systems can be implemented.

**Adaptability and flexibility of software:** Adaptability allows software to be modified as needed as the unique business processes need to be preserved. It also refers to how easy it is to customize the software (Bernroider & Koch, 2001). OS ERP gives unlimited access to the source code and increase the adaptability (Johansson & Sudzina, 2008). Flexibility refers to how flexible the software is to change in order to fit with the business processes and the requirements.

**Total cost/price:** Total cost includes price of the software, maintenance cost, expenses for the consultants and infrastructure cost (Wei et al., 2005). Johansson and Sudzina (2008) mentioned that Open Source ERP implementation reduces one third of the implementation cost then compared to proprietary ERP implementation, and it can reduce cost as the SMEs do not need costly and sophisticated hardware.

**Local support:** Local Support includes support from Suppliers (vendors/consultants). It is important for the smaller organizations as they have the employees who lack the education and training on potential technology (Sia, 2008) and also in terms of domain knowledge (Rao, 2000). For proprietary user it is important as they are locked in with one vendor. In terms of OS ERP support from large enough community can replace support from vendors.

**Domain knowledge of the suppliers:** It is important for the Suppliers and developer to know the industry. If the organization is manufacturing industry, it should source the system from the supplier or vendor who has experience in that industry (Rao, 2000) and provides industry specific best practices (Stefanou, 2001).

**Reliability:** Proprietary vendor tries to be highly reliable but Open Source community finds an error faster and solves it quickly while for proprietary it is much harder because same people have access to code always (Johansson & Sudzina, 2009).

**Ease of use:** Proprietary ERP tries to be more users friendly but community of users can make the OS ERP more-or-less acceptable for most of the users (Johansson & Sudzina, 2009).

**Customization:** Customization of code is important in terms of OS though it is not the only feature of OS ERP systems anymore, now MS Dynamics AX allows certain level of customization but the others are still not customizable. Customization ability of systems makes systems adaptable and flexible (Johansson & Sudzina, 2009).

**Functionality:** Proprietary ERP may offer more but in Open Source ERP they are less, may be easier to master them. Checking functionality of specific solution is an important factor (Johansson & Sudzina, 2009).

**Vendor reputation:** The reputation of the vendor in the market, how the previous customer evaluated them in terms of services (Johansson & Sudzina, 2009).

**Training:** Education and training from the vendors or the Suppliers for the key users in the implementing organization. It might be an important factor (Johansson & Sudzina, 2009).

**Upgrade:** Upgrading Open Source ERP is free but Proprietary ERP customers have to buy upgrade or pay an annual fee which can be an important issue in OS ERP selection (Johansson & Sudzina, 2009).

Summarized result of the literature review is presented in *Table 1*.

## Concluding Framework

A theoretical model was developed based on the frame of reference discussed above for the factors that influence SMEs to select an Open Source ERP. The theoretical model includes all the probable factors that may motivate SMEs to select Open Source ERP.

- Critical Success Factors for both Proprietary and Open Source ERP implementation that are related to ERP selection or evaluated at the time of selection have been discussed.
- The Selection criteria that are related to organizational size and Openness of the ERP systems have also been discussed. It is found that SMEs emphasize more on few criteria in ERP selection, while these criteria might be less important to larger organizations.
- The factors related to Openness of the ERP systems have been discussed. It is also found to influence the ERP selection by the SMEs.

## RESEARCH METHODS

This chapter presents a result from an empirical study which identifies the most important factors that may motivate the Small and Medium Sized Enterprises (SMEs) to select OS ERP. 18 selection factors were identified through an extensive literature review and presented in the theoretical model. Primary data is obtained based on that literature review from SMEs that are using Open Source ERP systems, vendors who are developing such solutions and from the consultants who work on behalf of vendors and provide guidance to firms on Open Source ERP solution issues. For this purpose two questionnaire were designed; one for SMEs and the other for Suppliers. These two questionnaires were comprised of various questions addressing which rationales are most

Table 1. Summarize the result of the literature review: factors that motivate SMEs to select an Open Source ERP

| | Al-Mashari et al. (2003) | Motwani et al. (2005) | Everdingen et al. (2000) | Loh and Koh (2004) | Johansson and Sudzina (2009) | Somers and Nelson (2001) | Baki and Kemal (2005) | Bernroider and Koch (2001) | Choon Ling Sia (2008) | Johansson and Sudzina (2008) |
|---|---|---|---|---|---|---|---|---|---|---|
| 'Training and Education' | ✓ | | ✓ | | ✓ | | | | | |
| 'Vendor Support' | | | ✓ | | ✓ | ✓ | | | ✓ | |
| 'Best fits with current business procedures' | | ✓ | ✓ | | ✓ | | | | | |
| 'Exhaustive analysis of current business processes' | ✓ | ✓ | | | | | | | | |
| 'Business Process Reengineering(BPR) and minimum customization' | ✓ | | | ✓ | | | | | | |
| Short Implementation time/ Speed of Implementation | | | ✓ | | ✓ | | ✓ | ✓ | | |
| Adaptability and flexibility of software' | | | | | ✓ | | ✓ | ✓ | | ✓ |
| Total Cost | | | ✓ | | ✓ | | | ✓ | | ✓ |
| Domain Knowledge of the supplier | | | | | ✓ | | | | | |
| Reliability | | | | | ✓ | | | | | |
| Ease of use | | | ✓ | | ✓ | | | | | |
| Customization | | | | | ✓ | | | | | |
| Integration | | | | | ✓ | | | | | |
| Functionality | | | ✓ | | ✓ | | | | | |
| Vendor Reputation | | | | | | | | | | |
| Decreased Reliance on Single Vendor | | | | | | | | | | ✓ |
| Reliance on large Community | | | | | ✓ | | | | | |
| Upgrades | | | | | ✓ | | | | | |

important in selecting OS ERP systems for SMEs. The respondents were provided with multiple alternatives to choose from. These questionnaires were then sent to those companies who are using Open Source ERP systems and to Suppliers of such ERP solutions. The aim for designing two separate questionnaires was twofold-getting the opinions of users i.e. SMEs about preferred reasons for selection of OS ERP solutions as well as getting the perception of the vendors and consultants about what they think motivated their customers to selection of Open Source ERP solutions. Both questionnaires were comprised of closed and open ended questions. Each questionnaire was split into two sections; where section 1 deals with basic information of the respondents while section 2 deals with importance of different factors in selection of Open Source ERP.

Responsible representatives from various companies were contacted through mail. Survey in a form of web based questionnaires was used to get the responds from a widespread respondent. In our case we have to obtain feedbacks from companies which were geographically dispersed. The survey questionnaires were made by using an internet based survey tool[1]. Individual emails were sent to all the respondents. E-mails contained a letter describing the purpose of the survey, why the respondents were chosen and a web link to web based survey questionnaire. The email was sent to SMEs on 12th of April, 2010 and to Suppliers on 19th of April, 2010. On 18th of April, 2010 a reminder was sent to SMEs who did not answer the questionnaire.

Moreover a questionnaire comprised of open ended questions was also sent to 'Prof. Rogerio Atem de Carvalho, D. Sc.' who is an OS ERP expert. The aim for this was to use the perception of expert in the analysis of results found through empirical findings. The opinion of Open Source ERP expert was collected by sending a questionnaire via e-mail. 'Prof. Rogerio Atem de Carvalho, D. Sc.' is a prominent researcher in the field of FOS-ERP and a consultant of ERP5 FOS-ERP. He

is a member and chair of the Brazilian Chapter of IFIP Working Group on Enterprise Information Systems and founder member of the IEE SMC Society Technical Committee on Enterprise Information Systems. He is also an Associate Editor of Enterprise Information Systems journal.

Target population for this study is all the Small and Medium Sized organizations who have implemented Open Source ERP but population cannot be taken into consideration as all these companies cannot be accessed entirely. All the Small and Medium Sized organizations who have implemented Open Source ERP can not be included in this study due to some practical limitations such as- there is no valid statistics in most of the countries about the number and list of the SMEs who have implemented ERP systems. In few countries there is statistics about the proprietary ERP implementation in the enterprises but it is not available when it comes to Open Source ERP systems. That is why finding out the real number and list of the SMEs who have implemented Open Source ERP would be really troublesome and time consuming. For example, in case of Sweden, statistics on all the registered companies are available to institution named 'Government's Statistical Bureau of Sweden'. According to the statistics of year 2008 about 30 percent of the enterprises use ERP systems to share information in the enterprises. It would be really problematic to find out how many SMEs out of that number use Open Source ERP. For this study objective/ random sampling could not be taken because in that case the exact number and list of SMEs that implemented Open Source ERP would be needed. The list must be assigned with numbers and then statistical random sample could be taken from the list. That is why the non probability (purposive and convenient) sampling technique is used in this study. For taking responses from the SMEs the convenience sampling was used. Castillo (2009) explains convenience sampling as a non-probability sampling technique where respondents are selected because of their easy availability for research. The sample of SMEs has been selected in a convenient way from customer lists available on Open Source ERP vendor's web sites. An email containing the link to the web based questionnaire survey[2] was sent to 50 SMEs who had valid contact addresses on the web sites of Open Source ERP vendors. The same mail was also sent to 'Community Mailing List' of WebERP and OpenERP.

To obtain information from the Suppliers (vendors/consultants) of the Open Source ERP systems, purposive sampling technique was used. The reasons for using a purposive sampling technique for vendors/consultants have been numerous such as; there might be existence of many Open Source ERP names in the internet but most of them are just a project registered in 'Sourceforge.net'. Many of them have websites but no evidence of having any customers or implementers. Statistical random sample technique could not been used in this case because there would have been a chance of selection of some Open Source ERPs that do not exist in reality or have no customer at all. That is why 8 vendors were selected purposefully who are prominent in the Open Source ERP market and who have cases of successful implementations. The purpose was to get trustworthy opinion for research. Polkinghorne (2005) describes purposive sampling as a technique when the focus is on obtaining rich information from more specific source rather than having a large amount of data. 20 consultants were selected based on the availability of their contact addresses from the website of those 8 vendors. The selection of consultants was also a convenient sampling. An e-mail containing the link to web based survey questionnaire[3] was sent to those 8 vendors and 20 consultants. A total of 24 responses were received from all respondents including SMEs and Suppliers (vendors/consultants). They were divided into two groups. Out of 24 respondents, 14 of them were users of Open Source ERP and rest of them i.e. 10 were Suppliers (vendors/consultants) who were developing Open Source ERP solutions or

providing implementation support to their users. Four collected questionnaires from the SMEs were not completed properly and hence were eliminated. Totally 20 correctly answered questionnaires were used for presenting and analyzing the results.

The expert has deep knowledge about Open Source ERP issues and hence was selected purposefully to acquire his opinion for analyzing the results obtained. Polkinghorne (2005) explains purposive sampling as a technique to get rich information from respondents and where the researchers select the participants based on their willingness to explain their experience to researcher. The expert was selected since he has involvement in research and development of Open Source ERP for long and has adequate knowledge about Open Source ERP and was willing to participate in the research. For quantifying, the data obtained from the Respondent (SMEs and Suppliers of OS ERP) a 5 point Likert Scale (4=Very Important, 3=Important, 2=Less Important, 1=Not Important, 0=Don't Know) is used and the mean value is taken to make a mean ranking in an ascending order of importance of the factors. Two different ranking of motivating factors of OS ERP were made based on the responds from the SMEs and Suppliers.

## EMPIRICAL FINDINGS

The empirical findings contain three perspectives. The results are presented in three sections explaining users' perspective i.e. the perspective of OS ERP implementer SMEs, perspective of the suppliers (vendors/consultants) of such OS ERP systems and perspective of the OS ERP expert.

### Users (SMEs) Perspective

Users (SMEs) who have participated in the survey are mostly from manufacturing and service industry. Most of the SMEs are small in size except a medium organization from Malaysia. WebERP is the mostly implemented ERP among those users.

The users are mostly from Asia and Europe while two of them are representing Africa and America. The respondent from USA wanted to be anonymous. Information of the users taken part in the study can be seen in the *Table 2*.

The responses of the SMEs about the factors motivated them to select Open Source ERP are presented in a mean ranking in an ascending order of importance in *Table 3* as mentioned in the research method that a general psychometric '5 point Likert Scale' is used to measure the importance of the factors that motivated SMEs.

'Reduced Cost' of the Open Source ERP solutions was considered very important to the SMEs when they were selecting ERP. Total cost of OS ERP includes zero or less licensing fees, less maintenance cost, less consultation and infrastructure cost. Due to the importance of less cost of OS ERP implementation 'Reduced Cost' termed as most important factor (mean: 3.8) by the SMEs.

Implementing organizations always prefer the ERP system which is easy to use and which best fits with organizational processes. Responses from the users (SMEs) also depict it. 'Ease of Use' and 'Functionality' are second most important factors

along with 'Support from the community' with a mean value of 3.6. Since Cost is the most important factor to the SMEs 'Support from the community' was also very important to them because reliance on the large community helps them to get rid of extra cost from Vendor/Supplier support during implementation or fixing problems.

'Implementation time' and 'Customization' were very important to almost half of the respondents during the selection because, the more the implementation time required the more cost added and Customization also resulted in high implementation cost. 'Business Process Re-engineering' was also important to the implementers since implementing organization wants to avoid it in order to keep unique business processes intact. These three factors were resulted as third most important factors in the study with a mean value of importance of 3.2.

'Best fit with the current Business processes', 'Increased Adaptability & flexibility' and 'Easy Integration with current systems' got the same mean value of importance, though 'Best fit with the current Business processes' was very important to more(40%) respondents than 'Increased

*Table 2. Users (SMEs) information*

| Company Name | Geo-graphical location | Industrial sector | Size of the organization | Implemented ERP | Responsibility of the respondents |
|---|---|---|---|---|---|
| Edoro Private Ltd. | India | Distribution | Small | OpenERP | IT Manager |
| NLTechno | France | Service | Small | Dolibarr | Programmer |
| ODIN Motor Company | The Netherlands | Manufacturing | Small | Dolibarr | Project Manager |
| Ulas Zipper | Turkey | Manufacturing | Small | WebERP | Consultant |
| Xuandoo | China | Distribution | Small | Opentaps | Business/Systems analyst |
| Webtech Resources | Kenya | Service | Small | WebERP | Consultant |
| Digital India | India | Manufacturing | Small | WebERP | Consultant |
| Profen Sdn. Bhd. | Malaysia | Manufacturing | Medium | Openbravo | Project Manager |
| JPL TSolucio, S.L. | Spain | Service | Small | WebERP | IT Manager |
| ----- | USA | Service | Small | Compiere | Chief Information Officer |

*Table 3. Mean ranking of the factors that may motivate SMEs to select OS ERP*

| Factors motivated to select an Open Source ERP | Very Important (%) | Important (%) | Less Important (%) | Not important (%) | Don't know (%) | Mean Value of Importance |
|---|---|---|---|---|---|---|
| Reduced Cost | 80 | 20 | 0 | 0 | 0 | 3,8 |
| Support from the community | 60 | 40 | 0 | 0 | 0 | 3,6 |
| Ease of Use | 60 | 40 | 0 | 0 | 0 | 3,6 |
| Functionality | 60 | 40 | 0 | 0 | 0 | 3,6 |
| Implementation Time | 50 | 30 | 10 | 10 | 0 | 3,2 |
| Business Process Re-engineering | 40 | 40 | 20 | 0 | 0 | 3,2 |
| Customization | 40 | 40 | 20 | 0 | 0 | 3,2 |
| Best fit with the current Business processes | 40 | 30 | 30 | 0 | 0 | 3,1 |
| Increased Adaptability & flexibility' | 20 | 70 | 10 | 0 | 0 | 3,1 |
| Easy Integration with current systems | 20 | 70 | 10 | 0 | 0 | 3,1 |
| High reliability | 40 | 30 | 10 | 20 | 0 | 2,9 |
| Education and training from Suppliers | 40 | 20 | 20 | 20 | 0 | 2,8 |
| Free Upgrades | 40 | 20 | 20 | 20 | 0 | 2,8 |
| Thorough analysis of current business processes | 30 | 20 | 50 | 0 | 0 | 2,8 |
| Supplier Support | 20 | 50 | 20 | 10 | 0 | 2,8 |
| Decreased reliance on Single Vendor | 20 | 50 | 10 | 20 | 0 | 2,7 |
| Domain Know-ledge of the vendors | 20 | 20 | 40 | 20 | 0 | 2,4 |
| Vendor Reputation | 0 | 40 | 40 | 20 | 0 | 2,2 |

Adaptability & flexibility' and 'Easy Integration with current systems' which were very important to only few respondents.

'High Reliability', 'Education and training from Suppliers', 'Free Upgrades', 'Thorough analysis of current business processes' and 'Supplier Support' were not that much important to the users while they were selecting OS ERP. 'Domain Knowledge of the vendors' and 'Vendor Reputation' got least importance to the respondents.

The respondents were also asked about the factors that should be given priority in the OS ERP selection in an open ended question but there were very few answers. Among the four respondents two of them identified 'Support from the Community' as most important. One of the other respondents mentioned 'top management needed to be convinced about Open Source con-

cept as it is not only about reduced price but also the community supports it provides'. The other respondent's opinion was 'Open Source is good for Africa'.

## Suppliers (Vendors/ Consultants) Perspective

Suppliers who have participated in the study are mostly consultant while few were vendors. Some suppliers deal with renowned OS ERP systems while some of the suppliers work with new or growing OS ERP systems with small customer bases. The vendors and Consultants information can be seen in the *Table 4*

The responses received from the Suppliers (vendors/consultants) about the factors they think motivated their customers to select the OS ERP

*Table 4. Suppliers (vendors and consultants) information*

| Company Name | Geo-graphical location | Vendor/ Consultant | ERP Solution Provide | Responsibility of the respondents |
|---|---|---|---|---|
| Compiere, Inc. | USA | Vendor | Compiere ERP and CRM | Sr. Director of Sales |
| xTuple | USA | Vendor | xTuple ERP: PostBooks Edition | CEO |
| NightLabs Consul-ting GmbH | Germany | Vendor | JFire | Architect & Lead De-veloper |
| SRL | Italy | Consultant | OpenERP | Software Developer |
| UAB 'Sandas' | Lithuania | Consultant | Open ERP | Project Manager |
| Vicus eBusiness So-lutions bv | Nether-lands | Consultant | vtiger CRM | Managing Director |
| Digitals India Secu-rity Products Pvt. Ltd | India | Consultant | WebERP | Manager(Tech.) |
| Moxx Consulting | India | Consultant | WebERP | Principal Consultant |
| Artoge | Nether-lands | Consultant | DOLIBARR | CEO |
| Mitija Australia | Australia | Consultant | OpenERP | Managing Director |

are presented in a mean ranking in an ascending order of importance in *Table 5*. As mentioned in the research method that a general psychometric '5 point Likert scale' is used to measure the level of importance the Suppliers think given by their customers when selecting their solution.

It is obvious that implementing organization analyze the functionality of ERP along with the cost, potential support from supplier and flexibility to customize the software in order to get maximum benefit from the systems. But according to suppliers perspective 'Functionality' and 'Increased Adaptability & flexibility' are prioritized more by their customers. Suppliers might have wanted to proclaim that apart from 'Reduced Cost' their customer become more interested because of 'Functionality' and 'Increased Adaptability & flexibility'. 'Reduced Cost' and 'Supplier Support' come after 'Increased Adaptability & flexibility' in the list with the same mean value of importance of 3.2, though more Suppliers (60%) assumed that 'Supplier Support' was important to their customer than 'Reduced Cost' (40%).

'Business Process Re-engineering', 'Best fit with the current Business processes' is the next important factor in the ranking with a mean value

of 3.1. 'Education and Training from Suppliers' goes after that in the ranking with a mean value of 3. The other factors were not that importantly admitted by the suppliers to be important to their customers. The interesting fact is that 'Support from the community' was one of the most important factors identified by the users which got least importance according to suppliers responses. With minimum mean value of importance of 1.7 it places at the bottom of the list.

The Suppliers were further asked about the 'Free Upgrades' of their OS ERP Systems. 60% of the vendors/consultants provide free upgrade of their solution to the user while 40% of them charge for it.

The Suppliers were asked to what extent they agree that Open Source ERP adoption increase the reliance on large community. 50% of the respondents strongly agree that the adoption of Open Source ERP decrease the reliance on single vendor, 25% disagree on that while rest 25% of the vendors/consultant remained neutral.

*Table 5. Mean ranking of the factors that the suppliers (vendors/consultants) think motivated their customer*

| Factors motivated to select an Open Source ERP | Very Important (%) | Important (%) | Less Important (%) | Not important (%) | Don't know (%) | Mean |
|---|---|---|---|---|---|---|
| Functionality | 50 | 40 | 10 | 0 | 0 | 3,4 |
| Increased Adaptability & flexibility | 40 | 50 | 10 | 0 | 0 | 3,3 |
| Reduced Cost | 40 | 40 | 20 | 0 | 0 | 3,2 |
| Supplier Support | 60 | 20 | 0 | 20 | 0 | 3,2 |
| Business Process Re-engineering | 20 | 70 | 10 | 0 | 0 | 3,1 |
| Best fit with the current Business processes | 30 | 50 | 20 | 0 | 0 | 3,1 |
| Education and training from Suppliers | 20 | 60 | 20 | 0 | 0 | 3 |
| Customization | 20 | 50 | 30 | 0 | 0 | 2,9 |
| Implementation Time | 20 | 50 | 10 | 20 | 0 | 2,7 |
| Ease of Use | 10 | 50 | 40 | 0 | 0 | 2,7 |
| Easy Integration with current systems | 10 | 60 | 20 | 0 | 10 | 2,6 |
| High reliability | 20 | 30 | 30 | 20 | 0 | 2,5 |
| Domain Knowledge of the vendors | 20 | 30 | 30 | 10 | 10 | 2,4 |
| Free Upgrades | 10 | 30 | 30 | 30 | 0 | 2,2 |
| Thorough analysis of current business processes | 0 | 30 | 50 | 20 | 0 | 2,1 |
| Support from the community | 0 | 20 | 40 | 30 | 10 | 1,7 |

## Perspective of Open Source ERP Expert

Prof. Rogerio Atem de Carvalho, D. Sc. was asked about different important factors in selection process of Open Source ERP to get experienced and detailed opinion. When the expert was asked about the 'Implementation Time' he replied: 'SME lead-time perception is different, they are used to faster decisions and process, simply because they have less people involved. SME also understand that since they are smaller, lead-time MUST be smaller'.

It is important for the implementing organization to analyze the business process to match it with the functionality of the ERP systems. When the expert was asked about this regarding small and medium sized company he replied: 'They know their business process well, because there are fewer process. However, they don't apply very complicated ERP selection processes. For

further query on 'Analyzing the functionality of the ERP solution' he added, 'Usually, they search for the 'most similar' ERP, and sometimes keep non-compliant process outside the ERP - in special the small ones. Although this can sound as an idiosyncrasy, their perception is that is less effort than adapting the company - or the system. It is interesting to say that there is a difference between the small and the medium company, and for the ERP realm I suggest that they should be considered in separate'.

By answering the question about 'changing the software to match the organizational requirements', he emphasized on evaluating small and medium company separately as he replied 'Again we should separate small from medium.' He further added, regarding the question of ability of the SMEs to change the OS ERP systems 'Probably small companies wouldn't do that, but some medium yes'.

Regarding Industry specific solutions he replied, 'Sure, industry specific solution is much better for the smaller, since they don't have money to customize the system a lot'.

When Mr. Carvalho was asked about his opinion on the vendor reputation he replied, 'Yes, but some users also check the community involvement'.

Regarding 'Education and training from Suppliers' he replied, 'Community is enough only for small cases. Sending someone (sometimes, only one or two persons!) to be trained in the vendor site is the most common solution'.

Regarding 'Supplier Support' and the 'Support from the community' Mr. Carvalho replied, 'There is a difference on Commercial Open Source and Community Open Source. Most successful FOS-ERPs are of the second type for sure. And the companies behind the ERP needs to earn money from the services, therefore, it is very hard for them to admit that (which is perfectly understandable)'.

For the question regarding cost of 'Supplier Support' he replied, 'Typically it is smaller than for P-ERP (proprietary) because they relay also in other open source technologies (database, operational system, office suite). Also, it is possible to find support from 'anyone who knows the system', including others than the main vendor, consultants etc. Although the adopter is free to choose, the support network generally is smaller, giving the smaller marketing work (less people know the system = less consultants)'.

Regarding the support from the community during the implementation Mr. Carvalho replied, 'Depends on the customization complexity. For environments not so complex, the user can do parameterization, for instance'.

Regarding cost to implement updates Prof. Carvalho pointed the individual case and problem as he answered, 'The same above, it depends on the problem but generally is less expensive than P-ERP'.

## ANALYTICAL DISCUSSION

The comparative representation of the results from two kinds of respondents (SMEs and Suppliers) is presented in *Table 6*. The difference between two mean values of importance for each of the factors is presented to make the reader comprehend for different factors how much disagreement is there between SMEs and Suppliers regarding importance of those factors. The average of two mean values for each of the factors will also be presented to find out comparatively which factors of Open Source ERP are most important that motivate SMEs to select Open Source ERP. The factors are illustrated in a Descending order of Average of the two mean value of importance in the *Table 6*.

As visible in *Table 6*, 'Reduced Total Cost' and 'Functionality' are the two most important factors on an average. Open Source ERP implementation reduce one third of the implementation cost then compared to proprietary ERP implementation (Johansson & Sudzina, 2008). That is why 'Reduced Total Cost' got priority by both types of respondents though in case of 'Reduced Total Cost' there is a significant difference of 0.6 between the two mean values. It indicates the suppliers' initiative to advertise their systems.

The empirical findings also revealed that. 'Functionality' of OS ERP got high level of importance to most of the SMEs, and most of the Suppliers also considered it important to their customers. The average mean value of importance for this factor is 3.5. Analyzing the functionality let the SMEs to select the right Open Source ERP which is similar to their organizational processes. The expert interview also revealed the same as Prof. R., A., De Carvalho mentioned 'Usually, they search for the 'most similar' ERP'.

SMEs identified 'Increased Adaptability & flexibility' as an important factor to evaluate before the selection, 3.1 mean value of importance from SMEs responds represents that. The Suppliers even identified it to be more important to their

*Table 6. Comparative ranking of factors that motivate SMEs to select OS ERP*

| Factors motivated to select an Open Source ERP | Mean value of Importance (SMEs) | Mean Value of Importance (Suppliers) | Difference | Average |
|---|---|---|---|---|
| Reduced Total Cost | 3,8 | 3,2 | 0,6 | 3,5 |
| Functionality | 3,6 | 3,4 | 0,2 | 3,5 |
| Increased Adaptability & flexibility | 3,1 | 3,3 | 0,2 | 3,2 |
| Ease of Use | 3,6 | 2,7 | 0,9 | 3,15 |
| Business Process Re-engineering | 3,2 | 3,1 | 0,1 | 3,15 |
| Best fit with the current Business processes | 3,1 | 3,1 | 0 | 3,1 |
| Customization | 3,2 | 2,9 | 0,3 | 3,05 |
| Supplier Support | 2,8 | 3,2 | 0,4 | 3 |
| Implementation Time | 3,2 | 2,7 | 0,5 | 2,95 |
| Education and training from Suppliers | 2,8 | 3 | 0,2 | 2,9 |
| Easy Integration with current systems | 3,1 | 2,6 | 0,5 | 2,85 |
| High reliability | 2,9 | 2,5 | 0,4 | 2,7 |
| Support from the community | 3,6 | 1,7 | 1,9 | 2,65 |
| Free Upgrades | 2,8 | 2,2 | 0,6 | 2,5 |
| Thorough analysis of current business processes | 2,8 | 2,1 | 0,7 | 2,45 |
| Domain Knowledge of the Vendors | 2,4 | 2,4 | 0 | 2,4 |
| Decreased reliance on Single Vendor** | 2,7 | ----- | ----- | ----- |
| Vendor Reputation** | 2,2 | ---- | ------- | ---- |

(** 100% reply could not be received from Suppliers)

customer which can be said from their responses with 3.3 mean value of importance. The reason of this factor is more important to Suppliers assumption is probably because of business aspect, as it is an attribute of the ERP systems which tells how flexible the software to edit or modify as per the needs of the customers and it is one of the factors that the Suppliers use for promotion of their systems. The importance of this to the customers can be linked with the necessity of the customization in the code. As visible in *Table 6,* customization is important to the SMEs. The easy and flexible customizability also got importance to SMEs on an average, as 'Increased Adaptability & flexibility 'got 3.2 average mean values.

'Ease of Use 'got higher importance to most of the SMEs though in Suppliers point of view it was not that important. The difference between these two values is 0.9 which is almost 1 point in the used Likert Scale. So the level of disagreement is high. It is normal expectation of all implementers to have an ERP system easy to operate. The answer was bit biased may be due the Suppliers predetermined claim about easiness of their systems. However, with an average mean value of 3.15 'Ease of Use' is an important factor.

'Business Process Reengineering' was identified by most of the Suppliers and SMEs to be important With an average mean value of importance of 3.15. The reasons behind 'Business Process Reengineering' of being important to the SMEs might be the cause of Standardization of the processes. 'Business Process Reengineering' might have been important from another perspective that is: the smaller organizations do not have enough resources to do extensive editing in code;

they might have been interested to the 'Business Process Reengineering' because they want to avoid this cost. The expert interview also revealed that 'Business Process Reengineering' is important to the SMEs to avoid editing the code of ERP Systems. Prof. Carvalho says, 'Probably small companies wouldn't do that, but some medium would'. Smaller organization cannot afford to change the Code as per their need because they want to avoid unnecessary cost further more SMEs are more flexible to adopt changes (de Carvalho & Johansson, 2009). And almost all the SMEs in this study are small in size, only one of them is medium. More involvement of the Medium organization might have made the result different.

On an average 'Best fit with the current Business processes' is an important factor to the SMEs in the selection processes and the Suppliers also identified it to be important to their customers. Due to the limited size SMEs normally have fewer processes specially the smaller organizations, which are generally less complex than the larger organizations and hence they easily could match them with the ERP Solutions. That is why they might have given importance to the ERP systems that are closest to their functionality. The expert interview also revealed the same as Mr. Carvalho mentioned, 'Usually, they search for the 'most similar' ERP, and sometimes keep non-compliant process outside the ERP - in special the small ones'.

The Suppliers expectation about importance given by their SME customers to 'Customization' was lower than importance given by SMEs. With an average mean value of 3.05 'Customization' is an important factor overall. Giving importance to 'Customization' and 'Business Process Reengineering' by SMEs at the same time is bit strange. The probable reason to indentify 'Customization' as important might be SMEs attempt to save certain unique business process which is the source of their competitive advantage.

'Supplier Support' got less importance to SMEs than Suppliers assumption. SMEs relied on the Community mostly. The mean value of importance of 'Supplier Support' identified by the SMEs is 2.8 which is less than the level of importance the Suppliers assumed their customer given, which is 3.2. Over all 'Supplier Support' can be said an important factor with the average mean value of 3. The reason for this factor to be less important to the SMEs may be the cost of support. Because the Vendor Support is not free even in some cases it can overweight the zero cost of the systems for example, in Sweden nowadays a consultant can charge even 1,500 SEK per hour for Open Source Software while Consultants expert in Microsoft Products charge almost half of the figure (Danielsson, 2007 cited in Johansson & Sudzina, 2008).

'Implementation Time' got importance to the SMEs with a mean value of importance of 3.2. It was very important to most of the SMEs because the lesser the time the lower the cost. Prof. R., A., De Carvalho also commented like this. As he says, 'SME lead-time perception is different; they are used to faster decisions and process, simply because they have less people involved. SME also understand that since they are smaller, lead-time MUST be smaller'. Over all, 'Implementation Time' is not that important as the average mean value of importance is under 3.

'Education and training from Suppliers' did not get importance to the SMEs. There might be several reasons, one of them is the insufficient education and training from the Suppliers, another reason can be the cost for the training. Another possible reason is that for the smaller organization the Community is enough as they have less functionality and those are less complex relatively. Prof. Carvalho makes it more clear as he says, 'Community is enough only for small cases. So they were just focusing on the preliminary education and training from the Suppliers and for the rest they rely on community.

'Easy Integration with current systems' comes after that in the list. The average mean value of importance 2.85 indicates it is not that important overall. 'High Reliability' also was not that important to the SMEs, and overall average mean value of importance is also not that high.

'Support from the community' is one of the most important factors identified by the SMEs. The high mean value of importance indicates it from the responds of the SMEs. With a high mean value of importance of 3.6 it is the second most important factor to SMEs. But according to the Suppliers point of view it is less important with the mean value of 1.7. That is why the average mean value of importance is also low. The difference between the two mean values of importance is 1.9 which is really a big number and it indicates a big difference between the SMEs expectations to the Community and the Suppliers acknowledgement about it. So it can be said that the opinion from the Suppliers does not reflect the real importance given by the SMEs on this factor. The Suppliers might have been biased in their opinion. It is commercial reason that might have biased them in their opinion. Prof. Carvalho's assessment is "the companies behind the ERP need to earn money from the services, therefore, it is very hard for them to admit that (which is perfectly understandable)." When the SMEs search for Open Source ERP solutions their expectations to the community is much more higher than their expectations to the Supplier because one of the most important benefits of deploying Open Source Software is that it decreases reliance on single supplier (Serrano & Sarriegi, 2006 cited in Johansson & Sudzina, 2008) and the 'Vendor Support' can be interpreted as support from the community (Johansson & Sudzina, 2008). That's why the 'Support from the community' got higher importance to the SMEs and in fact it can be termed as one of the most important factors to them though the Suppliers did not admit it.

On an average mean value of 2.6 'Free Upgrades' is a less important factor overall. According to SMEs point of view it got 2.8 mean value of importance. According to Suppliers assumption also it is less important and the mean value of importance is 2.2. The possible reason of 'Free Upgrades' for being less important to the Suppliers is all the Suppliers do not offer upgrades for free, 40% supplier's upgrades are not free.

'Thorough analysis of current business processes' was not that important to SMEs as the mean value of importance is 2.8 which is under 3. It indicates that to some SMEs it was very important but to most of them it was either important or less important. The Business Processes of the SMEs are very few and they know those very well and they do not need to analyze their business processes thoroughly. The expert Prof. R., A., de Carvalho also mentioned this as the reason for not analyzing business processes thoroughly, as he mentioned, "They know their business process well, because there are fewer processes". Suppliers also identified it to be less important to their customers.

The factor 'Domain knowledge of the vendors' or industry specific solution got less importance to the both types of respondents. With an average of 2.4 it is placed at the bottom of the table.

For the factors 'Decreased reliance on Single Vendor' and 'Vendor Reputation' 100% responds could not be get and hence comparison between two respondents point of view could not be done.

## Most Important Factors that Motivate the SMEs to Select Open Source ERP

Based on the average of the two mean values of importance for each of the factors represented in the *Table 6*, the top important factors were identified. The Suppliers in few cases might have not given the exact opinion, they might have thought about their business while answering the questions. It becomes clearer when one of the top important factors identified by the SMEs got lowest importance from the anticipation of the Suppliers.

So, the consideration is the factors that have average mean value of importance more than 3 will be considered as important factor to motivate SMEs to select Open Source ERP as 3 indicates 'Important' in the scale used in this study to measure the level of importance. These are mutually important factors identified from the result of the responds from both SMEs and Suppliers.

As subjective answer is understandable from the Suppliers for 'Support from the community' and as it is one of the most important factors identified by SMEs, 'Support from the community' is also included in the list. *Table 7* represents mutually top most important factors that may influence SMEs to select an Open Source ERP.

## FUTURE RESEARCH DIRECTIONS

This study was supposed to conduct on the SMEs but the study could include only one Medium sized organization which can be an implication for the future studies. As the medium organizations have bit more business processes and those are also bit complex than the smaller organizations have. So, their expectations to the Open Source ERP and

*Table 7. Top most important factors that influence SMEs to select an Open Source ERP*

| |
|---|
| *Reduced Total Cost* |
| *Functionality* |
| *Increased Adaptability & flexibility* |
| *Ease of Use* |
| *Business Process Re-engineering* |
| *Best fit with the current Business processes* |
| *Customization* |
| *Supplier Support* |
| *Support from the community* |

level of giving importance to different factors of Open Source ERP would also be different in some ways. It would be very interesting to study this.

The study was conducted on different SMEs having different geographical locations and which could be done for a single country with randomized selection.

There are many large organizations even some fortune 500 companies' also implemented Open Source ERP solution. It could also be very interesting to study the factors motivated them to overlook many prominent proprietary ERP.

No or few investigations are made on what happened after organization implemented open source ERP solutions. Are they satisfied once they deployed such systems? Moreover, did they face any problems or challenges after they adopted such open source ERP solutions? If so, how they overcame with those challenges? Investigating these issues will be of great interest and importance as it will also explore the real success rate and future scope of these Open Source ERP systems.

A research can be made to check the issues in developed countries and developing countries separately regarding Open Source ERP; and then to make a comparison between them. Because the licensing issues are different in developed and developing countries and this way there is a possibility that different results may be obtained for them.

## CONCLUSION

The ground of the chapter was to present a study that identifies the factors motivate SMEs to prioritize an Open Source ERP over the Proprietary ERP. The supplementary aim was to draw implications for the interested parties. Open Source ERP is gaining acceptance day by day. This can be due to the reason that the proprietary ERP systems are disheartening the users as they are facing various challenges once they implemented them. The other reason can be the maturity of Open Source

ERP solutions, with the passage of time this type of ERP systems are more matured and can be trusted. The concept of Open Source opened new way to collaborate, distribute, customization and use. Open Source ERP also gave this flexibility in enterprise computing area with its downsizing cost and customizability. It is developed from many distance places, hence more modular and hence there is no exact owner. Anyone can share, download, distribute and edit which make it more robust. It has a different view than the proprietary licensing and support. However, let's return to the Research Question: **What motivates the SMEs to select an open source ERP?**

Throughout the analysis that was done based on the empirical findings the discussion was directed to the answer of the research question.

The top most important factors that motivate SMEs to select an Open Source ERP are the following:

- Reduced Total Cost
- Functionality
- Increased Adaptability & flexibility
- Ease of Use
- Business Process Re-engineering
- Best fit with the current Business processes
- Customization
- Supplier Support
- Support from the community

In this chapter the SMEs were investigated regarding the importance of the ERP selection factors. Furthermore, the comparison of this result with the importance as suppliers thinking on their customers allowed us to see the difference between the two levels of importance and to identify mutually important factors. The importance of the motivating factors to select an Open Source ERP might be different from organization to organization. It might be dependent on the size, geographical location of the organization or many other issues.

From the discussion above it can be concluded that OS ERP gave an alternative to the SMEs enjoy the benefits of enterprise wide information systems at a low cost. And SMEs are willing to take these benefits. Since the SMEs have less and simple business processes they can easily find the appropriate ERP systems and OS ERP might be perfect choice for them. Large community from all around the world develops the OS ERP and for that it is more modular and more flexible to customize a module without hampering the others. It can be another matter to be interested about this sort of ERP. Large community of OS ERP replaces paid services of consultant of proprietary ERP. Community can fix a bug more quickly and can solve a problem quickly which is totally free. SMEs suffer from resources which are a drawback in using ERP systems since it required sufficient human resources along with sufficient fund. But one or two experts with the help of community can implement OS ERP which can really be an attractive deal for the SMEs.

## REFERENCES

Al-Mashari, M., Al-Mudimigh, A., & Zairi, M. (2003). Enterprise resource planning: A taxonomy of critical factors. *European Journal of Operational Research, 146*, 352–364. doi:10.1016/S0377-2217(02)00554-4

Baki, B. & Cakar, k. (2005). Determining the ERP package-slection criteria: The case of Turkish companies. *Business Process Management Journal, 11*(1), 75–86. doi:10.1108/14637150510578746

Bernroider, E., & Koch, S. (2001). ERP selection process in mid-size and large organizations. *Business Process Management Journal, 7*(3), 251–257. doi:10.1108/14637150110392746

Bruce, G., Robson, P., & Spaven, R. (2006). OSS opportunities in open source software — CRM and OSS standards. *BT Technology Journal, 24,* 127–140. doi:10.1007/s10550-006-0028-9

Castillo, J. J. (2009). *Convenience Sampling.* Retrieved March 17, 2010 from Experiment Resources.com, http://www.experiment-resources.com/convenience-sampling.html.

*Cereola, S.J. (2008).* The Performance Effects Of Latent Factors On Assimilation Of Commercial Open-Source Erp Software On Small-Medium Enterprises.

De Carvalho, R. A. (2006). Issues on Evaluating Free/Open Source ERP Systems. *Research and Practical Issues of Enterprise Information Systems,* 667-676. Springer-Verlag.

De Carvalho, R. A. (2009). *Free and Open Source Enterprise Resources Planning* (pp. 32–44). Hershey, PA: IGI Global.

De Carvalho, R. A. & Johansson, B. (2009). *Enterprise Resource Planning Systems for Small and Medium-sized Enterprises.*

Dreiling, A., Klaus, H., Rosemann, M., & Wyssusek, B. (2005). Open Source Enterprise Systems: Towards a Viable Alternative. *Proceedings of the 38th Hawaii International Conference on System Science.*

Everdingen, Y., Hillegersberg, J., & Waarts, E. (2000). ERP adoption by European midsize companies. *Communications of the ACM, 43,* 27–31. doi:10.1145/332051.332064

Holland, C. P., & Light, B. (1999). *A Critical Success Factors Model For ERP Implementation.* IEEE Computer Society Press.

Hong, K. K., & Kim, Y. G. (2002). The Critical Success Factors for ERP Implementation: an Organizational Fit Perspective. *Information & Management, 40*(1), 25–40. doi:10.1016/S0378-7206(01)00134-3

Johansson, B. (2008). Knowledge Diffusion in ERP Development: The Case Of Open Source Erp Downloads. *IFIP International Federation for Information Processing.* In León, G., Bernardos, A., Casar, J., Kautz, K., & DeGross, J. (Eds.), *Open IT-Based Innovation: Moving Towards Cooperative IT Transfer and Knowledge Diffusion* (*Vol. 287,* pp. 247–259). Boston: Springer. doi:10.1007/978-0-387-87503-3_14

Johansson, B., & Sudzina, F. (2008). ERP systems and open source: an initial review and some implications for SMEs. *Journal of Enterprise Information Management, 21*(6), 1741–0398. doi:10.1108/17410390810911230

Johansson, B., & Sudzina, F. (2009). Choosing Open Source ERP Systems: What Reasons Are There For Doing So? In Boldyreff, C. (Eds.), *OSS 2009, IFIP AICT 299.*

Kim, H., & Boldyreff, C. (2005). *Open source ERP for SMEs. ICMR.* U.K.: Cranfield University.

Loh, T. C., & Koh, S. C. L. (2004). Critical elements for a successful enterprise resource planning implementation in small-and medium-sized enterprises. *International Journal of Production Research, 42*(17), 3433–3455. doi:10.1080/00207540410001671679

Motwani, J., Subramanian, R. & Gopalakrishna, P. (2005). Critical factors for successful ERP implementation: Exploratory findings from four case studies. *Computers in Industry, 56,* 529–544.

Nah, F.F., Lau, J.L. & Kuang, J. (2001). Critical Factors for Successful Implementation of Enterprise Systems. *Business Process Management, 7* (3).

Parr, A. N., & Dr. Shanks, G. (2000). Taxonomy of ERP Implementation Approaches. *Proceedings of the 33rd Hawaii International Conference on System Sciences.*

Polkinghorne, D. E. (2005). Language and Meaning: Data Collection in Qualitative Research. *Journal of Counseling Psychology*, *52*(2), 137–145. doi:10.1037/0022-0167.52.2.137

Rao, S. S. (2000). Enterprise resource planning: business needs and technologies. *Industrial Management & Data Systems*, 81–88. doi:10.1108/02635570010286078

Sarkis, J., & Sundarraj, R. P. (2003). Evaluating Componentized Enterprise Information Technologies: A Multiattribute Modeling Approac. [Boston: Kluwer Academic Publishers.]. *Information Systems Frontiers*, *5*(3), 303–319. doi:10.1023/A:1025605529006

Sia, C. L. (2008). Impact of Organisational Resources on implementaion of ERP by an SME Firm: An Exploratory Study. *PACIS 2008 Proceedings.* Paper 111.

Smets-Solanes, J.-P., & De Carvalho, R. A. (2002). An Abstract Model for an Open Source ERP System: The ERP5 Proposal. *8th International Conference on Industrial Engineering and Operations Management,* Curitiba, Brazil.

Soh, C., Kien, S. S., & Tay-Yap, J. (2000). Cultural fits and misfits: is ERP a universal solution? *Communications of the ACM*, *43*(4), 47–51. doi:10.1145/332051.332070

Somers, T. M., & Nelson, K. (2001). The impact of critical success factors across the stages of enterprise resource planning implementation. *34th Hawaii International Conference on System Sciences,* Mavis, HI, pp 2936-45.

Stefanou, C. J. (2001). A framework for the ex-ante evaluation of ERP software. *European Journal of Information Systems*, *10*(4), 204–215. doi:10.1057/palgrave.ejis.3000407

Tawileh, A., Rana, O., Ivins, W., & McIntosh, S. (2006). Managing Quality in the Free and Open Source Software Community. *Twelfth Americas Conference on Information Systems,* Acapulco, Mexico.

Teltumbde, A. (2000). A framework for evaluating ERP projects. *International Journal of Production Research*, *38*(17), 4507–4520. doi:10.1080/00207540050205262

Valkov, S. (2008). Innovative concept of open source Enterprise Resource Planning (ERP) system. *International Conference on Computer Systems and Technologies - CompSysTech'08.*

Vidyaranya, B. G., & Cydnee, B. (2005). Success and failure factors of adopting SAP in ERP system implementation. *Business Process Management Journal*, *11*(5), 501–517. doi:10.1108/14637150510619858

Wei, C.-C., Chein, C.-F., & Wang, M.-J. (2005, April 18). J. (2005). An AHP-based approach to ERP system selection. *International Journal of Production Economics*, *96*(1), 47–62. doi:10.1016/j.ijpe.2004.03.004

## KEY TERMS AND DEFINITIONS

**Business Process:** Business process is a set of logically related task that is performed to achieve a specific and defined business goal.

**Business Process Reengineering (BPR):** Business Process Reengineering analyze and design workflows and process within an organization and put them back together in new set of business flows or sets of business flows.

**Consultant:** An outside organization or team responsible for the ERP implementation of an organization including selection of vendor, training for the staffs, planning, customization of systems, testing and implementation and after implementation services is called consultant.

**Customization:** Changing the code of the software in order to fulfill the specific requirements.

**Enterprise:** An enterprise is any kind of activity, operation or project that produces products or services. Fundamentally enterprises are tow types - Business enterprises and Social enterprises. Business enterprises produce product or provide services for earning profit. Social enterprises run for social purpose their success is measured in terms of social benefits rather than monetary benefits.

**Enterprise Resource Planning (ERP):** Organization wide software that integrates data, application and resource into a single, integrated software environment and thereby allows various departments to share information and communicate with each other.

**Open Source ERP:** The ERP system that follow the definition of Open Source defined by Open Source Initiative (OSI).

**Open Source Software:** Open Source Initiative (OSI) is a nonprofit organization work as a standards body for maintaining the Open Source definition to serve the software community. According to their definition Open Source means access to the source code but it should be distributed freely, the program must include source code and it must be in a readable form so that a programmer could modify the program, the license must allow modifications and the rights of a program must apply to all those to whom such program is redistributed.

**Small and Medium Sized Enterprises (SMEs):** According to EU definition of (2003) SMEs, in order to be considered as an SME an enterprise must have less than 250 employees and annual turnover not exceeding than 40 million euro and the firm cannot be owned by one or jointly by several large enterprise more than 25%.

**Suppliers:** Suppliers support implementing organization by supplying ERP systems, training, pre implementation and post implementation supports. They can be Vendors of the ERP systems or the Consultants.

**Suppliers Support:** Implementing organizations face technical or other problems during installation, implementation or after implementation period. Suppliers (Vendors/Consultant) support implementing organization to deal with these problems.

**Vendor:** The organization that develop the ERP Systems.

## ENDNOTES

[1] Internet based survey tool 'Kwik Surveys' is used. https://www.kwiksurveys.com

[2] https://www.kwiksurveys. com?s=KIOHLN_f1e899b9

[3] https://www.kwiksurveys. com?s=KIKLOM_cba7a44b

# Chapter 4

# Open Source as a Strategic Asset:
## Evidence from the Financial Industry

**Carmen de Pablos Heredero**
*Rey Juan Carlos University, Spain*

**David López Berzosa**
*IE Business School, Spain*

**Andres Seco**
*Caja Guadalajara, Spain*

## ABSTRACT

*Caja Guadalajara has succeeded in the migration from privative to open source systems. In this book chapter the authors describe the process of open source software implementation in Caja Guadalajara and the main motives for the success achieved. The case they present can mean an inspiration for the implementation of further open source ERP systems in this company of other ones.*

*The size of the company, the absence of organizational conflicts, the clearness of objectives on information and communication technology possibilities, the training and knowledge in private and open source possibilities, the belief and motivation towards open source solutions and the trust of the top management on the technical areas have become relevant factors for achieving success in this project.*

## INTRODUCTION

Open source migration (F/OSS) was first applied in the sixties. In the nineties it becomes a quite consolidated business alternative. Since then, the free software implementation process has been studied from both, a technical point of view (Raymond, 1999; Hunter, 2006; Berry, 2008) as well as an economic emergent possibility in the market (Lerner and Tirole, 2002; Lerner and Tirole, 2005; Riehle, 2007; Rossi, 2009).

Free software migration means an efficient solution in terms of costs, specially for small and medium size companies and in contexts demand-

DOI: 10.4018/978-1-61350-486-4.ch004

ing great technological resources, as it is the case of the financial industry (Lerner and Tirole, 2005; Riehle, 2007; Lakhan and Jhunjhunwala, 2008). The implementation of free software integrated systems promotes the innovation in firm's worldwide (David and Steinmueller, 1994; Shiff, 2002; Hippern and Krogh, 2003; Osterloh and Rota, 2007, Contini and Lanzara, 2009). Most experiences that have just been started in the twenties keep still in progress today (UOC Report, 2009, López et al., 2010).

Firms must maintain a culture centered in offering the best services to the final users. In our information society users must be the builders apart from consumers (West, 2010). Free software developments can offer an opportunity to this fact since final users can be easily involved in the design process. Open source fosters a culture of sharing and collaboration in which users take a prominent role therefore leading innovation and technology adoption (Von Hippel, 2005).

In this chapter we describe the processes of selecting and implementing an open source integrated management system in a financial company in Spain, Caja Guadalajara. The main objectives of the chapter include,

1. To show the process of the decision making when choosing open source software at firms
2. What the main critical success factors are when implementing open source integrated management systems at firms
3. What the main advantages of implementing open source integrated systems at firms are

Although we have not exactly built the research over the implementation of the ERP in the case we have chosen, we show the experience of the company with the integral systems they have decided to migrate. We consider anyway that this case can be of reference for firms trying to migrate their ERP systems into open source software.

## BACKGROUND

Caja Guadalajara is a Savings Local Bank founded in 1961 in the Guadalajara Region in Spain. It is a small size financial firm specialized in families and small and medium firms. It develops its main activity in the Guadalajara province and it maintains 75 offices opened and 72 automatic teller machines located in 90 different locations. Being a small size firm in its industry it has made a special emphasis in optimizing limited resources. Computing resources are amongst those resources where the company has tried to make the best in the equilibrium "excellence and resource optimization".

The Computing Department in Caja Guadalajara is composed by eleven people that offer computing services to 550 users as well as a regional network of teller machines.

The department is divided into the following areas:

**Business organization**: Coordination and development of internal business processes conducted by different business units.
**Development**: where the different data mining activities and the support for business applications are located. Different handmade software applications are developed here for the specific needs of some departments.
**Communications and systems**: Rest of computer related tasks: technical assistance, telecommunications, physical architecture, logical security, systems integration, IT I+D. The central computer is externalized in the so-called financial CEUS. The financial CEUS is grouped in other banks of similar characteristics that share the outsourcing of the financial services and the host, as it is the case of Caixa Penedés, Caja Circulo, Caixa Manlleu, Caixa Pollensa, Caja Jaén and Caja Guadalajara.

In this sense we observe how different "Spanish Cajas", as saving banks, co-operate by sharing costs and resources related to ICT. This co-operation also allows them to achieve a higher degree of innovation while preserving knowledge and still remain entrepreneurial.

From the computing department a very positive attitude towards open source alternatives has been practiced. As we have previously mentioned, the fact that we are dealing with a small size firm lacking of resources promotes even more the motivation towards the search of more efficient computing solutions from the cost-benefit perspective. As far as Caja Guadalajara is concerned, open source software has always been considered as an alternative of great interest for the firm. As the CIO indicates "it only costs the time of someone who is already working for the firm". The CIO is at the same time a person highly motivated towards the use of free software tools who, himself, keeps a great experience in these tools.

From the computing area, a great stability of the computing systems has been sought and the technical areas of the firm recognize that private solutions are not stable at all. Besides, as they are experts both in open source and privative (legacy) solutions they can conduct a rigorous cost-benefits analysis before choosing a technological option. In the period from 1996 to 2006, different open source solutions have been tried and, at the same time, some other legacy software solutions have been maintained in the company.

In the year 2007, the firm decides to migrate towards open source software as the main technological framework for every office desktop. This initiative initially driven by the technical area of the firm was supported from the very beginning by the corporate division. According to managers interviewed a key aspect for having unquestioned support from non-technical areas have been the trust the organization has in its technical department and its proven expertise in open source and ICT service management.

It is considered a priority to evolve towards open source environments that allow them some independence from software providers and in this way be able to reach more stability and control of their own ICT infrastructure. The person in charge of the Organization and Systems in the firm points out as a decisive factor the need of not losing the know-how in previous proprietary software which is becoming obsolete yet still very important for the running business processes still in place.

The savings on software licenses and the possibilities to remove redundant applications facilitated the decision to migrate. Apart from this, open source software allows better development environments for prototyping and software testing than proprietary alternatives: "The products are more homogenous and it allows a lot of modularity amongst the components, besides we have always specially appreciated the fact to dispose of the source code,..., they allow a best self-management of the firm's business processes" according to the CIO of the company.

## MAIN FOCUS OF THE CHAPTER

### Issues, Controversies, Problems

In all the efforts towards a change in the organization, it is important to define precisely the present state as the basis upon which to define the goals and the required resources to get there. In this sense, it is also convenient to analyze different alternatives: the available technological resources, and to what extent these technological resources will affect the firm's process and the strategic or organizational decisions that take part in the management of change.

Initially the company had as its main computing infrastructure Microsoft Windows NT and related hardware and software. It is important to note that Microsoft opted to terminate support services for this computing platform by the end of 2004.

The context affecting the management of change specific to this company had been:

- Induced migration from corporate to avoid similar situations in the future.
- Then end of support services hence requiring a fast-track alternative.
- Highly formalized working profiles: they are designed for a concrete profile, and they must respond to specific industry needs. In total 400 working positions with strict security and procedural requirements had to be migrated.
- Highly motivated IT managerial positions towards the possibilities of open source software.
- High degree of involvement of managers, users and technical positions in the project. The CEO consistently promoted a quite active communication policy, to foster user's acceptance and support levels of the new software, and the support in the execution of the project. There is a constant support of the top management and the rest of managerial positions to the project.
- There is a positive organizational climate with absence of conflicts and where workers seem to be quite close. There is trust, what makes it easier the implementation of the free software and the possibilities of success at the firm.

## The Decision to Migrate to Open Source Software

The first pilot experience involving open source takes place in 1999, with the migration of one of the UNIX servers used for a long time to manage data and processes.

The positive effects of this project did cheer up the implementing team to develop other initiatives involving open source software, for instance renewing internet firewalls and security systems related to the regional network of automatic teller machines.

Later on, from year 2004 until year 2006, all the office servers were substituted by Debian servers, which are open source, in a progressive way. Debian servers allow the processing of a higher number of functions at a reduced cost of ownership.

Finally a large migration project, affecting desktop hardware and software starts in 2007, follows the inertia previously started in the organization and mainly motivated by the obsolescence of the Windows NT system. The decision to give up the Microsoft technical assistance implied an opportunity for the migration process. This pattern of adoption is consistent with extant literature (Lopez and de Pablos 2010; de Pablos and Lopez 2010).

## The Technological Tools used in the Project

The open source software tools chosen for the migration projects that have taken place in Caja Guadalajara span a large set of internal business processes either security (Firewalling, Encryption), network services (VoIP, Internetworking) as well as software programming or software applications.

## Planning and Implementation Steps

The two principles in which the planning and implementation of open source software is based in Caja Guadalajara are the following ones,

1. The creation of an ISO 9660 image that allows a technological base upon which applications and services are further implemented.
2. The selection of the software tools to cover all the needs according to the following aspects,

- ◦ Functionality: the final selection of the software applications must satisfy the particular and daily needs of each user.
- ◦ Corporate image: the user must perceive that his/her working profile is aligned with the company image and his/her specific profile.
- ◦ Personalization: the configurations are active or non active according to the considerations of the user or area to which each user belongs to.
- ◦ Security: the user must be able to execute the applications that he or she has been authorized to.

The technical team in Caja Guadalajara has worked in an interoperable environment that enforces single-sign-on behavior thus making daily use of applications simpler for end users. Arguably open source has been key to achieve interoperable services and applications.

High levels of automation in processes related to software maintenance and upgrade have been achieved thanks to extensive use of open source since early stages of new software planning. According to CIO: "open source facilitates remote installation and unattended configuration of multiple work positions customized to different requirements....a complete functional building can be finished on average in 30 minutes or less".

In the migration process the security issues have been a constant concern for the organization. The fact that Caja Guadalajara is located in the bank industry makes it especially sensitive to this issue. It is critical to take the needed measures to avoid that the working profiles or the rest of the software applications and the data and customers are not exposed to external attacks or failures. This is the reason why they rely on the SUSeLinux System. It presents a group of security characteristics over the Linux System. This system was initially developed by the American National Security Agency and greatly accepted worldwide.

## The Cost of the Migration

According to the people responsible for the migration project in Caja Guadalajara expense savings have been achieved in the following:

- Software licences related to operating systems, applications, security.
- Longer utilization of existing hardware: up to 3 times for office servers and 1.5 times for user desktops.
- Higher availability of systems and services.

Caja Guadalajara estimates that since open source was adopted by the company as a strategic option in 2007 total expense savings add up to 0.8 million euros on a yearly basis.

## The Keys for the Change Management

The management of change has been basically based in two main principles, (1) planning and (2) communication.

## A Correct Planning

The firm has followed a structured approach, by respecting all the defined phases and making a special emphasis on avoiding disruptions to employees. According to the CIO of the company: "we do our best to keep employees unaware of any technical change, they just keep working on the same software the day after any migration"

A clear grouping of services in five different areas:

- Identification services: access to the system, access to applications and services, user identification and user accounting.
- Administrative services: routine maintenance, remote assistance, integrity checks and updates.
- Data backup services.

- Standard Software services: providing controlled roll-over of new updates and new functionalities.
- Personalized services: Applications or services which are customized to specific users or requirements.

## A Proper Communication Strategy

In which the benefits of these technologies have been explained to every employee including management staff. An intensive training program aimed at minimizing chance resistance and adoption of new software.

## Results for the Migration

In the last part of the semester 2007, the first application prototypes where internally developed under the framework of a strategic program termed PROA-NG aimed at renewing existing software in every regional branch and business unit. Since then, the company has been immersed in a process of continuous improvement based on user's feedback reporting any failure or potential improvement. As of 2010 the program is still in place confirming the idea that software migration in large organizations is a continuous, incremental process of change and adoption. Nowadays, given that initial objectives have been accomplished (avoiding vendor lock-in), the strategic program PROA-NG envisions a complete set of open source tools and applications for every employee at the company.

## Benefits

Caja Guadalajara as a small financial company of 320 employees and with revenues in 2008 of 9 million Euros has managed to save due to open source up to 0.8 million Euros on a yearly basis.

An important innovation in the company has taken place: reduction of technological dependence and therefore less exposure to external ICT providers as well as greater capacity to align ICT with strategic and budgetary needs.

From a technical point of view, migrating to open source has produced: higher systems availability rates, fewer upgrades and a total absence of software viruses. Moreover a higher level of flexibility in software applications and interoperability between different technological systems is observed as a result.

The CIO affirms "Now we have the control, by avoiding the technological dependence according to different providers", the returns and the stability of the system are higher than the expected. Response times have been minimized for the solution of problems and the recovery of hardware problems".

A simple and operative work environment has been achieved. In words of the people responsible of different areas: "The environment is very friendly for the employees". The simplicity of GNU/Linux, the mobility and multimedia attributes have allowed it.

In words of the managers of the firm "we wanted to offer a more attractive and useful desktop office. A new Java-based environment has been designed, which mimics previous functionalities thereby minimizing learning curve for final users.

Final user satisfaction is related with their own participation in the development and implementation of the system. Workers must face the differences between an old and new system. The user's involvement in the implementation of the new system is of key importance and offers a very interesting point of view for the final success or failure of the project. Users are involved many times in the project, in the process of implementation of the new computing system, in the definition of the needs about the new system of global management and in the implementation of the global management system (De la Rosa et al., 2010). This pattern of behavior is consistent with other results in the literature and more specific in open innovation.

Holland and Light (1999) and Al Mashari et al. (2003) point out that the final user satisfaction is related with the continuous process of queries and the training that the users receive on the new system. The degree of final satisfaction is very important when defining the different models of internalization of the new system in the firm. Probably Ives and Olson (1983) have developed one of the most complete methodologies to measure the degree of IT satisfaction of final consumers. It has been implemented with success in firms and sectors of different nature and it seems a very useful tool to be applied in the concrete case of the implementation of free software tools.

To further acquire more insight regarding the initiative a group of employees at Caja Guadalajara have been interviewed. For this part of the analysis we apply the model of critical success factors we have developed in previous research (De Pablos and De Pablos, 2008) based in the analysis of five main groups of variables affecting to the final results in ERP implementations (the decision-making policy of the firm in the ERP selection, implementation and use the training characteristics of the people involved in the ERP implementation and final use, the organisational inertia in the firm and the final internal user satisfaction).

## Keys for the Success

In words of the CIO "the key of the success has been the involvement of the managerial positions and the trust of the employees, very friendly with the possibilities of open source software". The firm has with not doubt bet on innovation according to the new technological possibilities.

The capacity of the firm's adaptation to the new situation is dependent on the management of the change. In this group of explaining variables we include the selection, implementation and the use of the selected system, the existence of managerial support, the clarity of the procedures established

for the required business process redesign, the effectiveness in the project management and the "good relationships" amongst all the agents taking part in the implementation process. We explain the previous aspects,

## The Existence of a Managerial Support Group

Finney and Corbett (2007) mention in their study that this is the most cited aspect in the literature review. The recent interviews we developed with consultancy groups specialized in the implementation of ERP software in firms (SAP, Accenture, AtosOrigin, 2008-2010), mention that the existence of managerial support is key for the final success of the projects since it provides of leadership, resources and talent. To reach the expected results in the implementation of a new computing system, it is important the collaboration of support of all the employees in the firm.

## The Existence of Clear Work Procedures when the Business Process Reengineering is taking Place

The implementation of new technologies requires of the redesign of the business processes (Hammer, 1994). Very often, the implementations do fail because the effort of processes change is under-estimate. Motwani et al. (2002) suggest that the organization must be prepared to provide key changes in any business process. The process of change that accompanies the whole implementation is critic since it helps to overcome the state of uncertainty of the persons working for this kind of projects. In the management of change of a project of implementation of a new computing system, the firm must work on three main aspects: information, training and compromise (Casacuberta, 2003).

## The Effectiveness of the Management of the Project

The plans for the management of the projects coordinate and control the various and complex activities of the projects (Bravo and Santana, 2010): the implementation of a new managerial system requires of making work together different firms specializations in a period of time, demanding additional efforts on the daily managerial efforts. For this reason, it is important to consider and dedicate time to the following tasks (De Pablos, 2004): 1. to promote a plan of formal implementation, 2. dedicate realistic time to the project. 3. celebrate periodic meetings around the project, 4. to count on with a problem solving leader, 5. To include in the work teams to members that are at the same time interested parts in the project.

## The Existence of a Compromise coming from all the Parts of the Firm

Then a communication plan is required (Falkowski et al., 1998, Marbert et al, 2003), effective decision makers and a good motivation for the team. As far as we consider that free software systems are information systems that allow the integration of the information in all the functional parts in the organization, it is important to count on with the required support in all this areas. Everyone in the firm must be completely responsible for the whole system and the key users of each department must have cleared the different phases for the implementation of the project (Ahmed, 2005).

## The Use of Different Methodologies for the Implementation of the Project

Can be of interest for this complex systems, since they offer a group of steps that allow the management of the project and offer pieces of advice to the final users and needed work teams for each of the phases (Rossi, 2006): 1. The preparing of the project, 2. The planning of objectives, results and actions, 3. The development of the project, 4. The final preparation, 5. The management of change of the project.

## The Existence of Support to the Different Actors taking Part in the Implementation

The provider of the technology, the external services, etc. is very important in order to get equilibrium between the solutions that can be acquired in the market and the solutions that best fit the organization (Hammer, 1994, Targowski, 2009). The objectives that the firm tries when implementing the global system must be defined in the document elaborated once that the functional analysis is finished. The design report must show the situation of the system before and after the business process reengineering has taken place.

## The Training of the People Involved in the Implementation of the System and the Final Use

The user systems are all the people that take part in the project to get the final product (García Bravo, 2000). For this reason, we can consider that all the members in the organization are potential final users since they are going to use or modify the information of the system. Monforte Moreno (1995) refers to the organization of computing system as a group of independent functions, that are independent from the rest of the organization and that have mainly to do with the system's development, programming and exploitation processes, including the analysis tasks and the maintaining of the system. McLeod (2000) proposes an organizational schema adapted to the cycle life model that appears in figure 1. The main character of the implementation process must be the Chief Information Officer (CIO). In an individual level a group of supervisors of different system areas with less control.

The training policies must be oriented to increase the individual abilities of the human resources implied in the implementation and use of the new systems. They must be accompanied by policies of rewards and motivation oriented to the application and abilities obtained in the final use (Von Hippel, 1986).

## The Organizational Inertia in the Firm

The organizational inertia refers to the culture, values and ways of expression in the firm (De Pablos and De Pablos, 2008). The organizational change implies leaving a group of structures, procedures and behaviors to some different ones to improve the final results. The management of change means the application of a group of concepts, techniques and methodologies that will make possible the complex migration from an initial non desired status to another final one (Hammer, 1994). It must be started by a challenge, something that must be changed. We must distinguish between people that must decide what to change, since they count on with responsibilities in the firm and people working in the processes that must be listened too. Once that the change has taken place, there will be people informed and trained in the new process, and people that have just been informed (Bitzer, 2005). These circumstances are going to promote an impact in the change, in a positive or negative way.

The process must be the axis for the change (Davenport and Prusak, 1998). The organizations develop their objectives by means of processes. A process is a group of tasks that take place under different functionalities or specializations. In this sense, we can affirm that a process is transfunctional (Davenport, 1998). This concept is very important for the considerations of change at firms. Firstly because the change effort will have an impact in the whole process, since any task is just a part in the process, and secondly because the change in any part of the process will have its impact in other processes of the same or

different nature. This way changes in the organizational processes will have their impact in the decision making processes or vice versa. Then, firms can take into account with models of change oriented to processes that help to reduce the fear to change and create enough energy for the team work (Cummings, 2004). It is then important to define specific objectives for the change, to define advantages and disadvantages for the change, plan a training that accompanies the change efforts and communicate the change efforts and make the employees take part on it.

In different interviews we have followed with employees working at Caja Guadalajara we have checked a very positive feedback on these policies for the investment and implementation of open source software (Table 1).

The previous aspects show the following positive aspects derived in the implementation process:

- **An efficient response** to the change of management
- A **careful evaluation of the human and material resources** that the firm has
- A **careful planning of the whole propriety software** we try to migrate by including the training and support costs.
- **A leadership that enthusiasm** the innovation in the firm

Here we show some of the main characteristics of a proper leadership that helps the implementation of new technological tools in the firm and we have tried to test in Caja Guadalajara.

According to *planning aspects,*

- The leader offers clear objectives by taking into account the considerations of the rest decision makers in the firm. He or she does not just impose them.
- He or she helps in the understanding of different objectives.

*Table 1. Policies for decision making about the investment and implementation of open source software*

| 1. Different functions have been established for the decision makers in the implementation of free software in the firm |
| --- |
| 2. The firm has developed group responsibilities |
| 3. The firm has developed individual responsibilities |
| 4. The firm has trained employees in the implementation of the free software tools |
| 5. The firm has trained external collaborators for the implementation of the open source tools |
| 6. The firm has communicated potential final users about the change of the software |
| 7. A specific rewards policy has been developed for the workers that take part in the implementation of the open source software |
| 8. The firm has established a conduct code related to the use of OSS |
| 9. The firm has developed programs, meetings or recommended readings of the new software solution |
| 10. The firm has offered information about Acts protecting data |
| 11. The firm has established ethical responsibilities for each worker according to his/her tasks |
| 12. The firm promoted the integration of the workers in professional associations |

According to the *performance*,

- The leader offers the information and needed resources for the project
- The leader gets interest for the final results and the difficulties in the way and he or she accompanies the project always it is required
- The leader is tolerant
- The leader provides of rich feedback

In the *personal relationships* and communication with the rest of the team,

- It is possible to speak with the leader even under pressure situations
- He or she does not make any distinction in the personal relationships with the rest of the team work
- The leader enables the information flows, inside the team work and the rest of the environment that allows avoiding the rumors of panic.
- The leader listens very actively, this means; between other things he or she dies not interrupts and tries to be in others place.
- Offers and receives trust
- The leader is a quite easy-going person

In the *leadership style and the management* of the team,

- The leader lives the team problems
- The leader respects the personal timing of collaborators
- The leader leads but does not order. He is just another worker with a responsibility.
- The leader is easily available
- The leader has clear ideas
- The leader delegates in other persons at the firm
- The leader thanks and provides of recognition
- The leader recognizes individual merits of each of his/her collaborators

In the *participation of collaborators* for the management and the decision making process,

- The leader values the positive effects of the ideas and collaborators although he/she doesn't follow them
- The leader asks collaborators before making key decisions on the project, especially if they have consequences in their work.
- The leader is opened to change

In the *personal career* of the team work,

- The leader promotes the training, development and continuous learning of the group
- The leader promotes the enrichment and evolution of the team
- The leader can be in the role of leader-coach whenever it is required

In all concerning with *his/her own self-managerial* situation,

- The leader does not hide his/her mistakes. He or she learns from them.
- The leader is honest

In all concerning to *health work situations*,

- The leader is worried about a healthy physical environment.
- The leader tries the rewards system is reasonable and offers satisfaction

In all concerning with the *searching for resources*,

- The leader counts on with good contacts outside the team, and it is very useful for the search of the required resources for the final performance.
- In most of the cases, this "good leader" behavior allows us identifying in a realistic way the leader in firms

In a survey directed to workers of Caja Guadalajara we have tried to emphasize the following qualities of the leader of the OSS implementations: respect, authority, empowerment, trust, motivation, delegation and vision (Table 2).

The main restrictions for this integrated project to open source software migration comes from two different places; in one hand the need to maintain an operative business full time, with the main objective of trying not to interrupt the

critical services. Apart from this, there were some budgetary restrictions. An automatic integration with the pre-existent services was required, they had to operate normally.

## CONCLUSION

In this chapter we present a case of success in the implementation of global open source software solutions in a Spanish firm operating in the banking industry: Caja Guadalajara.

We have analyzed some aspects that from the literature review have been considered of importance in the implementation of new information technologies at firms and applied then to the specific case of open source software implementation.

The small size, the youth of the company, the absence of organizational conflicts, the clarity of objectives on information and communication technologies, the knowledge of both open and proprietary software environments, the belief and motivation towards open source software transmitted to all the workers have been relevant factors to have success in the project. The management of the change and the leadership of the CIO at the company have been of key importance for the final performance.

To make this migration possible, some factors that have conditioned the project have been taken into account. Amongst the main ones, we can describe:

- The total cost ownership: less than 30% over the initial estimation with privative alternatives, namely Microsoft. What it implies is that the investment should be limited with plenty functionality.
- The need to integrate the information and the managerial options with the preexistent services. It implies that the new software must be compatible with the previous environments to keep on maintaining the service.

*Table 2. Perception of the attributes of the leader is OSS projects at the firm*

| |
|---|
| 1. The leader fixes reachable and agreed objectives. He does not impose them |
| 2. He helps understanding objectives |
| 3. He enables the information and the required resources for daily work |
| 4. He maintains interest for the difficulties that appear in the projects and "helps" whenever is needed |
| 5. He is tolerant |
| 6. He offers good feedback |
| 7. It is possible to speak with him even under pressure situations |
| 8. He does not make distinctions in the relationships with the rest of employees |
| 9. He offers information about the team and the environment that allows avoiding rumors and panic |
| 10. He listens to others actively |
| 11. He offers and gets trust |
| 12. He is an outgoing person |
| 13. He lives the team problems |
| 14. He respects his collaborators personal time |
| 15. He leaders and does not oblige |
| 16. He is easy to access |
| 17. He is clear in ideas |
| 18. He delegates part of decision making process |
| 19. He thanks and provides of acknowledge |
| 20. Facing foreign teams, he acknowledges the individual merits of each of his collaborators |
| 21. He evaluates the positive aspects of his collaborators ideas, although he does not always follow them |
| 22. He normally takes into account other team members opinions before making decisions on the Project, especially if the decisions have impact on their own work or results |
| 23. He is opened to change |
| 24. He promotes continuous training and learning actions |
| 25. He promotes the mutual enrichment and evolution of his team |
| 26. He can be on the role of leader-coach whenever is needed |
| 27. He does not hide his errors, but learn from them |
| 28. He is honest and sincere |
| 29. He is worry for maintaining a healthy work environment |
| 30. He tries that the reward system to be reasonable and satisfying |
| 31. He maintains good contacts outside the team |

- The flexibility of open source software has been of great importance to perform the different works without interrupting daily business activity and has assured a coexistence with the precious environment.

- The active participation of Caja Guadalajara, in the dilemma of maintaining the required daily processes and be able to execute the project with a minimum of possible interruptions.

On decreasing the risks in the execution of the project, the proofs of the new system have been performed in applications that are considered not to be critic in the organization. This way they have tried to avoid problems in the daily services that the company is offering. It is the typical strategy of gradual adaptation, where the different services that where operational is preserved. As the CIO explains "The computing positions in the company present a very concrete profile and they must answer to a group of needs of the industry that are not similar to a multi-purpose working place".

In the execution of the project, software testers play an essential role. Early users of the system tried the new software and a very valuable feedback is provided to the firm which in turn enables adaptation and improvement. In this sense, the internal customer becomes a very useful tool when trying to reach an optimal security control

# REFERENCES

Ahmed, O. (2005). *Migrating from proprietary to Open Source: Learning Content Management Systems*. Doctoral Dissertation, Department of Systems and Computer Engineering, Carleton University, Ottawa, Ontario, Canada.

Al-Mashari, M., Al-Mudimigh, A., & Zairi, M. (2003). Enterprise Resource Planning: a taxonomy of critical factors. *European Journal of Operational Research, 146*, 352–364. doi:10.1016/S0377-2217(02)00554-4

Berry, D. M. (2008). *Copy, rip, Burn: the Politics of Copyleft and Open Source*. London: Pluto Press.

Bitzer, J. (2005). The impact of entry and competition by Open Source Software on Innovation Activity. *Industrial Organization 051201*, EconWPA.

Bravo, E. & Santana, M. (2010). El impacto de la implantación de los Sistemas de Planeamiento de Recursos Empresariales ERP en el desempeño individual. *AMCIS Proceedings*, paper 265.

Casacubierta, D. (2003). *Collective creation*. Barcelona: Gedisa.

Contini, F., & Lanzara, G. (2009). *ICT and innovation in the Public Sector*. New York: Palgrave MacMillan.

Cummings, M. (2004). Work groups, structural diversity, and knowledge sharing in a global organization. *Management Science, 50*(3), 123–156. doi:10.1287/mnsc.1030.0134

Davenport, T. (1998). Putting the enterprise into the enterprise system. *Harvard Business Review*, (June): 98–123.

Davenport, T., & Prusak, E. (1998). *Working knowledge, how organizations manage what they know*. Boston: Harvard Business Review School Press.

David, P.& Steinmueller, E. (1994). Information Economics and Policy. *Special Issue on The Economics of Standards, 6*(3-4), December.

De La Rosa, G., & Valentín, M. Fernandez.Renedo, C.; López, D.; De Pablos, C & De la Puerta, E. (2010). Productivity models in knowledge intensive service activities. *Grand Challenge in service week*, University of Cambridge, 22nd September 2010, UK.

De Pablos, C. (2004). *Ilustraciones de la aplicación de Tecnologías de información en la empresa española*. Madrid: ESIC.

De Pablos, C., & De Pablos, M. (2008). Elements that can explain the degree of success of ERP systems implementation. In Cruz-Cunha, M. M. (Ed.), *Social, Managerial and Organizational Dimensions of Enterprise Information Systems*. Hershey, PA: IGI Publishing.

De Pablos, C., & López, D. (2010). The implementation of free software in firms: an empirical analysis. *The International Journal of Digital Accounting Research, 10*(3), 45–67.

Falkowski, G., Pedigo, P., Smith, B., & Swamson, D. (1998). A recipe for ERP success. Beyond Computing. *International Journal of Human-Computer Interaction, 16*(1), 5–22.

Finney, S., & Corbett, M. (2007). ERP implementation: a compilation and analysis of critical success factors. *Business Process Management Journal, 13*(3), 329–347. doi:10.1108/14637150710752272

García Bravo, D. (2000). *Sistemas de información en la empresa. Conceptos y aplicaciones.* Madrid: Pirámide.

Hammer. 1994. *Reengineering the corporation: A manifesto for business revolution.* Boston: HarperBusiness.

Hippern, L., & Krogh, S. (2003). Open source software and the private-collective innovation model: Issues for organization science. *Organization Science, 14*(2), 241–248.

Holland, C. P., & Light, B. (1999). A critical success factors model for ERP implementation. *IEEE Software*, (May/June): 30–36. doi:10.1109/52.765784

Hunter, H. (2006). *Open Source Data Base Driven Web Development.* Oxford, UK: Chandos.

Ives, B., & Olson, M. (1983). The measurement of User Information Satisfaction. *Management of Computing, 26*(10), 519–529.

Lakhan, R., & Jhunjhunwala, V. (2008). Open Source in Education. *EDUCAUSE Quarterly, 31*(2), 32–40.

Lerner, J., & Tirole, J. (2005). The Economics of Technology Sharing: Open Source and Beyond. *The Journal of Economic Perspectives, 19*(2), 99–120. doi:10.1257/0895330054048678

López, D., & De Pablos, C. (2010). Profiling F/OSS Adoption Modes: An Interpretive Approach. *IFIP Advances in Information and Communication Technology,* 319, 354-360. Springer, Boston.

Mabert, V., Soni, A., & Venkatamara, M. (2003). Enterprise Resource Planning: managing implementation process. *European Journal of Operational Research, 146*(2), 302–314. doi:10.1016/S0377-2217(02)00551-9

McLeod, R. (2000). *Management Information Systems.* D.F., Mexico: Prentice Hall.

Monforte Moreno, M. (1995). *Sistemas de Información para la Dirección.* Madrid: Pirámide.

Motwani, J., Mirchandani, M., & Gunasekaran, A. (2002). Successful implementation of ERP Projects: evidence from two case studies. *International Journal of Production Economics, 75,* 83–96. doi:10.1016/S0925-5273(01)00183-9

Osterloh & Rota. (2007). Open source software development, just another case of collective invention. *Research Policy, 36*(2), 157–171. doi:10.1016/j.respol.2006.10.004

Raymond, E. (1999). The Cathedral and the bazaar. *Knowledge. Technology and Policy, 12*(3), 23–49. doi:10.1007/s12130-999-1026-0

Riehle, D. (2007). The Economic Motivation of Open Source: Stakeholder Perspectives. *IEEE Computer, 40*(4), 25–32.

Rossi, C. (2009). Software Innovativeness: a comparison between proprietary and free/open source solutions offered by Italian SMEs. *R & D Management, 39*(2), 153–169. doi:10.1111/j.1467-9310.2009.00547.x

Rossi, D. (2006). Decoding the green open source software puzzle: A survey of theoretical and empirical contributions. *The Economics of Open Source Software Development,* 22nd IEEE International Parallel and Distributed Processing Symposium, New York.

Shiff, T. (2002). The Economics of Open Source Software: a survey of the early literature. *Review of Network Economics, 1*(1), 66–74.

Targowski, M. (2009). *The enterprise systems approach. social, managerial, and organizational dimensions of enterprise information systems. The Enterprise Systems Approach. Social, Managerial, and*. Organizational Dimensions of Enterprise Information Systems.

UOC (2009) UOC Report. *The use of open source in Public Administrations in Spain*, Universitat Oberta de Calalunya, Report.

Von Hippel. (2005). *Democratizing Innovation*. Cambridge, MA: MIT Press, April 2005.

Von Hippel, E. (1986). Lead Users: A Source of Novel Product Concepts. *Management Science*, *32*(7), 791–805. doi:10.1287/mnsc.32.7.791

West, J., & Mace, M. (2010). Browsing as the killer app: Explaining the rapid success of Apple's iPhone. *Telecommunications Policy*, *4*(34), 241–267.

## ADDITIONAL READING

Akkermans, H., & Van Helden, K. (2002). Vicious and virtuous cycles in ERP implementation: a case study of interrelations between critical success factors. *European Journal of Information Systems*, *11*(1), 35–46. doi:10.1057/palgrave/ejis/3000418

Ang, J. S. K., Sum, C. C., & Yeo, L. N. (2002). A multiple-case design methodology for studying MRP success and CSFs. *Information & Management*, *39*(4), 271–281. doi:10.1016/S0378-7206(01)00096-9

Esteves, J., & Pastor, J. (2001). Analysis of critical success factors relevance along SAP implementation phases. *Proceedings of the Seventh Americas Conference on Information Systems*, 1019-1025.

Fui-Hoon, F., Zuckweiler, K. M., & Lee-Shang, J. (2003). ERP implementation: Chief Information Officers' Perceptions on Critical Success Factors. *International Journal of Human-Computer Interaction*, *16*(1), 5–22. doi:10.1207/S15327590I-JHC1601_2

Moor, J. H. (1985). What is computer ethics? *Metaphilosophy*, *16*(4), 266–275. doi:10.1111/j.1467-9973.1985.tb00173.x

Nah, F., Lau, J., & Kuang, J. (2001). Critical factors for successful implementation of enterprise systems. *Business Process Management*, *7*(3), 285–296. doi:10.1108/14637150110392782

Parker, D. (1988). Ethics for Information Systems Personnel. *Journal of Information Systems Management*, *5*, 44–48. doi:10.1080/07399018808962925

Rosario, J.G. (2000). On the leading edge: critical success factors in ERP implementation projects. *Business World*, May, 21-27.

Smith, A. (2009). New framework for enterprise information systems. *International Journal of CENTERIS*, *1*(1), 30–36.

Sommers, G., & Nelson, C. (2003). A taxonomy of players and activities across the ERP project life cycle. *Information & Management*, *41*(3), 257–278. doi:10.1016/S0378-7206(03)00023-5

Summer, M. (1999). *Critical success factors in enterprise wide information management systems projects*. Proceedings of 5th Americas Conference on Information Systems, 232-234.

Tiwari, R., et al. (2007) *Mobile Banking as Business Strategy: Impact of Mobile Technologies on Customer Behaviour and its Implications for Banks*. Working Paper, Germany. Retrieved Feb. 2007

Umble, E. J., Haft, R. R., & Umble, M. M. (2003). Enterprise Resource Planning: implementation procedures and critical success factors. *European Journal of Operational Research, 146*, 241–257. doi:10.1016/S0377-2217(02)00547-7

Wang, E., Sheng-Pao, S., Jianj, J. J., & Klein, G. (2008). The consistency among facilitating factors and ERP implementation success: A holistic view of kit. *Journal of Systems and Software, 81*, 1601–1621. doi:10.1016/j.jss.2007.11.722

## KEY TERMS AND DEFINITIONS

**Business Process Reengineering:** It is a radical redesign of a process in order to reach great results.

**Caja de Ahorros (Saving Bank):** Financial entities that operate in a similar way as a bank and also offers social benefits for firms and individuals operating in a certain region in Spain.

**Change:** To give a different form or appearance to; transform.

**Critical Success Factors:** (CSFs) are the critical factors or activities required for ensuring the success of your business.

**ERP System:** Enterprise Resource Planning, a business management system that integrates all the facets of the business, including planning, manufacturing, sales, etc.

**Information and Communication Technologies:** Tools to treat information, they can be composed by telecommunications technologies, as for example telephone, cable, satellite and radio, and digital technologies, as for example computers, information networks and software.

**Managerial Support:** Help offered and promoted by the managers in a firm.

**Open Source Software:** Software that can be read, modified and re-distributed in a free way.

**Processes:** A series of operations performed in the making or treatment of a product or service.

**Team:** A group of two or more individuals who interact dynamically to achieve a shared objective.

# Chapter 5
# Developing Business Model with Open Source Enterprise Resource Planning

**Swanand J. Deodhar**
*Management Development Institute, India*

**Kulbhushan C. Saxena**
*Management Development Institute, India*

**Rajen Gupta**
*Management Development Institute, India*

**Mikko Ruohonen**
*University of Tampere, Finland*

## ABSTRACT

*Open source approach to software development has been used to develop the so-called 'horizontal infrastructure' software such as databases and application servers. However, there is an increasing acceptance of open source approach for developing business applications like enterprise resource planning (ERP) software. Indeed, organizations are building business models around ERP and similar business application developed using open source. In this chapter, the authors analyze the business model of one such open source ERP and explain increasing importance of software licensing and partner networks in FOS-ERP business models.*

## INTRODUCTION

Open source software represents an alternative to the predominant proprietary mode of software development and distribution. In its simplest form, open source represents a licensing paradigm that allows users to access, modify, and redistribute the product (Lerner & Tirole, 2002). When these licensing norms are applied to software; the outcome is what is known as open source software. In other words, open source software is the software that grants its users the right to access the source-code, modify it and redistribute it.

DOI: 10.4018/978-1-61350-486-4.ch005

Apart from licensing regimes, the development process of OSS products is distinctly at odds with the traditional proprietary software development (von Hippel & von Krogh, 2003). As a user can redistribute the software on his/her own without requiring an authorization of the original creator of the software, OSS is most often provided at no monetary cost. This provision, along with the licensing norms, is distinctly different from proprietary model's key source of revenue i.e. software license sale. This feature of OSS, being acutely deviant from the established economic theories, has attracted researchers to the field of OSS (von Krogh & Spaeth, 2007).

Traditionally, open source as an approach was used for developing projects that could be used for 'horizontal infrastructure' of an organization (Fitzgerald, 2006). Examples include database systems, application servers and operating systems. However, there is an increasing use of open source approach for developing business applications like enterprise resource planning and customer relationship management systems (Fitzgerald, 2006).

This transition across software types is far from obvious. There are at least two issues that differentiate open source ERP from other 'horizontal infrastructure' software developed using open source approach. First, users of business applications may have little interest in the technological aspect of the software. Therefore, unlike the vertical infrastructure projects like databases and application servers, end user may not participate in the product development for business applications developed using open source approach (Ågerfalk & Fitzgerald, 2008). Secondly, the functional requirements for business applications may not be uniformly understood by all members of the community and therefore, there might be a need for a more emphasis on planning and requirement elicitation prior to actual development (Fitzgerald, 2006).

In summary, extending open source approach to developing business applications like ERP is unclear and hence there is a need to explore business models built around open source business applications. In this chapter, we explore one such ERP software that follows the open source approach to software development and licensing and has combined it with proprietary approach to create a hybrid business model. The chapter uses software business model framework proposed by Rajala et.al (2003) to explain business model developed around the studied ERP product.

## SOFTWARE BUSINESS MODELS

In this section, we provide a brief review of the term business model and provide the conceptualization of business model adopted for this study. This exercise is important as there is little consensus in organizational research literature about the term business model (Morris et.al, 2005). Thus to bring uniformity in readers' perception about business model, we explicitly define the term business model as we perceive and employ in this chapter. We also describe the business model framework by Rajala et.al (2003) which we use to analyze the business model of the product under study. We culminate the section by once again highlighting the focus of the chapter.

### Business Models

Although there is some research in understanding the role of business model in firm's performance (Zott & Amit, 2008) there is no unanimously acceptable definition of 'business model' construct (Hedman & Kalling, 2003; Morris et.al, 2005). As Morris et.al (2005) posited, organizational researchers have treated business model at three levels: revenue model of a firm, organization's design, and organization's strategic direction.

Clearly, none of these perspectives can individually serve the purpose of this chapter. Instead, we need a more inclusive conceptualization of the term business model. We therefore adopt the definition of business model as given by Morris et.al (2005). The definition is as follows: "A business model is a concise representation of how an interrelated set of decision variables in the areas of venture strategy, architecture, and economics are addressed to create sustainable competitive advantage in defined markets" (Morris et.al, 2005; p: 727). Thus in the context of this study, business model represents different aspects from creation of offerings to their delivery to the customer.

## Software Business Models

Business models as a term has origins in rise of e-commerce (Mahadevan, 2000). Consequently, there has been considerable work on understanding business models pertaining to software industry (Rajala et.al, 2003; Rajala & Westerlund, 2007). However, as the aim of this chapter is to analyze a business model of a software product, we had to choose a suitable framework designed for this particular purpose. Additionally, the framework had to match definition of business model adopted for the purpose of this study. Thus, the chosen framework had to deal with all dimensions of business model and not focus on certain aspects only. With these constraints in mind, we chose a framework for analyzing software business models as suggested by Rajala et.al (2003). This framework conceptualizes a software business model along four dimensions: product strategy, revenue model, distribution model, and services and implementation.

Rajala et.al (2003) define product strategy as the *composition of product and service proposition and the way development work is organized* (Rajala et.al, 2003; p: 6). Revenue model focuses on *how an organization can generate monetary returns from a given software*. Distribution model defines *the way marketing of product and services is organized as well as actual sale of the product* (Rajala et.al, 2003; p: 9). The fourth dimension, services and implementation aspects of the software business model defines *how product and services are dispatched and deployed to customers* along with the mode of carrying out software maintenance and post-purchase services. It is important to note here that there are several sub-dimensions to each of these four aspects. Table 1 provides an overview of each of the dimensions and the constituent sub-dimensions.

In applying this framework to our study, we mapped each of four dimensions of the framework to analyze the business model of the product being studied.

## BUSINESS MODEL OF OPENBRAVO ERP

As the aim of the chapter was to develop the understanding of Openbravo ERP's business model, we interviewed personnel responsible for four dimensions of software product business model as explained above. Initially, Chief Executive Officer of Openbravo ERP was approached for gaining the access for the study. Once the access was granted, chief technology officer was

*Table 1. Software Product Business Model Framework as given by Rajala et.al (2003)*

| Dimension | Sub-dimensions |
|---|---|
| Product strategy | Customized product solution, product platform, uniform core product, modular product family, standardized online services |
| Revenue logic | Effort, cost or value based pricing, license sales and royalties, revenue sharing, hybrid models and loss-leader pricing, others |
| Distribution model | Direct contact with customers, reseller or agent model, re-publisher or OEM model, distributor or dealer model, partner network |
| Maintenance and services | IT consulting and customer specific system work, System integration projects, software deployment, online services, self service |

interviewed to understand the product strategy. This was followed by interviews with the Product engineering manager and business development manager. Lastly, the partner network manager was interviewed. Due to geographical constraints, interviews were conducted online and recorded. For conducting interview, a case study protocol was developed that included interview questions. Later they were transcribed and content-analyzed. For content analysis, Rajala et.al's (2003) framework was used as a template.

## Evolution of OpenBravo ERP

Openbravo ERP was initiated as an open source product. The software was developed by a team of developers who did consulting in enterprise resource planning in local companies and educational institutes in Spain. These developers initiated the development of ERP software by using number of open source technologies. As the CTO of Openbravo stated:

*"It was a project started by a group of local software developers in Pamplona, Spain and they had an objective to serve local companies with an ERP [...] They had previously done a project for a local university, University of Navarra and they thought that developing a web-based ERP would be an interesting project."*

At foundation, the firm was not named as Openbravo; it was named as Tecnicia. Company was backed by venture capital funding and received multiple funding rounds (see Table 2). Investors included *Adara Venture Partners*, *Amadeus Capital Partners*, *GIMV*, and *Sodena*. It was not until 2006 when Tecnicia decided to adopt open source licensing regime for their ERP software. First driver for changing the licensing regime was the use of open source technologies in developing Openbravo ERP. This was also clear from following comment from the community director of Openbravo:

*"We are web-native [and] based on open standards [such as] XML, HTML, and XHTML. We run on open source stack [in which] we use MySQL, Apache, Java, Pentaho, [and] Jasper; we obviously rely on work of many other communities to put together our solution."*

The CTO of Openbravo further elaborated the relationship between technology and adoption of Open source license:

*"To begin with they [founders] decided that they wanted to license it [Openbravo ERP] under an Open source license primarily because they wanted to leverage Open source technology components. Because they were embedding technology components, they decided that the overall project was to be licensed under Open source license."*

Targeted at small and medium enterprises, OpenBravo ERP managed to generate significant dissemination. As per the data collected from the

*Table 2. Evolution of OpenBravo ERP (Openbravo, 2010)*

| Time | Milestone |
|------|-----------|
| 2001 | Tecnicia is founded in Pamplona Spain |
| Jan 2006 | Openbravo is founded. It secures the funding of five million Euros. |
| Oct 2006 | Openbravo is ranked number one project on SourceForge |
| Feb 2007 | Openbravo becomes the founding member of the Open Solutions Alliance. This was in order to encourage application interoperability and best practices |
| Jan 2008 | Openbravo Professional Subscription launches, providing customers guaranteed support |
| May 2008 | Openbravo secures second round of venture capital funding worth 9.1 million Euros |
| Nov 2008 | Openbravo reaches one million downloads on SourceForge |
| April 2009 | Launch of Openbravo Forge which is basically a platform where community members can interact |
| Jan 2010 | Launch of Openbravo exchange which is an open source portal created. It's an open source distribution portal dedicated to ERP solutions and extensions |

news items published on OpenBravo's web site, OpenBravo ERP released the source code under an open source license in April 2006 and was immediately recognized as one of the promising OSS products. In September 2006, OpenBravo ERP was ranked number three on Source Forge (one of the largest hosting platforms for open source products) and in October 2006, OpenBravo ERP was ranked number one OSS product on SourceForge.net, which at that time hosted one hundred and thirty thousand products. On January 5, 2007, the product reached two hundred thousand downloads and it reached five hundred thousand in February 2008.

OpenBravo ERP was also successful in securing considerable venture capital funding. Its first round of funding was worth five million Euros and was received in January 2006. The product also succeeded in getting partners through its partner program launched in March 2007. In May 2008, OpenBravo ERP received twelve million Euros as a venture capital funding. As of July 2009, OpenBravo's partner network consisted of over one hundred partners in forty countries. Partners not only contributed to product dissemination but also to product development as many partners also participated in creating vertical specific extensions and localization modules.

## Product Strategy

As explained earlier, there are five categories of product strategies that a software business model can adopt (Rajala et.al, 2003): *customized software, product platform, uniform core product, modular product family* and *standardized online services.* Examining the product strategy of OpenBravo ERP, it can be argued that the core of OpenBravo ERP is a platform on top which domain specific extensions and localization projects can be developed. As the manager for product development platform of OpenBravo ERP stated:

*"From version 2.50 on; we have introduced a modularity concept which means that you can have your OpenBravo installation, plug-in additional capabilities into it. [...] You have dozens of localization packages for OpenBravo ERP [...] all these things [extensions in the form of plugins] circulate around the main products"*

Thus it can be concluded that OpenBravo ERP followed the modular product family as a product strategy. This strategy is further bolstered through suitable licensing regime. OpenBravo ERP is licensed under OpenBravo Public License (OBPL) which is derived from an older OSS license known as Mozilla Public License (MPL). Under OBPL, core part of the software product (section of the entire code base that can be used to develop and deploy additional functionality) is released under standard open source licensing norms where user has the access and right to modify the source code. However proprietary extensions can be developed on top of the core. Such extensions, being proprietary, are not governed by the license which governs the software product's core. As the Chief Technology Officer of OpenBravo ERP stated:

*"[Mozilla Public License] had an advantage of being very commercial friendly because implementers of the system could have decided to have not only open source extensions but commercial extensions on top of OpenBravo so as to have maximum flexibility to the users. So we chose Mozilla Public License because of that."*

This way OBPL allowed OpenBravo ERP to operate under modular product strategy as community could use the core as the platform and develop domain-specific extensions and localization projects that may be open source or proprietary in nature. This approach has been successful for OpenBravo ERP as it also allows others to build their business models on top of core of the software. As the business development manager stated:

*"We allow commercial modules to be created and we host them on our exchange and allow [creators to] distribute them. So [for] the commercial module, an author gets paid. [...] we build most capabilities into the platform so that the software author [the one who writes the extensions in the form of plugins] can have his IP protected and he can commercialize and get revenues on top of the professional edition."*

## Revenue Model

As mentioned earlier, Rajala et.al (2003) identified five categories of revenue models that may be employed by software business models: *effort, cost or value based pricing, license sales and royalties, revenue sharing, hybrid models and loss-leader pricing, and others*. Open source edition of OpenBravo ERP is given for free in order to develop the user-base for the product. On the other hand, the enterprise edition is the revenue source where users need to buy subscriptions for using the enterprise editions. The business development manager explained the role of the two editions:

*"From the community perspective the key to the business model is dissemination [...] the community edition has this dissemination force [...] they [organizations using community edition] can simplify their business and if they want to go forward and maximize their business then they are going to go for professional [...]".*

*"The commercial module an author gets paid for; it runs on top of our commercial edition that requires subscription"*

Thus, it is proposed that OpenBravo ERP follows the hybrid model where the hybridity is in different modes of revenue generation. One mode is through *sale of services and maintenance of the software* while the other mode is through *sale of extensions to the core functionality*. In a typical

case, a user who subscribes to the enterprise edition pays a subscription fee and then can avail both services and the software extensions. Similar to the product strategy, licensing regime facilitated revenue model choice. OBPL as a licensing regime facilitates the hybrid revenue model. OBPL allows development of commercial extensions which are available with enterprise edition of the software and therefore allow OpenBravo ERP to price the subscription of its professional edition accordingly.

## Distribution Model

Distribution model of OpenBravo ERP is partner-dependent. More specifically, OpenBravo ERP gets implemented as well as maintained and serviced by the global partner network. Open-Bravo as a firm only involves itself in training and certifying partners as well as a second level of support which can be availed by its partners through subscription contracts. As the following quotes suggest, OpenBravo as a firm depends entirely on partners to also provide maintenance support to the end users.

*"So whatever business we do, we do through partners. Whatever services we provide to end customers are also through partners [...] Even it happened that we have lost some opportunities because they wanted to work directly with us. It happened in India also when our partnership network was pretty new; that was the time when people did not want to work with the partner, they wanted to work with the vendor directly." [Partner network manager, OpenBravo ERP]*

*"People who participate in the community, that post on forums that log defects, that make contributions are system integrators, value added resellers that implement the product at the end customers. We have an indirect distribution channel both from our commercial standpoint but also*

*from community standpoint." [Chief technology officer, OpenBravo ERP]*

Thus, distribution model of OpenBravo ERP falls in the fifth category termed by Rajala et.al (2003) as *partner network*. The rationale for developing a partner-based distribution model was explained in the following manner:

*"The goal was to build a very scalable business model for the ERP [...] the model is to interact with the service providers actually working with end customers. So we don't sell directly to the end customers" [Business development manager, OpenBravo ERP]*

The partners usually receive customer leads that are generated by OpenBravo's internal business development team. As the business development manager explained:

*"It's very important to be able turn web-traffic into leads. So we pass our leads to our partners and key part is automating that. We are looking to build a volume business; a certain amount of marketing automation in terms of taking in traffic, scoring it in an automated way and then handing it off to the best partner."*

For passing on leads to partners, the rating of that partner is used to assess if the partner has enough competency to serve that particular customer. As partner network manager of Open-Bravo stated:

*"If you see he is a gold-certified partner that means he has enough experience of handling critical projects. He has some number of satisfied customers behind him. It shows the maturity of the partner. So that is how we determine the maturity of the partner. For us it is an indicator to decide which partner to go for which project."*

Partners are further classified into three categories as per their own business model: independent software vendors, value added resellers and system integrators. Table 3 explains the distinction between different business models of partners of OpenBravo:

## Services and Implementation

As stated earlier, OpenBravo does not provide any services to the end-customer directly. Thus, its direct service offerings are not to the end customers but to the partners.

*"So whatever business we do, we do through partners. Whatever services we provide to end customers are also through partners [...] Even it happened that we have lost some opportunities because they wanted to work directly with us. It happened in India also when our partnership network was pretty new; that was the time when people did not want to work with the partner, they wanted to work with the vendor directly." [Partner network manager, OpenBravo ERP]*

*Table 3. Types of partners (OpenBravo, 2010)*

| Type of Partner | Partner's Business Model |
|---|---|
| System Integrator (SI) | SIs provide implementation and integration services to government as well as private organizations in collaboration with pre-sales and customization services offered by OpenBravo |
| Independent Software Vendor (ISV) | ISVs embed solutions into the OpenBravo ERP. ISVs are also allowed to re-brand the product and getting on-site and online technical support from Openbravo. |
| Value Added Reseller (VAR) | Build a scalable business on top of OpenBravo ERP. VARs provide implementation and customization services to small and mid-sized businesses. VARs can also build and globally distribute their own modules |

The services can be classified in two categories: services for knowledge transfer where OpenBravo can train and certify partner organizations and services based on knowledge exploitation where OpenBravo can use its deeper insights into the software to provide services like specialized consultation and custom product development. The aim of these services is to enable partners to achieve successful implementation and support to the end customers. Table 4 outlines the services provided by OpenBravo ERP.

When we employ the framework by Rajala et.al (2003), it can be seen that OpenBravo's services and implementation model falls under online services category because OpenBravo does not provide services directly to the end user but provides the technical and consulting aid to its partners. In this chapter, we focused on under-

standing the business model of OpenBravo ERP. Table 5 provides a concise description of the business model of OpenBravo ERP.

## IMPORTANT ASPECTS OF A FOS-ERP BUSINESS MODEL

The chapter started with an aim of understanding of business model of an open source ERP product. For the analysis purpose, software business model template developed by Rajala et.al (2003) was used. In this section, we discuss important aspects of the FOR-ERP business model.

To begin with, software licensing seems to be playing a much wider role in contrast to existing literature on OSS licensing choice that focuses largely on role of licensing in attracting develop-

*Table 4. Services and implementation model (OpenBravo, 2010)*

| Service Offerings | Description | Knowledge Transfer/Exploitation |
|---|---|---|
| Implementation Consulting | A project team with local knowledge and expertise to implement OpenBravo (targeted at end-users and is provided through partners) | Knowledge transfer |
| Maintenance Support | Professional maintenance services to keep OpenBravo ERP implementation updated and in line with user requirements (targeted at end-users and is provided through partners) | Knowledge transfer |
| Training | In-class and online courses on OpenBravo functionality, methodologies and customization (service with knowledge transfer as the focus, targeted at partners) | Knowledge transfer |
| Certification | Online certification exams to officially demonstrate partners' knowledge of and experience with OpenBravo (service with knowledge transfer as the focus, targeted at partners) | Knowledge transfer |
| 2nd Level Support | Ticket based support directly from the OpenBravo experts to help partners with any issue (service with knowledge exploitation as the focus, targeted at partners) | Knowledge exploitation |
| Specialized Consulting | Consultative support to complement partner's own team with complex project requirements or in demand peaks (service with knowledge exploitation as the focus, targeted at partners) | Knowledge exploitation |
| Outsourcing | Custom development services for complex requirements or to complement partner's own team (service with knowledge exploitation as the focus, targeted at partners) | Knowledge exploitation |

*Table 5. Business model of OpenBravo ERP*

| Aspect of the business model framework | Positioning of OpenBravo ERP |
|---|---|
| Product strategy | Modular software family (allows the development of extensions and localization modules on top software's core) |
| Revenue model | Hybrid revenue model (presence of two editions of the software. Community edition to build user-base while enterprise edition to generate revenue through subscription) |
| Distribution model | Partner network (allows OpenBravo to build a scalable business model and achieve faster localization of the ERP software) |
| Services and Implementation | Online services (provides enabling and certifying services to partners who in turn can conduct implementation and maintenance to end users) |

ers to the project as well as ensuring adherence to the norms of OSS (Sen et.al, 2008; Singh & Phelps, 2009). For example, Sen et.al (2006) posited developer appeal as a antecedent to a license choice. However, in case of OpenBravo ERP, license not just affected the product strategy but also facilitated the revenue model and distribution model. Emergence of OS licenses such as Affero General Public License (AGPL) that is exclusively important for OSS products distributed over networks highlight the impact licensing can have over the software distribution model. Thus, it can be proposed that FOS-ERP business models should be employed under licensing regime that facilitate majority of the business model aspects and not just software development.

The second important aspect is the participation of partners in the business model. Traditionally, partners were treated as a distribution channel. However, in case of OpenBravo ERP, partners' role as contributors to software localization was acutely highlighted by the respondents.

In case of proprietary ERP software, role of partners in product development may be restricted because proprietary licensing regime does not allow users to either access or modify the source code of the product (von Hippel & von Krogh, 2003). However, in case of OpenBravo ERP in particular and FOS-ERP in general, partner network can be leveraged not only as the distribution channel but also as product development resource. As the Chief Technology Officer of OpenBravo ERP stated:

*"Our community is made of three constituents. From one side we have end users which I would say, as I said before, is probably the minority of our community and second ones are people that implement the products... the projects at their customers. So they are system integrators and value added resellers that provide services around our product but they choose to work in the pure community vault without any commercial relationship with us and third constituents are our business partners that are people that provide services but they choose to do it on professional edition and having commercial relationship with us"*

The partner network manager and product development manager of OpenBravo outlined the role played by partners in product development:

*"if someone wants us to deliver some results that are in the roadmap and that's why in the backlog, faster that person; and we welcome this; first can collaborate with us in terms of delivering some piece of functionality themselves and we include this functionality as a contribution to our product and this thing we envision as a more interesting collaboration to join one of our teams which is working on features that are of interest to that particular person and the community and work with us on delivering this feature [...] it is actually for our community members and partners it's a great training experience because they work with the OpenBravo developers and actually learn a lot OpenBravo technologies, OpenBravo development, OpenBravo platform functionality and so on an so forth."* [Product development manager, OpenBravo ERP]

Benefit of involving partners in software development includes faster localization of the software as well as extension of the software to multiple business domains. Business development manager of OpenBravo narrated an anecdote where the partners collaborated to localize a product extension:

*"We see lot of these Indian partners with commercial operations in west and development operations in India and he has developed a Hotel management vertical. It's really a micro-vertical because it is specifically for bed and breakfast types. He is commercializing on top of our professional edition [...] he writes it in English but guess what! We can pair him up with Spanish guys they can do the translation and Spanish people can sale his hotel management system in Spain, they get commission on it, he gets the royalty and we get cut for being the enabler for all of this."*

Clearly, partners associated with an FOS-ERP product can be leveraged by the organization as both distribution model as well as product development resource.

## FUTURE RESEARCH DIRECTIONS

Although ERP has been studied from the user perspective, the adoption of open source as an alternative approach for software business model is particularly interesting as open source represents a change that is visible for ERP vendor rather than the end-user. As chief technology officer of Open-Bravo ERP indicated, *most end-users of ERP are little aware about the underlying technology and may not choose an ERP for it being open source.* In other words, research on FOS-ERP necessitates the incorporation from the vendor perspective in organizational research on ERP. With the need of incorporating vendor's business model is overall organizational research in ERP, we can suggest at least two future research dimensions: *organizational success factors for adoption of business models based on FOS-ERP* and *comparative studies on adoption issues between FOS-driven and proprietary ERP products.*

Organizational factors affect the success of a technology products (Sivadas & Dwyer, 2000) as well decision to adopt open source as a business model (Bonaccorsi et.al, 2006). However, in the context of ERP, success factor studies have taken the user perspective and have studied factors affecting adoption of an ERP. There is very little understanding if organizational factors affect the success of an ERP in general and open source ERP in particular. We believe that our exploration of a business model based on FOS-ERP would instigate ERP success factor research from the vendor perspective.

On the other hand, researchers exploring ERP success factor from user perspective may need to give open source ERP a fresh start as open source software has an implicit perception of risk from the user perspective (Bonaccorsi et.al, 2006). On the other hand, users can participate in the product development at a much early stage. Thus it is worthwhile to examine if perception of high risk associated with open source software is compensated in some sense by a more transparent development process. Once a clear understanding of what affects the success of an open source ERP product from users' perspective, a comparative analysis of success factors of proprietary and open source ERP would be the next logical step.

## REFERENCES

Ågerfalk, P. J., & Fitzgerald, B. (2008). Outsourcing to an Unknown Workforce: Exploring Opensourcing as a Global Sourcing Strategy. *Management Information Systems Quarterly*, *32*(2), 385–409.

Bonaccorsi, A., Giannangeli, S., & Rossi, C. (2006). Entry Strategies Under Competing Standards: Hybrid Business Models in the Open Source Software Industry. *Management Science*, *52*(7), 1085–1098. doi:10.1287/mnsc.1060.0547

Fitzgerald, B. (2006). The Transformation of Open Source Software. *Management Information Systems Quarterly*, *30*(2), 587–598.

Hedman, J., & Kalling, T. (2003). The Business Model Concept: Theoretical Underpinnings and Empirical Illustrations. *European Journal of Information Systems*, *12*, 49–59. doi:10.1057/palgrave.ejis.3000446

Hippel, E. v., & Krogh, G. v. (2003). Open Source Software and the "Private-Collective" Innovation Model: Issues for Organization Science. *Organization Science*, *14*(2), 209–223. doi:10.1287/orsc.14.2.209.14992

Lerner, J., & Tirole, J. (2002). Some Simple Economics of Open Source. *The Journal of Industrial Economics*, *50*(2), 197–234. doi:10.1111/1467-6451.00174

Mahadevan, B. (2000). Business Models for Internet-Based E-Commerce: An Anatomy. *California Management Review*, *42*(4), 55–69.

Morris, M., Schindehutteb, M., & Al, J. (2005). The Entrepreneur's Business Model: Toward a Unified Perspective. *Journal of Business Research*, *58*, 726–735. doi:10.1016/j.jbusres.2003.11.001

Openbravo. (2010). *Global Partner Program*. Retrieved April 2, 2010, from Openbravo Web Site: http://www.openbravo.com/partners/become-partner/global-partner-program/

Openbravo. (2010, January). *Openbravo Backgrounder*. Retrieved March 30, 2010, from Openbravo Web Site: http://www.openbravo.com/docs/openbravo-backgrounder_January2010.pdf

Openbravo. (2010). *Openbravo Services*. Retrieved April 2, 2010, from Openbravo Web site: http://www.openbravo.com/services/

Rajala, R., Rossi, M., & Tuunainen, V. (2003). A Framework for Analyzing Software Business Models. *Proceedings of the European Conference on Information Systems 2003, Conference on Information Systems - New Paradigms in Organizations, Markets and Society,* June 18-22, 2003, Naples, Italy

Rajala, R., & Westerlund, M. (2007). Business Models - a new Perspective on Firms' Assets and Capabilities. Observations from the Finnish Software Industry. *International Journal of Entrepreneurship and Innovation*, *8*, 115–125. doi:10.5367/000000007780808039

Sen, R., Subramaniam, C., & Nelson, M. L. (2008). Determinants of the Choice of Open Source\ Software License. *Journal of Management Information Systems*, *25*(3), 207–239. doi:10.2753/MIS0742-1222250306

Singh, P. V., & Phelps, C. C. (2009) Determinants of Open Source Software License Choice: A Social Influence Perspective. Available at SSRN: http://ssrn.com/abstract=1436153

Sivadas, E., & Dwyer, F. R. (2000). An Examination of Organizational Factors Influencing new Product Success in Internal and Alliance-based Processes. *Journal of Marketing*, *64*(1), 31–49. doi:10.1509/jmkg.64.1.31.17985

von Krogh, G., & Spaeth, S. (2007). The Open Source Software Phenomenon: Characteristics that Promote Research. *The Journal of Strategic Information Systems*, *16*(3), 236–253. doi:10.1016/j.jsis.2007.06.001

Zott, C., & Amit, R. (2008). The Fit between Product Market Strategy and Business Model: Implications for Firm Performance. *Strategic Management Journal*, *29*(1), 1–26. doi:10.1002/smj.642

## ADDITIONAL READING

Bonaccorsi, A., & Rossi, C. (2003). Why Open Source software can Succeed. *Research Policy*, *32*(7), 1243–1258. doi:10.1016/S0048-7333(03)00051-9

Campbell-Kelly, Martin & Garcia-Swartz, D.D. (2010). The Move to the Middle: Convergence of the Open-Source and Proprietary Software Industries. *International Journal of the Economics of Business*, *17*(2), 223–252. doi:10.1080/13571516.2010.483091

Dahlander, L., & Magnusson, M. (2008). How do Firms Make Use of Open Source Communities? *Long Range Planning*, *41*(6), 629–649. doi:10.1016/j.lrp.2008.09.003

Hippel, E. v. (2005). *Democratizing Innovation*. Cambridge, MA: The MIT Press.

Lakhani, K. R., & Hippel, E. v. (2003). How Open Source Software Works: "Free" User-to-User Assistance. *Research Policy*, *32*(6), 923–943. doi:10.1016/S0048-7333(02)00095-1

Lakhani, K. R., & Wolf, R. (2005). Why Hackers Do What They Do: Understanding Motivation and Effort in Free/Open Source Software Products. In Feller, J., Fitzgerald, B., Hissam, S., & Lakhani, K. (Eds.), *Perspectives on Free and Open Source Software* (pp. 3–22). Cambridge, MA: MIT Press.

Srivardhana, T., & Pawlowsk, S. D. (2007). ERP Systems as an Enabler of Sustained Business Process Innovation: A Knowledge-Based View. *The Journal of Strategic Information Systems*, *16*(1), 51–59. doi:10.1016/j.jsis.2007.01.003

Vitari, C., & Ravarini, A. (2009). A Longitudinal Analysis of Trajectory Changes in the Software Industry: The Case of the Content Management Application Segment Segment. *European Journal of Information Systems*, *18*(3), 249–263. doi:10.1057/ejis.2009.13

West, J., & O'Mahony, S. (2008). The Role of Participation Architecture in Growing Sponsored Open Source Communities. *Industry and Innovation*, *15*(2), 145–168. doi:10.1080/13662710801970142

Xua, Q., & Ma, Q. (2008). Determinants of ERP Implementation Knowledge Transfer. *Information & Management*, *45*(8), 528–539. doi:10.1016/j.im.2008.08.004

## KEY TERMS AND DEFINITIONS

**Business Model:** The mechanism that links creating of offerings to delivery of offerings.

**Distribution Model:** An approach making the product/service available to the customer.

**Product Strategy:** An approach specifying product development and product positioning.

**Software Product:** Packaged software that can be purchased off-the-shelf by the customers.

**Software Product Industry:** A subsection of a software primary industry where the organizations are involved in development of software products.

# Chapter 6
# Free and Open Source ERP:
## Distinction, Direction, Co-Existence, and Potential

**Torben Tambo**
*Aarhus University, Denmark*

**Christian Koch**
*Aarhus University, Denmark*

## ABSTRACT

*With the proliferation of commercial Packaged ERP (P-ERP) systems in today's enterprises, many reasons exist to look for alternatives in the quest for innovation, business development, cost, agility and dependency. P-ERP provides a solid and proven business support, an ecosystem of consultancies and integrators, senior management having gained confidence over the last 20 years, and commercially based support and development. This leaves companies with still more expensive P-ERP costs, still less flexibility, a still harder push to lose possibilities for differentiation, still more homogenised business processes, and absence of flexibility to change suppliers and systems. FOS-ERP offers an answer to most of these questions, but is facing issues in market penetration. In this chapter, barriers of FOS-ERP are reviewed; proposals are made on how to manage barriers. An approach managing co-existence of P-ERP and FOS-ERP is suggested. Concluding, FOS-ERP is seen as a strong option for enterprises in the future, but a clear understanding and distinction must be the offset, barriers needs to be managed, and optimal co-existence will in most cases be the realistic scenario.*

DOI: 10.4018/978-1-61350-486-4.ch006

## INTRODUCTION

In a book on Free and Open Source Enterprise Resource Planning Systems (FOS-ERP), we believe it is beneficial to look at the actual meaning and business account of FOS-ERP particularly in contrast to Standard or Packaged ERP Systems (P-ERP) (Pollock & Williams 2009). Traditionally, Open Source Software (OSS) has been viewed as something positive; the group of innovative fiery souls sitting in dark attics and making global software systems in a democratic spirit. Fitzgerald (2006) describes the transformation to a more professionalised Open Source system called OSS 2.0. The professionalised FOS-ERP has a convergence towards a classical view of P-ERP as something static. Sen (2007) points out the risk that open source projects are not sufficiently oriented towards user requirements. Our observation is based on viewing P-ERP as dynamically redefining itself (Koch 2007).

Traditionally, discussions on ERP have been unitary: Do you have an enterprise-wide ERP or not; and if you do, it is probably one large whole with little flexibility. In many cases, ERP is not monoliths of business information processing; various software packages and systems fill out specialised roles probably using the general ERP as a common repository, a transaction system and for master data management (O'Brien & Marakas 2008). This is supported by the movement towards service-oriented architectures (SOA) and as described in (Microsoft 2010, SAP 2010, Oracle 2010) the opening of most P-ERP towards development of user modules, value-added reseller (VAR) add-ons and Enterprise Integration Architectures (EIA) to interface with external systems. There is a demand for openness in the P-ERP world that works both as a competitor to FOS-ERP, but also tries to mimic the advantages of OSS. This creates obstacles to and potentials for FOS-ERP. These will be discussed further below.

FOS-ERP should be an attractive option for any enterprise wanting to search for alternatives to existing, costly and inflexible enterprise systems (Johanson & Sudzina 2009). FOS-ERP provides flexibility, influence, broad networked contacts and probably reduced costs. However, it seems that FOS-ERP from the emerging period 2003-2008 still has some way to go to gain the same momentum as e.g. positive Open Source cases, such as Linux, Firefox or StarOffice (Bitzer 2004). Despite decent growth rates FOS-ERP seems difficult to spot in the statistics, individual cases remain "exotic" (Compiere 2008).

It is the general assumption in this chapter that FOS-ERP or certain variants of FOS-ERP is beneficial to most enterprises in many cases (Lemos 2008). The overall perception of FOS-ERP is, however, that many barriers exist in the enterprises' understanding of FOS-ERP; the attractiveness, the assumed market-orientation and the enterprises ability to operate a FOS-ERP (Gruman 2007). In addition, FOS-ERP should be viewed in light of innovation and technology management, namely management of information technology. Ågerfalk and Fitzgerald (2008) emphasise attention to the strength of open source development models to instate distributed and globalised development. Their approach to view customer and (open source) community responsibilities and obligations has been very beneficial to this chapter.

Issues contributing to the understanding of FOS-ERP are vendor identification and confidence. Normally, P-ERP is purchased through a combined reseller and consulting company representing the duality of software and services. With FOS-ERP, the software reselling is somewhat different, not imposing an issue in other open source scenarios, but probably critical in senior management optics of risk management (Lin 2008, Goode 2005).

Attractiveness of FOS-ERP should be a multitude of decision parameters of the user enterprise (Hauge et al 2010). Here, regular ERP acquisition or purchasing processes must be viewed – including value of decision parameters, such as partial upgrades, totality of infrastructure and applications, security issues, learning curve and technology cultures of the enterprise. Fitzgerald (2006) found that more mature open source projects pay attention to these more enterprise-oriented issues.

Open source (Kavanagh 2004) and innovation should be a closely linked discussion (Harison & Koski 2009, Krogh 2003, Hicks & Pachamanova 2007). In realising that one company cannot manage all aspects of innovation, large communities of contributors have proven to be an alternative and attractive option (Ajila & Wu 2007). Open architectures and interoperability are addressed in (Joode & Egyedi 2005, Anand & Ganesh 2006). When discussing innovation within ERP, there is the dichotomy of ERP for operational effectiveness and ERP for strategic positioning (Porter 1996). Grant et al. (2006), however, adds scepticism to the expectations of ERP in many enterprises.

## Method

The method applied in the study of this chapter is a qualitative (Myers 1997; Klein & Myers 1999) and interpretive desk-study. It is based on the information system tradition of observing and understanding information technology within its context in organisation, application and business (Baskerville and Wood-Harper 1998, Mathiassen and Nielsen 2008). The ERP observation offset is previous contributions and studies of ERP and ERP communities (Koch 2001, Koch 2007). Recent methodological contributions may also be found in Ågerfalk et al. (2009). An account on technological insight of information systems research on ERP is found in (Koch et al. 2010).

Furthermore, as offset for this chapter, a comprehensive case study has been made (Lee 1989) in which a large company applied both P-ERP, FOS-ERP components and on a large scale bespoke development centred on open standards (Tambo 2010). A number of senior management positions are compiled through adjacent information systems studies, particularly regarding senior managements' mindset in terms of responsibilities and liabilities of vendors. Background and considerations from P-ERP projects are enacted as a lens for reaching a better understanding of the organisational and technological factors surrounding FOS-ERP (Cunningham & Jones 2005).

This chapter is scientific-oriented, but includes experience of practitioning within ERP development and implementation, and action research of ERP in real-life contexts (Kock 2007). As this chapter is seeking to introduce a relatively broad scope of FOS-ERP, this is done at the expense of a full scientific justification of all aspects. The combined practitioner – science view is believed to support the discussion by summarizing discussions with business executives (Dalle et al. 2008). The co-existence model developed in this chapter is derived by merging neo-classical n-tier models of Java 2 Enterprise Edition (Singh et al. 2002, Tomascheck 2010) with guidelines published on P-ERP development and interoperability strategies as discussed in (Farhoomand 2007, Oracle 2010, Microsoft 2010). Each tier is discussed within its potential openness potentials using either P-ERP or FOS-ERP.

This chapter first introduces the context of ERP in its business information system. Then a distinction of FOS-ERP is made, particularly regarding management understanding and creation of confidence. This is followed by a presentation of responsibilities of business software in relation to various internal and external compliance requirements. Subsequently, a strategy for FOS-ERP is suggested to open-mindedly position itself in co-existence with P-ERP following a chosen strategy of positioning within application architectures. Finally, this chapter makes suggestions for further research.

## BACKGROUND

ERP systems (Sadagopan 2004, Koch 2001) have developed over time, from mainframe systems of the 1980s, to client-server systems of the 1990s, to largely multi-tiered systems running on thin presentation platforms – mostly HTML-inspired – in the first decade of the 2000s (Pollock & Williams 2009, O'Brian & Marakas 2008). Business data and processes have also changed from silos and OLTP to integrated, orchestrated services strongly aligned to formal business processes. Where ERP is facing difficulties in adaption is in dealing with informal and social/organisational processes, agility and innovation/differentiation (Markus & Tanis 2000, Koch 2007).

ERP as a rigid definition in the enterprise has generally troubled researchers. ERP can assume differing roles over time. Some roles deliberate and well planned, other less intended roles can be derived out of corporate subcultures and determinism of other professions (Kerr et al. 2007); research has also addressed this as drift of the technology in its organisational context (Ciborra 2000). ERP implementation projects are some of the most difficult change projects in most companies, and has a track record of failure on either cost, quality or time. Koch (2007) discusses intrinsic creeping of scoping during the implementation project as a major contributor the project failure.

The realm of ERP is assumed to be more diverse in the coming years than over the last decade, since:

- No vendor can be specialist in any field or industry
- Particularly modern supply chain requirements for very close interactions between companies might mean a partial dissolving of the ERP as a monolith; a fact highly recognised within the marketing push of the leading ERP actors

- IT organisations under pressure cannot accommodate all business requirements, and must let some business priorities free to be organised by the business stakeholders themselves
- SOA, SaaS and cloud-computing will mean unprecentended competition on price and functionality within certain domains, where even the strongest IT strategy might accept that there is better and cheaper solutions just out of the net
- Growing compliance requirements force specialised solutions to meet such challenges.

In a corporate position where consolidation of ERP on large, inflexible, expensive monolithic P-ERP is the only option, this following aims at giving a frame for assessing FOS-ERP as the potential alternative. Enterprises are viewed as a whole – governmental, private and NGO – where P-ERP is applicable, FOS-ERP is also to be considered (Waring & Maddocks 2005, Tomascheck 2010, Bitzer 2004, Silverman 2008).

## DISTINCTION

ERP systems are normally the most critical IT systems of the enterprise by representing master data, tying business processes together and generating the foundation for the operational reporting (Pollock & Williams 2009, Sadagopan 2004). Management would desire the highest level of confidence and reliance in the ERP, and especially senior management would regard ERP as an unchallenged governor of business processes even if uncontrolled behaviour successively enters the system (Kerr et al 2007).

Traditionally, confidence in ERP is created out of a multiplicity of factors. Below is listed a set of factors derived from discussions carried out within the project described in (Tambo 2010):

1. The supplier's legal, professional and moral responsibility in case of ERP implementation default. Management can claim "that we chose the right product, our advisers supported us, but something out of our hands failed".

2. An irrational belief amongst senior management that if P-ERP projects fail, there is an infinite liability from the software manufacturer or the consultancy to compensate and correct all issues; no manufacturer and/or consultancy enter business without having the customer signing a contract waiving infinite compensation.

3. The concept of inherence of knowledge business processes from state-of-the-art by using high-class P-ERP and corresponding consultancies; this concept might be questioned by

    a. the organisation will most probably not accept superimposing of externally derived business processes

    b. most organisations have to be shaped out of their intrinsic characteristics

    c. consultancies might port knowledge between or within industries without having to focus on particular ERP

    d. over time, it is possible that business processes become more general, more public domain and FOS-ERP can encompass a broad spectre of business processes as well as P-ERP.

4. In the relation between vendor and senior management level, P-ERP is observed as a warranty for agility and innovation; new software updates; new business requirements should easily be adapted into the P-ERP and offered to the business. However, P-ERP is largely subjected to operational procedures requiring meticulous version management; profound testing; bundling of features into release management packages with contingency procedures; thus P-ERP might secure stability but not agility.

As a more diverse platform, FOS-ERP could better accommodate change (Hicks & Pachamanova 2007) and should be regarded less or equally susceptible to cross-silo side-effects in upgrade situations. These arguments and more make it justifiable to strongly consider FOS-ERP, as no paramount argument meets the one ERP approach as to the other.

FOS-ERP can originate from many actors and sources some more voluntary, some more commercially oriented (Krishnamurthy & Tripathi 2007, Boyer & Robert 2006, Campbell-Kelly & Garcia-Swartz 2009). Just to mention a few:

1. consultancies having done this earlier and now giving software away for free to obtain consultancy contracts

2. vendor-backed initiatives organised as associations or interest groups

3. business associations, indirect business actors and other with secondary financial motives

4. external influence, e.g. from tooling makers doing free business components that can act as an ERP system, such as business components for .Net, Java or Joombla.

Origination do probably not play an overly role in FOS-ERP system, but a thorough understanding is equal to an active risk management, and a decision of the governance structure for e.g. participation, self support, funding, sharing, collaboration etc. Lack of transparency within OSS might impose a problem in regards to credibility (Campbell-Kelly & Garcia-Swartz 2009).

## RESPONSIBILITY

Larger enterprises are often highly concerned with legal responsibilities of enterprise software (O'Brien & Marakas 2008, Pollock & Williams 2009) given the serious potential impact of downtime, errors, lack of scalability, secure flaws, etc.

Loss of profit, customer confidence and product damages need to be catered for. This is among other things supported with

- Legal frameworks for the software particularly reducing liabilities and indemnities
- Legal frameworks for operational services, e.g. SLA
- Operational and governance frameworks e.g. ITIL
- Business history successes, often underpinned using reference customers, case stories and argumentative statistics.

In such cases, software is purchased from suppliers with the strongest track records, and financially weaker, but more innovative suppliers are omitted.

Most software vendors recognise this fact which over the last ten years has led to a continuously stronger concentration of vendors within P-ERP for large corporations; today, basically Oracle and SAP with Sage, Infor, Microsoft Agresso, Lawson and Epicor in a tier-2 role. The legal frameworks of software vendors and operational services providers have increasingly been strengthened; no one will be able to financially to justify full liability for the customers systems under all circumstances.

P-ERP is typically a matter of very long customer-supplier relationships (Ford et al. 2003). In very few cases, the customer will be able to impose a substantial financial liability on a supplier. Most likely, the supplier has a legal framework which cannot hold him liable. The relationship will eventually be so tainted that it will have to end knowing that a switch of systems might cost 100+ MUSD and take several years to accomplish. This intricate customer-supplier catch needs strong attention in watching companies' options for alternatives.

Over time, financial responsibility will simply not be sufficient to enter into an agreement with a P-ERP supplier. Support organisation of the P-ERP

supplier can be an argument, but is fully paid for by the customer. All in all, this leads to a position where there is no basic argument in the line of responsibility for P-ERP rather than FOS-ERP.

## EMPIRICAL FRAMEWORK STUDIES

Where does FOS-ERP come from and who will supply you with these? ERP systems are never simple to develop. Likely, they require both software development skills at very high level and domain knowledge, or at least generic business process knowledge, at an intricately detailed level. Recently, it was found that Google funded 80% of Wikipedia, and Linux has been relying highly on heavy funding from engaged stakeholders, such as HP, Oracle and IBM. The development of FOS-ERP is mostly, presumably, not done by a bunch of idealists. Much FOS-ERP is most likely done by individuals and organisations with financial interest in establishing services associated with the free and open concept (Campbell-Kelly & Garcia-Swartz 2009, Dahlander & Magnusson 2005). Within an organisation and community view, FOS-ERP contributors may be:

- Groups of interest – with or without professional sponsors – open source developers
- ERP vendors with interest in augmenting traditional business with added functionality beyond existing support organisation
- Secondary suppliers giving functionality to link to ERP; e.g. postal services offering shipping systems; bar code scanner vendors offering scanner packages
- Consultancies supplying or supporting FOS-ERP packages to get the contracts of implementation, adaption and operation
- Academia and research initiatives providing services to support their merits

Open source software's association with individuals is discussed in Giuri et al. 2008, Koch 2008.

In most cases, commercial backing of FOS-ERP is not a problem – with many large and smaller consultancies already being deeply engaged into FOS-ERP. As with P-ERP, implementation and operation is by far the lion's share of the cost of ERP projects. Concern should instead be given to specific requirements of the enterprise. Here the enterprise's general IT strategy is central.

## COMPLIANCE

In addition to financial responsibilities of ERP vendors, there are other aspects to consider when acting on the markets: In many cases, certain tests and compliancy measures have to be passed to be able to do business within specific areas. The compliance can be related to certain legal, regulatory, institutional and traditional national or super-national business foundations. Table 1 provides selected issues to review ERP for compliance (adapted from Silverman 2008).

Compliance is largely a matter of quality within a context. Generally, the OSS model is recognised to secure a good quality in e.g. Linux, and existing FOS-ERP apparently shows no less quality than P-ERP. Quality in OSS development is discussed in (Zhao & Elbaum 2003, Bitzer et al. 2007, Bonaccorsi & Rossi 2003, Hansen et al. 2009, Sowe et al. 2008, Yu 2008). Particularly the formation of communities around OSS is a strength surpassing P-ERP which has a more unilateral vendor-customer relationship. OSS communities often include academia, consulting, users and general vendors who can provide a more holistic setting around the development process (Stam 2009, Dahlander & Magnusson 2005, David & Shapiro 2008, Krogh 2003).

*Table 1. ERP within compliance management*

| Compliance type | Compliance enforcement organisation | ERP implications |
|---|---|---|
| Fiscal | Local, regional, national, bilateral or multilateral laws and practices of taxation, excise, sales tax/value-added tax and duties. E.g. EU's 6th VAT directive, Danish Law of Bookkeeping; etc. | P-ERP is often 'type approved' like cars; FOS-ERP will probably have to be approved on individual basis. The approval process might not be formal, but P-ERP users will be regarded more on a standard basis than FOS-ERP users. |
| Corporate, financial governance | GAAP, IFRS, SOX | It takes many resources to comply with terms and business process requirements of these frameworks. FOS-ERP might comply with the spirit but lack something on the detailed level. Many organisations do, however, choose to embed these guidelines in governing procedures and not relate them directly to the concrete ERP system. |
| Process | FDA, GMP, HAACP, DIN, ISO | To justify compliance through a transaction system is attractive. Given the relatively strict enforcement, FOS-ERP has much to prove to support companies in this field. |
| Product | Issues such as traceability, testing, quality data, configuration, options, change, commercial terms | Compliance on product issues is attractive to obtain agility in the market. FOS-ERP could provide particular options in this field. |
| Delivery | Shipping according to transportation regulations. Sales or adherence contracts. AEO, C-TPAT, WCO, SAFE. | Global supply chains are incessantly reshaping; new actors mean new requirements. Anti-terrorism and anti-whitewash measures impose though requirements on ERP; interesting if FOS-ERP communities can deal with this. |

## COEXISTENCE FRAMEWORK OF FOS-ERP WITH P-ERP

In this paragraph, a framework is presented for the use of FOS-ERP within business environments where P-ERP plays various roles targeting business processes or delivering a breadth of infrastructural components.

P-ERP is the main technological trajectory is the general assumption in this chapter. However, different possibilities do exist. Before P-ERP, bespoke ERP was commonplace and provided strong alignment but troublesome operational management (Pollock & Williams 2009, Tambo 2010, Graham & Koch 2001). Pollock & Williams (2009) also envision a more mixed approach as alternative to large P-ERP.

### Co-Creation in P-ERP

Most ERP manufacturers support various levels of adaption, co-creation and third-party solutions (Koch 2007, Oracle 2010, SAP 2010, Microsoft 2010).

Adaption has been a classic approach to make P-ERP fit with business processes. Data tables, logics or user interfaces have been augmented with whatever the user company wanted. This was early found effectively blocking upgrade paths and patch kit compatibility. Several vendors introduced a layered approach to distinguish between core ERP and adaptations. Furthermore, most ERP systems now support per-user configuration of user interfaces. E.g. on most data tables, Oracle E-business suite has 15 user-defined fields which are also included in upgrade paths. Application Programming Interfaces (API) has also gained some popularity in adapting P-ERP without tampering the core. P-ERP's enabling of SOA and XML technology has expanded even more with possibilities of transactional transparency and application adaption.

Most P-ERP vendors are conducting a gradual system of adaptations reaching from user freedom and down to inclusion of adaption in the core offerings. This can be illustrated with inspiration from Sadagopan (2004) and the vendors' websites (see Figure 1)

In other words, a company-specific solution might turn into industrial solutions which then again might be approved and eventually included in the functional core. Dynaway (2010) describes this in relation to Microsoft Dynamics Shop Floor Control module.

*Figure1. Control and level of integration of ERP modules*

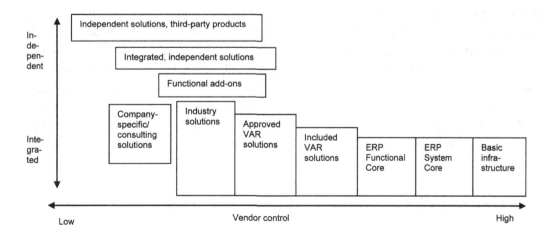

In presentations of ERP vendors, ecosystems have become a critical sales parameter. Exchange of company-specific/consulting solutions is encouraged. Directories of solution providers are offered. User groups are encouraged and supported along with conferences and trade shows.

ERP vendors, consultancies and solution providers form a community around a commercial P-ERP which should be understood in relation to strength, offerings and corporate interrelatedness (Ford et al 2003) in considering alternatives, when FOS-ERP is to be assessed. Each major ERP vendor represents commercial communities with combined turnover counted in billions EUR. This is what FOS-ERP has to compete against.

## Co-Existence and Interoperability

In the implementation of FOS-ERP, is it most likely that the enterprise already has a P-ERP for most of its business processes. FOS-ERP will henceforth probably have to enter a co-existence with P-ERP; several different options for doing so exist, a range of these are shown below. Notably within co-existence, there is a series of issues to address within sharing and integration of business data, business logics and system infrastructure´, such as servers, clients, identities, authentication and authorisation. These are also listed below to underpin the overall issue of how to create architectures for the use, particular use within co-existence, of FOS-ERP and P-ERP.

The enterprise's incentive for FOS-ERP must position itself with the co-existence as a given fact. A strategic framework is suggested to position FOS-ERP with this context:

- Embedded into the P-ERP framework
- Augmenting the P-ERP within functional and domain-specific areas
- Parallel operation with the P-ERP most likely using an EIA (Enterprise Integration Architecture) to integrate the major software components
- Sharing of infrastructural resources and repositories
- Sharing business components wherever possible
- Embed into user interfaces using e.g. SOA and mash-ups
- Disconnected with only manual or file-loads as data exchange; this might apply in cases of web applications including SaaS, customer applications, supplier applications and other external applications for e.g. banking, tax reporting, customs services.

Most FOS-ERP must be assumed to comply with the basic n-tier or multi-tier model of enterprise computing (Fowler 2002) and basically work as (what is commonly known as) a web application (O'Brian and Marakas 2008). To display this further, Table 2 has been developed with inspiration from Singh et al (2002), Sadagopan (2004) and Fowler (2002) regarding the layered approach to business information systems. Additionally, FOS-ERP are displayed under the option of either embed or include itself into existing information systems structures with an artifactual fusion (Intra-ERP), or FOS-ERP will remain at distance, avoiding overlapping and retaining its own boundary integrity (Extra-ERP).

The column Extra-ERP reflects, to some degree, more interoperability, whereas the Intra-ERP has a higher portion of co-existence (Joode & Egeydi 2005). The co-existence creates equivalence among FOS-ERP and commercial third-party software products. FOS-ERP still has to cope with organisational barriers, but may penetrate considerably easier than in all-or-nothing scenarios.

*Table 2. FOS-ERP co-existence and interoperability overview*

| | **Intra-ERP** | **Extra-ERP** |
|---|---|---|
| Session and security layer | Authentication and authorisation given from the P-ERP system. | Independent authentication and authorisation, or retrieve this information from a common enterprise wide repository e.g. using LDAP. |
| Data layer | Using embedded API's or direct access to the database or the ERP-system; using the P-ERP's designated interface tables; using tables and supporting functions (sequences, indices, constraints) of the P-ERP's database but with tables created within the overall security framework of the P-ERP. | Using self-declared area of the P-ERP's database, or a database unrelated to the P-ERP. |
| Database business logic layer | Given strong use of extensive database logics or stored procedures (database-based programming), these can be used according to their documentation to share logics between FOS-ERP and P-ERP. | The FOS-ERP will make its own use of the database regardless of the implementation of the P-ERP. Although considerations might be given to common issues, such as language coding, numerical sizes, string lengths. |
| Application persistence layer | The FOS-ERP establishes access to the P-ERP database through the given objects of the persistence layer. | The FOS-ERP uses its own persistence framework probably given out of the implementation framework, e.g. J2EE and.Net. |
| Application business logic layer | The FOS-ERP uses (part of) the same logics and functionalities as the regular P-ERP. Useful for validation and non-core functionality, e.g. "GetCustomerAddress", "FormatDate". | The FOS-ERP is application-wise independent of the P-ERP. |
| Business process orchestration framework, e.g. BPEL | Use, supplement or extend existing functionalities | Use or do not use orchestration related or unrelated to P-ERP. |
| Development tools | FOS-ERP must decide upon when to use general programming languages, e.g. Java or C#, or when to use P-ERP native languages, e.g. X++, C-SIDE or ABAP. Along with this modelling, testing and operational tools must be addressed. | Tools of own preference could be chosen. Novel tools could provide leading edge benefits like Ruby on Rails or Haskell. The open source community as such offers an abundance of development tools. |
| Application presentation layer | FOS-ERP developed using the same user interface foundation (GUI) as the P-ERP. | GUI of its own. Adapt to enterprise front-ends. Use an XML output stream for mash-ups. |
| Client | If any client executor is required, this must be used if FOS-ERP and P-ERP are to share application presentation layer. | Few applications are client-based in the future, but client components may be installed for distinction of the application and enrichment of the GUI. |

## USER PERCEPTION

The monolithic approach of P-ERP has among other things been promoted by the promise that users can work within identical and easily recognisable graphic user interfaces (Pollock & Williams 2009). Additionally, data should be far more consistent across functional segments and enterprise workflows should be better supported. As suggested above, this is contradicted in part by P-ERP being challenged within

- Business partners' introduction of self-service websites each within different GUI
- Widespread use of company-specific adaptations of P-ERP, each introducing changes to the standard system
- The opening of P-ERP at several tiers for integration, shared business logics, co-creation and value-added reseller solutions – each opening also introducing added complexity and divergence from the standard system.

For the individual user, using the ERP system in daily assignments, these complexities do not have much impact on the single system level, but many users might incur troubles in finding a direction through over-complex P-ERP. Presumably, users should be viewed from position, engagement, degree of self-determination and requirements for innovation. The distinction between ERP for operational effectiveness versus competitive advantage is interesting, and proposing FOS-ERP appealing far more to users and companies seeking competitive advantage through differentiation.

There seems to be a contour of FOS-ERP attracting more sophisticated companies and users. Sen (2007) criticises an over-simplified view on OSS particularly with respect to usability and support of business users and suggest professionalisation within OSS communities. Bonaccorsi and Rossi (2003) describe OSS from a diffusion view where the broader network of the developer community provides user organisations with more options of choice. Lin (2008) clearly states the necessity for a higher skill level within companies adopting FOS-ERP, but also heads for the broader network. The study of Subramaniam et al. (2009) emphasises the perseverance of users through OSS projects leading to an indication that requirements for in-depth understanding are stronger with FOS-ERP than with P-ERP. Sowe et el. (2008) looks at the knowledge sharing through OSS projects including developers, experts and non-developers (users) also suggesting a high degree of commitment and insight at the user/company side. Gwebu and Wang (2010) have studied smaller OSS projects than ERP, but conclude that OSS and OSS users can benefit from inexpensive, innovative, quality software. Furthermore, this study contributes to a deeper comprehension of users' perception and mindsets on why to engage in OSS.

User and company typologies seem critical in understanding the adoption of FOS-ERP. Typologies might prove useful for both vendor and purchasers of FOS-ERP in avoiding mistakes or reposition themselves. The technical view on FOS-ERP architectures suggested in Table 2 may also be included in the assessment and planning of the software-based work-design of companies and users to highlight pitfalls and make decent risk analyses.

## DIRECTIONS FOR FUTURE RESEARCH

FOS-ERP has to offer a distinct proposition to the companies. Selling it as 'real ERP, just less license cost' is not an argument creating trustworthiness. FOS-ERP must make distinctive offerings in terms of particular business solutions, openness, transparency, co-creation and innovation.

FOS-ERP does not necessarily change the dominating part of the supplier community found in the ERP market, namely the consulting supplier. As consulting is generally regarded as the most expensive part of the implementation the argument for FOS-ERP is generally quite weak. Consultancies could actually resell FOS-ERP just as any other product, and still run a fair earning. The FOS-ERP community along with research has to provide solutions requiring fewer consultancies and more empowerment of the user organisation to increase outcome (Lin 2008).

The social and managerial understanding of the corporate infrastructure is in many cases closely linked to the P-ERP system with the schism of having P-ERP, e.g. SAP, conducting and appropriating business flows, and on the other hand knowing that there are organisations insisting on doing things their way (Ciborra 2000, Kerr et al. 2007, Koch 2007). Further research in FOS-ERP will probably, in a better way than P-ERP, yield solutions for softening ERP's control aspect (Markus & Tanis 2000) and provide more empowerment and less rigid structures.

To create a more realistic competiveness of FOS-ERP, the co-existence aspect needs to be highlighted making it fit into known sockets of existing information systems architectures. Contemporary frameworks need to be addressed. Research is also of interest in adding new potentials to the market possibilities as various tendencies could predict a dissolving of the traditional monolith observation of ERP and enterprise computing with the high rate growth of extra-organisational service-oriented architectures (SOA), software as a service (SaaS), business-to-business web-solutions and cloud computing/services.

## CONCLUSION

The billion dollar business of P-ERP has undergone major changes since ERPs where just understood as monoliths able to fulfil any mechanistic requirement given appropriate license payments. P-ERP companies have all introduced co-creation, value-added reseller solutions, third-party approval schemes, and generally invites to engagement of users in an open source work style. Contrary to this, companies using P-ERP are facing continued challenges in keeping the application strategies intact: Software-as-a-service (SaaS) provides new, specialised features at unprecedented rates, self-service websites are popping up, spreadsheet-based niche solutions are being self-composed by users and P-ERP is being used beyond intended scope. This creates a space for FOS-ERP, but also challenges the concept of FOS-ERP heavily as something different.

Since P-ERP is in a phase of change as a monolithic strategic artefact, FOS-ERP is to be understood as partially, selectable choices fulfilling particular requirements within a business, but with little chance of getting around every aspect of the company.

FOS-ERP bears the same characteristics as P-ERP in its connection to knowledge communities and particularly consultancies. FOS-ERP does not change this situation dramatically; professional consultancies can provide services of P-ERP as well as FOS-ERP. The decision on FOS-ERP is up to the IT management and the senior management of the enterprise; the rewards are straightforward, but risks are more vague and uncertain, so it is a matter of active risk taking.

Finally, FOS-ERP is in any case expected to play a stronger role in the future given an observed "inadequacy crisis" of P-ERP: SAP's Open Source Integration and Community Network initiatives are strong examples of this. Oracle and Microsoft Dynamics have had options for user-driven development for several years. Getting to the bottom of the issue, FOS-ERP is a matter of technological governance – or taste. Is it the way to go, or are commercially supplier-backed solutions the choice? This contribution hopefully provides managers with a little more background to decide.

## REFERENCES

Agerfalk, P., & Fitzgerald, B. (2008). Outsourcing to an Unknown Workforce: Exploring Opensourcing as a Global Sourcing Strategy. *Management Information Systems Quarterly*, *32*(2), 385–409.

Agerfalk, P., Fitzgerald, B., & Slaughter, S. (2009). Flexible and Distributed Information Systems Development: State of the Art and Research Challenges. *Information Systems Research*, *20*(3), 317–328. doi:10.1287/isre.1090.0244

Ajila, S. A., & Wu, D. (2007). Empirical study of the effects of open source adoption on software development economics. *Journal of Systems and Software*, *80*, 1517–1529. doi:10.1016/j.jss.2007.01.011

Anand, S. & Ganesh, J. (2006) Towards Enterprise Agility Through Effective Decision Making. *SETLabs Briefings, 4* (1).

Baskerville, R., & Wood-Harper, A. T. (1998). Diversity in information systems action research methods. *European Journal of Information Systems*, *7*, 90–107. doi:10.1057/palgrave.ejis.3000298

Bitzer, J. (2004). Commercial versus open source software: the role of product heterogeneity in competition. *Economic Systems, 28,* 369–381. doi:10.1016/j.ecosys.2005.01.001

Bitzer, J., Schrettl, W., & Schöder, P. (2007). Intrinsic motivation in open source software development. *Journal of Comparative Economics, 35,* 160–169. doi:10.1016/j.jce.2006.10.001

Bonaccorsi, A., & Rossi, C. (2003). Why Open Source software can succeed. *Research Policy, 32,* 1243–1258. doi:10.1016/S0048-7333(03)00051-9

Boyer, M., & Robert, J. (2006). *The Economics of Free and Open Source Software: Contributions to a Government Policy on Open Source Software.* Montreal: CIRANO.

Campbell-Kelly, M., & Garcia-Swartz, D. D. (2009). Pragmatism, not ideology: Historical perspectives on IBM's adoption of open-source software. *Information Economics and Policy, 21,* 229–244. doi:10.1016/j.infoecopol.2009.03.006

Ciborra, C. (2000). *From Control to Drift: The Dynamics of Corporate Information Infrastructures.* Oxford.

Compiere (2008). *Seven Years and Still Growing with Compiere Open Source ERP.* Retrieved from http://www.compiere.com/downloads/success-stories/compiere-erp-ss-pharmanord.pdf

Cunningham, S. J., & Jones, M. (2005). *Autoethnography: a tool for practice and education.* In CHINZ; Vol. 94 Proc. of the 6th ACM SIGCHI conf. on Computer-human interaction: making CHI natural.

Dahlander, L., & Magnusson, M. G. (2005). Relationships between open source software companies and communities: Observations from Nordic firms. *Research Policy, 34,* 481–493.

Dalle, J. M., David, P. A., den Besten, M., & Steinmueller, W. E. (2008). Empirical issues in open source software. *Information Economics and Policy, 20,* 301–304. doi:10.1016/j.infoecopol.2008.09.001

David, P. A., & Shapiro, J. S. (2008). Community-based production of open-source software: What do we know about the developers who participate? *Information Economics and Policy, 20,* 364–398. doi:10.1016/j.infoecopol.2008.10.001

Dynaway (2010). *About Dynaway.* Retrieved from http://www.dynaway.com/en-GB/aboutdynaway/Pages/Default.aspx

Farhoomand, A. (2007). Opening up of the Software Industry: The Case of SAP. *Communications of the Association for Information Systems, 20*(49).

Fitzgerald, B. (2006). The transformation of open source software. *Management Information Systems Quarterly, 30*(3).

Ford, D., et al. (2003). *Managing Business Relationships 2ed.* London: Wiley.

Fowler, M. (2002). *Patterns of Enterprise Application Architecture.* Boston: The Addison-Wesley.

Giuri, P., Rullani, F., & Torrisi, S. (2008). Explaining leadership in virtual teams: The case of open source software. *Information Economics and Policy, 20,* 305–315. doi:10.1016/j.infoecopol.2008.06.002

Goode, S. (2005). Something for nothing: management rejection of open source software in Australia's top firms. *Information & Management, 42,* 669–681. doi:10.1016/j.im.2004.01.011

Graham, I., & Koch, C. (2001). Tailor or configure? – Challenges in designing IT for support of Business Processes. In *Proceedings of WMSCI 2001.*

Grant, D., Hall, R., Wailes, N., & Wright, C. (2006). The false promise of technological determinism: the case of enterprise resource planning systems. *New Technology, Work and Employment, 21*(1). doi:10.1111/j.1468-005X.2006.00159.x

Gruman, G. (2007). *Is Open Source The Answer to ERP? CIO.COM*, February 15, 2007. Retrieved from http://www.cio.com/article/28812/Is_Open_Source_The_Answer_to_ERP_ [Accessed 20.03.2010]

Gwebu, K. L., & Wang, J. (2010). Seeing eye to eye? An exploratory study of free open source software users' perceptions. *Journal of Systems and Software, 83*(11), 2287–2296. doi:10.1016/j.jss.2010.07.011

Hansen, K. M., Jónasson, K., & Neukirchen, H. (2009). *An Empirical Study of Open Source Software Architectures' Effect on Product Quality*. Engineering Research Institute, University of Iceland, Technical report VHI-01-2009, July 2009

Harison, E., & Koski, H. (2009). Applying open innovation in business strategies: Evidence from Finnish software firms. *Research Policy, 39*, 351–359. doi:10.1016/j.respol.2010.01.008

Hauge, Ø., Ayala, C., & Conradi, R. (2010). Adoption of open source software in software-intensive organizations – A systematic literature review. *Information and Software Technology, 52*, 1133–1154. doi:10.1016/j.infsof.2010.05.008

Hicks, C., & Pachamanova, D. (2007). Backpropagation of user innovations: The open source compatibility edge. *Business Horizons, 50*, 315–324. doi:10.1016/j.bushor.2007.01.006

Johansson, B., & Sudzina, F. (2009) Choosing Open Source ERP Systems: What Reasons Are There For Doing So? In Boldyreff, C., Crowston, K., Lundell, B. & Wasserman, A.I. (eds) *Open Source Ecosystems: Diverse Communities Interacting 5th IFIP WG 2.13 International Conference on Open Source Systems*, OSS 2009, Skövde, Sweden, June 3-6, 2009. Proceeding

Joode, R.v.W.d, & Egyedi, T.M. (2005). Handling variety: the tension between adaptability and interoperability of open source software. *Computer Standards & Interfaces, 28*, 109–121. doi:10.1016/j.csi.2004.12.004

Kavanagh, P. (2004). *Open Source Software – Implementation and Management*. New York: Elsevier.

Kerr, D.V., Houghton, L., Burgess, K. (2007) Power Relationships that Lead to the Development of Feral Systems. *Australasian Journal of Information Systems, 14* (2).

Klein, H. K., & Myers, M. (1999). A Set of Principles for Conducting and Evaluating Interpretive Field Studies in Information Systems. *Management Information Systems Quarterly, 23*(1), 67–97. doi:10.2307/249410

Koch, C. (2001). *ERP-systemer, erfaringer, ressourcer, forandringer.* (In Danish: ERP systems – experiences, resources, change.) Copenhagen: Ingeniøren-bøger.

Koch, C. (2007). ERP – a moving target. *International Journal of Business Information Systems, 2*(4), 426–443. doi:10.1504/IJBIS.2007.012544

Koch, C., Olsen, M., & Tambo, T. (2010) How little do we need to know about Enterprise Resource Planning (ERP)? -A critical review of information systems research on ERP. *Proceedings of the 33rd Information Systems Research Seminar in Scandinavia*

Koch, S. (2008). Effort modeling and programmer participation in open source software projects. *Information Economics and Policy, 20*, 345–355. doi:10.1016/j.infoecopol.2008.06.004

Kock, N. (Ed.). (2007). Information Systems Action Research – An Applied View on Emerging Concepts and Methods. *Integrated Series on Information Systems 13.*

Krishnamurthy, S., & Tripathi, A. K. (2009). Monetary donations to an open source software platform. *Research Policy, 38*, 404–414. doi:10.1016/j.respol.2008.11.004

Krogh, G. v. (2003). Community, joining, and specialization in open source software innovation: a case study. *Research Policy, 32*, 1217–1241. doi:10.1016/S0048-7333(03)00050-7

Lee, A. S. (2009). A Scientific Methodology for MIS Case Studies. *Management Information Systems Quarterly, 13*(1), 33–50. doi:10.2307/248698

Lemos, R. (2008). Open-source ERP grows up. [Accessed 20.03.2010]. *InfoWorld*, (april): 22. Retrieved from http://www.infoworld.com/t/applications/open-source-erp-grows-615?page=0,1.

Lin, L. (2008). Impact of user skills and network effects on the competition between open source and proprietary software. *Electronic Commerce Research and Applications, 7*, 68–81. doi:10.1016/j.elerap.2007.01.003

Markus, M. L., & Tanis, C. (2000). The Enterprise System Experience - From Adoption to Success. In Zmud, R. W., & Price, M. F. (Eds.), *Framing the domains of IT management: projecting the future through the past* (pp. 173–207). Cincinatti, OH: Pinnaflex.

Mathiassen, L. & Nielsen, P.A., (2008). Engaged Scholarship in IS Research. *Scandinavian Journal of Information Systems*.

Microsoft. (2010). *Microsoft Dynamics*. Retrieved from http://community.dynamics.com

Myers, M. D. (1997). Qualitative Research in Information Systems. *Management Information Systems Quarterly*, (Jun): 97, 241–242.

O'Brien, J. A., & Marakas, G. (2008). *Management Information Systems*. McGraw-Hill.

Oracle (2010). *Oracle E-Business Suite Knowledge Zone*. Retrieved from http://www.oracle.com/partners/en/knowledge-zone/applications/021473.htm

Pollock, N., & Williams, R. (2009). *Software and Organisations: The biography of the enterprise-wide system or how SAP conquered the world*. Oxon: Routledge.

Porter, M. E. (1996). What is strategy? *Harvard Business Review*, (Nov-Dec): 1996.

Sadagopan, S. (2004). Enterprise Resource Planning. *Encyclopedia of Information Systems*, 169-184.

SAP. (2010). *SAP Ecosystem and Partners Sharing Best Practices with Sap Communities*. Retrieved from http://www.sap.com/ecosystem/communities/index.epx

Sen, R. (2007). Waiting For Usable Open Source Software? Don't Hold Your Breath! *Communications of the Association for Information Systems, 20*, 382–392.

Silverman, M. G. (2008). *Compliance management for public, private and nonprofit organizations*. New York: McGraw-Hill.

Singh, I., Stearns, B., & Johnson, M.Enterprise Team. (2002). *Designing Enterprise Applications with the J2EETM Platform* (2nd ed.). Reading, MA: Addison-Wesley.

Sowe, S. K., Stamelos, I., & Angelis, L. (2008). Understanding knowledge sharing activities in free/open source software projects: An empirical study. *Journal of Systems and Software, 81*, 431–446. doi:10.1016/j.jss.2007.03.086

Stam, W. (2009). When does community participation enhance the performance of open source software companies? *Research Policy, 38*, 1288–1299. doi:10.1016/j.respol.2009.06.004

Subramaniam, C., Sen, R., & Nelson, M. L. (2009). Determinants of open source software project success: A longitudinal study. *Decision Support Systems, 46*, 576–585. doi:10.1016/j.dss.2008.10.005

Tambo, T. (2010) Bespoke ERP - A Systems View On Enterprise Management. In Hosni et al. (eds), *Proceedings of the 19th Conference of the International Association for Management of Technology.* Maimi: IAMOT.

Tomaschek, N. (2010). *Einführung Eines Open Source CRM ERP System in einem mittelständisches unternehmen.* Saarbrücken: VDM Verlag.

Waring, T., & Maddocks, P. (2005). Open Source Software implementation in the UK public sector: Evidence from the field and implications for the future. *International Journal of Information Management, 25*, 411–428.

Yu, L. (2008). Self-organization process in open-source software: An empirical study. *Information and Software Technology, 50*, 361–374. doi:10.1016/j.infsof.2007.02.018

Zhao, L., & Elbaum, S. (2003). Quality assurance under the open source development model. *Journal of Systems and Software, 66*, 65–75.

## ADDITIONAL READING

Al-Mashari, M. (2002). Enterprise resource planning (ERP) systems: a research agenda. *Industrial Management & Data Systems, 102*(3), 165–170. doi:10.1108/02635570210421354

Cheliotis, G. (2009). From open source to open content: Organization, licensing and decision processes in open cultural production. *Decision Support Systems, 47*, 229–244. doi:10.1016/j.dss.2009.02.006

Collins, H., Gordon, C., & Terra, J. C. (2006). *Winning at Collaboration Commerce.* Amsterdam: Elsevier.

Elliot, M. S., & Scacchi, W. (2002). *Communicating and Mitigating Conflict in Open Source Software Development Projects. Working Paper,* Institute for Software Research, UC Irvine, Fall 2002.

Esteves, J. & Pastor, J. (2001). Enterprise Resource Planning Systems Research: An Annotated Bibliography. *Communications of AIS 7* (8).

Ferran, C., & Salim, R. (2008). *Enterprise resource planning for global economies: managerial issues and challenges.* London: Information Science Reference. doi:10.4018/978-1-59904-531-3

Laudon, K., & Laudon, J. (2009). *Management Information Systems – Managing the Digital Firm* (11th ed.). New York: Prentice Hall.

Lengnick-Hall, C. A., Lengnick-Hall, M. L., & Abdinnour-Helm, S. (2004). The role of social and intellectual capital in achieving competitive advantage through enterprise resource planning (ERP) systems. *Journal of Engineering and Technology Management, 21*(4), 307–330. doi:10.1016/j.jengtecman.2004.09.005

Nicholson, N., Audia, P. G., & Pillutla, M. M. (Eds.). (2005). *The Blackwell Encyclopedia of Management, Organizational Behavior (Blackwell Encyclopaedia of Management)* (Vol. 11). Oxford, UK: Blackwell.

Nielsen, P. A., & Kautz, K.-H. (2008). *Software Processes and Knowledge: Beyond Conventional Software Process Improvement.* Aalborg: Software Innovation Publisher.

Norris, G., Hurley, J. R., Hartley, K. M., & Dunleavy, J. R. (2000). *E-business and ERP – Transforming the Enterprise. PriceWaterhouseCoopers.* New York: Wiley.

Pykäläinen, T., Yang, D., & Fang, T. (2009). Alleviating piracy through open source strategy: An exploratory study of business software firms in China. *The Journal of Strategic Information Systems, 18*, 165–177. doi:10.1016/j.jsis.2009.10.001

Svejvig, P. (2010). *Enterprise Systems and Institutions - Theorizing about Enterprise Systems in Organizations Using Institutional Theory - A Case Study Approach.* Department of Management, Aarhus School of Business, Aarhus University. PhD Thesis.

Umble, E. J., Haft, E. J., & Umble, M. M. (2003). Enterprise resource planning: Implementation procedures and critical success factors. *European Journal of Operational Research, 146*(2), 241–257. doi:10.1016/S0377-2217(02)00547-7

Watt, D. (2003). *E-business Implementation: A guide to web services, EAI, BPI, e-commerce, content management, portals, and supporting technologies.* Oxford: Butterworth-Kleinemann.

Weber, S. (2004). *The success of open source.* Cambridge: Harvard University Press.

## KEY TERMS AND DEFINITIONS

**Co-Existence:** The ability to operate two or more software products, versions or families concurrently in the same business environment. Often an open or service-oriented application architecture is required to do so. Measures must be taken on licensing, change management, operational responsibilities, business case evaluation, etc.

**Community:** Fundamental actors in ERP business are typically the customer (user organisation), the consultant and the software manufacturer. Observations show that several other stakeholders and knowledge institutions influence ERP, such as universities, press/media, user groups, conferences, rumours, buzz, and advisories like Gartner and Forrester. Decision making and organisational issues tend to be affected from these communities. A community understanding is in many cases essential for the full understanding of life cycles with ERP – company interaction.

**Compliance:** The issue of adhering a business concept or process to a set of commonly agreed rules. The rule-sets can be written or unwritten, company internal or external, statutory or voluntary, national or international, etc. Both social, economic and technical issues might be governed in terms of compliance.

**Consultant:** Most ERP manufacturers including FOS-ERP leave implementation and services of ERP systems to independent consultant companies. These companies can have from 1 to 100.000 employees. The traditional understanding of a 'consultant' as a particular person of professional insight advising a company at a managing level is in ERP more a question of manpower and establishment of skilled project-teams.

**Eco-System:** The sum of proponents within a professional community contributing to the idea of spreading the positive message of the value of a certain technology. Typically members of the eco-systems are not directly paid, but have an indirect economic or idealistic interest in forwarding the message.

**Infrastructure:** The basic structures enabling any higher level of system or process. For servers the infrastructure might be networks and power. For ERP systems the infrastructure might be database and application servers and appropriate clients.

**Monolith:** The classic understanding of an ERP system as fully encompassing all demands of a company within one "blackbox" system. The opposite is e.g. modularised systems, service-oriented architectures, enterprise integration architectures, and co-existence.

**Partner:** Similar to consultant with the probably difference that partners sometimes are resellers and might sell competing products. Partners might have special knowledge within a country, certain industries or business segments.

**Responsibility:** The idea that one actor is bound to another actor by certain social, legal, ethical, technical or economical obligations. In a narrow sense a responsibility is only economical, but in this sense imposes serious users of definition, scope and delimitation. In ERP business responsibilities manufacturer – customer and consultant – customer is typically limited to timely information and exercising of professional best practices.

# Chapter 7
# Legal Issues with FOS–ERP:
## A UK Law Perspective

**Sam De Silva**
*Manches LLP, UK*

## ABSTRACT

*Whilst there are numerous benefits for a business from procuring a ERP on the basis of FOS licensing terms, there are a number of legal risks which need to be considered. These legal risks include: (a) assuming all FOS licences are the same; (b) uncertainty as to the enforceability of FOS licences; (c) lack of clarity in relation to the legal characterisation of FOS licences; (d) risk of poor performance; (e) risk of IPR infringement claim; (f) issues arsing from reciprocity; (g) legal challenges to FOS licences; and (h) the issues arising from the missing contractual provisions. The chapter outlines these legal risks and provides recommendations as to how to mange such risks.*

## INTRODUCTION

At its simplest level, free/open source (FOS) is a way of licensing software and this chapter accordingly begins with a reminder of why we need software licences and what they typically include in a conventional model.

It is from that basis that the different approach taken in FOS licensing is introduced. This chapter outlines the key features of FOS licences (in particular the most common FOS licence, the GNU General Public Licence) and considers the key legal issues and risks to be considered when licensing an ERP using FOS. These legal risks include:

- assuming all FOS licences are the same;
- uncertainty as to the enforceability of FOS licences;
- lack of clarity in relation to the legal characterisation of FOS licences;
- risk of poor performance;

DOI: 10.4018/978-1-61350-486-4.ch007

- risk of IPR infringement claim;
- issues arsing from reciprocity;
- legal challenges to FOS licences; and
- the issues arising from the missing contractual provisions.

This chapter is based on the laws of England and Wales as at 15 October 2010.

## BACKGROUND

To understand some of the legal risks a business could encounter with using a ERP licensed on the basis of a FOS licence, it is useful to explain how ordinary (i.e. proprietary) software is licensed.

As a general comment there is only a limited amount of literature and research on the legal issues with FOS-ERP. It should be acknowledged that much of the literature on open source software is from the perspective of developers who regard the social ideal of shared software and the developers' community above all other ideals (such as securing a revenue model), without acknowledging some of the legal difficulties with open source licensing (such as those canvassed in this chapter) (James, 2003).

### Software Copyright and the Need for Licensing

Property is simply a bundle of rights to own, use and prevent others from using something, for example, a plot of land, a car or a house. Intellectual property is a bundle of rights that protects applications of ideas and information that have commercial value (Cornish and Llewelyn, 2010). Intellectual property rights (IPRs) give creators certain exclusive rights over the knowledge and information they create to prevent others using it without permission (Gower, 2006).

IPRs cover a wide variety of subject matter, but in respect of software the principal right is copyright (although database rights and patents can also apply). In this chapter, the focus is on copyright. However, software patents should not be ignored and are increasingly likely to apply to software products. They represent a separate area of risk, however, they are beyond the scope of this chapter.

Under English law, software is automatically protected by copyright, as soon as the code is expressed in a material form such as writing (Korn, Oppenheim and Sol Picciotto, 2007). Unless varied by contract, the first owner of the copyright in software is its author, except that in the case of software created during the course of employment, it is the employer rather than the employee (Section 11 of the Copyright, Designs and Patents Act 1988).

Copyright places a number of restrictions upon use, which include:

- permanent and temporary copying, either of the program as whole or a substantial part, either of the source or object code, including writing code in any language which is substantially based on it;
- communicating to the public (for example, making it available on a website to other than authorised users) of all or a substantial part;
- making an adaptation, arrangement or other altered version, including a translation into another computer language; this includes repurposing of any elements, for example, combination or incorporation with other software or other copyright works;
- distribution or rental;
- de-compilation of a program, unless it is for the purpose of creating an interoperable program;
- possessing or disseminating an infringing copy. (Korn, Oppenheim and Sol Picciotto, 2007).

It is the owner of the copyright who has the right not to have its copyright works "infringed" by the above acts and has the right to claim damages or a court order preventing further restricted acts if an infringement is found to have taken place.

A software licence is a legally binding contract which makes lawful what would otherwise be copyright infringement. It is usually made between the owner of the relevant software copyright and someone wanting to use or distribute the software. It will have many terms relating to the commercial basis of the deal, but it is the scope of the licence in terms of permitted use and the extent to which changes can be made to the code that are crucial to the FOS issue.

## The Importance of Source Code

Source code is essentially the blueprint for the software product. It describes the algorithms, techniques and data structures which comprise the program, as written by a software engineer. The instructions contained in the source code are translated (or "compiled") into object code, a symbolic code which is not readily understandable to the engineer. Object code is ultimately "linked" into an executable program (i.e. the code which operates the hardware), which again is not readily understandable to the engineer. In summary, if a party has access to the source code version of a software product and it has the requisite skill it is able to modify the code to enhance or change what the software does.

For software development companies which invest a significant amount of time and resources in developing its products, the traditional position has been that the source code is the "crown jewels" of their business. Accordingly, most software development companies keep their source code confidential and do not release it to third parties, including customers (who usually receive just the executable or object code). If a program needs to be changed, for example, to enhance its functional-

ity or fix bugs, software engineers must generally have access to the source code.

As explained below, it is the feature of allowing third parties to have open access to source code which gives FOS its name, and which differentiates it from closed source software (the norm for proprietary software products).

## Proprietary Software Licensing

In order to exploit software commercially, a supplier can either:

- sell ownership of the software outright, transferring ownership of the related IPRs; or
- retain ownership of those IPRs and "license" the use of the software.

Software licensing is the most common route, primarily because it enables the supplier to generate revenue from multiple end users by granting multiple licences. In addition, licensing allows the supplier to further develop the software with a view to producing other exploitable products.

Licence agreements are a flexible contractual tool, the structure and content of which can be widely adapted to suit the requirements of the parties concerned. In business to business arrangements there is often a written contract between the two parties which is formally executed by signature. On the other hand, in the consumer space it is more common to see shrink wrap or click wrap licences as a means of executing a licence agreement between the software vendor ("licensor") and the customer ("licensee").

A thorough examination of all elements of a typical software licence is beyond the scope of this chapter. However, in order to understand what is special about an FOS licence, it is worth pointing out certain common elements which appear in most proprietary software licences.

## Scope of Licence

The licence agreement will typically contain restrictive terms limiting the scope of what the licensee can do with the software, ranging from mere use on a single PC, to modification and distribution of the software. Usually, the software will be provided in executable form only, in other words, with no source code being made available.

Proprietary software typically comes at a monetary cost (although products such as Adobe Reader amply demonstrate the exception to the rule). In corporate licensing, the price may be expressed by reference to the number of copies of software which are installed. So, proprietary software is usually neither open (in terms of source code visibility) nor free (in terms of cost).

A number of other restrictions may be imposed under the licence, and the licensee will need to consider whether they are acceptable in each case.

## Key Benefits of Proprietary Licensing

Considering the list of restrictions common to proprietary licensing (from which we have presented but a small selection above), what, from the licensee's perspective, are the benefits of this mode of licensing?

Firstly, a proprietary software license will often contain a number of software warranties by the licensor. A warranty is a contractual promise which, if not satisfied, gives rise to a right to sue for damages. There will typically be a warranty that the software will comply with the relevant specification, or that it will run on a particular combination of hardware and operating system.

A proprietary software licence may also contain indemnities. An indemnity is a stronger form of contractual protection than a warranty; a party that has the protection of an indemnity has an automatic right to full reimbursement of the losses to which the indemnity relates.

As with all contractual terms, the relative bargaining position of licensor and licensee will strongly influence the extent of the nature and scope of the warranties and indemnities provided to the licensee.

IPR related warranties and indemnities are common in proprietary software licences. These protect the licensee in circumstances where use of the software turns out to breach the IPRs of a third party (a circumstance in respect of which it is usually reasonable to expect the software licensor, as developer of the product, to take the risk).

It is useful to examine the types of FOS licences and the key features of such licences.

## TYPES OF FOS LICENCES

A business should not assume that all FOS licences are the same. There are many hundreds of FOS licences in use, varying widely in length, clarity, intent and legal effect. The FOS licences range from the intrusive, "copyleft" GPL through to short licences containing virtually no express terms.

The initial starting point for any business considering licensing a ERP using FOS is to:

- identify the FOS licence terms under which the ERP is made available; and
- assess whether the licence attaches any particular terms.

A leading FOS service provider provides a regularly updated table of the top 20 FOS licences in use and their estimated popularity. Table 1 shows this as at October 2010.

The following three observations can be made from Table 1:

- Firstly, the prevalence of the GPL, which accounts for about half the FOS world. These are the FSF licences with the more stringent "copyleft" terms. The four GPL licences together account for nearly 60%

*Table 1. Top 20 open-source licences (October 2010)*

| Rank | License | % |
|------|---------|---|
| 1. | GNU General Public License (GPL) 2.0 | 46.80% |
| 2. | Artistic License (Perl) | 8.80% |
| 3. | GNU Lesser General Public License (LGPL) 2.1 | 8.77% |
| 4. | GNU General Public License (GPL) 3.0 | 6.46% |
| 5. | BSD License 2.0 | 6.24% |
| 6. | MIT License | 6.10% |
| 7. | Apache License 2.0 | 4.43% |
| 8. | Code Project Open 1.02 License | 2.76% |
| 9. | Microsoft Public License (Ms-PL) | 1.61% |
| 10. | Mozilla Public License (MPL) 1.1 | 1.19% |
| 11. | Eclipse Public License (EPL) | 0.54% |
| 12. | Common Public License (CPL) | 0.51% |
| 13. | GNU Lesser General Public License (LGPL) 3.0 | 0.47% |
| 14. | zlib/libpng License | 0.40% |
| 15. | Academic Free License | 0.38% |
| 16. | Common Development and Distribution License (CDDL) | 0.32% |
| 17. | Open Software License (OSL) | 0.28% |
| 18. | Mozilla Public License (MPL) 1.0 | 0.24% |
| 19. | Ruby License | 0.23% |
| 20. | PHP License Version 3.0 | 0.22% |

[Source: Black Duck FOS Resource Center. Retrieved: http://www.blackducksoftware.com/FOS/licenses on 15 October 2010]

of the total FOS licence world, with GPL version 2 (GPLv2) alone accounting for 46%; its cousin the Lesser GPL version 2 (LGPLv2) accounts for nearly 9%; and the GPL version 3 (GPLv3) and LGPLv3 (both published in June 2007) account for 5% and 0.5% respectively.

- Secondly, and next in popularity, are the academic licences accounting for around 10%. These include the more liberal and permissive BSD and MIT licences, each also in the top 10.

- Thirdly, the top four licences account for approximately 75% of the total, and the top 10 licences for greater than 90%.

The remainder of this section examines the more common types of FOS licences.

## The GNU General Public Licence (GPL)

The GPL is probably the most famous FOS licence, as it is the licence under which Linux is distributed. Version 1 of the GPL was issued in 1989. Version 2 (GPLv2), the licence Linus Torvalds chose to apply to the Linux kernel, was issued in 1991. Version 3 (GPLv3) was published in its final form and adopted on 29 June 2007.

Of all the common FOS licences, the GPL has the strongest obligations in relation to reciprocity. The power of these provisions has led to the characterisation of the GPL as a viral licence, it spreads itself by "infecting" proprietary code with GPL licensed code.

The GPL has been interpreted as meaning that the whole of any work whatsoever that can be said to contain any portion of GPL licensed code, or be derived from it, must itself be licensed under the GPL. This means that even if the new work contains only snippets of code from the original GPL code, and even if that new work itself is made up from a series of files, only one of which contains a portion of GPL code, the entire work must itself be licensed under the GPL if it is to be "distributed" or "published".

This interpretation of the GPL has lead to the production of the "Lesser GPL" (or "LGPL"). The LGPL excludes infection where the LGPL code simply links to proprietary code. This is used to license Linux libraries so that these can link to proprietary software products created to run on a Linux platform.

With no judicial determination in the UK on the validity and effect of the GPL the position remains untested not entirely clear. Understandably, the GPL risk of infection has led to some fear on the part of some businesses who depend on the sanctity of their proprietary code for their livelihoods and a reluctance to use such FOS software in their projects.

As is usual with FOS licences, the GPL disclaims all warranties as far as possible, although it does envisage the possibility that the licensor may wish to give some form of warranty (usually in return for a fee).

In addition to providing no warranty, the GPL provides no indemnity protection against infringement claims by third parties. It also contains a clause which seeks to prevent the licensee from suing the licensor in the event of a claim being brought by a third party. It should be noted that the effect of UK law on the enforceability of such exclusions of liability is largely untested.

## The Berkeley Software Distribution (BSD)

The BSD licence was written by the University of California, Berkeley, and was originally used to distribute their Unix variant. It was altered in 1999 to remove a clause that required acknowledgement to be made of all the contributors to the code on any advertising for a software release. This clause had led to the necessity of a vast array of names being added to advertisements and consequently upsetting their presentation. For this reason BSD licences are often distinguished as being "new style" or "old style", but the only difference is the clause requiring acknowledgement on advertising.

If the GPL lies on one extreme of FOS licences in relation to reciprocity, the BSD lies on the other. There is no requirement for any derived works to be licensed in any particular way. It is up to the licensee to decide what he wants to do. The licensee may charge for the code, alter it substantially, slightly or not at all, refuse to disclose the source code and release it on any

terms he wishes. The only requirement the BSD imposes is for subsequent releases to contain an acknowledgement and copyright notice.

The BSD, like the GPL, attempts to disclaim all warranties. As for the GPL, it is questionable whether such an exclusion will have the effect intended under UK law. The BSD also contains no indemnity provisions.

## The Mozilla Public Licence (MPL)

MPL is a licence written by the Mozilla Foundation. In the late 1990s, facing heavy competition from Microsoft's Internet Explorer, Netscape decided to release the source code to its browser, Netscape Navigator, in order to promote its adoption. The licence was released under terms which evolved into the current MPL, under which Navigator's present day successor, Firefox, is licensed.

The MPL lies somewhere between the BSD and the GPL in its provisions for reciprocal licensing. Like the GPL, it requires modifications of the MPL source code by the licensee to be released under the MPL. However, this does not apply where the MPL code and proprietary source code are contained in different files, even where the MPL code links to the proprietary code and the combined work is released as a single product. In this respect it is more like the LGPL, as it allows proprietary code to run on top of and link to the MPL code without requiring the proprietary code to be released. MPL goes further by explicitly stating that the combination of the two types of code may be released as a single product. This reflects the fairly commercial approach of the Mozilla Foundation, which is wary of scaring companies away from using MPL licensed code with provisions analogous to the viral parts of the GPL.

As with the GPL and BSD, the MPL seeks to exclude warranty protection as far as possible, and as before the extent to which that would be successful under UK law remains untested.

As with the other two licences there are no explicit indemnity provisions in the MPL. However, there is a requirement where the licensor is aware of any infringement proceedings being brought by a third party that they make a note in a separate file of the facts of the case (that they are aware of) and who to contact. Although this will only work where the licensor is aware of the claim, it does at least give the licensee the possibility of notice.

## KEY LEGAL RISKS OF FOS

### Enforceability of FOS Licences

One important legal question that relates to FOS licences is the extent to which they are enforceable. Unfortunately, there is no UK case law on the subject which means that there is no certainty as to how a court would interpret any of the licences, or even whether it would enforce them at all. Certain bodies take an active interest in policing compliance with FOS licensing terms.

In the US the Free Software Foundation checks adherence to the GPL and threatens companies that it sees as breaching the GPL with litigation. To date, all such cases have settled before reaching trial.

Although there have been no UK cases, in Germany, GPL-violations.org has made claims against Sitecom, Fortinet, D-Link and Skype:

- Sitecom. In 2004 the German lower regional court of Munich confirmed a temporary injunction preventing the distribution of FOS in breach of the GPL's requirements. The defendant, Sitecom, had used netfilter/IP-tables without providing access to the source code. The court ruled that Sitecom was not entitled to use the netfilter/ip-tables code for its proprietary products and prohibited it from distributing them. The court, upholding the decision made at the interim hearing, held that the GPL licence

terms had been validly agreed between the parties by way of standard licence terms and conditions and that the defendant was in breach of the licence.

- Fortinet. In April 2005, gpl-violations.org brought an action against Fortinet UK for using GPL software in firewall and anti-virus products and trying to conceal the fact using cryptographic techniques. The Munich district court granted a preliminary injunction against Fortinet Ltd., banning further distribution of those products until they complied with the GPL.

- D-Link. In 2006, gpl-violations.org brought a claim in Frankfurt against D-Link for selling a data storage device using the Linux kernel without enclosing the GPL text, disclaiming any warranty or disclosing the source code. The court in its July 2006 ruling treated section 4 of the GPL as a condition subsequent which, when broken, revoked D-Link's licence to use the software.

- Skype. In July 2007 it was reported that Skype had been found in breach of the GPL by a Munich regional court. The breach was said to involve the way in which Skype had distributed a VoIP handset using an embedded Linux kernel, having failed to supply the source code with the handset. Welte reported in May 2008 that Skype had accepted that judgment and withdrawn its appeal.

GPL-violations.org maintains that its success in these cases has meant that it has not had to bring any new actions in Germany for the last year or so and publicises its approach to litigation as focusing on achieving publication of the source code rather than damages.

Despite the enforcement of the GPL in Germany, there is no guarantee that it would be enforced in the UK. One key issue with anyone attempting to enforce the terms of any FOS licence is the extent to which they would be entitled to do so in the UK courts. UK copyright law favours the individual author and does not easily adapt to a situation where there are hundreds of collaborators to a single work. Joint ownership of copyright arises where collaborators are working to a common design. However, where the software is being developed as and when the developers feel like it (as is often the case), it could be difficult to claim any real common design process giving rise to joint ownership. In such a case, a court might break the work up into smaller pieces corresponding to each author's contribution to the code. If the relevant portion qualified for copyright protection and it had been used in violation of its licence then it could be sued upon. However, there are real practical difficulties in associating one piece of code with one author.

## Characterisation of the FOS Licences

Another key question to answer is whether the licence in respect of FOS is a bare copyright licence or a contractual licence? The distinction is important for three main reasons:

- The terms of a contractual licence can be enforced against both the licensor and licensee. In a bare copyright license, the licensee cannot bring a claim against the licensor.
- When interpreting a contractual licence, a court may imply or disallow terms in certain circumstances to give effect to the presumed intentions of the parties or public policy.
- If a FOS licence is characterised as a contractual licence, it is possible that the remedy of specific performance might be granted by a court against a licensee breaching its terms. This would be a powerful remedy if used to compel a licensee to provide access to source code. If the FOS licence

is characterised as a bare copyright licence only (not a contract), the only relief available would be damages, an account of profits (or a hybrid of the two) and an injunction to restrain further infringement.

The publicly-expressed view of the Free Software Foundation (FSF), now supported by the US Court of Appeals decision in the *Jacobsen* case before settlement in February 2010 (see under the heading "Legal challenges to FOS" below) is that the GPL is a bare copyright licence with conditions attached and that breach of those conditions automatically results in the loss of the licence to distribute.

However, some commentators still characterise the FOS licences as a contractual licence. The rationale is as follows:

- It starts off as a unilateral contract, in other words, an offer made to the world by the author to use its software in compliance with the FOS licence conditions.
- In respect of GPL, the normal requirement to communicate acceptance is waived by the licensor under section 5 of GPLv2 so that when the software is modified or distributed, the offer is accepted by conduct and a bilateral contract is created (section 5 of GPLv2 states "*...by modifying or distributing the Program (or any work based upon the Program), you indicate your acceptance of this License to do so...*").

It should be noted that GPL does not have any express governing law or jurisdiction terms and that consequently for any GPL case outside the USA, complex conflicts of law issues may arise.

## Risk of Poor Performance

FOS software is usually supplied without any kind of warranties or guarantees, although these may be offered to a limited degree in the more "commercial" versions of FOS software, for example, those promoted by major vendors such as Sun Mircosystems (now known as Oracle America, Inc).

The reliability and robustness of FOS can deteriorate if members of a community contributing to a code base move on to other projects. A small company with limited IT development capabilities may consider that the possibility of support "falling away" due to circumstances outside its control is a possibility which is too difficult to contemplate. However, with careful selection of deployed products, and a proper risk assessment, proponents of FOS would argue this risk can be mitigated.

A customer considering deploying FOS software in its business should consider the extent to which a proprietary software vendor would provide certain warranties in any event. It would be extremely surprising, for example, for a proprietary software vendor to warrant that the software they are supplying will provide uninterrupted and error-free operation. A customer should consider what protection they would expect from a warranty, and see if they could get it elsewhere. The lack of explicit warranty protection may therefore not be as important as it may first seem – rather, it should be another factor that is put into the equation when considering FOS against proprietary software.

## Risk of IPR Infringement Claim

This is important in the context of FOS licences, particularly against copyright infringement claims by third parties. Proprietary software licences will often give an indemnity to the licensee against any claims for copyright infringement brought against them by third parties as a result of their use of the code. However, with FOS software, such indemnities are not common. There are three main reasons for this:

- A single piece of FOS software will sometimes have had hundreds, if not thousands of contributors to it. Each contributor will probably own the copyright in their contribution to the code. This means that there are a large number of potential claimants in an infringement suit, which makes risk very difficult to manage. Checking the provenance of every line of code to ensure that there is no infringement of copyright is extremely difficult, if not impossible.
- The licensor is often providing the code free of charge. It would be unusual for an indemnity to be given where there was no money received in return. However, note that some companies such as Red Hat (a Linux supplier) that use FOS software as part of their commercial model will give an indemnity, and the GPL does allow for this.
- There has been a large measure of fear injected into users of FOS software by high profile litigation (see under the heading "Legal Challenges to FOS").

The risk with the lack of indemnity protection is that:

- if a third party claims to own IPRs in the FOS-ERP which a business has deployed; and
- in the absence of a valid licence from the third party, the business is infringing the third party's copyright (and possibly also patents). The result is that the business would be required to cease use of the ERP and/or pay royalties or damages.

It is entirely possible that by deploying FOS-ERP, a third party may allege ownership of the IPRs in that software. However, the ability of a third party to demand royalties in respect of a product a business considered was free does raise the need to consider, at the outset of an FOS–ERP deployment, whether there is a real ability to substitute the deployed product in the event that unreasonable royalty fees are demanded or the product must be withdrawn from use.

## Reciprocity (The "Forcing Restriction")

This refers to the restrictions which most FOS licences impose upon subsequent licences of "downstream" programs that use their code. These licences require certain types of program based on their code to be licensed on the same terms as the source code. This reciprocal licensing of IP is often referred to as "copyleft", to emphasise the fact that it seeks to subvert the traditional approach to copyright.

Ironically, copyleft relies upon copyright to take effect. It works by giving the proprietor and original licensor the rights to terminate the licence where the licensee has developed the software and has licensed the derived works on terms different to those upon which the initial code was licensed. When this licensee licenses a derived work in breach of the copyright licence, the original licence is terminated meaning that the licensee is then infringing copyright by continuing to use and distribute the software.

As stated above the risk with reciprocity is that, in incorporating FOS code into a business' own closed source product, the licence terms of the FOS component oblige the business to make the combined product available as FOS software when it is distributed. This risk is considerable if the FOS software is licensed under the GNU GPL (with its reciprocity provisions as described above). This phenomenon is referred to by those in traditional software circles as the GPL "infection" risk.

Reciprocity obligations do not arise due to use of FOS software; they arise when modified or improved software (a derivative work, in copy-right terminology) is distributed. Therefore, if a business uses Linux as an operating system on its computers, but does not distribute Linux outside of the company, the reciprocity obligations of the Linux GNU GPL licence will not bite. In most cases given that the ERP would be used for internal business purposes only, this risk is not relevant.

However, if a business modifies Linux and distributes its modified version to others, that business must license those modifications – including the source code – to everyone under the terms of the GPL. Therefore, it is critically important that when a business modifies FOS-ERP software (including Linux) it should seek legal advice to determine whether it is creating a derivative work.

Many people have interpreted the GPL to mean that any software which interacts with running GPL code must be freed under the GPL reciprocity provisions. This is not true, and the best example is the Linux operating system. The Linux kernel is licensed under the GPL, but there are now many closed commercial applications (such as Oracle) available on UNIX which have not fallen foul of the GPL "forcing" restrictions.

## Legal Challenges to FOS

The FOS licences have been subject to various court cases. The following section examines some of the key cases.

## USA: The SCO-Linux Cases

This is a long-running series of US cases between SCO Group (SCO) and various GNU/Linux end-users and distributors and Novell.

In 1990 AT&T, which had created the UNIX operating system in 1969, sold all its rights in UNIX to Novell. In 1995 Novell sold certain parts of its UNIX business to the Santa Cruz Operation and in 2000 Santa Cruz Operation sold its entire UNIX business to Caldera Systems, which then changed its name to SCO Group.

SCO began making statements that it owned the rights to UNIX and that it would seek royalties from GNU/Linux users and distributors. Novell then claimed that the copyright in UNIX had not been assigned in the 1995 sale and began registering the copyrights to certain UNIX products. SCO filed actions claiming slander of title. In the meantime, SCO had begun actions against two other GNU/Linux distributors, IBM (alleging that IBM was in breach of a contract with SCO when IBM provided source code for the GNU/Linux code base) and Red Hat. SCO also sued some of its users (including AutoZone and DaimlerChrysler) who had stopped using SCO's UNIX for GNU/Linux. On 10 August 2007, the federal district court judge decided that Novell had retained the copyright to UNIX and not assigned it to SCO. On 14 September 2007 SCO filed for Chapter 11 bankruptcy protection. The IBM case was administratively closed on 20 September 2007 as a consequence, but the Novell case lives on as at spring 2010.

## USA: Jacobsen vs. Katzer and Kamind Associates, Inc.

Of considerable concern to the FOS movement was the US case of *Jacobsen v Katzer and Kamind Associates, Inc*. At an interim hearing, the US District Court for the Northern District of California found that breach by the licensees of their obligations under a non-exclusive FOS licence gave rise to a claim for breach of contract rather than a claim for copyright infringement. Leading members of the FOS community including the OSI, SFLC, Linux Foundation and Creative Commons Corporation submitted as amici curiae a brief supporting an appeal from the District Court's decision. On 13 August 2008, the US Court of Appeals for the Federal Circuit vacated the District Court's decision, finding that the licensees' obligations were conditions limiting the scope of the licence and not independent contractual covenants. By failing to comply with those conditions, the licensees

had acted outside the scope of the licence and therefore an action for copyright infringement could be brought by the licensor. The injunction application was remanded back so that the District Court could make a finding on the licensor's likelihood of success on the merits. The litigation finally concluded with a settlement agreement on 19 February 2010, nearly four years after the case was launched, with the defendants agreeing to pay Mr Jacobsen USD 100,000 and accepting a permanent injunction against copying or modifying the software material at issue.

## USA: FSF vs. Cisco Systems, Inc.

On 20 May 2009, the FSF announced the settlement of its long running dispute with Cisco. In the early 2000s, Linksys Group, Inc. adopted for its wireless broadband router a chipset from US "system on a chip" maker Broadcom Corp. which included a Linux distribution customised for Broadcom by CyberTAN Technology, Inc., a Taiwanese company. In 2003, Linksys was bought by Cisco Systems, Inc. for USD 500 million. Linksys declined to publish the relevant source code, and the FSF became involved in 2004/2005, seeking source code publication from Cisco. In the absence of an acceptable settlement FSF sued Cisco in the New York District Court in December 2008. Under the settlement, Cisco agreed to appoint a Free Software Director for Linksys (FOS compliance officer) who would be required to make ongoing compliance reports to the FSF; to notify Linksys customers of their rights under the GPL; to publish compliant licence notices; to make complete, corresponding and up-to-date source code available on its website; and to make a monetary contribution to the FSF.

## Other USA Litigation

Considering the widespread popularity of FOS and the GPL in particular, aside from the SCO, Jacobsen and Cisco litigation there remains surprisingly little in the way of US case law on the enforcement of FOS licences against licensees. However, the dearth of reported cases may be misleading to the extent that the FSF and, more recently, the SFLC have taken active roles in the USA in ensuring compliance with the GPL outside the courts. In September 2007 the SFLC launched the first US copyright infringement lawsuit based on non-compliance with the GPL. It has filed a number of further lawsuits since then and most have settled out of court.

## UK: FSF Europe and BT's Home Hub

One case that is reported to have attracted some notice, however, was the intervention by FSF Europe over BT's Home Hub, a network device that utilises the Linux kernel. BT was challenged by FSF Europe for distributing the Home Hub without making available the firmware source code. BT admitted that the Home Hub used Linux kernel version 2.6.8.1 under GPL v2, but stated that it also used proprietary software which it claimed was not subject to the GPL. In January 2007 FSF Europe notified BT of its claim that it was breaching the GPL. Since then BT has published source code for certain parts of the firmware but FSF Europe argued that some of the necessary code was still missing, saying that the GPL required publication of a top level Makefile (a file used to assist compilation), the scripts that would be used to generate a firmware image and also a script or file containing configuration information for certain library files. In spite of FSF Europe's claims, no further action appears to have been taken against BT.

## MISSING CONTRACTUAL PROVISIONS

There are many contractual provisions which a licensor may wish to include in a software licence, but which FOS licences do not include. For example, there are no clauses:

- setting out the governing law of the licence and dealing with the parties' submission to the relevant court's jurisdiction;
- applying non-litigation dispute resolution processes (such as mediation or arbitration);
- allowing provisions which are unenforceable to be severed or read down without affecting other provisions in the licence;
- regulating assignment of the licence;
- dealing with confidentiality of information exchanged in the context of the transaction;
- dealing with costs and taxes;
- dealing with insolvency or termination;
- stipulating the licence as the entire agreement of the parties; or
- other contractual "boiler plate" clauses to aid interpretation and enforcement. (James, 2003)

The above are useful protections for a licensor and in their absence could expose the licensee to a certain degree of risk.

## CONCLUSION

Anyone considering adopting a FOS-ERP in their business should do so with a full consideration of the risks. This chapter outlined the key legal risks in using FOS. Such legal risks include:

- assuming all FOS licences are the same;
- uncertainty as to the enforceability of FOS licences;
- lack of clarity in relation to the legal characterisation of FOS licences;
- risk of poor performance;
- risk of IPR infringement claim;
- issues arsing from reciprocity;
- legal challenges to FOS licences; and
- the issues arising from the missing contractual provisions.

Ultimately, lawyers and IT managers are risk managers, and the risks outlined in this chapter can often be managed to achieve a commercially acceptable solution. It is critically important that the whole of the relevant FOS licence is reviewed. This legal analysis should be carried out alongside a careful technical analysis of the proposed ERP deployment. This joint analysis should consider the interactions between any closed source code and the FOS code, and whether the applicable FOS licence requires mandatory redistribution of closed source code which interacts with the FOS code.

# REFERENCES

Copyright, Designs and Patents Act 1988.

Cornish, W., & Llewelyn, D. (2010). *Intellectual Property: Patents, Copyright, Trade Marks and Allied Rights* (7th ed.). Sweet and Maxwell.

James, P. (2003) Open Source Software: An Australian Perspective. In Fitzgerald, B. & Bassett, G (Ed), *Legal Issues Relating To Free and Open Source Software* (pp. 63-88). Essays in Technology Policy and Law Volume 1, Queensland University of Technology School of Law.

Korn, N., Oppenheim, C., & Picciotto, S. (2007). *IPR Issues and Software: A Briefing Document*. In collaboration with JISC Legal and OSS Watch. Retrieved 15 October 2010: http://www.jisc.ac.uk/media/documents/projects/iprissuesrelatingto-softwarefinal.pdf

Robert Jacobsen v (1) Matthew Katzer (2) Kamind Associates Inc., 13 August 2008.

Treasury, H. M. (2006). *Gowers Review of Intellectual Property*. Norwich, CT: The Stationery Office.

# ADDITIONAL READING

Black Duck White Paper. (n.d.). *GPLv3 Summary*. Retrieved 15 October 2010: http://www.blackducksoftware.com/resources/whitepapers#managingos

Carvalho, R. A. (2006). Issues on evaluating Free/open source ERP sysyems. In *Research and Practical Issues of Enterprise Informations Systems* (pp. 667–676). New York: Springer Verlag New York Inc.doi:10.1007/0-387-34456-X_72

Dreiling, A., Klaus, H., Rosemann, M., & Wyssusek, B. (2005) *Open Source Enterprise Systems: Towards a Viable Alternative*. 38th Annual Hawaii International Conference on System SciencesHawaii.

Kim, H., & Boldyreff, C. (2005). *Open Source ERP for SMEs*. Third International Conference on Manufacturing ResearchCranfield, U.K.

Palamida White Paper. (n.d.). *Is Open Source Software Putting Your PCI Compliance at Risk?* Retrieved 15 October 2010: http://www.palamida.com/themes/resources/Palamida_WhitePaper_PCIComplianceAtRisk.pdf

Riehle, D. (2007). *The Economic Motivation of Open Source: Stakeholders Perspectives*. Computer IEE Computer Society, 25-32.

Rosen, L. (2005). *Open Source Licensing: Software Freedom and Intellectual Property Law*. Prentice Hall.

The Software Freedom Law Center. (Version 1.5.1 3 March 2008). *Legal Issues Primer for Open Source and Free Software Projects*. Retrieved 15 October 2010: http://www.softwarefreedom.org/resources/2008/foss-primer.pdf

## KEY TERMS AND DEFINITIONS

**Copyleft:** The principle that a modification or derivative of a work (software, manuals etc) should be distributed on the same basis as the original work, i.e. with the same freedom to copy, modify (therefore with access to the source code) and distribute. Some call this a "viral" obligation, because it causes the self replication of the copyleft principal for all distributed and derivative works. Not all Freeware is copyleft – a licence might allow the user to distribute modified or derivative work on terms that do not grant these freedoms (James, 2003).

**FSF or Free Software Foundation, Inc:** The organisation formed for the GNU Project and now an advocate of open source free software, found at www.gnu.org/. FSF promotes 3 forms of licence: 1) the general public licence; 2) the lesser general public licence; and 3) the GNU free documentation licence (James, 2003).

**Freeware or Free Software:** Does not necessarily mean the software is supplied at no charge. What it refers to is the freedom of use – usually, freedom to distribute and modify the software (therefore with access to the source code) and to use pieces of the software to make new programs. However, the expression does not necessarily mean that there are no restrictions on use or distribution. Freeware could be on terms that require any on-licensing or any distribution of derivative works to be on the same terms as the original software (i.e. a "copyleft" requirement). Similarly, "free documentation" used in open source parlance generally refers to a particular level of freedom to copy, modify and redistribute it, with or without the payment of a fee (James, 2003).

**Netfilter/IP-Tables:** A tool providing networking functionality to the Linux kernel. Netfilter/IP-tables is a standard part of all modern Linux distributions.

**Open Source:** Is where software is distributed in both source code (ie human readable programming language) and in the executable (machine readable) form. Open source does not necessarily imply that the code is made available on a "copyleft" basis or that it is "freeware". For the canonical definition of Open Source and the nine principles of it, originally written by Bruce Perens, see www.opensource.org/docs/definition_plain.html (James, 2003).

**Viral Obligation:** Is a licensing obligation that distribution of the software – and of software which is derived from the original software – be on the same basis as the original code's licence, ie the means by which "copyleft" principal is effected in a licence. The expression is not one the FSF and other open source proponents find flattering (James, 2003).

# Chapter 8
# Tailoring FOS-ERP Packages:
## Automation as an Opportunity for Small Businesses

**Klaus Wölfel**
*Technische Universität Dresden, Germany*

**Jean-Paul Smets**
*Nexedi SA, France*

## ABSTRACT

*Free/Open Source software (FOSS) has made Enterprise Resource Planning (ERP) systems more accessible for Small and Medium Enterprises (SMEs) including overseas subsidiaries of large companies. However, the consulting required to configure an ERP to meet the specific needs of an organization remains a major financial and organizational burden for SMEs. Automatic ERP package configuration based on knowledge engineering, machine learning and data mining could be a solution to lessen the burden of the implementation process. This chapter presents two approaches to an automation of selected configuration options of the FOS-ERP package ERP5. These approaches are based on knowledge engineering with decision trees and machine learning with classifiers. The design of the ERP5 Artificial intelligence Toolkit (EAT) aims at the integration of these approaches into ERP5. The chapter also shows how FOS-ERP can boost Information System (IS) research. The investigation of the automation approaches was only possible because the free source code and technical documentation of ERP5 was accessible for TU Dresden researchers.*

DOI: 10.4018/978-1-61350-486-4.ch008

## INTRODUCTION

Enterprise Resource Planning (ERP) systems are said to enable organizations to manage their resources efficiently and effectively by providing a total and integrated solution for their information processing needs (Nah, Lau, & Kuang, 2001). Due to technical and economical restrictions, ERP systems traditionally have been focused on larger organizations. In recent years however, a turn of the market towards Small and Medium Enterprises (SMEs) can be observed (Deep, Guttridge, Dani, & Burns, 2008). Adam and O'Doherty (2000) show that SMEs are as likely to be interested in ERP as multinational organizations. ERP packages are being viewed as a key factor for gaining competitive advantage in the SME sector and empirical findings confirm these expectations (Koh & Simpson, 2007).

However, Morabito, Pace, and Previtali (2005) identify a lack of human and financial resources as well as lock-in risks as major problems that SMEs face when adopting ERP technology. They often do not have dedicated teams for implementation and software maintenance and cannot spend as much money on Information Technology (IT) as large enterprises, which in turn makes them more vulnerable to the risk of lock-ins in ERP packages when requirements change after implementation.

FOS-ERP systems are considered a viable alternative for SMEs as they tackle their specific problems. They not only help to save license costs, but they also prevent lock-in. As their source code is free to everyone they lower the barrier for third parties to perform modifications. (Campos, Carvalho, & Rodrigues, 2007).

Business models, where SMEs access ERP functionalities through the Internet could further alleviate the SME-specific problems and broaden the ERP market (Adam & O'Doherty, 2000). Recently Software as a Service (SaaS) is associated to this kind of business model (Hofmann, 2008). By providing applications directly through the Internet, SaaS eliminates installation and update tasks, thus saving clients from maintenance work and reducing IT expenses by on-demand pricing (Wang et al., 2008).

Despite these promising perspectives the consulting effort remains a financial burden for an ERP implementation project (Janssens, Kusters, & Heemstra, 2007). Although ERP systems are cheaper and easier to implement for SMEs than for large enterprises (Morabito et al.), SMEs may face challenges in affording major consulting support (Snider, Da Silveira, & Balakrishnan, 2009; Kinni, 1995). FOS-ERP help to save license costs, but implementation costs are often far exceeding the costs for ERP package licenses. Thus the greatest savings can be achieved during implementation (Timbrell & Gable, 2002).

To make implementation less complex and less costly, ERP vendors try to reduce the amount of knowledge required for the implementation by various degrees: cutting down functionality, designing package templates or giving customers and system integrators a common implementation methodology (Timbrell & Gable, 2002). Functionality cut-down and package templates are static approaches and therefore only suit a defined group of companies sharing common business needs. A common implementation methodology does not permit the CEO of a small business to configure his ERP all on his own. Therefore, we propose automation as an alternative or complemental approach to ERP package tailoring for small businesses.

Off-the-shelf ERP packages are implemented mainly by configuration (Brehm, Heinzl, & Markus, 2001). Automating this configuration process would lessen the burden of the implementation process and make ERP more accessible for SMEs. The vision is that a packaged ERP system will be automatically configured based on a questionnaire filled out by the Chief Executive Officer (CEO) of a small business. The first example of such automation is the SaaS "TioLive" which uses various wizards to automate the configuration of the FOS-ERP system "ERP5".

However, current technology is still very simple. To further pursue this vision, two approaches for automating the configuration of packaged ERP Software based on questionnaires are investigated: knowledge engineering with decision trees and classification based on machine learning algorithms. The public availability of source code and technical documentation allows to analyze ERP5's configuration options and to implement the automation approaches in the ERP5 system. This will make those wizards more intelligent and will allow to provide a solution which matches the requirements of a small business far better than before.

Integrating these prototypes with the existing ERP5 Configurator technology will turn the basic configuration wizards into an automated system that can accomplish the bulk of the work needed to configure ERP5 for a specific adopting organization. In a SaaS-based setup, this basic configuration could then be refined by human IT consultants on demand over the Internet. Thus, the customer would experience the tailoring process of his ERP package as an integrated online service. Such a service could be called "Cloud Consulting".

## RESEARCH QUESTIONS AND DESIGN

The research objective is to investigate the automation of the adaption of a packaged ERP to the specific business needs of a SME. This is done on the basis of the FOS-ERP package ERP5 by Nexedi. Brehm et al. (2001) call this adaption "tailoring" and identify several types of ERP package tailoring with different impact on the ERP system. To reach the research objective, the following questions have to be answered:

- Which tailoring options are most likely to be suited for automation generally and in the case of ERP5 specifically?

- How can these ERP5 tailoring options be automated?

Our procedure to answer these questions is based on the design science paradigm. The idea is to better understand and solve human and organizational problems by creating innovative artifacts and applying them (Hevner, March, & Park, 2004). The artifacts we created are building blocks of an automated configuration system. The first type of artifact consists of a decision tree that shows how ERP parameters can be configured based on expert knowledge. The second type of artifacts is prototypical code examples that use classifiers to show how an ERP can be configured based on data mining. The third artifact is a prototype for three ERP5 modules that helps to create questionnaires and decision trees in ERP5 that can be used for data mining and form the basis for future automatic configuration. Configuration use cases have been applied to the designed artifacts to test the viability of the approaches.

The information necessary to implement these approaches was gathered through expert interviews, desk research and an exemplary configuration case. Important information sources were ERP5's technical documentation and source code as well as previous configuration projects. The procedure to design the automation artifacts was roughly based on the design as a search process (Hevner et al., 2004), covering the problem identification phase and the solution design phase. Only the first steps of the design science process (Offermann, Levina, Schönherr, & Bub, 2009) have been conducted up until now. In order to strengthen research rigor we have applied the input artifact selection approach as suggested by Gräning, Wendler, Leyh, & Strahringer (2010). Using this approach to assess artifacts a researcher intends to build his research on has proven the inherent suitability of FOSS for the purpose of design science research.

## ERP5: THE UNDERLYING FOS-ERP PACKAGE

ERP5 is a FOS-ERP project, born in 2001 at the initiative of two French companies, Nexedi and Coramy. Nexedi is the main developer of ERP5 which was first deployed at Coramy, an apparel producer (Smets-Solanes, 2002). Since then it is developed and used by a growing international community from France, Brazil, Germany, Bulgaria, Japan, Russia, Poland and Senegal among others (Monnerat, Carvalho, & Campos, 2008). ERP5 targets SMEs as well as larger organizations (Nexedi SA, n.d.). Apart from apparel, it has been deployed in various industries, among them aerospace, automotive, e-commerce, software service companies, a central bank, a hospital and a government agency (Smets, 2008).

The ERP5 framework is based on the Python programming language, the Zope Application Server, its content management framework (CMF) and other third-party Zope components. The Zope Object Database (ZODB) provides persistence of data in a NoSQL fashion. Querying is conducted by ZSQLCatalog, which implements an object-to-relational indexing scheme to make use of fast relational databases like MySQL. This allows using standard SQL for searching and reporting. All the technologies that ERP5 builds upon are also open source software. All ERP5 functions are accessed through a web-based interface. A generic workflow engine is used to implement the supported business processes. What makes ERP5 fundamentally different from other ERP systems is:

- its abstract model which defines only five classes to represent all business processes within one and between multiple organizations and
- its document-centric approach to implement these business processes.

Other than a data- or process-centric paradigm, the document-centric approach focuses on the operational documents, their fields and document workflows. It assumes that every business process relies on a series of documents and that the architecture of an organization is discoverable through the list of operational documents which support this organization. The fields of the documents represent the data and their relations. The document-flow in a company corresponds to the workflows of its business processes (Atem de Carvalho & Monnerat, 2007; Smets, n.d.).

ERP5 defines an underlying abstract core model which is the base for representing all kinds of business processes. This Unified Business Model (UBM) has been described by Smets-Solanes and Atem de Carvalho (2003). The Name ERP5 is derived from the five abstract core classes that make up the UBM and help to consistently implement new or specialized components:

*Resource* is the base class for all abstract resources that are needed to realize a business process. Examples for resources in ERP5 are skills that are linked to persons, currencies, services, products and components of products. Relations between resources are defined for example to describe the needed components for products in Bills of Material (BOMs).

*Node* is a business entity that sends and receives resources. A node can be a physical entity, like a factory, that sends products and receives raw material, or an abstract entity, like a bank account that sends and receives money. Nodes have capacities which are either stock capacity or production capacity. Minimum and maximum amounts of resources that the node can contain or produce are defined in inequalities the node must satisfy.

*Movement* describes the movement of a resource from a source node to a destination node. For example the shipping of a product from a supplier to a client is a movement that can be represented by a delivery line in a packing list.

119

The payment following the delivery is another movement where money is sent from one bank account to another bank account.

*Path* defines the way and the conditions how a destination node receives a resource from a source node. As a trade condition it can define the standard price of a resource for a certain client or from a certain supplier. Paths also represent assignments of persons to projects for a period of time, so they can have a start and an end date.

*Item* is a physical instance of a resource. Items split an abstract movement of a resource between two nodes into movements of traceable items that can have a serial number and can define how they are being shipped.

These abstract core classes are related to each other: A movement contains multiple items and is related to a source node, a destination node and to a resource that is moved between the two nodes. Similar, a path is related to a source and destination node and to the resource whose path attributes it defines.

## ERP PACKAGE TAILORING

## Tailoring Types Best Suited for Automation

Adopting an ERP package requires its adaption to the specific business needs of an organization. ERP systems are often viewed as *off-the-shelf* software, which means that they are usually implemented by setting parameters in the package to adapt their functionality to business requirements. This form of implementation, called *configuration*, is usually distinguished to *modification* which refers to changing the source code of a package. Modification is considered typical for *custom-built* software (Brehm et al., 2001).

Brehm et al. (2001) argue that ERP systems do not fit into this traditional distinction. They use the term *tailoring* to refer to both, configuration and modification as well as many options in be-

tween. They suggest a typology of nine different ERP tailoring types shown in Figure 1. The order in which the tailoring types are presented in the Figure 1 are roughly derived from the "impact" they have on the ERP system as well as on the ERP adopter, beginning with "lighter" tailoring types at the top of Figure 1 to "heavier" tailoring types at the bottom. For the ERP system, impact means how severely it is being changed if a tailoring option is applied. For the ERP adopter, impact means how much effect is required to employ a tailoring type (Brehm et al., 2001).

The impact of tailoring on the ERP system also affects automation. The heavier the ERP system is changed through tailoring, the more complicated is the required automation logic to facilitate the tailoring. *Configuration* is the tailoring type with the lowest impact. The possible values for each configuration parameter are bounded by the value range of the configuration parameter. They can be further narrowed by defining a set of configuration cases that the automation method should support. This set could contain:

- all theoretical possible configuration cases,
- all realized configurations in the past plus a predefined set of possible values or
- a set of viable values defined by a function.

Thus, the solution space of automated configuration is bounded and configuration is predictable.

Brehm et al. (2001) place *bolt-ons* at the low-impact end of their typology. They remark that the impact of bolt-ons is debatable because their quality depends on the communication between ERP vendor and bolt-on developer. They further argue that the risk of a release-lag between the ERP system and bolt-on version can be an issue when updating the ERP system. Both considerations also apply for the suitability of including bolt-ons in an automated tailoring process. Choosing, installing and configuring bolt-ons can be suitable for automation, if ERP vendor and bolt-on developer collaborate on the automation process.

*Figure 1. Typology of ERP tailoring types adapted from Brehm et al. (2001)*

| Tailoring Type | Description | Layer |
|---|---|---|
| Configuration | Setting of parameters to choose between different executions of processes and functions | All layers |
| Bolt-ons | Implementation of third-party package designed to work with ERP system and provide industry-specific functionality | All layers |
| Screen masks | Creating new screen masks for data in- and output | Application and/or database layer |
| Extended reporting | Programming of extended data output and reporting options | Communication layer |
| Workflow programming | Creating of non-standard workflows | Application and/or database layer |
| User exits | Programming of additional software code in an open interface | Application and/or database layer |
| ERP programming | Programming of additional applications, without changing the source code (in vendor's computer language) | All layers |
| Interface development | Programming of interfaces to legacy systems or third-party products | Application and/or database layer |
| Package code modification | Changing the source-codes ranging from small changes to change whole modules | Can involve all layers |

Especially FOSS business models favor bolt-on automation. If the source code of the ERP system and the bolt-on are available in public Version Control Systems (VCSs), then the integration and automatic configuration of bolt-ons can be automatically tested for each version of the ERP system and the bolt-on.

For heavier tailoring types, automation logic would be more complex. Source code often has to be generated automatically. For *screen masks, extended reporting* and *workflow programming*, a combination of automation with easy to use graphical design tools could be a solution. For *user exits, ERP programming* and *interface development*, an automation system could gather the required information from the user through questionnaires and generate a rough code structure that would be the base for a final implementation by a human consultant. Whether the higher tailoring types are suitable for automation also depends on how generic functionalities are implemented in the ERP system and how easy it is to reuse existing data models and functions as building blocks for new functionalities.

In *package code modification*, the automation would have to "understand" the whole ERP system to be able to do modifications and calculate their impact. Also, the automation system itself would have to be adapted on every update of the ERP system. The automatic generated code would then have to be regenerated automatically to reflect the changes.

The impact of tailoring on the ERP system is not only affected by the type of tailoring, but also by *how extensively* a tailoring type is used (Brehm et al., 2001). This factor also influences the suitability of tailoring for automation. Using the configuration type of tailoring more extensively means for automation that more configuration options are automated and that for each configuration option, more configuration cases are considered by the automation system. A system, that automates more extensive configuration, has to ask more questions to the ERP adopter in the configuration process and consists of more complicated automation logic, for example larger and thicker decision trees.

121

We experienced the influence of extensiveness to automation during the creation of a decision tree to automate the configuration of company sites in ERP5 (see section "Automation Procedure and Approaches"). In its draft version, the site decision tree aimed to support a higher number of the theoretical possible configuration cases with a deep site hierarchy. This resulted in a complicated decision tree consisting of too many and too difficult questions. The improved version of the decision tree achieves – with reduced complexity – faster and easier configuration for many standard configuration cases relevant to SMEs at the cost of leaving apart some edge cases covered by the draft version.

The mentioned considerations indicate that the impact of tailoring on the ERP system might be a viable indicator for the suitability of tailoring for automation. Therefore, our research is based on the hypothesis:

The lower the impact of tailoring on the ERP system, the more likely it is that the tailoring is suitable for automation.

Following this hypothesis, configuration is the tailoring type which is most likely suitable for automation, depending on how extensively it is used. Therefore, the automation approaches and prototypes presented in the following sections concentrate on automating the configuration type of tailoring. Automating other tailoring types like *screen mask* generation, *extended reporting*, and *workflow programming* is topic for future research. Once automation has been implemented for multiple tailoring types with different degrees of impact, the hypothesis can be tested by analyzing the effectiveness of the automation implementations and the effort necessary to implement them.

Brehm et al. (2001) argue that tailoring increases the degree of fit between the features and functions of an ERP package and the business processes of a particular organization. They hypothesize that "the greater the impact of tailoring on the ERP..., the more likely it is that...the system will meet the needs of the business" (p. 7).

*Configuration* is the tailoring type with the lowest impact in Brehm et al.'s typology. From an ERP adopter's point of view this means that if the gap between the ERP package functionality and the business needs is too big to be filled by configuration, tailoring types with greater impact are required. From an ERP package design point of view however, an alternative to automate tailoring types with a higher impact can be considered: designing the ERP package to be more generic and to offer wider configuration choices.

Following this alternative, automating consists of two parts: Automating the configuration of an ERP package and enhancing the ERP package in a way that more tailoring tasks that currently require tailoring types with a higher impact can be achieved solely by configuration. Therefore our investigations concentrate on the automation of the configuration type of ERP package tailoring.

## Tailoring Options in ERP5

Most of ERP5's tailoring options do not map unambiguously to Brehm et al.'s tailoring typology, however a rough categorization is presented in Figure 2. Similar to Brehm et al.'s typology which refers to the general three-layer model of application systems, the last column in Figure 2 refers to the three layers in ERP5, where tailoring can take place: Business Templates, Property Sheets and Zope Products.

*Business Templates* assemble applications from configuration parameters, forms, views, reports, workflows, document types based on ERP5 core classes and Property Sheets, modules, custom scripts or actual documents based on ERP5 document types. All these are objects in the ZODB. Most tailoring is realized in this object space through-the-web. The first configuration step of a new ERP5 Instance is the installation of the required business templates. Basic automation for this procedure is already implemented in ERP5's configuration system. Then, tailoring is conducted by setting attribute values of existing

*Figure 2. Categorization of ERP5 tailoring options*

| Tailoring Type | ERP5 Tailoring Options | ERP5 Layer |
|---|---|---|
| Configuration | Choosing modules and workflows, defining site preferences, categories, business processes and security | Business Templates |
| Bolt-ons | Installing third-party Business Templates; adding Property Sheets / Zope Products, if data model extensions / auxiliary core functionalities are required | Business Templates, Property Sheets and Zope Products |
| Screen masks | Creating form views, fast input forms and Page Templates in custom skins | Business Templates |
| Extended reporting | Designing search forms and create SQL- or Python reports with ERP5 Report Wizard | Business Templates |
| Workflow programming | Creating custom workflows and implement associated actions and worklists | Business Templates |
| User exits | Creating new modules, document types, actions, forms, jumps and interactions based on existing types | Business Templates and Property Sheets |
| ERP programming | Creating Zope Products to provide core extensions or to integrate external libraries | All layers |
| Interface development | Designing XML Import- and Export conduits; Creating python scripts for invocation through XML-RPC | Business Templates and Property Sheets |
| Package code modification | Modify core ERP5 Business Templates, Zope Products or standard Property Sheets - not meant to be necessary by ERP5 design philosophy | All layers |

objects, copying and modifying objects or creating new objects. These objects can be packaged as a new custom business template containing the results of all tailoring at this level.

Referring to the general three-layer model of application systems, the implementation of the communication layer is completely contained in Business Templates. The "PortalSkins" tool which is part of the CMF is used to manage forms, corresponding action scripts and page template views in layers, called "skins", which allow to customize all user interface related objects without touching the originally installed objects. Interface methods to communicate with other application systems over XML-RPC are also defined in PortalSkins. Business Templates are also involved on the application-layer as they contain workflows, reports and the actual ERP5 modules and document types which are assembled through-the-web based on the core classes and Property Sheets.

*Property Sheets* define the ERP5 data model. Each property sheet can be reused by any core class as well as by document types defined in Business Templates. Although arbitrary attributes can be set and accessed in the ZODB for rapid prototyping, automatic indexing and dynamically generated accessors are only available for attributes defined in Property Sheets. However, as Document types, forms and workflows can easily use attributes already defined in existing Property Sheets and as ERP5's standard attributes are very generic, the need for new properties is very rare (Gorny, Nowak, & Perrin, 2008). Whole new modules can often be designed by assembling document types out of multiple standard Property Sheets.

*Zope Products* are the place where ERP5 core components are defined, including the classes of the UBM. As they contain core application logic, they are comparable to the application layer of the general three-layer model of application systems. ERP programming can involve the development of Zope Products, if extensions to the ERP5 core model are required or external libraries should be included. Bolt-ons might provide additional Zope Products to extend the ERP5 core model for industry-specific requirements. Zope Product development would also happen in case of package code modification, though theoretically it should not be necessary in an ERP5 implementation process.

The ERP5 tailoring options have been allocated in Figure 2 to tailoring types according to their maximum possible impact weight. In practice, the impact of most tailoring options is lower than the usual impact of the tailoring type to which they have been assigned.

*Configuration* is the most commonly used tailoring type in ERP5. Many tailoring options that involve high-impact tailoring types in complex cases can be accomplished solely by configuration in simple cases. Definition of site preferences is the tailoring option that fits best to the traditional understanding of configuration as it consists of instance-wide configuration parameters that alter the behavior of ERP5 functionalities. TioLive's configuration systems already automates some configuration-type tailoring options like the choice of locale dependent accounting business templates, configuring default site preferences and generation of initial documents, for example the adopter's organization and its employees.

*Definition of security groups* and *Categories* can also be implemented purely by configuration and are therefore considered suitable for automation. Still, they have a great effect to the behavior of ERP5. This is the reason why the automation approaches presented later are applied to automate category configuration. Group definition is related to category configuration, as users can be assigned to security groups dynamically based on multiple categories.

*Category* configuration highly influences the behavior of ERP5. Categories help to classify business objects and to build hierarchies. They define not only the structure of the company, but also the company's view of the world in a taxonomy. Every business object in ERP5 can be associated to one or several categories. Categories can aggregate multiple nodes into a meta node or multiple resources into a meta resource.

*Group definition* consists in configuring how users are categorized from a security point of view (Smets, n.d.). In ERP5's security concept, users are assigned to groups automatically based on categories. Each category can have a security codification. Group names are constructed out of the codifications of the categories they depend on.

*Bolt-ons* have a low impact in ERP5 if they consist solely of Business Templates as they can be installed automatically and assure version compatibility. The impact will be higher if bolt-ons include core extensions in form of extra Zope Products that subclass ERP5 core classes to add industry-specific functionalities.

*Screen masks* are assembled in ERP5 out of configurable form field objects. This type of tailoring mainly consists of creating "fast input forms" to optimize data input for critical business processes (Smets, n.d.). The impact of ERP5 fast input implementation is higher, if complex user interfaces are designed for special purposes like point of sales.

*Extended reporting* is conducted in ERP5 to extend standard PDF rendering forms with statistics such as inventory, average price or with custom visual design. ERP5 Report Wizard helps to generate reports with SQL- or Python reports (Smets, n.d.). Different reporting engines are available using direct PDF generation with reportlab or OpenOffice for generating reports in different office formats.

*Workflow programming* will be required, if ERP5's standard workflows are not sufficient to fulfill the adopter's needs. In simple cases, only configuration of standard workflows is necessary. If new actions are programmed or the implementation of existing actions is changed, then programming of python scripts will be involved and impact of this tailoring type will be possibly higher.

*User exits and ERP programming* cannot be clearly separated in ERP5. New modules with new document types can be designed in ERP5 in a way that is closer to configuration than to programming. Since forms and document types are just objects in the ZODB, the impact of creating new modules or changing existing modules merely depends on how many existing objects, actions or Property Sheets can be reused in the process. This is additionally supported by techniques like "Proxy Fields" that make sure that custom form fields based on other existing form fields adapt automatically to changes in new versions of ERP5 (see Courteaud, 2009).

*Package code modification* should theoretically not happen in an ERP5 implementation process. ERP5's design philosophy strives to make the package code general enough to accomplish adaption to different business needs by employing lighter tailoring types. In cases where the core package code is still not general enough, the open source nature of ERP5 favors the improvement of package code in the public source code repositories over custom changes that only serve one adopter and aggravate package updates.

*Configuration* has been identified as the tailoring type which is most suitable for automation. Thanks to its abstract model, ERP5 is a very generic application system, thus many ERP5 tailoring tasks can be accomplished solely or partly by configuration and still have great effect on how ERP5's functionalities behave. The best example is *category definition*, which is clearly a configuration type of tailoring and vastly influences ERP5's functionalities. Therefore the next section presents two approaches to automate ERP5 category configuration and the procedure we used to implement these approaches.

## AUTOMATION PROCEDURE AND APPROACHES

To automate category configuration in ERP5 the following information had to be gathered first: the category configuration process, the use of selected categories in ERP5 and possible configuration values. Therefore ERP5's source code and technical documentation were analyzed. Expert interviews were conducted with Nexedi staff. Additionally,

past configuration projects were analyzed and an example configuration was conducted. Additional information for possible configurations was retrieved by desk research from reference models, especially those described by Scheer (1997). In this process we realized that it is difficult to adapt reference models to the case of ERP5, because ERP functionalities are implemented in a more general way in ERP5 than in other ERP systems.

Two approaches to automate category configuration based on artificial intelligence have been investigated. Both approaches share the idea to ask the adopting organization a list of questions and then automatically generate the category configuration based on the given answers. The first approach is based on knowledge engineering, The second approach is based on machine learning.

The idea of the knowledge engineering approach is to manually define a set of rules. These rules encode expert knowledge on how to configure categories based on answers to a list of questions. We chose decision trees to represent these rules. The user is guided through a list of questions which are represented by the nodes of the tree. The branches of the tree perform the actual category configuration and decide which question comes next.

After the initial information search, the assumptions about category configuration were evaluated by expert questionnaires sent to Nexedi staff. The decision trees were then built based on the answers to these questionnaires.

Figure 3 shows the site decision tree as drawn by the decision tree design prototype. It illustrates how a single decision tree can fulfill two contradicting goals for automatic configuration: Support as many configuration cases as possible and ask few questions in simple cases for quick configuration. In the simplest case, only one question is asked, and a default site is created. If the user has less than 20 sites, a flat list of site names is created, for more than 20 sites hierarchy levels of continents and/or countries are created, depending on the geographical distribution of sites.

Another example for decision tree based configuration is the group decision tree. The group category is used in ERP5 to define juridical structure (subsidiaries) as well as structure based on subordination and is as such part of representing positions in a company. It defines how responsibility and decision power is delegated. By asking simple questions like "Do you have subsidiaries?", "Do you decide alone or do you let somebody decide for you?", "Do you define positions in your company?" or "Do you have profit/ and loss analysis per division or business unit in your company?" the group decision tree gathers the needed information for configuration step for step. In the simplest case (which is quite common for small businesses) the owner of a company decides all alone and only one group for the whole company is necessary. In more complex cases groups

with multiple levels like "company_name / subsidiary_name / accounting" or "company_name / business_unitA" will be created.

The drawback of the knowledge engineering approach is the "knowledge acquisition bottleneck" (Sebastiani, 2002). The decision tree must be manually defined by an ERP implementation expert with the aid of a knowledge engineer. Extensive knowledge about the ERP system, the specific configuration option and about related requirements of businesses is necessary. Possible configuration cases have to be anticipated. For many categories it is impossible to cover all cases. The configuration cases supported by the decision tree have to be narrowed. Therefore we investigated another approach which allows an automation system to learn new configuration cases and evolve continually: learning classi-

*Figure 3. The site decision tree*

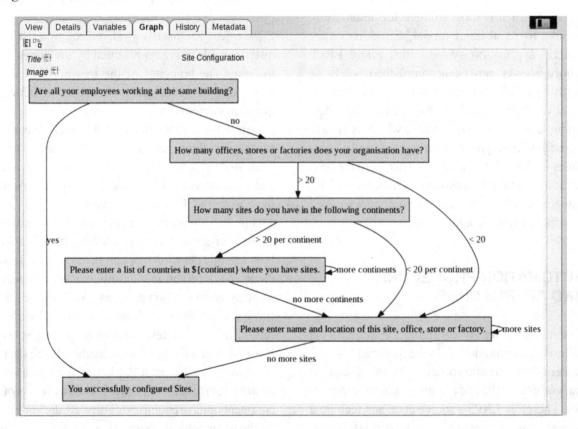

fiers. We created two working examples, one for configuration based on free text questions, and one for questions with predefined answers. Both use Bayesian Learners as classifiers.

The classification of free text questions works similar to Spam filters. For example, let us assume we have a quite general question, like "What does the organization sell, offer or produce?" and a data set with free text answers to this question and corresponding configurations of the product_line category. For a given sub category like "product_line / fish", every answer to a question is categorized either to support this subcategory (the corresponding configuration contains the subcategory) or to not support it (the corresponding configuration does not contain the subcategory). There could be answers that have a corresponding configuration containing "product_line / fish" and those that do not. Then the two classes are "product_line_fish" and "product_line_not_fish" and every answer is either assigned to one or the other, just like emails are assigned to the categories "Spam" and "Not Spam".

For question sets, where possible answers are defined for each question, those are first converted into Boolean questions. For example there could be a question "What types of clients do you have?" with a list possible answers such as 'consumer', 'business', 'administration', 'not-for-profit'. This question is then converted into multiple Boolean questions, like "client-types_consumer?", "client-types_business?" etc. Each of these questions can be answered with yes or no.

The advantage of the machine learning approach over the knowledge engineering approach is that it is easier to manually classify multiple answer sets than to build and tune a set of rules or a decision tree "since it is easier to characterize a concept extensionally (i.e. to select instances of it) than intensionally (i.e. to describe the concept in words, or to describe a procedure for recognizing its instances)" (Sebastiani, 2002, p. 10).

The SaaS model of TioLive also favors the machine learning approach. Once an initial training set is available, the first instances for new TioLive adopters can be configured automatically. These initial configurations can then be improved manually by human consultants. The improved instances together with the answer sets provided by the TioLive adopters are then the new high quality training sets. Therefore, the automatically constructed classifiers continually evolve to support different and new business requirements to category configuration.

Our tests gave promising results in correctly assigning product lines and roles based on the answers they learned. However, the data sets we used were very small. To validate our approach, many example configurations and corresponding answers to the configuration questions are needed. Therefore, we implemented a prototype to directly define the questions in ERP5 and collect the answers together with a corresponding configuration. The idea is to give these questions to students that create a sample configuration for a small business. Together with the answers to the configuration questions, it will be input to the learning classifiers. Once more learning data in form of answers and corresponding configuration data is available, the results then can be compared to the results of using other learning algorithms like, Support Vector Machines or Decision Tree Learners as classifiers.

## IMPLEMENTATION OF THE ERP5 AI TOOLKIT

FOS-ERP enables researchers to implement investigated approaches directly into an ERP system. We created the ERP5 AI Toolkit (EAT), a collection of modules that help to implement artificial intelligence in ERP5. EAT consists of:

- a question management tool to create, collect and evaluate different types of configuration questions,
- a design tool that helps to create decision trees and questionnaires and
- an answer collection tool for data mining to collect answer data as input for learning classifiers and as a data basis for question evaluation.

Figure 4 shows the question management tool. It allows to create and collect different kinds of configuration questions, for example Boolean questions, free text questions or questions with multiple possible answers. A special "document question" allows to upload documents in the questioning process, for example a spreadsheet with an ERP5 category configuration to connect the answers with a corresponding configuration as input for the learning classifiers. A validation workflow is attached to each question to allow question evaluation with the objective to identify redundant and overcomplicated questions for elimination or reformulation.

The design tool allows to relate questions to each other to create questionnaires and decision trees. Every node in the decision tree graph corresponds to a question. Different answer ranges can be defined for every question. Each leads to one of the next possible questions. These answer ranges represent the branches in the decision trees. They are defined by Boolean expressions in the Python programming language and represent the condition under which the branch gets activated (see Figure 5). The expression is not bound to the answer of the last question, it can take any data in the system into account. The expressions of all branches of a common node must be mutually exclusive, so that only one arrow can be activated at a time. Scripts can be defined for every branch to take actions based on the user's input.

The graphs of the designed decision trees can be painted automatically (see Figure 3). The prototype heavily reuses the ERP5 Workflow component, and could therefore be implemented in very short time. We implemented the decision trees we created during our research with the EAT design tool to validate its functionality. Simple questionnaires, like exams, where all questions

*Figure 4. The question management tool showing a selection question*

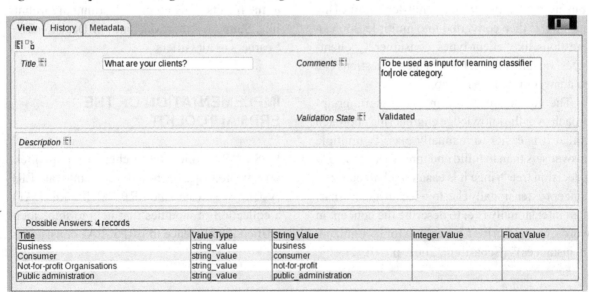

*Figure 5. The design tool showing a question node related to a boolean question (The assigned answer ranges are shown with condition and destination node.)*

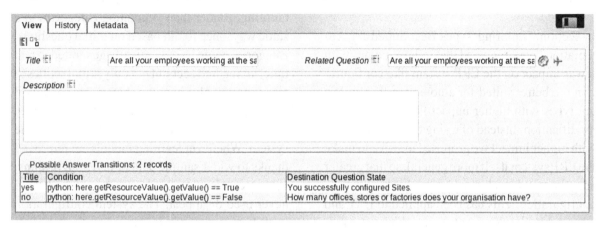

are displayed in a fixed linear order can be designed in the same way. In this case, every question has only one answer range, which is "All Answers", so the expression returns always "True".

In a questioning process, the forms to display a particular question are implemented for each question type in the question management tool. The order, in which the questions are displayed, is defined by the corresponding decision tree or questionnaire. The answer collection tool (see Figure 6) collects all answers of a questioning process. In configurations and exams, the effort of a question can be measured based on the time it takes to answer the question. This effort may then serve as an indicator for question evaluation.

The purpose of distributing the functionalities of the EAT is that questions can be used in a very general way in ERP5 serving different purposes. The same questions can be used for student exams as well as in a configuration decision tree.

In the future, an initial configuration of TioL-ive should be accomplished automatically. If this basic configuration is then improved by a human consultant, the altered configuration together with the answers in the configuration process will be new input for the learning classifiers. Thus the system will become smarter with every successful implementation.

*Figure 6. The answer collection tool showing an answer set for the site decision tree*

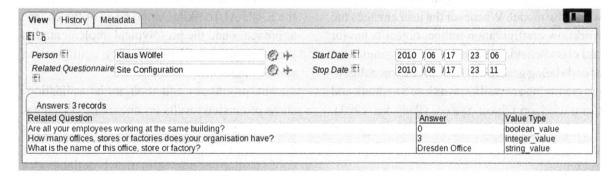

## PERSPECTIVE: REFLEXIVE TAILORING

In section "Tailoring Types Best Suited for Automation" we concluded that tailoring types with lower impact on the ERP system like configuration are better suited for automation than tailoring types with higher impact like package code modification. Instead of trying to automate types with higher impact we proposed to strive to make the ERP system itself more general, so that greater adaption can be achieved by solely changing the configuration. This has been applied to EAT and our machine learning prototypes which automatically change category configuration. However, whenever the business needs of the adopter of the ERP change, the ERP configuration has to be adapted accordingly which requires again deep knowledge of the ERP system and therefore external consulting which is often unpractical for small businesses. Automation approaches designed for initial configuration through the generation of static data or source code no longer apply to the problem of updating the initial configuration. The introduction of reflexivity in ERP package tailoring could lead to a different analysis. Rather than by defining an automation system outside the ERP and generating configuration from this system, the automation system itself could become part of the ERP. This is what already happens in ERP5 with workflows and accessors. Workflows in ERP5 are defined as ERP5 objects. Python meta-object protocol is used to generate dynamically reified accessors – rather than source code – which are always synchronized with the workflow model. Whenever the user changes the workflow configuration online, object behavior and class behavior changes without a single line of code being generated. Reflexive approaches to programming are well known since Smalltalk and Common Lisp Object System (Paepcke, 1993). They had a great influence on ERP5 design and explain how its source code base could remain as compact.

The idea of reflexive programming could be extended to create a new paradigm: reflexive tailoring. Rather than generating categories in a static way, once for all based on initial questions, categories could be dynamically generated in real time, taking into account not only initial replies to questions but also how the system has been used until then by the user and how the user would reply again to the same questions after having used the system. Whenever learning models are improved thanks to wider sample data or better algorithms, new categories are added; categories which were never used disappear. The system configuration itself becomes dynamic, providing to users better configuration everyday without requiring any regeneration steps. Reflexive tailoring could also help to implement context-aware process design (Rosemann & Recker, 2006) to adapt the configuration of the ERP to changes in legislations or changes in market trends.

Future research will be required to analyze how reflexive tailoring impacts Brehm et al.'s tailoring typology and introduces new perspectives for configuration automation of ERPs.

## CONCLUSION

Regarding our research questions, we have identified configuration as the type of ERP package tailoring best suited for automation. We chose category definition as the configuration option to automate for the FOS-ERP package ERP5. Thanks to its FOS nature, we could apply the investigated automation approaches to ERP5 and implement the ERP5 AI Toolkit. On the basis of the chosen approaches and the prototypical implementation we showed how ERP5 category configuration can be automated.

The prototypes and their initial validations show promising results for automatic configuration of selected ERP5 categories. The prototypes have shown that decision trees are well suited for configuration options with narrowly defined value ranges. When configuration is more complex, it becomes more difficult to explicitly convert expert knowledge into decision trees. For these cases data mining using classifier algorithms seems to be a solution. The code examples we created showed that it is possible to configure categories based on text mining with open questions as well as based on questions with discrete values. While these results are promising there are many aspects that need further investigation.

Most importantly, sample data has to be collected to feed the learning classifiers. This would allow to refine the example code, to compare the results of the current implementation with the results of using other types of classifiers and to select the categories best suited for the data mining approach.

The technological base for collecting sample data has been created with the EAT, but more questions have to be added to the question management tool. Once we have gathered a large pool of configuration questions, then the next step will be identifying unnecessary ones. Decision Tree Learners generated from sample data could be used to filter out all questions which have the lowest influence in category classification. The overall objective is to find the smallest set of questions that covers the biggest range of possible configurations.

Also the decision trees have to be elaborated to cover more configuration cases on the one hand and to be simpler for the user on the other hand. The display of the questions in a questioning process should include automatically painted graphs for categories with multiple hierarchical levels. More sample data will allow to test the decision trees and refine them.

Converting the prototype into a production system with real ERP adopters replying to the configuration questions and working with the automatically configured instances will allow a better validation of the investigated approaches. When automatic category configuration runs in production, we will begin to automate other ERP5 configuration options, like workflow alternatives, security definitions, or business rules.

Then, an initial automatic configuration of ERP5 could be conducted for a small business based on a questionnaire replied by the owner or CEO. This basic configuration could then be improved by a human consultant. In the case of a FOS-ERP system like ERP5, the barrier for third parties to perform higher-impact tailoring is lowered by the free availability of the package source code. Using this approach with the TioLive SaaS, it could be offered as an integrated online service, named Cloud Consulting. Adopting an ERP this way would make it much more achievable for SMEs.

## REFERENCES

Adam, F., & O'Doherty, P. (2000). Lessons from enterprise resource planning implementations in Ireland - towards smaller and shorter ERP projects. *Journal of Information Technology, 15*, 305–316. doi:10.1080/02683960010008953

Brehm, L., Heinzl, A., & Markus, M. L. (2001). Tailoring ERP systems: A spectrum of choices and their implications. In *Proceedings of the 34th Annual Hawaii International Conference on System Sciences, Maui, Hawaii*. New York: Institute of Electrical and Electronics Engineers.

de Campos, R., de Carvalho, R. A., & Rodrigues, J. S. (2007, May). *Enterprise modeling for development processes of open-source ERP*. Paper presented at the 18th Production and Operation Management Society Conference, Dallas, TX.

de Carvalho, R. A., & Monnerat, R. (2007). ERP5: designing for maximum adaptability. In Oram, A., & Wilson, G. (Eds.), *Beautiful code* (pp. 339–351). Sebastopol, CA: O'Reilly Media.

Deep, A., Guttridge, P., Dani, S., & Burns, N. (2008). Investigating factors affecting ERP selection in made-to-order SME sector. *Journal of Manufacturing Technology Management, 19*(4), 430–446. doi:10.1108/17410380810869905

Gorny, B., Nowak, Ł., & Perrin, J. (2008, March 28). *How to use property sheets*. Nexedi & ERP5 Community. Retrieved July 7, 2010, from http://www.erp5.org/HowToUsePropertySheets

Gräning, A., Wendler, R., Leyh, C., & Strahringer, S. (2010). Rigorous Selection of Input Artifacts in Design Science Research – TAVIAS. In *AMCIS 2010 Proceedings*. Paper 51.

Hevner, A. R., March, S. T., & Park, J. (2004). Design science in information systems research. *Management Information Systems Quarterly, 28*(1), 75–105.

Hofmann, P. (2008, July–August). ERP is dead, long live ERP. *Internet Computing, IEEE, 12*(4), 84–88. doi:10.1109/MIC.2008.78

Janssens, G., Kusters, R. J., & Heemstra, F. (2007, June). Clustering ERP implementation project activities: A foundation for project size definition. In S. Sadiq, M. Reichert, K. Schulz, J. Trienekens, C. Moller, & R. J. Kusters (Eds.), *Proceedings of the 1st international joint workshop on Technologies for Collaborative Business Processes and Management of Enterprise Information Systems, Funchal, Portugal* (pp. 23–32). Portugal: Institute for Systems and Technologies of Information.

Kinni, T. B. (1995). Process improvement, part 2. *Industry Week, 244*(4), 45.

Koh, S. C. L., & Simpson, M. (2007). Could enterprise resource planning create a competitive advantage for small businesses? *Benchmarking: An International Journal, 14*(1), 59–76. doi:10.1108/14635770710730937

Monnerat, R. M., de Carvalho, R. A., & de Campos, R. (2008). Enterprise systems modeling: the ERP5 development process. In *Proceedings of the 2008 ACM symposium on Applied Computing* (pp. 1062–1068). New York, NY: ACM.

Morabito, V., Pace, S., & Previtali, P. (2005). ERP marketing and Italian SMEs. *European Management Journal, 23*(5), 590–598. doi:10.1016/j.emj.2005.09.014

Nah, F. F. H., Lau, J. L. S., & Kuang, J. (2001). Critical factors for successful implementation of enterprise systems. *Business Process Management Journal, 7*(3), 285–296. doi:10.1108/14637150110392782

Nexedi, S. A. (n.d.). *Nexedi opensource on demand*. Retrieved May 10, 2010, from http://www.nexedi.com

Offermann, P., Levina, O., Schönherr, M., & Bub, U. (2009). Outline of a design science research process. In *Proceedings of the 4th International Conference on Design Science Research in Information Systems and Technology, Philadelphia, PA*. New York, NY: Association for Computing Machinery.

Paepcke, A. (1993). *Object-Oriented Programming: The CLOS Perspective*. Cambridge, MA: MIT Press.

Rosemann, M., & Recker, J. (2006). Context-aware process design: Exploring the extrinsic drivers for process flexibility. In Latour, T., Petit, M. (eds.): *The 18th International Conference on Advanced Information Systems Engineering. Proceedings of Workshops and Doctoral Consortium* (pp. 149–158). Namur University Press, Luxembourg, Grand-Duchy of Luxembourg

Scheer, A. (1997). *Wirtschaftsinformatik: Referenzmodelle für industrielle Geschäftsprozesse (7., durchges. Aufl.)*. Berlin: Springer.

Sebastiani, F. (2002). Machine learning in automated text categorization. *ACM Computing Surveys, 34*(1), 1–47. doi:10.1145/505282.505283

Smets, J.-P. (2008, March). *ERP5 industries overview*. Nexedi SA. Retrieved May 11, 2010, from https://www.myerp5.com/kb/web page module/233

Smets, J.-P. (n.d.). *ERP5 implementation*. Nexedi SA. Retrieved October 10, 2009, from https://www.myerp5.com/kb/documentation section/consultant/consultant-Front.Page/consultant-Implementation.Process/view (Restricted)

Smets-Solanes, J. (2002). ERP5: *a technical introduction*. Paper presented at Linux Tag, Karlsruhe, Germany. Available from http://cps.erp5.org/sections/free/erp/linuxtag.pdf/view

Smets-Solanes, J., & Carvalho, R. Atem de. (2003, July–August). ERP5: a next-generation, open-source ERP architecture. *IT Professional, 5*(4), 38–44. doi:10.1109/MITP.2003.1216231

Snider, B., Da Silveira, G., & Balakrishnan, J. (2009). ERP implementation at SMEs: analysis of five Canadian cases. *International Journal of Operations & Production Management, 29*(1), 4–29. doi:10.1108/01443570910925343

Timbrell, G., & Gable, G. (2002). The SAP ecosystem: a knowledge perspective. In *Proceedings of the Information Resources Management Association international conference* (pp. 1115–1118). Hershey, PA: Information Resources Management Association.

Wang, L., Tao, J., Kunze, M., Castellanos, A. C., Kramer, D., & Karl, W. (2008). *Scientific cloud computing: early definition and experience. In 10ᵗʰ IEEE international conference on High Performance Computing and Communications* (pp. 825–830). New York, N.Y: Institute of Electrical and Electronics Engineers.

## KEY TERMS AND DEFINITIONS

**Classifier:** Function that groups its input parameters into a set of classes. In the case of automatic category configuration, the classifier categorizes each response to a configuration question in two classes for each category: a class in favor of the particular category and a class against the particular category.

**Configuration:** The lightest form of ERP package tailoring. It consists of setting parameters in the ERP system.

**Decision Tree:** Can be used for solving a classification problem using the knowledge engineering approach. The input to the decision tree is a set of attributes and the tree returns a decision. In the case of category configuration, a decision tree decides which categories are to add to the ERP instance.

**Knowledge Engineering:** A problem solving approach in which expert knowledge is encoded into a computer system, for example by manually defining a set of rules.

**Machine Learning:** A problem solving approach in which learner algorithms are trained with example data to solve future problems based on the characteristics of the examples.

**Tailoring:** Adapting an ERP package to the specific requirements of a business which adopts the ERP package.

**Universal Business Model (UBM):** The underlying model of ERP5. It consists of five abstract core classes which are used to represent all kinds of business processes in ERP5.

# Chapter 9
# SMEs and FOS-ERP Systems:
## Risks and Opportunities

**Constantinos J. Stefanou**
*Alexander Technological Educational Institute of Thessaloniki, Greece*

## ABSTRACT

*Free/Open Source Enterprise Resource Planning (FOS-ERP) software is an emerging phenomenon having the potential to revolutionize the ERP market worldwide. This chapter focuses on the FOS-ERP market for Small and Medium-sized Enterprises (SMEs) and aims at informing managers, scholars, students and researchers of the opportunities and the related risks for SMEs wishing to adopt and implement a FOS-ERP solution. It is widely accepted that SMEs, which have limited capital and other resources, are among the organizations to be benefited by the existence of FOS-ERP by acquiring a system similar to that used by large enterprises. At the same time there are certain risks in adopting a FOS-ERP solution such as security issues and hidden costs. Guidelines for SMEs to eliminate these risks are provided. In order to define the backdrop of FOS-ERP systems, Web 2.0, cloud computing and Open Source Software (OSS) are also discussed.*

## INTRODUCTION

Free/Open Source (FOS) software in general and Free/Open Source ERP systems (FOR/ERPS) in particular are gaining interest in providing an alternative solution to proprietary integrated enterprise software (De Carvalho, 2006). Re-cently, open source has become a part of the IT infrastructure of organizations (Madsen, 2009). However, FOS-ERP software is still viewed with much skepticism by the majority of enterprises worldwide despite reduced IT budgets due to economic recession (Jutras, 2009). It is also true that academic research on FOS-ERP is rather

DOI: 10.4018/978-1-61350-486-4.ch009

limited and deficient (De Carvalho, 2009) a fact that significantly contributes to the skepticism and the blur surrounding the FOS-ERP phenomenon.

Although at first sight it seems that all enterprises are to be benefited by the existence of FOS-ERPS, it is argued in this chapter that FOS-ERPS is not a suitable solution for all enterprises. Hidden costs and costs that incur in the long run need to be taken into consideration regarding the adoption of FOS-ERPS in relation to the business and IT strategy planning. Users' information requirements have to be accommodated by software which purpose is to be as simple to be implemented as possible but this is not always the case with FOS-ERP. The objective of the chapter is to identify the opportunities available for SMEs adopting a FOS-ERP solution as well as the risks associated with this decision. The chapter aims at informing scholars, students and researchers having an interest in this emerging area of business software. In a practical level, it will provide managers with information and knowledge required in making the right decisions regarding the acquisition of FOS-ERP software.

The chapter is organized as follows: Next section discusses cloud computing and Open Source Software (OSS) in order to define the backdrop of FOS-ERP systems. The section that follows provides a literature review on FOS-ERP and the subsequent one presents the opportunities and risks for SMEs regarding the adoption and implementation of FOS-ERP systems. The final two sections provide suggestions for future research related to adoption of FOS-ERP systems by SMEs and final conclusions.

## CLOUD COMPUTING AND OPEN SOURCE SOFTWARE

Cloud computing, the technological platform that allows users, organizations or individuals, to access and use computer resources via the internet, has recently emerged as one of the most promising

and revolutionizing approaches of computing. It is also becoming a significant market trend in the field of Information and Communication Technology (ICT). According to WinterGreen Research (2009), cloud computing market comprised of search engines, communications technology, and application development, is expected to reach $160.2 billion by 2015 compared to $36 billion in 2008.

Web 2.0 and Open Source are seen as the perfect background for cloud computing (Sharif, 2009). It is apparent that the undeniable success of Web 2.0 social networking applications has certainly facilitated the promotion of the idea of collaborative software. It is also a driver for the acceptance of the notion that the internet can be a respected, secure transportation platform, even for critical business applications such as the integrated enterprise systems on which all or most of the enterprises' core functions depend upon. As far as ERP is concerned, according to Wu and Lao (2009), Web 2.0 may be used to reduce the cost, improve the quality and lower the risk of ERP implementations. Web 2.0 can provide, for example, a repository system of knowledge and experiences that supports ERP application implementations. The authors notice that higher-quality ERP implementations at reduced costs with lower risks can be achieved through the collective power of a large group of people. This is not achieved, for example, in the case of traditional collaborative software development where developers work on a given project with a common goal; instead, Web 2.0 ERP implementation synthesizes on the various experiences of collaborators who work in diverse situations and try to solve different problems or model unique business processes. This formulates a new model of ERP implementation, taking advantage of emerging Web 2.0 technologies such as wiki and social tagging systems which facilitate knowledge classification and enrichment; collaborative documentation and knowledge databases can be stored in the cloud to facilitate and enlighten future ERP projects.

Open source software allows users to have access to the software's code. This allows every user to modify the software according to specific business needs. At the same time, a worldwide community of users contributes to the efforts for making the software better and customizable in order to provide solutions and satisfy various needs with fewer code errors and limitations. Free access to its source code alone does not render software the open source status; according to the Open Source Initiative (www.opensource.org) free redistribution of the license is among the criteria that OSS should comply to.

Service Oriented Architecture (SOA) and Application Server Provider (ASP), largely facilitated by broadband internet communication, are two paradigms that should not be confused with the open source model. In these delivery models, providers give access to their hardware and software resources on-demand upon an all-inclusive fee. Software as a Service (SaaS), an extension of the ASP model, has undeniably many benefits especially for SMEs. It has been argued that large enterprises will not yet adopt the SaaS paradigm for mission-critical applications although they will use SaaS in certain occasions, such as to support infrequently used applications or applications that are shared with partners outside the company (Wohl, 2010). SaaS benefits for SMEs include lower costs for acquiring an advanced application in a much faster time than implementing the application in-house, reduced total cost of ownership, improved reliability and support offered by the service provided, greater flexibility and no need for building a complex on-premise IT architecture.

SaaS platforms are also used to distribute ERP systems. Brocke et al (2009) distinguish between hybrid service oriented ERP systems and fully service oriented ones. Common service oriented ERP systems do not allow for the integration of non-vendor specific services in contrast to the fully service oriented ERP systems which enable a "best-of-the-breed" approach and allows the

combination of software components from different software vendors (Brocke et al., 2009). The later approach results in increasing flexibility as the required applications are combined according to specific business needs. Despite its importance, this is yet an under researched subject and it has been recently acknowledged that there is certainly a need for studies on emerging business models for service oriented ERP (Enquist & Skielse, 2010).

Open source software, either downloaded and installed to a company's server or provided as a SaaS, requires that individuals do not just have access to use an application via the internet or in house; rather they are collaborating with each other sharing knowledge aiming at achieving a common goal, that is to make the software better (see e.g. www.opensource.org). Users can incorporate their own modifications in the code and develop new versions of the software. Therefore, OSS can be described as a combination of the software delivery and development models. King (2010) states that OSS is software that the developers of the product have released back to the community for reasons such as to make it better, faster or expand its features set beyond the original conception of the project. The community of developers can extend a product over a period of time and the extensions can then be included into the main product in the very next release. According to Riehle (2007) there are two different categories of open source software; the first type includes open source software developed by members of a community where there are not any market-entry barriers and the second one includes commercial open source software, which is developed for profit by an individual or organization. In the later case, vendors are not interested in selling the software per se but in selling services associated with the software, such as its provision, maintenance, and support to end-users.

It follows from the discussion above, that open source software has to be viewed and researched by a much wider angle in order to access its potential in the IT industry. It is not a surprise then that OSS is of interest to a wide range of disciplines including economics, public policy, psychology and sociology (see, e.g., Hars & Qu, 2002; Krogh & Hippel 2006). Several issues related to OSS are under researched, such as the coordination of the activities of the members of the development team and the management of open source projects with growing complexity or the optimal licensing of open source software (Lerner & Tirole, 2005). In contrast, proprietary software is developed by software houses using their own protocols, software architectures and file formats and it is licensed to be used, but not sold, by customers on premises. Vendors do not allow or at the best limit severely the right of the buyers to extend the functionality of a product (King, 2010). The same happens with the hosted application paradigm, where licensed applications bought by a customer are hosted by third-parties.

Next section will present FOS-ERP in more detail followed by a discussion on the advantages and the disadvantages of FOS-ERP for the SMEs.

## FOS-ERP SYSTEMS AND SMES

SMEs is the backbone of the economic environment of many countries around the world. SMEs are facing today the challenge of a continuous changing, globalized and extremely competitive economic environment. Advances in the information and communication technologies as well as the widespread phenomenon of web-based applications and markets impose even in the small companies the need to invest in modern integrated, enterprise-wide information systems in order to remain competitive.

However, SMEs differ significantly from large enterprises as far as information technology (IT) acceptance and information systems (IS) acquisition practices are concerned (Buonanno et al., 2005; Ramdani & Kawalek, 2009).

ERP systems are enterprise-wide modular software packages that provide fully integrated business processes using a common database and offering data visibility and information from various viewpoints. ERP systems have the potential of greatly enhancing organizational performance and establishing competitive advantage (Davenport, 1998). However, SMEs face high costs in their effort to integrate and make more competitive their business processes or they are tied-up in a single vendor when they adopt a smaller but still a propriety packaged solution (De Carvalho, 2009). The complexity of standard ERP systems makes their evaluation a multifaceted issue (Stefanou, 2001) and hardly suits SMEs which need a flexible, low cost and easy to implement integrated business information system in order to meet the challenges of the ongoing competitive environment. In addition, standard ERP systems provide SMEs with functionality which is largely unexploited. Therefore, it is in the interest of SMEs to consider the adoption of FOS-ERP software as a low cost alternative to large propriety ERP systems (De Carvalho, 2009).

Seethamraju and Seethamraju (2008) provide a discussion of the external and internal factors forcing SMEs to adopt ERP systems. External factors are, for example, e-procurement initiatives forcing SMEs to adapt to them if they want to stay in the market and powerful supply chain partners who require their partners to upgrade their information systems in order and achieve transactional efficiency. Internal factors, such as the need to remain competitive and cost-efficient, force SMEs to acquire ERPS in order o streamline their processes and reduce costs. Among SMEs, those that are likely to acquire an ERP package are companies with a greater perceived relative advantage, organizational readiness, top management support and larger size (Ramdani et al., 2009).

Understandably, the penetration of standard ERP systems in the mid-market segment is not too high. SMEs have limited resources and they cannot afford to acquire, implement and operate a standard ERP solution offered by large ERP vendors such as SAP and Oracle. It is also true that, until recently, SMEs attracted limited attention by vendors of large ERP packages or in any case SMEs were certainly not their first priority. This situation changes today; saturation of the ERP marker for the big clients and pressures from the OSS front have reversed this trend. Many traditional EEP vendors, SAP being no exception, have developed products that aim at mid market clients. These are pre-configurable, limited functionality and low cost options compared to the state-of-the-art systems. Recently, another significant option, FOS-ERP systems, became available to SMEs and seem to be of an increasing interest today either as a result of dissatisfaction with proprietary ERP systems or as a result of maturity in the open source phenomenon (Johansson & Sudzina, 2008).

However, the question which is the best way for companies to acquire software remains unanswered. In a recent study of ERP selection criteria based on literature review, Johansson and Sudzina (2009) could not conclude whether open source or proprietary solutions are more suitable for the majority of the organizations. It is widely accepted, however, that SMEs are among the organizations that are to be benefited by the FOS-ERP trend for a variety of reasons (see e.g. Bueno & Callego, 2010), many of which were presented above. At the same time and despite positive prospects, many issues have to be resolved and there are certain risks in adopting a FOS-ERP solution. Both anticipated benefits and risks for SMEs are discussed in the following section.

## FOS-ERP OPPORTUNITIES AND RISKS FOR SMES

During the last fifteen year ERP systems emerged as a revolutionary way to integrate business processes and provide competitive advantage to adopters. Today, open source software seems to be the new revolutionary initiative in the information technology arena and Free/Open Source ERP will become potentially a significant part of this emerging phenomenon.

Open source software should not be confused with free software, although there are free or low cost open source applications available. The idea behind FOS-ERP is the information and knowledge sharing among collaborators who update the software offered on a come-and-go basis. Customers have more control on choosing software applications and components that suits their business needs as well as their budgets without a long term commitment to a complex and costly commercial ERP system.

FOS-ERPS have the potential to revolutionize the way SMEs acquire and use enterprise information systems, which in their commercial offering are complex, rigid and costly but, if implemented successfully, they can retain or provide a competitive advantage for the adopting organization. Not only medium-sized but also small companies have now the opportunity to use FOS-ERPS in order to respond quickly to changing market conditions by adopting technologies similar to what the big enterprises are using worldwide during the last 15 years.

FOS-ERP systems, such as Compiere, Openbravo, ERP5, TinyERP, and WebERP, to name but a few, are gaining everyday a higher rate of acceptance by companies having limited budgets for IT spending but wishing to implement an enterprise-wide, integrated business information system. It has been recently reported that in the Sourceforge.net website, which provides free hosting to open source ERP development projects, 2058 open source ERP projects can be identified (Bueno & Gallego 2010) in contrast to about 356 open source ERP projected registered in 2007 (Johansson & Sudzina, 2008). This comparison provides an indication of the increasing importance of FOS-ERP in the ERP market, although, the impact of most of these projects is, quite predictably, not significant (Bueno & Gallego 2010). Still, FOS-ERP, due to certain weaknesses discussed below, has a long way to go before it can be a creditable and respected alternative to propriety ERP software, especially for large enterprises.

## FOS-ERP Opportunities for SMEs

Serrano and Sarriegi (2006) argue that there are 3 main reasons, among others such as easier management of licenses, to choose an OSS ERP system: a) Increased adaptability; ERPs need always to be implemented in order to match the business processes and local regulations. Companies, having full access to the ERP source code are facilitated in the software customization. b) Decreased reliance on a single supplier; organizations that acquire a proprietary ERP are highly dependent on the source code's owners such as developers and distributors. c) Reduced costs; proprietary ERP licenses are expensive compared to low cost or free licenses of open source software. The above reasons indicate that the benefits of adopting OSS are rather greater for ERP software than for other types of software applications.

According to De Carvalho and De Campos (2006) lower costs and access to source code are the main reasons attracting companies to FOS-ERP systems. Benefits are likely to be greater for new firms. A newly established midsize company may enjoy a huge competitive advantage in acquiring FOS-ERP technology for two, mainly, reasons; Firstly, the company has not yet established rigid business processes that are hard to be modified. Thus, it has more flexibility to adapt to the software or vice versa in order to support unique business needs and processes regarded as competitive. Of course, it has also the option to implement the processes embedded in the preconfigured application. Secondly, the company can hire at the outset knowledgeable consultants who have experience in that particular system.

Johansson and Sudzina (2009) argue that ease and speed of implementation, price, vendor support and reliability are the basic criteria upon which organizations base their decision to acquire ERP systems. Taking this for granted, the first two criteria are in favor of FOS-ERP systems as these systems are considered much cheaper and are implemented more easily than large scale ERP systems. It should be noted, however, that if midsize companies wish to expand by acquiring other companies, customization of the ERP software is inevitable and costs will increase. Integration with other partners in the supply chain generates the same problem. It has been argued that a percentage of SMEs needs at some point of time to customize their ERP systems to the same way larger firms do, in which case more customization will be necessary (Gruman, 2007). As far as vendor support and reliability is concerned, it seems that FOS-ERPs have to go a long way before convincing customers of their value. Nevertheless, FOS-ERPs offer a greater degree of freedom and flexibility to the adopting organizations. There is a decreased reliance on a single supplier, reduced costs and the adaptability of the software to core business processes is certainly greater than that of propriety ERP (Serrano & Sarriegi, 2006).

If follows from the above, that the availability of FOS-ERP software provides an important opportunity for SMEs to become competitive for the following reasons: Companies keep low their initial capital spending, control spending for software support, get, almost always, free product updates (King, 2010) and have greater freedom in adapting the software to their core business. In addition, FOS-ERP software is more flexible than the standard large ERP packages. Table 1 presents the advantages and disadvantages of FOS-ERP software compared to propriety ERP software for SMEs.

*Table 1. Advantages/disadvantages of FOS-ERP software compared to Propriety ERP software for SMEs*

| System characteristics and costs | Free Open Source ERP (FOS-ERP) | Propriety ERP (P-ERP) |
|---|---|---|
| Acquisition cost | free or not free but lower than P-ERP | high cost for license per user |
| Total Cost of Ownership (TCO) | uncertain but maybe high in the long-run | high but predictable |
| Source code openness | high | low |
| Upgrades | depended on community, low cost | vendor releases, high cost |
| Support | community, consultants | vendor, consultants, users' blogs |
| Software stability/reliability | rather uncertain | vendor reliance, rather certain |
| Functionality | satisfactory, uneven between the various solutions | high but not fully utilized by SMEs |
| Scalability | low | high |
| Flexibility /Adaptability to business processes | high | low |
| Implementation - costs | easier - low | difficult - high |
| Customization - costs | easier - low usually | difficult - high |
| Maintenance costs | low for SaaS ERP higher for downloaded FOS-ERP | high |
| Maintenance services | uncertain | vendor, consultants |
| Consultants availability | low | high |
| Consultants cost | high, uncertain in the long run | known market rates, anticipated |
| User training costs | lower than P-ERP | high |
| Documentation | maybe incomplete and not regularly updated | complete /regularly updated |
| Vendor lock-in | low or non-existent | high |
| Exit cost | low | high |

## FOS-ERP Risks for SMEs

It has been argued by many authors that cost is probably the main or even the sole factor upon which SMEs base their decisions to acquire and implement an FOS-ERP system. In that respect FOS-ERPs are a serious alternative to propriety ERPs as FOS-ERP vendors will often provide the product license at no cost but may charge customers for support or software updates (King, 2010). However, generally the price of acquiring the licenses to use software is low relative to Total Cost of Ownership (TCO). It has also relatively low importance compared to the costly tasks performed during system acquisition and full-cycle operation (Krivoruchko, 2007).

Thus, what matters in the long run is not the initial capital spending for acquiring the software but the TCO and this is a magnitude that can be easily overlooked by SMEs. Economides and Katsamakas (2006) emphasize that open source software can be used for free but costs incur for implementing, learning, operating, supporting and maintaining activities. Consider, for example, that the fees paid to a consultant for implementing a FOS-ERP may overweight the zero cost of the license (Johansson & Sudzina, 2008). Additionally, customization and maintenance, if the company cannot take care of them internally, they will be certainly high cost activities reducing any benefits arising from zero cost licenses. There are also questions regarding high system availability and reliable support as well as data security and accessibility.

FOS-ERPs are yet to be accepted by the majority of companies as a reliable and trustworthy way to implement an ERP system due to certain weakness beyond TCO. Such a weakness is for example the deployment processes of most FOS-ERP projects, which is not centrally managed. Many FOS-ERP transform the responsibility of following an appropriate development process to the partner side offering either specific development-support tools or compatible packaged tools (De Carvalho & Monnerat, 2008). The creator organization needs also to create and manage a community around the FOS-ERP project, in order to keep it alive and sound, and find new customers for the system (De Carvalho, 2009).

Other weaknesses is the lack of specialized consultants at least as far as the not so well known FOS-ERPs are concerned and managers' perceptions about the actual value of using FOS-ERPs. Goode (2005), by analyzing responds form Australia's 500 top companies, found that managers are reluctant to acquire OSS due to limited support, lack of available resources, lack of time needed to implement the software and even because they perceive little value for adopting open source technology in their businesses.

FOS–ERP may also be not yet the right choice for midmarket companies that wish to expand and join supply chains where larger companies operate standard propriety ERP packages. The same holds true for integration or expansion via acquisition of other companies. In such cases, it is difficult to achieve systems compatibility and an enormous amount of effort and money will be needed with questionable results. Table 2 summarizes the main risk factors of adopting FOS-ERPs by SMEs presented above and provides guidance for FOS-ERP acquisition in relation to certain characteristics of SMEs.

*Table 2. SMEs characteristics and FOS-ERPs*

| SMEs Characteristics, Policy, and Strategy | Recommended solution |
|---|---|
| Expansion with acquisition of other companies | P-ERP |
| Integration with other companies | P-ERP |
| Partner in expanded supply chain | P-ERP |
| Compliance to legislation (e.g. Sarbanes-Oxley Act, Accounting, etc) | P-ERP |
| Extensive customization needed to support core business processes | FOS-ERP |
| Limited capital budgets | FOS-ERP |
| Limited resources (IT infrastructure, IT staff) | FOS-ERP |

## FUTURE RESEARCH DIRECTIONS

Despite the importance of FOS –ERP for modern mid-sized companies, research on the subject is quite limited. The growing penetration of FOS-ERP especially in the SMEs market, calls for future research that should analyze and provide frameworks and guidelines for the selection process, the implementation and the operation of FOS-ERP. Although the need for evaluation and additionally a method for FOS-ERP evaluation has been proposed by de Carvalho (2006) academic research in this domain is deficient. The ex-post evaluation of FOS-ERP systems is also of paramount importance in identifying its impact on the organization especially as there is no currently any research reporting on FOS-ERP success rates (De Carvalho, 2009). Web 2.0 ERP implementation is a collaborative approach quite different from the traditional software development. Research is needed to evaluate the merits and drawbacks and identify key success factors of this new paradigm providing an assessment of its potential customer value.

## CONCLUSION

Cloud computing, Web.2.0 and open source software have the potential to revolutionize the way business software is developed and distributed. The impact of these emerging technologies is also evident in the ERP market. OSS provides companies with a compelling alternative to the traditional way of acquiring software (King, 2000). SMEs have now the opportunity to acquire integrated, company-wide business software critical for their operations in a continuous globalised and competitive environment, which in the past only large companies could afford. However, the acquisition of FOS-ERP software is not always a safe investment without risks and drawbacks.

The chapter presented opportunities and risks available to SMEs wishing to acquire and implement ERP systems resembling that used by big enterprises, taking advantage of the availability of the FOS-ERP solutions in the cloud computing universe. Low capital budgets, limited IT infrastructures, tight contracts and vendor lock-in are barriers for most SMEs to acquire a propriety ERP system but SMEs have now the option to implement an FOS-ERP solution in their effort to remain competitive. The growth of FOS-EPR market is spectacular and it is expected to increase in the coming years, a fact that provides an indication of the relevance of FOS-ERP systems mainly to SMEs.

This endeavor, however, as it has been argued above, is not without risks; firstly, the TCO of implementing a FOS-ERP solution is not easily anticipated and there are indications that can be very high in the long run. A high TCO will absorb resources, the value of which is difficult to be assesses and calculated at the outset, and this could be devastating for the adopting company. Secondly, the functionality of the software may be quite limited in case of SMEs which wish to expand, add, modernize or reengineer their business processes, and have substantial new information requirements. The same holds true in the case SMEs need to be partners in supply chains where information systems' compatibility and efficiency is required. Thirdly, data security, accessibility and availability in case of hosted/web-based applications are not guaranteed. This is maybe not a critical problem for newly established companies, but it can be a serious one for companies operating in the marker for a long time and especially when critical decisions they make are based on these data.

To eliminate these risks, SMEs should look at how large the FOS-ERP software developer community is, the number of installations the specific FOS-ERP software to be adopted by the company has, as well as how long the FOS-ERP project has been running. A proven comprehensive set of tools offered by the FOS-ERP solution facilitating configuration and implementation is also required. Technical, organizational, operational, and financial risks associated with FOS-ERP software should not be overlooked. Finally, it should be certainly noted, that a clearly articulated strategy, business goals and vision is of paramount importance in making the right decision as far as the adoption of an FOS-ERP or a P-ERP solution is concerned.

## REFERENCES

Brocke., J. vom, Schenk, B. & Sonnenberg C. 2009. Organizational Implications of Implementing Service Oriented ERP Systems: An Analysis Based on New Institutional Economics. In: Abramowicz, W. (Ed.). *BIS 2009, LNBIP 21,* 252–263, 2009, Springer-Verlag Berlin Heidelberg.

Bueno, S., & Gallego, M. D. (2010). Evaluating acceptance of OSS-ERP based on user perceptions. In Sobh, T. (Ed.), *Innovations and Advances in Computer Sciences and Engineering, Springer Science+Business Media B.V.* doi:10.1007/978-90-481-3658-2_10

Buonanno, G., Faverio, P., Pigni, F., Ravarini, A., Sciuto, D., & Tagliavini, M. (2005). Factors affecting ERP system adoption. *Journal of Enterprise Information Management, 18*(4), 384–426. doi:10.1108/17410390510609572

Davenport, T. H. (1998). Putting the enterprise into the enterprise system. *Harvard Business Review, 76*(4), 121–131.

De Carvalho, R. A. (2006). Issues on Evaluating Free/Open Source ERP Systems. In *Research and Practical Issues of Enterprise Information Systems* (pp. 667–676). Springer-Verlag. doi:10.1007/0-387-34456-X_72

De Carvalho, R. A. (2009). Free/Open Source Enterprise Resources Planning. In Gupta, J. N. D., Rashid, M. A., & Sharma, S. K. (Eds.), *Handbook of Research on Enterprise Systems* (pp. 32–44). Hershey, PA: Information Science Reference. doi:10.4018/978-1-59904-859-8.ch003

De Carvalho, R. A., & de Campos, R. (2006). A Development Process Proposal for the ERP5 System. *IEEE International Conference on Systems, Man, and Cybernetics,* October 8-11, 2006, Taipei, Taiwan, 4703-4708.

De Carvalho, R. A., & Monnerat, R. M. (2008). Development support tools for Enterprise Resource Planning. *IEEE,*Computer.org/ITPro

Economides, N., & Katsamakas, E. (2006). Two-Sided Competition of Proprietary vs. Open Source Technology Platforms and the Implications for the Software Industry. *Management Science, 52,* 1057–1071. doi:10.1287/mnsc.1060.0549

Enquist, H., & Skielse, G. J. (2010). Value Propositions in Service Oriented Business Models for ERP: Case Studies, in W. Abramowicz and R. Tolksdorf (Eds.) *BIS 2010, LNBIP 47,* 268–279, Springer-Verlag Berlin Heidelberg.

Goode, S. (2005). Something for nothing: management rejection of open source software in Australia's top firms. *Information & Management, 42,* 669–681. doi:10.1016/j.im.2004.01.011

Gruman, G. (2007). More Midmarket firms choose open-source ERP. *Computerworld*

Hars, A., & Qu, S. (2002). Working for Free? Motivations for Participating in Open-Source Projects. *International Journal of Electronic Commerce, 6,* 25.

Johansson, B., & Sudzina, F. (2008). ERP systems and open source: an initial review and some implications for SMEs. *Journal of Enterprise Information Management, 21*(6), 649–658. doi:10.1108/17410390810911230

Johansson, B., & Sudzina, F. (2009). Choosing Open Source ERP Systems: What Reasons Are There For Doing So? In Boldyreff, C. (Eds.), *OSS 2009, IFIP AICT 299* (pp. 143–155). IFIP International Federation for Information Processing.

Jutras, C. (2009). SaaS ERP: Trends and observations. *An Aberdeen Report*

King, S. (2010). Implementing Open Source Software. In Simon, P. (Ed.), *The Next Wave of Technologies; Opportunities from Chaos.* New York: John Wiley & Sons.

Krivoruchko, J. (2007). The Use of Open Source Software in Enterprise Distributed Computing Environments. *IFIP, Vol.24: Open source development, adoption and innovation.*

Lerner, J., & Tirole, J. (2005). The Scope of Open Source Licensing. *Journal of Law Economics and Organization, 21,* 20–56. doi:10.1093/jleo/ewi002

Madsen, M. (2009). The role of open source in data integration. *Third nature Technology Report.*

Ramdani, B., Kawalek, P., & Lorenzo, O. (2009). Predicting SMEs' adoption of enterprise systems. *Journal of Enterprise Information Management, 22*(1/2), 10–24. doi:10.1108/17410390910922796

Riehle, D. (2007). The economic motivation of open source: stakeholders perspectives. *Computer, IEE. Computers & Society, 40*(4), 25–32.

Seethamraju, R., & Seethamraju, J. (2008). Adoption of ERPs in a Medium-sized Enterprise - A Case Study. *19th Australasian Conference on Information Systems*, pp.887-896.

Serrano, N. S., & Sarriegi, J. M. (2006). Open Source Software ERPs: A New Alternative for an Old Need. *IEEE Software, 23*(3), 94–97. doi:10.1109/MS.2006.78

Sharif, A. M. (2010). It's written in the cloud: the hype and promise of cloud computing. Invited Viewpoint in *Journal of Enterprise Information Management, 23*(2), 131–134.

Stefanou, C. J. (2001). A Framework for the Evaluation and Selection of ERP Systems. *European Journal of Information Systems. Special Issue on IT Evaluation, 10*, 204–215.

von Krogh, G., & von Hippel, E. (2006). The Promise of Research on Open Source Software. *Management Science, 52*(7), 975–983. doi:10.1287/mnsc.1060.0560

WinterGreen Research. (2009). Worldwide Cloud Computing -- Markets Reach $160.2 Billion by 2015. *Press Release*, Lexington, Massachusetts (July 24, 2009).

Wohl, A. (2010). Software as a Service. In Simon, P. (Ed.), *The Next Wave of Technologies; Opportunities from Chaos* (p. 105). New York: John Wiley & Sons.

Wu, H. & Cao, L. (2009). Harnessing Web 2.0 for ERP Implementations. *IEEE Software*.

## KEY TERMS AND DEFINITIONS

**Application Server Providers (ASPs):** ASPs are vendors who procure and resell a customized application to a customer upon an all-inclusive fee.

**Cloud Computing:** Cloud computing is the technological platform that allows users, organizations or individuals, to access and use computer resources via the internet.

**Service Oriented Architecture (SOA):** According to CBDI Forum (http://everware-cbdi.com/cbdi-forum) SOA can be defined as the policies, practices and frameworks that enable application functionality to be provided and consumed as sets of services published at a granularity relevant to the service consumer using a single, standards-based form of interface.

**SME:** According to the European Commission, enterprises qualify as micro, small, and medium-sized enterprises (SMEs) if they fulfill the criteria laid down in the adopted Recommendation of May 2003: Micro (< 10 Headcount, ≤ € 2 million Turnover, ≤ € 2 million Balance sheet total), Small (< 50 Headcount, ≤ € 10 million Turnover, ≤ € 10 million Balance sheet total), and Medium-sized (< 250 Headcount, ≤ € 50 million Turnover, ≤ € 43 million Balance sheet total).

**Software as a Service (SaaS):** SaaS is an improved extension of the ASP model, where providers host themselves or use a third-party and license configurable applications to users over the internet through a subscription model or distribute them freely if they can generate revenues from other sources such as advertisement.

**Web 2.0:** The term Web 2.0 denotes collectively web applications that facilitate social interaction, networking and collaboration in the virtual environment of the Web.

# Chapter 10
# An Exploratory Investigation of the Barriers to the Adoption of Open Source ERP by Belgian SMEs

**Kris Ven**
*University of Antwerp, Belgium*

**Dieter Van Nuffel**
*University of Antwerp, Belgium*

## ABSTRACT

*Notwithstanding the increasing interest in open source ERP (OS-ERP) products in the past few years, their adoption by Belgian organizations is still very limited. To gain more insight into this phenomenon, we performed an exploratory investigation of which barriers inhibit the adoption of OS-ERP by Belgian SMEs. Based upon our previous research, we identified two main barriers, namely a lack of functionality and a lack of support. Next, we performed a screening of the Belgian OS-ERP market to investigate the functionality and support offered by various OS-ERP products. This allowed us to determine how the perceptions of organizations compare to the actual market for OS-ERP in Belgium. Our results provide more insight into the barriers to the adoption of OS-ERP by Belgian SMEs and provide various avenues for future research.*

## INTRODUCTION

In the past decade, open source software (OSS) has evolved significantly and has become a viable solution for organizations. The adoption of OSS has taken place in three different waves. The first

DOI: 10.4018/978-1-61350-486-4.ch010

wave of OSS adoption was focused on server-side applications such as Linux and Apache. This can be explained by the fact that most OSS development initially focused on horizontal domains such as Internet applications, developer tools and technical tools (Fitzgerald, 2005). As a result, server-side applications were the most mature OSS products available and were among the first OSS products to be adopted by organizations. Thanks to the increasing involvement of commercial software vendors in OSS development, many mature OSS products have appeared in other domains as well (Fitzgerald, 2006; Brydon & Vinning, 2008). The second wave of OSS adoption seems to be centering around the adoption of open source desktop software, such as OpenOffice.org and Firefox. Public administrations in particular have been rather active in exploring the possibilities of migrating towards OSS on desktop computers (Ven, Van Nuffel, & Verelst, 2007). Lately, several OSS products have become available in the enterprise application domain such as Enterprise Resource Planning (ERP), Supply Chain Management (SCM), Customer Relationship Management (CRM), and Enterprise Content Management (ECM). Hence, the OSS phenomenon has been gradually penetrating the whole software stack, going from the infrastructural level to the business application level. It has been argued that some OSS products may have the potential to gain entrance to and disrupt the commercial enterprise software market (Brydon & Vinning, 2008). The third wave of OSS adoption may therefore involve the adoption of open source enterprise software. In this chapter, our focus is on the adoption of open source Enterprise Resource Planning (OS-ERP). It can be observed that among the various open source enterprise software products, OS-ERP products are slowly gaining acceptance in organizations (Davis, 2008). It has also been noted that a relatively large number of new OSS projects are gradually appearing in this area (Johansson & Sudzina, 2008; Johansson & Sudzina, 2009).

Since the adoption of OS-ERP is a rather new phenomenon, it has not been studied extensively in academic literature yet and several authors have called for additional research on this topic (Kim & Boldyreff, 2005; de Carvalho, 2009; Davis, 2008). Some of the early studies in this domain have suggested a number of advantages of OS-ERP that may generate the interest of organizations to adopt. These advantages include:

increased adaptability of the software thanks to the availability of the source code, possibility to realize cost savings, and reduced vendor lock-in (Serrano & Sarriegi, 2006; Johansson & Sudzina, 2008; de Carvalho & Johansson, 2010; Davis, 2008). A recent study among Belgian organizations has, however, shown that the adoption of open source enterprise software—including OS-ERP—is lagging far behind the adoption of OSS for desktop or server-side use (Ven, 2008). This suggests that several barriers exist with respect to the organizational adoption of OS-ERP. Given the fact that ERP systems are crucial for supporting the business activities of organizations, it is reasonable to expect that organizations may be rather hesitant to rely on an open source solution for their ERP needs. It has been suggested that possible reasons for this low degree of adoption include the lack of reliable, maintainable and scalable OS-ERP solutions (Davis, 2008).

In this chapter, we will provide more insight into the barriers that currently exist to the organizational adoption of OS-ERP. Since research has shown that small and medium-sized enterprises (SMEs) use different selection criteria and make use of different ERP software than large organizations (Bernroider & Koch, 2001), we need to restrict the scope of our research in order to increase the reliability of our findings. We will therefore focus on the adoption of OS-ERP by SMEs. This choice is based on a number of reasons. First, the market of ERP software that is specifically targeted towards SMEs is growing (Deep, Guttridge, Dani, & Burns, 2008). Most large organizations have already adopted ERP, and SMEs therefore represent an interesting opportunity to ERP vendors to further expand their business. Many SMEs are also a supplier for large organizations and therefore experience the need to integrate their IT infrastructure with that of their customers (Hallikainen, Kivijrvi, Rossi, Sarpola, & Talvinen, 2002). Furthermore, as SMEs become more mature, they will require the same ERP-functionality as large organizations, albeit on a different scale (Deep et al., 2008). Although SMEs often start with custom developed ERP systems, they will require a more stable ERP product that offers opportunities for the future once the SME grows and matures (Bernroider & Koch, 2001). Second, SMEs form the backbone of the European Union (EU) economy. The European Commission officially defines an SME in terms of employees as an organization consisting of less than 250 employees (European Commission, 2003). In 2008, SMEs represented 99.8% of all organizations, 67.4% of the labor force, and 57.9% of the added value in the EU (European Commission, 2009a). Finally, previous research has suggested that OS-ERP seems particularly interesting for SMEs (Johansson & Sudzina, 2008; de Carvalho & Johansson, 2010; Davis, 2008; de Carvalho, 2009; Kim & Boldyreff, 2005). The websites of several OS-ERP products also reflect their focus on SMEs (Davis, 2008). In this chapter, we will specifically focus on the adoption of OS-ERP by Belgian SMEs. Similar to the European situation, SMEs constitute a prominent role in the Belgian economy, as they represented 99.8% of all organizations, 66.9% of the labor force, and 57.7% of the value added in 2008 (European Commission, 2009b). The aim of this chapter is to perform an exploratory investigation into the barriers that currently exist to the adoption of OS-ERP by Belgian SMEs.

The rest of this chapter is structured as follows. We start by providing a brief literature review on the use of proprietary ERP (P-ERP) products by SMEs in general and Belgian SMEs in particular. The results from these studies are useful to provide the context of the adoption of OS-ERP by SMEs. In the following section, we focus on the current status of the adoption of OS-ERP by Belgian organizations. Given the low level of adoption, our focus will be on determining what organizations perceive to be the main reasons for not adopting OS-ERP. We subsequently investigate how these perceptions relate to the current market for OS-ERP in Belgium by investigating the functional-

ity offered by OS-ERP products and the level of support that is currently available to Belgian organizations. We continue with a discussion in which we identify the most important barriers to the adoption of OS-ERP by Belgian SMEs. We further suggest several topics for future research. Finally, our conclusions are offered.

## LITERATURE REVIEW

Given the paucity of research on OS-ERP, it is interesting to start from the general literature on (P-)ERP by considering which selection factors are used by SMEs when selecting ERP software. We will briefly summarize previous research and discuss which selection factors are considered important by Belgian SMEs by drawing upon our previous empirical research. Notwithstanding the fact that this research was focused on ERP software in general, it can be expected that many of these selection factors are also relevant in the context of the adoption of OS-ERP. Although OS-ERP may compare favorably or unfavorably to P-ERP with respect to each of these selection factors, prior research has argued that it is interesting to consider how such selection factors relate to the adoption of OS-ERP (Johansson & Sudzina, 2009). A recent study has found that although the relative importance of various selection factors differ between P-ERP and OS-ERP, the same set of selection factors proved relevant for both (Benlian & Hess, 2010).

## Use of ERP by SMEs

It is generally known that the adoption of ERP systems by SMEs exhibits some particular characteristics, compared to large organizations. SMEs differ from large organizations on the following aspects (Bernroider & Koch, 2001; Mabert, Soni, & Venkataramanan, 2003):

- *Applied selection criteria:* SMEs use more operational and less strategic motives to choose among the different ERP systems.
- *Information gathering:* SMEs utilize a smaller number of, and less expensive, information methods to acquire information.
- *Team structure:* fewer people are involved to take the decisions within SMEs.
- *Project duration:* the lead time of the project is shorter within SMEs.
- *Cost:* the overall cost for SMEs is significantly lower.
- *ERP systems considered and selected:* the ERP market for SMEs typically consists of smaller suppliers and vendors.

Within the context of this study, it is interesting to further elaborate on the selection criteria that are used by SMEs. An overview of the most important selection factors identified in literature can be found in Table 1 (Baki & Cakar, 2005; Bernroider & Koch, 2001; Chau, 1995; Deep et al., 2008; Keil & Tiwana, 2006; van Everdingen, Van Hillegersberg, & Waarts, 2000). These selection factors can be divided in a number of categories. Factors can refer to the ERP system itself or the vendor of the system (Chau, 1995; van Everdingen et al., 2000). Some authors argue that the former category should even be further refined in factors that target the attributes of the ERP product, and factors that relate to the implementation (Keil & Tiwana, 2006). It can also be observed that some factors have a technical nature (e.g., flexibility), while other factors have a non-technical nature (e.g., cost). It must also be noted that the importance attributed to the selection criteria differs between hierarchical organizational levels: managers value operational factors, whereas owners attach the most weight to strategic factors (Chau, 1995).

## Use of ERP by Belgian SMEs

In previous research, one of the authors of this chapter investigated the importance that Belgian SMEs attribute to various selection factors (Van Nuffel & De Backer, 2010). This research applied a qualitative case study methodology (Eisenhardt, 1989; Yin, 2003). In this study, informants within SMEs that recently acquired an ERP system were interviewed. The sample consisted of eighteen SMEs. To select these SMEs, the researchers used a purposeful sampling procedure. The SMEs had completed both the acquisition and implementation of an ERP system to ensure that organizations could provide a well-founded assessment of the suitability of the selected ERP system and the success of the corresponding implementation. The case selection was also controlled for sector, magnitude of the organization and the use of external knowledge.

*Table 1. Selection factors used by SMEs (based on Baki & Cakar, 2005; Bernroider & Koch, 2001; Chau, 1995; Deep, Guttridge, Dani, & Burns, 2008; Keil & Tiwana, 2006; van Everdingen, Van Hillegersberg, & Waarts, 2000)*

| Cost | Purchase cost | Maintenance cost |
|---|---|---|
| | Implementation cost | |
| ERP system | Functionality | Organizational Fit |
| | Flexibility | Integration |
| | Ease of Customization | Adaptability |
| | Reliability | Usability |
| | Compatibility | |
| ERP vendor | Vendor Reputation | Industry References |
| | Market position | Domain knowledge |
| | International support | |
| Other factors | Optimization business processes | Fit with business processes |
| | Fit with organizational structure | |

Table 2 provides the most important selection factors used by the organizations included in the case study. This table also displays the number of SMEs that used each selection factor. The selection factors are listed in decreasing order of importance. It should also be mentioned that only factors encountered within three or more SMEs are included in Table 2. Generally, Belgian SMEs seem to highly value selection factors related to the functionality provided by the ERP system, the system's flexibility, the cost and time span of implementation, and key vendor characteristics. Full results are discussed in Van Nuffel and De Backer (2010).

## OS-ERP ADOPTION IN BELGIUM

As part of a larger research project on the adoption of OSS by Belgian organizations, Ven (2008) conducted a survey across 111 Belgian organizations. The sample was constructed by random sampling and included organizations from various sizes and sectors. One question of this survey inquired to which extent 13 types of OSS products were used. Respondents were asked to report their extent of adoption of each of these types of OSS using a 7-point Likert scale (ranging from "no usage"

*Table 2. Overview of selection criteria applied by Belgian SMEs*

| Selection factor | Number of SMEs |
|---|---|
| Fulfill requirements | 18 |
| Vendor's reputation | 14 |
| Implementation cost | 14 |
| Flexibility | 14 |
| Optimize business processes | 10 |
| Vendor's market position | 8 |
| Avoid customization | 7 |
| Industry references | 6 |
| Implementation time | 6 |
| Vendor's domain knowledge | 5 |

to "to a very large extent"). Respondents were informed that the category "enterprise software" included (but was not limited to) ERP, CRM and data warehousing. A summary of the responses is shown in Figure 1. The horizontal bars indicate the average extent of adoption of the various types of OSS products. As can be seen, the adoption of open source enterprise software is lagging far behind the adoption of OSS for desktop or server-side use. More specifically, 84 out of 107 (78.5%) organizations indicated to be using no open source enterprise software at all (four organizations did not reply to this question in the survey). Although it would appear that a reasonable number of organizations indicated to be using open source enterprise software (i.e., 21.5%), their extent of adoption was very limited. Of the 23 organizations that made use of open source enterprise software, only three organizations (2.8%) indicated to be using open source enterprise software to a large extent. Interestingly, 18 out of 23 organizations had at least 100 employees, suggesting that the adoption of open source enterprise software is primarily undertaken by medium-sized organizations. This is consistent with the recommendation of de Carvalho and Johansson (2010) that OS-ERP is primarily suited for medium-sized organizations. Overall, these findings suggest that several barriers exist with respect to the organizational adoption of OS-ERP.

We also explored which reasons exist for the non-adoption of OS-ERP by Belgian SMEs. As part of the same research discussed in the previous section (i.e., Van Nuffel & De Backer, 2010), informants in nine SMEs and one selection consultant were asked for their reasons for not adopting an OS-ERP product. The SMEs all decided to adopt an ERP system, but did not select an OS-ERP product. The selection consultant is an independent party that assists SMEs in selecting appropriate ERP software that fits their needs. This selection consultant is not affiliated in any way with specific P-ERP or OS-ERP vendors and only assists in the selection process; the actual

*Figure 1. Use of open source software by Belgian organizations (Ven, 2008)*

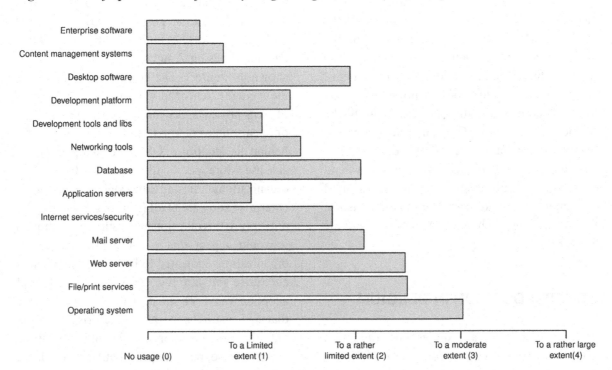

implementation of the ERP-system is left to other consultants. This selection consultant was well-informed about the Belgian ERP market. Although OS-ERP systems are taken into account by the selection consultant—especially when composing the so-called longlist—he has not recommended the use of an OS-ERP to any of its clients yet, and did not expect to do so in the near future.

Based on our data, we identified two important reasons for the non-adoption of OS-ERP. These reasons each relate to a set of selection factors identified in the literature review (see Table 2). A first barrier that was mentioned is a *lack of functionality* (cf., fulfill requirements, flexibility, and optimize business processes). Some organizations perceived that OS-ERP was not able to provide all the functionality that was required by the SME. Other organizations were not convinced that OSS in general or OS-ERP in particular was sufficiently mature and considered

it unsuitable for organizational use. It has also been noted in literature that a misfit between the functionality required by an organization and the functionality offered by the OS-ERP product is a major problem (Johansson & de Carvalho, 2009; Johansson & Sudzina, 2008). Second, organizations mentioned a *lack of external support* for OS-ERP (cf., vendor's reputation, vendor's market position, industry references, and vendor's domain knowledge). Organizations perceived that it was difficult to obtain technical expertise on OS-ERP since only a few consultants offer services related to the implementation of OS-ERP. Consistent with the research on ERP selection factors, organizations particularly expressed concerns about the ability of these consultants to provide reliable support for OS-ERP. Many of these consultants were considered too small, to be lacking reference implementations, unable to provide reliable support at all times, and not internationally active (which means that the foreign branches of the

SME cannot be served by the same consultant). Vendors of OS-ERP systems therefore do not seem to possess the characteristics desired by SMEs as listed in Table 2. In order to mitigate the perceived risks affiliated with these OS-ERP vendors, SMEs should increase their available internal technical ICT knowledge. However, SMEs were very reluctant to do so. The main reason for this is that it is difficult for SMEs to acquire sufficiently skilled resources (e.g., Caldeira & Ward, 2002). One organization expressed a specific concern with respect to the lack of support. This organization did not consider an OS-ERP system because if the ERP implementation failed, it would be very difficult to determine whether the OS-ERP consultant or the developers of the OS-ERP product are responsible. The organization further feared that if the cause of the failure was due to a lack of quality of the OS-ERP product, it would become very difficult to receive compensation. Previous studies have also identified the issue of the availability of support as an important issue in the adoption of OS-ERP (e.g., Davis, 2008; Johansson & Sudzina, 2008; Benlian & Hess, 2010).

## OS-ERP MARKET IN BELGIUM

We performed an exploratory investigation into the Belgian OS-ERP market to explore how these perceptions of organizations relate to the actual market conditions. First, we analyzed which functionality was offered by the most important OS-ERP products. This way, we could determine whether OS-ERP products were missing functionality compared to their proprietary counterparts. Second, we explored the availability of support for OS-ERP products. We focused on whether the OS-ERP product could provide any reference implementations and whether officially certified consultants for OS-ERP products were available. This allowed us to gain insight in whether organizations could rely on sufficient external support when adopting OS-ERP.

## Functionality of OS-ERP Products

In order to analyze the functionality offered by various OS-ERP products, we started by compiling a list of OS-ERP products. To this end, we used the SourceForge (http://www.sourceforge.net) and Freshmeat (http://www.freshmeat.net) websites. On SourceForge, we searched for products in the category "Office/Business–Enterprise–ERP". On Freshmeat, we searched for projects using the keyword "ERP". In order to identify the most popular OS-ERP products, we sorted both results based on the interest each open source project received. The results from SourceForge were sorted based on the number of downloads and the list from Freshmeat was based on its popularity measure. It must be noted that these measures do not fully reflect the actual use and adoption of these OS-ERP products in practice. The download of an OS-ERP product does not necessarily result in its actual adoption and use. In addition, there are other means by which the software can be obtained (e.g., through a consultant or via the version control system). However, it can be argued that popular OS-ERP products will also receive a higher number of downloads. A similar reasoning was used in the study of Johansson and Sudzina (2008). The first 20 results from both sorted lists were taken, since these products generally included the most important OS-ERP products. In order to address the potential shortcomings of sampling from SourceForge and Freshmeat, we did a manual check to verify that all OS-ERP products that are frequently mentioned in academic, practitioner, and Internet literature were included in our sample. This also addressed the issue that not all OS-ERP products are listed on SourceForge or Freshmeat. Our final list contained 36 OS-ERP products.

However, not all of these products offer the full range of functionality that is generally expected from ERP products. For example, several of these products are in essence accountancy information systems with some additional features. The same issue was noted by Davis (2008), who argued that additional research should assess whether the various OS-ERP products offer the required ERP functionality. We addressed this issue by performing a screening of the functionality offered by each OS-ERP product. Hence, a list of functionality offered by ERP products was needed. Since, to the best of our knowledge, no academic publication exists that provides such a list of functionality, we turned to practitioner literature. More specifically, the "ERP & Accountancy Guide" of Datanews was used (Datanews, 2006). Datanews is a weekly IT-magazine for professionals in Belgium. However, it has also published a special report on ERP and accountancy software which includes a market overview. This overview is generally considered a useful indication of which modules are included in the various ERP products. This overview is, however, focused on proprietary ERP products. We therefore used the list of modules included in the Datanews market overview as a basis to perform an evaluation of the functionality of the OS-ERP products that we identified.

An overview of the functionality offered by the various OS-ERP products is included in Figure 2. For each OS-ERP product, it was determined whether it provided each of the 21 modules by using information that was publicly available on the website of the OS-ERP product. A circle in Figure 2 means that it could be confirmed that a specific module is present in the OS-ERP product. It must be noted that the scores in Figure 2 are a rough assessment of the functionality supported by each OS-ERP product. The names of the modules are sometimes quite broad, while the presence or absence of a module is indicated by a binary variable. The names of the modules in our overview also do not always map directly to the terminology used by the OS-ERP products. We therefore provide a rough assessment of the OS-ERP products concerning their functionality and accept this as a limitation of our study. However, to our knowledge, no such screening has been performed before in literature. Our assessment is therefore useful in providing a general overview

of the OS-ERP products and could be a basis for future studies. It can further be expected that if an OS-ERP product does not support a large number of modules in the broad sense, it is doubtful that the product is a likely candidate to be adopted by organizations.

As can be seen, some OS-ERP products offer a wide range of modules, while other OS-ERP products offer rather limited functionality. In order to gain more insight into our data, we performed a hierarchical cluster analysis. The variables indicating the presence or absence of a module were dichotomized with a value of "1" meaning the module was present, and a value of "0" meaning the module was not present. A solution with 3 clusters was the easiest to interpret. The first cluster consisted of the first 12 products in Figure 2 and represented those products that can be considered to offer the most complete set of modules (clusters can easily be identified in this table by the alternating background color). Unsurprisingly, this list contains many widely known OS-ERP products such as Compiere, OpenBravo and Adempiere. Concerning GNU-enterprise, it must be noted that although it contains a wide set of modules, several of them are still in development and not completely finished. It must also be noted that Adempiere Brazil is essentially an extension to Adempiere to comply with the Brazilian laws and taxing schemes but is completely identical to Adempiere. As a result, we obtained a shortlist of 10 OS-ERP products that can be considered mature based on the functionality that is offered. The second cluster contains 12 products that primarily offer the functionality of an accountancy information system with some additional ERP-oriented modules. Although they offer sufficient functionality to support the accounting needs of an organization, they miss several key features of an ERP system, making it difficult to consider them "true" ERP systems. Depending on the needs of the organization, however, they may cover the required functionality of an organization. Finally, we have a cluster

*Figure 2. Functionality offered by OS-ERP products*

| Product | Ledger | Financial Reporting | Accounts Receivable | Accounts Payable | Multicurrency | Invoicing | Order Processing | Inventory | Purchase Order | Warehouse Management | Manufacturing/Bill of Materials | Production Planning | Human Resources Management | Contact Management | Customer Relationship Management | Business Intelligence | Business Process Management | Supplier Relationship Management | Supply Chain Management | Procurement | Marketing |
|---|---|---|---|---|---|---|---|---|---|---|---|---|---|---|---|---|---|---|---|---|---|
| Adempiere | • | • | • | • | • | • | • | • | • | • | • | • | • | • | • | • | • | • | • | • | • |
| Adempiere Brazil | • | • | • | • | • | • | • | • | • | • | • | • | • | • | • | • | • | • | • | • | • |
| ApacheOFBiz | • | • | • | • | • | • | • | • | • | • | • | • | | • | | | | | • | • | • |
| CK-ERP | • | • | • | • | • | • | • | • | • | • | • | • | | • | | | | • | | | |
| Compiere | • | • | • | • | • | • | • | • | • | • | • | • | | • | | | | • | | • | • |
| ERP 5 | • | • | • | • | • | • | • | • | • | • | • | • | | • | | | | • | • | • | • |
| GNU Enterprise | • | • | • | • | • | • | • | • | • | • | • | • | | • | | | | • | • | • | • |
| OpenBravo | • | • | • | • | • | • | • | • | • | • | • | • | | • | | • | • | • | | • | • |
| OpenERP | • | • | • | • | • | • | • | • | • | • | • | • | | • | | | | | | • | • |
| Opentaps | • | • | • | • | • | • | • | • | • | • | • | • | | • | | • | | • | | • | • |
| Postbooks | • | • | • | • | • | • | • | • | • | • | • | | | • | • | | | | | • | |
| WebERP | • | • | • | • | • | • | • | • | • | • | • | | | • | | | | | | • | |
| AbanQ | • | • | • | • | • | • | | | | | | • | | | | | | | | | |
| ARIA Business Management | • | • | • | • | • | • | • | • | | | | | | | | | | | | | |
| BlueERP | • | • | • | • | | • | • | • | • | | | | | • | • | | | • | | • | |
| FrontAccounting | • | • | • | • | • | • | • | • | | | • | | | | | | | | | | |
| Gazie | • | • | • | • | • | | | | | | | | | | | | | | | | |
| JFire | • | • | • | • | | • | • | | | | | | | • | • | | | | | | |
| LedgerSMB | • | • | • | • | • | • | | • | | | | | | | | | | | | | |
| OfBiz Neogia | • | • | • | • | • | • | • | | | | | • | | | • | | | | | | |
| OpenBlueLab | • | • | • | • | • | | | | | • | | | | • | • | | | | | | |
| Project Open | • | • | • | | | • | • | • | • | | | | • | • | • | | | | | | |
| Tryton | • | • | • | • | • | • | • | • | • | • | | | | | | | | | | | |
| uzERP | • | • | | | | • | • | | • | | | • | | • | • | • | | | | | |
| Achievo | | | | | | | | | | | | | • | • | • | | | | | | |
| Bots OS EDI | | | | | | | | | | | | | | | | | | | | | |
| Dolibarr | | | | | | • | • | • | • | | | | | • | • | | | | | | |
| Kalpa | | | | | | | | | | | | | | | | | | | | | |
| MaxDB | | | | | | | | | | | | | | | | | | | | | |
| Opencrx | | | | | • | • | | | | | • | | | • | • | | | • | | | • |
| OrangeHRM | | | | | | | | | | | | | • | | | | | | | | |
| Plazma | | | | | | • | | | | | | | | • | • | | | | | | • |
| REDPOS | | | | | | | | | | | | | | | | | | | | | |
| TNTConcept | | • | • | • | | | | | | | | | | • | | | | | | | |
| Tutos | | | | | | • | | • | | | | | | • | | | | | | | |
| Vtiger | | | | | • | • | • | • | • | | | | | • | | | | | | | • |

Legend:
•: Module is present in product
Note: products are sorted alphabetically within each cluster.

of 12 products that lack many key features of an ERP system and that tend to focus on a particular application. Several products are, for example, essentially HRM (e.g., OrangeHRM) or CRM (e.g., Vtiger and Opencrx) applications.

## Support for OS-ERP Products

Having determined which functionality is offered by the various OS-ERP products, we continued by assessing to which degree support is available to organizations that are interested in adopting OS-ERP. We focused hereby on the shortlist of 10 products, since those have been shown to offer a rather complete feature set.

As shown in Table 2, an important selection factor in the adoption of ERP for Belgian SMEs is that the vendor is able to present reference projects ("industry references"). These reference projects demonstrate that the product can be implemented in a real-life environment. We therefore determined to which degree reference projects were available for the various OS-ERP products. We restricted ourselves to using the information that is publicly available on the website of the OS-ERP vendor. Evidently, the installed base of the OS-ERP product is likely to be larger than suggested by the cases mentioned on the various websites. However, the exact number of users of an OS-ERP product cannot be accurately determined since the software can be freely downloaded and installed without the knowledge of the OS-ERP vendor. Hence, we do not intend this to be an indication of the total customer base of each OS-ERP product. Nevertheless, these cases are highlighted by the OS-ERP vendors to attract the interest of potential customers. These potential customers will also rely on the information on the vendor's website to obtain information about the maturity and support of the OS-ERP product.

An overview of the number of reference projects for each OS-ERP product is shown in Table 3. Since our focus in this chapter is on the Belgian market, we distinguished between reference projects in Belgian organizations, organizations in the neighboring countries (The Netherlands, France, and Germany), other countries in the EU, and the rest of the world. Each cell in the table shows the number of reference projects in a specific region for a specific product. In case the website did not contain any information with respect to reference projects, a dash has been used.

It can be seen in Table 3 that OpenBravo, Apache OFBiz, Opentaps, and Compiere have the largest number of reference projects. However, the number of reference projects in Belgium is very limited. Only Compiere, OpenERP and Apache OFBiz make mention of a reference project in Belgium. Opentaps and OpenBravo are also able to present one and two reference projects, respectively, in the neighboring countries. Concerning ERP5, it must be noted that our information refers to the Tiolive product. Tiolive is a SaaS (Software as a Service) version of ERP5 that offers the same functionality, but is offered through a hosted web platform. The reference projects that are listed on the official ERP5 website refer to two successful implementations of this SaaS version of ERP5. The ERP5 website further states that this SaaS version is recommended for SMEs, and that 8,000 organizations are making use of Tiolive. It is further surprising to see that 3 out of 10 OS-ERP products did not list any information about reference projects on their website (i.e., Adempiere, CK-ERP, and WebERP). Notwithstanding the fact that these products were found to have a rather complete set of functionality, they fail to provide any evidence that the software has been implemented by organizations. This may be a considerable barrier to their adoption by organizations.

Next, we investigated to which degree each OS-ERP product has officially recognized partners that guide the selection, implementation and maintenance. We limited ourselves to those consultants that are officially recognized by the OS-ERP vendor since this can be considered a sign of quality. Potential customers will prefer to rely on

*Table 3. Reference projects for selected OS-ERP products*

| Product | Belgium | Neighbours[a] | European Union | World | Total |
|---|---|---|---|---|---|
| Adempiere | – | – | – | – | – |
| Apache OFBiz | 1 | 5 | 10 | 42 | 58 |
| CK-ERP | – | – | – | – | – |
| Compiere | 2 | 6 | 5 | 5 | 18 |
| ERP5[b] | 0 | 0 | 1 | 1 | 2 |
| OpenBravo | 0 | 2 | 40 | 22 | 64 |
| OpenERP | 1 | 4 | 2 | 2 | 9 |
| Opentaps | 0 | 1 | 10 | 18 | 29 |
| Postbooks | 0 | 0 | 0 | 6 | 6 |
| WebERP | – | – | – | – | – |

*Legend:*

*a: France, The Netherlands, Germany*

*b: Data for Tiolive*

*–: No data available*

a partner that is officially recognized, quite similar to the adoption of proprietary ERP systems (Keil & Tiwana, 2006). Nevertheless, it must be noted that our overview will underestimate the actual number of consultants providing services for OS-ERP. Given our focus on the Belgian market, we distinguished between consultants that are active in Belgium, The Netherlands, France, Germany, and the rest of the EU.

As can be seen in Table 4, officially recognized consultants are available in Belgium for 5 OS-ERP products (Apache OFBiz, Compiere, ERP5, OpenBravo, and OpenERP). The large number of consultants available for OpenERP can be explained by the fact that OpenERP is an open source project initiated by a Belgian company, thereby stimulating the development of an ecosystem consisting of various local organizations that support the further development and implementation of OpenERP. A similar situation exists with the OpenBravo project that has its origins in Spain, where it has more than 30 listed reference projects and partners. Concerning ERP5, it must again be noted that our data refers to the

Tiolive product. The official ERP5 website does not publish a list of partners, but refers to the Tiolive website where a number of partners are listed for the SaaS version of ERP5. It was also noted that two OS-ERP products did not list any officially recognized partners on their website (i.e., Adempiere and CK-ERP). The Postbooks project seemed primarily US-oriented, and did not list any other partners than the organization that was driving the further development of the project.

## DISCUSSION

Our previous research suggested that a lack of functionality and a lack of support may be important concerns in the adoption of OS-ERP. Based on our screening of the functionality of and support options for OS-ERP in the preceding section, we can now assess how these concerns compare with the Belgian OS-ERP market.

The analysis of the functionality offered by the OS-ERP products showed that several products had a large set of features. More specifically, 10

*Table 4. Partners for selected OS-ERP products*

| Product | Belgium | The Netherlands | France | Germany | European Union |
|---|---|---|---|---|---|
| Adempiere | – | – | – | – | – |
| Apache OFBiz | 2 | 0 | 3 | 7 | 17 |
| CK-ERP | – | – | – | – | – |
| Compiere | 2 | 2 | 3 | 3 | 11 |
| ERP5[a] | 1 | 0 | 5 | 0 | 2 |
| OpenBravo | 3 | 3 | 2 | 2 | 49 |
| OpenERP | 18 | 4 | 29 | 3 | 16 |
| Opentaps | 0 | 0 | 0 | 0 | 3 |
| Postbooks | 0 | 0 | 0 | 0 | 0 |
| WebERP | 0 | 1 | 0 | 0 | 7 |

*Legend:*

*a: Data for Tiolive*

*–: No data available*

OS-ERP products were found to be rather comprehensive in this respect. However, there were also a large number of OS-ERP products that have a rather to very limited set of functionality. Hence, it may be difficult for organizations to separate the wheat from the chaff. The fact that a large number of OS-ERP products with limited functionality exist may also contribute to the perception of organizations that important functionality is missing from OS-ERP products in general. It must also be noted that we did not investigate to which degree each module is implemented in the OS-ERP products. For example, several OS-ERP products were found to have an "invoicing" module. However, we did not investigate which specific features were supported by this module, such as whether the module is able to cope with the various legal and tax requirements surrounding the invoicing process in different countries (this may be an important requirement if the organization is active in several countries). As a result, the actual functionality offered by the various OS-ERP products may be less than suggested by Figure 2. In addition, it was sometimes difficult to determine which functionality was supported by

each OS-ERP product. This was caused by the fact that some websites offer very general information about the supported features or modules, or offer this information in various places. This may be a concern for potential adopters who may find it difficult to obtain clear and complete information about the OS-ERP product.

Concerning the support available for the 10 OS-ERP products, it was surprising to establish that four of them were not able to present reference projects and/or to offer officially approved partners in various countries. It can be observed in Table 4 that—with the exception of Open-ERP—the number of consultants is rather low in Belgium, as well as in The Netherlands, France, and Germany. It has indeed been noted that the certification process for OS-ERP consultants is still in its early phases (de Carvalho & Johansson, 2010). Although it can be expected that the number of certified partners will increase in the future, this is still an important issue for organizations. A related potential problem is that most of these partners are small and locally oriented organizations instead of medium to large organizations that are active in several countries. Hence, if the

SME has offices abroad, it may not be able to use the same consultant in its various offices. This is also an important concern since the globalization process has led an increasing number of SMEs to be active in multiple countries (de Carvalho & Johansson, 2010). In addition, the website of only 6 out of the 26 Belgian OS-ERP partners made mention of one or more reference projects that were performed by the partner itself. Although the absence of this information on the website does not necessarily mean that the other consultants have not performed any OS-ERP implementations in the past, it may still be a concern for potential customers. Hence, notwithstanding the fact that reference implementations of the OS-ERP product are available in other EU countries, successful implementations within Belgium may be more difficult to find.

Overall, based on this screening, it appears that a lack of functionality should not necessarily be a major barrier to the adoption of OS-ERP. However, it appears that a lack of support is still an important issue and is probably one of the most important barriers to the further adoption of OS-ERP. This is also consistent with the conclusions of Benlian and Hess (2010) who have found that product-related criteria (e.g., functionality) are more important in the adoption of P-ERP, while implementation-related criteria (e.g., support) are more important in the adoption of OS-ERP. It also reflects their observation that organizations are generally rather satisfied with the functionality offered by OS-ERP, while they are quite dissatisfied with the ease of obtaining support (Benlian & Hess, 2010).

It was also interesting to observe that the website of several OS-ERP products was primarily oriented towards a technical audience, emphasizing the further development of the product and how one can contribute, instead of listing information that is relevant to organizations that are considering to adopt the product (such as featuring a number of reference projects and referring to partners that can assist in the selection and implementa-

tion process). This is actually a serious concern, since the adoption of an ERP system represents a significant investment for an SME. More specifically, it has been established that the adoption of an ERP system frequently ranks within the top 5 of investments of Belgian SMEs (Van Nuffel & De Backer, 2007). Hence, OS-ERP vendors should pay sufficient attention to providing information that is relevant in supporting a business decision and to create trust in the OS-ERP product.

Based on our screening, it can be concluded that finding a suitable OS-ERP product may be a difficult search for organizations, since only a few products seem sufficiently developed at this time to be adopted by organizations. Taking into account the functionality and support offered by the various OS-ERP products, we expect the following OS-ERP products to be the most likely candidates to be adopted by organizations: Apache OFBiz, Compiere, ERP5 (mainly Tiolive), OpenBravo, OpenERP, and Opentaps. This list was obtained by starting from the list of 10 OS-ERP products that were found to have a large feature set and by eliminating those products that could not present any reference projects or approved partners in the EU. Specifically concerning the Belgian market, we would be inclined to exclude Opentaps, since only a single reference implementation and no partners were available in Belgium or its neighboring countries. This selection is quite consistent with the set of OS-ERP products considered by Johansson and Sudzina (2008) based on the recommendation of an OS-ERP consultant. Their selection included: Compiere, OpenBravo, TinyERP (which has been renamed to OpenERP), Opentaps, Facturalux, and WebERP (Johansson & Sudzina, 2008). Facturalux (which has been renamed to AbanQ) was excluded in our list due to the limited set of functionality (although it could be useful for organizations looking for an accountancy information system), and the lack of English documentation. WebERP was excluded due to the lack of reference projects and a rather low number of partners. The addition of Apache

OFBiz may be explained by the progress this project has made since the study of Johansson and Sudzina (2008).

## FUTURE RESEARCH

Given its exploratory nature, our study has a number of limitations that give rise to various suggestions for further research.

A first limitation of our study is that we have focused on the situation in Belgium. Hence, our findings with respect to the availability of reference projects and external support do not necessarily hold for other regions and countries. It can indeed be noted that regional differences can be very important in this respect. Given the fact that the OpenERP project originated in Belgium (and Walloon in particular), it has many consultants available in Belgium and France, while to a lesser extent in the other EU countries. Another example is OpenBravo, that originated in Spain and where it can present several reference projects and partners. Hence, future research could focus in the situation in other countries.

A second limitation is that we used a binary variable to indicate the absence or presence of a particular module in the assessment of the functionality of the various OS-ERP products. As mentioned before, our overview does not indicate to which degree the functionality is actually supported by each product and therefore provides a rough indication of the supported functionality. The results derived from Figure 2 should therefore be treated with some caution. It would be interesting that future research tries to gain a more fine-grained insight into the functionality offered by OS-ERP products. One way would be to use an empirical, case-based approach in which the requirements of a real-life ERP system of a number of organizations are taken and matched with the functionality offered by a set of OS-ERP

products. This would provide empirical evidence with respect to whether the functionality of OS-ERP products is sufficient.

Future research could also be conducted on determining which OS-ERP products are adopted by organizations. Based on our screening, we have identified a list of six products that we expect to be most likely candidates to be adopted by organizations. A survey across a large number of organizations could provide more insight into the extent to which OS-ERP products are adopted and which specific products are selected by organizations. Such studies should also capture the purpose of, and the functionality that needs to be supported by, the OS-ERP system. This would avoid bias in the results when it would appear that an organization adopted a specific product for their ERP system, while it is only used to support a specific domain. For instance, some organizations may adopt an OS-ERP system primarily to cover their accounting needs and have no interest in using it to support their HRM or CRM needs. This would be important information for other organizations considering to adopt an OS-ERP product.

Finally, we would like to call for additional empirical research on the organizational adoption of OS-ERP, since those studies can provide more insight in how organizations perceive these products. Such studies could either focus on the barriers to or enablers for the organizational adoption of OS-ERP. Such studies could also compare the perception of organizations to the various claims made in the literature. For example, several studies on OS-ERP have suggested that the avoidance of vendor lock-in is an important advantage of OS-ERP (e.g., de Carvalho & Johansson, 2010; Serrano & Sarriegi, 2006). This reasoning is based on the fact that the source code of OS-ERP is freely available, making the organization independent from a specific vendor for support and further updates. However, our screening has shown that there are only a few partners available in some countries.

This means that organizations are still dependent on a limited number of consultants to support their OS-ERP product. Future studies could therefore provide more insight into whether organizations actually still perceive vendor lock-in an important advantage in such contexts.

## CONCLUSION

At this moment, OS-ERP is not considered a viable solution by most Belgian organizations and its adoption is very limited. We therefore conducted an exploratory investigation into which barriers inhibit the adoption of OS-ERP by Belgian SMEs. To this end, we started from the general ERP literature and further built upon our own previous research on the adoption of ERP by Belgian SMEs. Our empirical work identified two main barriers: a lack of functionality and a lack of support. We subsequently performed a screening of the Belgian OS-ERP market to investigate the functionality and support offered by various OS-ERP products. This allowed us to determine how the perceptions of organizations compare to the actual Belgian OS-ERP market. It was shown that 10 OS-ERP products seemed rather complete in terms of functionality, although many other products were found to be missing specific functionality. Overall, this suggests that it is possible to find OS-ERP products with sufficient functionality. However, the support available for OS-ERP products in terms of the availability of reference projects and certified partners appeared problematic. This suggests that a lack of support is one of the main barriers to the further adoption of OS-ERP. Vendors offering OS-ERP products should address this issue in order to boost the further adoption of OS-ERP. Based on this screening of the market, a list of 6 OS-ERP products was identified that appear to be the most likely candidates to be adopted by organizations, i.e., Apache OFBiz, Compiere, ERP5 (mainly Tiolive), OpenBravo, OpenERP, and Opentaps.

Given the exploratory nature of this study, this study has identified several interesting avenues for future research.

## REFERENCES

Baki, B., & Cakar, K. (2005). Determining the ERP package-selecting criteria: the case of Turkish manufacturing companies. *Business Process Management Journal, 11*(1), 75–86. doi:10.1108/14637150510578746

Benlian, A., & Hess, T. (2010). Comparing the relative importance of evaluation criteria in proprietary and open-source enterprise application software selection: a conjoint study of ERP and office systems. *Information Systems Journal.* (Early view)

Bernroider, E., & Koch, S. (2001). ERP selection process in midsize and large organizations. *Business Process Management Journal, 7*(3), 251–257. doi:10.1108/14637150110392746

Brydon, M., & Vinning, A. R. (2008). Adoption, improvement, and disruption: Predicting the impact of open source applications in enterprise software markets. *Journal of Database Management, 19*(2), 73–94. doi:10.4018/jdm.2008040104

Caldeira, M. M., & Ward, J. M. (2002). Understanding the successful adoption and use of IS/IT in SME's: an explanation from Portuguese manufacturing industries. *Information Systems Journal, 12*(2), 121–152. doi:10.1046/j.1365-2575.2002.00119.x

Chau, P. Y. K. (1995). Factors used in the selection of packaged software in small business: views of owners and managers. *Information & Management, 29*, 71–78. doi:10.1016/0378-7206(95)00016-P

Datanews. (2006, September). *Erp & accountancy guide.* Appendix to number 32.

Davis, A. (2008). Enterprise resource planning under open source software. In Ferran, C., & Salim, R. K. (Eds.), *Enterprise resource planning for global economies: Managerial issues and challenges* (pp. 56–76). Hershey, PA: Information Science Reference. doi:10.4018/978-1-59904-531-3.ch004

de Carvalho, R. A. (2009). Free and open source enterprise resources planning. In Gupta, J. N. D., Sharma, S., & Rashid, M. A. (Eds.), *Handbook of research on enterprise systems* (pp. 32–44). Hershey, PA: IGI Global. doi:10.4018/978-1-59904-859-8.ch003

de Carvalho, R. A., & Johansson, B. (2010). Enterprise resource planning systems for small and medium-sized enterprises. In Ramachandran, M., & de Carvalho, R. A. (Eds.), *Handbook of research on software engineering and productivity technologies: Implications of globalization* (pp. 373–381). Hershey, PA: IGI Global.

Deep, A., Guttridge, P., Dani, S., & Burns, N. (2008). Investigating factors affecting ERP selection in made-to-order SME sector. *Journal of Manufacturing Technology Management, 19*(4), 430–446. doi:10.1108/17410380810869905

Eisenhardt, K. M. (1989). Building theories from case study research. *Academy of Management Review, 14*(4), 532–550.

European Commission. (2003). *Commission recommendation of 6 may 2003 concerning the definition of micro, small and medium-sized enterprises (2003/362/ec)* (Vol. 46) (No. L124/36).

European Commission. (2009a). *European SMEs under pressure: Annual report on EU small and medium-sized enterprises 2009*.

European Commission. (2009b). *SBA fact sheet*. Belgium.

Fitzgerald, B. (2005). Has open source software a future? In Feller, J., Fitzgerald, B., Hissam, S. A., & Lakhani, K. R. (Eds.), *Perspectives on free and open source software* (pp. 93–106). Cambridge, MA: MIT Press.

Fitzgerald, B. (2006). The transformation of open source software. *Management Information Systems Quarterly, 30*(3), 587–598.

Hallikainen, P., Kivijrvi, H., Rossi, M., Sarpola, S., & Talvinen, J. (2002). Evaluating IT investments: Selection of ERP software in finnish SME's. In *Proceedings of the 13th Australian conference on information systems (ACIS 2002)*.

Johansson, B., & de Carvalho, R. A. (2009). Management of requirements in ERP development: A comparison between proprietary and open source ERP. In *Proceedings of the 24th annual ACM symposium on applied computing, Honolulu, Hawaii, March 9–12, 2009* (pp. 1605–1609). New York: ACM.

Johansson, B., & Sudzina, F. (2008). ERP systems and open source: an initial review and some implications for SMEs. *Journal of Enterprise Information Management, 21*(6), 649–658. doi:10.1108/17410390810911230

Johansson, B., & Sudzina, F. (2009). Choosing open source ERP systems: What reasons are there for doing so? In C. Boldyreff, K. Crowston, B. Lundell, & A. I. Wasserman (Eds.), *Open source ecosystems: Diverse communities interacting, proceedings of the 5th IFIP WG 2.13 international conference on open source systems (OSS 2009), Skövde, Sweden, June 3–6, 2009* (Vol. 299, pp. 143–155). Berlin: Springer.

Keil, M., & Tiwana, A. (2006). Relative importance of evaluation criteria for enterprise systems: a conjoint study. *Information Systems Journal, 16*, 237–262. doi:10.1111/j.1365-2575.2006.00218.x

Kim, H., & Boldyreff, C. (2005). Open source ERP for SMEs. In *Proceedings of the 3rd international conference on manufacturing research (ICMR 2005)*, Cranfield, UK, September 6–8, 2005. Cranfield, U.K.: Cranfield University.

Mabert, V. A., Soni, A., & Venkataramanan, M. A. (2003). The impact of organisation size on enterprise resource planning (ERP) implementations in the US manufacturing sector. *Omega, 31*(3), 235–246. doi:10.1016/S0305-0483(03)00022-7

Serrano, N., & Sarriegi, J. M. (2006). Open source software ERPs: A new alternative for an old need. *IEEE Software, 23*(3), 94–97. doi:10.1109/MS.2006.78

van Everdingen, Y., Van Hillegersberg, J., & Waarts, E. (2000). ERP adoption by European midsize companies. *Communications of the ACM, 43*(4), 27–31. doi:10.1145/332051.332064

Van Nuffel, D., & De Backer, C. (2007). Ook kleine ondernemingen hebben een ERP-pakket nodig. *Informatie, 49*(1), 35–39.

Van Nuffel, D., & De Backer, C. (2010). *ERP acquisition within SMEs: A holistic study.* (Working paper)

Ven, K. (2008). *The organizational adoption of open source server software: An information systems innovation perspective.* Unpublished PhD dissertation, Universiteit Antwerpen, Antwerp, Belgium.

Ven, K., Van Nuffel, D., & Verelst, J. (2007). The migration of public administrations towards open source desktop software: Recommendations from research and validation through a case study. In Sowe, S. K., Stamelos, I., & Samoladas, I. (Eds.), *Emerging free and open source software practices* (pp. 191–214). Hershey, PA: IGI Publishing. doi:10.4018/978-1-59904-210-7.ch009

Yin, R. K. (2003). *Case study research: Design and methods* (3rd ed.). Newbury Park, CA: Sage Publications.

## ADDITIONAL READING

Bi, C., Zhao, L., Liu, J., & Shu, H. (2008). Analysis of open source software in enterprise informatization. In Xu, L., Tjoa, A., & Chaudhry, S. (Eds.), *Research and practical issues of enterprise information systems II* (*Vol. 1*, pp. 669–676). Boston, MA: Springer. doi:10.1007/978-0-387-75902-9_75

Chen, R.-S., Sun, C.-M., Helms, M. M., & Jih, W.-J. (2008). Role negotiation and interaction: An exploratory case study of the impact of management consultants on ERP system implementation in SMEs in Taiwan. *Information Systems Management, 25*(2), 159–173. doi:10.1080/10580530801941371

Daffara, C. (2009). *The SME guide to open source software, 4th edition.* Retrieved December 17, 2010 from http://smeguide.conecta.it/smeguide.pdf.

Davenport, T. H. (1998). Putting the enterprise into the enterprise system. *Harvard Business Review, 76*(4), 121–131.

de Carvalho, R. A. (2006). Issues on evaluating free/open source ERP systems. In Tjoa, A., Xu, L., & Chaudhry, S. (Eds.), *Research and practical issues of enterprise information systems* (*Vol. 205*, pp. 667–675). Boston, MA: Springer. doi:10.1007/0-387-34456-X_72

Dreiling, A., Klaus, H., Rosemann, M., & Wyssusek, B. (2005). Open source enterprise systems: Towards a viable alternative. In *Proceedings of the 38th Hawaii international conference on system sciences (HICSS'05)*, Waiikoloa, HI, January 3–6, 2005 (p. 227b). Los Alamitos, CA: IEEE Computer Society.

Erbizzoni, E., Teli, M., Campagnolo, G., De Paoli, S., & D'Andrea, V. (2006). Free/open source ERP and translation processes: Four empirical cases. In Tjoa, A., Xu, L., & Chaudhry, S. (Eds.), *Research and practical issues of enterprise information systems* (*Vol. 205*, pp. 695–704). Boston, MA: Springer. doi:10.1007/0-387-34456-X_76

Fitzgerald, B. (2009). Open source software adoption: Anatomy of success and failure. *International Journal of Open Source Software and Processes*, *1*(1), 1–23. doi:10.4018/jossp.2009010101

Grabski, S. V., & Leech, S. A. (2007). Complementary controls and ERP implementation success. *International Journal of Accounting Information Systems*, *8*(1), 17–39. doi:10.1016/j.accinf.2006.12.002

Hauge, O., Ayala, C., & Conradi, R. (2010). Adoption of open source software in software-intensive organizations - a systematic literature review. *Information and Software Technology*, *52*(11), 1133–1154. doi:10.1016/j.infsof.2010.05.008

Hong, K.-K., & Kim, Y.-G. (2002). The critical success factors for ERP implementation: an organizational fit perspective. *Information & Management*, *40*(1), 25–40. doi:10.1016/S0378-7206(01)00134-3

Howcroft, D., & Light, B. (2008). IT consultants, salesmanship and the challenges of packaged software selection in SMEs. *Journal of Enterprise Information Management*, *21*(6), 597–615. doi:10.1108/17410390810911203

Imtiaz, A., Hauge, J., & Chen, S. (2007). Collaboration within the tool-and-die manufacturing industry through open-source modular ERP/CRM systems. In Camarinha-Matos, L., Afsarmanesh, H., Novais, P., & Analide, C. (Eds.), *Establishing the foundation of collaborative networks* (*Vol. 243*, pp. 469–476). Boston, MA: Springer. doi:10.1007/978-0-387-73798-0_50

Jadhav, A. S., & Sonar, R. M. (2009). Evaluating and selecting software packages: A review. *Information and Software Technology*, *51*(3), 555–563. doi:10.1016/j.infsof.2008.09.003

Johansson, B. (2008). Knowledge diffusion in ERP development: The case of open source ERP downloads. In León, G., Bernardos, A., Casar, J., Kautz, K., & De Gross, J. (Eds.), *Open IT-based innovation: Moving towards cooperative IT transfer and knowledge diffusion* (*Vol. 287*, pp. 247–259). Boston, MA: Springer. doi:10.1007/978-0-387-87503-3_14

Loh, T., & Koh, S. (2004). Critical elements for a successful enterprise resource planning implementation in small- and medium-sized enterprises. *International Journal of Production Research*, *42*(17), 3433–3455. doi:10.1080/00207540410001671679

Lundell, B., Lings, B., & Lindqvist, E. (2010). Open source in Swedish companies: Where are we? *Information Systems Journal*, *20*(6), 519–535. doi:10.1111/j.1365-2575.2010.00348.x

Malhotra, R., & Temponi, C. (2010). Critical decisions for ERP integration: Small business issues. *International Journal of Information Management*, *30*, 28–37. doi:10.1016/j.ijinfomgt.2009.03.001

Momoh, A., Roy, R., & Shehab, E. (2010). Challenges in enterprise resource planning implementation: state-of-the-art. *Business Process Management Journal*, *16*(4), 537–565. doi:10.1108/14637151011065919

Morgan, L., & Finnegan, P. (2010). Open innovation in secondary software firms: an exploration of managers' perceptions of open source software. *SIGMIS Database*, *41*(1), 76–95.

Morton, N. A., & Hu, Q. (2008). Implications of the fit between organizational structure and ERP: A structural contingency theory perspective. *International Journal of Information Management, 28*(5), 391–402. doi:10.1016/j.ijinfomgt.2008.01.008

Muscatello, J. R., Small, M. H., & Chen, I. J. (2003). Implementing enterprise resource planning (ERP) systems in small and midsize manufacturing firms. *International Journal of Operations & Production Management, 23*(8), 850–871. doi:10.1108/01443570310486329

Nicolás, R. B., & Jaime, N. C. (2006). Enterprise applications: Taking the open source option seriously. In Avison, D., Elliot, S., Krogstie, J., & Pries-Heje, J. (Eds.), *The past and future of information systems: 1976–2006 and beyond* (*Vol. 214*, pp. 107–118). Boston, MA: Springer. doi:10.1007/978-0-387-34732-5_11

Olhager, J., & Selldin, E. (2003). Enterprise resource planning survey of Swedish manufacturing firms. *European Journal of Operational Research, 146*(2), 365–373. doi:10.1016/S0377-2217(02)00555-6

Poon, P.-L., & Yu, Y. T. (2010). Investigating ERP systems procurement practice: Hong Kong and Australian experiences. *Information and Software Technology, 52*(10), 1011–1022. doi:10.1016/j.infsof.2010.04.003

Rist, O., & McAllister, N. (2005). ERP. *InfoWorld, 27*(32), 43–47.

Ven, K., & Mannaert, H. (2008). Challenges and strategies in the use of open source software by independent software vendors. *Information and Software Technology, 50*(9/10), 991–1002. doi:10.1016/j.infsof.2007.09.001

Ven, K., & Verelst, J. (2008). The impact of ideology on the organizational adoption of open source software. *Journal of Database Management, 19*(2), 58–72. doi:10.4018/jdm.2008040103

Ven, K., Verelst, J., & Mannaert, H. (2008). Should you adopt open source software? *IEEE Software, 25*(3), 54–59. doi:10.1109/MS.2008.73

Verville, J., & Halingten, A. (2003). A six-stage model of the buying process for ERP software. *Industrial Marketing Management, 32*(7), 585–594. doi:10.1016/S0019-8501(03)00007-5

Verville, J., Palanisamy, R., Bernadas, C., & Halingten, A. (2007). ERP acquisition planning: A critical dimension for making the right choice. *Long Range Planning, 40*(1), 45–63. doi:10.1016/j.lrp.2007.02.002

## KEY TERMS AND DEFINITIONS

**Consultant:** A third party that assists an organization in the selection, implementation, and/or configuration of an ERP system.

**Enterprise Resource Planning (ERP):** ERP systems support the business processes of an organization. An ERP system is an integrated application suite consisting of different ERP modules and provides a company-wide information system.

**Enterprise Resource Planning (ERP) Module:** An ERP system consists of various modules that each provide the functionality required for a functional domain within an organization. These modules can often be bought separately, depending on the needs of the customer. Frequently used modules include accountancy, invoicing, customer relationship management and marketing.

**Open Source Enterprise Resource Planning (OS-ERP):** ERP systems that are distributed under an open source software license.

**Open Source Software:** Software that is licensed under a license that is compliant with the Open Source Definition (see http://www.opensource.org/osd.html). In general, such license provides users the right to view, modify, and redistribute the source code of the application.

**Small and Medium-Sized Enterprise (SME):** Within Europe, an SME is defined as an organization that consists of less than 250 employees, that has a turnover of maximum €50 million, and that has a balance sheet total of at most €43 million.

**Reference Project:** An ERP consultant generally mentions a number of reference projects on its website to illustrate that the consultant has already successfully completed the implementation of the ERP system in a number of organizations. This should convince potential customers that this ERP system and consultant would also be a good solution for their organization.

**Partner:** A partner is a consultant that is officially recognized by the vendor of the ERP system. Such partners generally enjoy a privileged relationship with the ERP vendor. Towards potential customers, the partnership also acts as a guarantee that the consultant is a reliable party to guide the implementation of the ERP system.

**Vendor:** A vendor is the company that develops and markets an ERP system. This can be either a proprietary or an open source ERP system.

# Chapter 11
# Security Management Issues for Open Source ERP in the NGN Environment

**Mirjana Stojanovic**
*University of Belgrade, Serbia*

**Vladanka Acimovic-Raspopovic**
*University of Belgrade, Serbia*

**Slavica Bostjancic Rakas**
*University of Belgrade, Serbia*

## ABSTRACT

*This chapter aims to provide a critical evaluation of security issues and potential solutions related to the use of free and open enterprise resource planning (FOS ERP) systems in highly dynamic and heterogeneous next generation networks (NGN). The authors first present a brief state of the art with respect to technologies, features and applicability of the existing security solutions for ERP systems. Second, they address security issues in FOS ERP systems. Further, they consider research directions concerning NGN infrastructure security, with a particular focus to the importance of building advanced security management systems. Properly defined service level agreement between the customer and the provider represents a starting point for provisioning of secure services with the required quality. The authors also propose policy-based security management architecture, in a wider context of quality of service management system.*

## INTRODUCTION

Development of free and open source (FOS) technologies in enterprise resource planning (ERP) has gained a strong momentum in the past few years and resulted in a number of mature solutions that had been successfully applied in practice[1]. Among numerous advantages of FOS ERP, the most obvious are the absence of expenses for software purchase and installation, reduction of operational expenses and efficient customization/upgrade according to specific enterprise needs.

DOI: 10.4018/978-1-61350-486-4.ch011

Security is an integral part of any software development. Key aspects that affect the degree of software dependability include the expertise to develop a secure product, quality of development tools, the level of testing carried out before releasing the product and the matured practices followed throughout the development cycle (Vadalasetty, 2003).

Communication requirements of the enterprise market differ for the small office/home office (SOHO), small and medium enterprise (SME), large enterprise and international corporation. However, advances in networking technologies create a new opportunity for all of them to become more efficient and competitive by interconnecting sites, deploying collaborative applications, increasing remote access of telecommuters and mobile users, and integrating heterogeneous telecommunication services over the same network (Stojanovic & Acimovic-Raspopovic, 2009).

The future telecommunications infrastructure will be built upon the concept of next generation network (NGN). NGN refers to an architecture of telecommunication core and access networks, which assumes transport of all information and services over a common network, typically built around the Internet Protocol (IP). In the NGN environment, many access networks may exist using various wired or wireless technologies. New service providers could enter and exit the market everyday. There is a strong need for end-to-end quality of service (QoS) provisioning, according to specific user requirements. Besides, support of generalized mobility is required, which is defined as "the ability for the user or other mobile entities to communicate and access services irrespective of changes of the location or technical environment" (International Telecommunication Union – Telecommunication Standardization Sector [ITU-T], 2004, p.2). Finally, an essential feature of NGN should be the disappearing distinction between users and the network. Deployment of IP services should be based on virtual networks that divide the transport network into multiple self-managed

subsystems. Under such circumstances, service providers need to define appropriate strategies quickly to address the business market, increase revenue, stay competitive, and increase market share (Mordelet, Festraets, & Wang, 2006).

This chapter aims to provide a critical evaluation of security issues and potential solutions related to the use of FOS ERP in a highly dynamic and heterogeneous NGN environment. We first present a brief state of the art with respect to technologies, features and applicability of the existing security solutions for ERP systems. Second, we address security issues in FOS ERP systems. Further, we consider research directions concerning NGN infrastructure security, with a particular focus to the importance of building advanced security management systems.

The objective of our research is to address the following open questions:

- Are FOS ERP tools more or less vulnerable than the commercial ones?
- Are security problems posing limitations to the applicability area of FOS ERP?
- How can services that are provided through a heterogeneous NGN environment be secured?
- What is the role of security management system, and which principles should be applied for designing such a system?

## BACKGROUND

ERP system tends to provide a complete business solution at the enterprise level. It assembles software modules like marketing, sale, user support, supply chain, distribution, industrial resource management, process design and development, quality, human resources, finances and account-keeping, information services. The most widespread commercial solutions of ERP software (proprietary ERP, P-ERP) include SAP AG, Oracle, PeopleSoft, SAGE, Microsoft Business Solutions, etc. Contemporary ERP systems assume integration of business processes with the enterprise communication infrastructure and the Internet, which may include collaborative business, e-procurement, e-commerce (De Búrca & Fynes, 2003).

In spite of obvious advantages of ERP systems, statistic research has shown low rate of successful implementations (Somers & Nelson, 2004; Iskanius, 2009). Many ERP implementations have been difficult, long lasting and expensive. Experiences have also shown that commercial ERP implementations represent projects of high risk for SMEs, particularly if the cost overruns the projected budget (Cereola, 2008). For that reason, FOS ERP systems are often targeted to enterprises whose requirements are not covered by standard software. Similar circumstances apply to organizations that need continuous adaptation of the software to changing processes and needs. Atem de Carvalho and Johansson (2010) provide an in-depth comparative analysis of FOS ERP and P-ERP adoption for SMEs, regarding concept, requirements and preliminary design, detailed design and implementation, and operation.

Security of ERP systems includes the needed operations to avoid the loss of information, the prevention of physical and logical attacks to the system or the insurance of the buildings facing human or natural errors. Although security of FOS ERP systems has been recognized as an important issue, so far it has not been sufficiently addressed in the literature.

Van Holsbeck and Johnson (2004) state that "for most enterprises, ERP security starts with user-based controls where authorized users log in with a secure username and password". Enterprises then limit a user's system access based on their individual, customized authorization level. Role-based security mechanisms allow the definition of different levels of access rights. Users are allowed to view and change only the data they need for their work. A security system based on usernames, passwords, and authorization

codes is difficult to keep up to date with employee promotions, terminations, and reassignments; new customers, contracts and business partners; and frequent installations of new and updated software modules (Russell, 2006).

Marnewick and Labuschagne (2005) claim that the security must form an integral part of ERP system and propose a generic information security framework for ERP systems. The framework consists of three interdependent components: people, technology and policy. The security framework is mapped on the ERP model to provide the organization with a clear understanding of which security issues must be addressed within which ERP component. Hertenberger (2005) proposes a reference framework for security in ERP systems relying on approach that employs open source principles.

Hendrawirawan, Tanriverdi, Zetterlund, et al. (2007) identify the following major challenges in auditing ERP security:

- Complexity of ERP systems, which leads to security vulnerabilities;
- Lack or inadequacy of ERP tools for security audit;
- Customization of ERP systems to specific enterprise needs, which may inhibit the deployment of standardized security solutions;
- Lack of experts who are trained in ERP security;
- Inadequate attention to ERP security during deployment.

Information assurance implicitly assumes that the network devices responsible for encrypting, forwarding and sending packets are trustworthy. For that reason, there is a compelling need to develop architectures, algorithms, and protocols to realize a dependable network infrastructure (Chakrabarti & Manimaran, 2002). Another problem appears in the case of rapid changes of resource availability, e.g., due to failure of a network segment. This problem is generally related to security policies and adaptive mechanisms, which may be efficient in securing mission critical services from different kinds of attacks (Zou, Duffield, Towsley, & Gong, 2006).

Securing network services and infrastructure becomes extremely important as the Software as a Service (SaaS) paradigm is rapidly emerging in both P-ERP and FOS ERP deployment. SaaS is a software deployment model in which an application is licensed for use as a service that is provided to customers on demand. The SaaS provider may host the application on his own private server farm or deploy it in on a third party cloud computing infrastructure service. Rane (2010) addresses the major security issues that must be carefully considered when enterprise applications migrate to the cloud, including data security, data segregation, network security, identity management and sign-on security.

Zunnurhain and Vrbsky (2010) identify possible security attacks on clouds including wrapping attacks, malware-injection attacks, flooding attacks and browser attacks. A wrapping attack appears if the user account and password are duplicated in the login phase. In a malware-injection attack, the attacker creates a normal operation, and then embeds in it another (false) command. A flooding attack occurs when an attacker generates false data (e.g., resource requests or some type of executable code), which might consume a large amount of the user's machine resources. A browser attack assumes disruption of the signature and encryption data, which are being exchanged between the Web browser and Web server. The authors also emphasize that, in the case of failure, it is not always clear who is the responsible party.

## SECURITY ISSUES IN FOS ERP SYSTEMS

Evaluation of FOS ERP system security is not straightforward, because different users and environments may pose different security requirements, and, consequently, differently evaluate the same product. For that reason, when evaluating a product, the enterprise should first identify its own security requirements.

ERP applications may be highly vulnerable to external security threats. Weak passwords can be easily broken; however, some of the most damaging hacks come "in the form of social engineering where users are tricked into freely divulging their credentials" (Van Holsbeck & Johnson, 2004). On the other side, the opportunities for insider's frauds and systems abuses have increased significantly with the deployment of a single automated system that manages accounts, employee benefits and other confidential information. For that reason, integrated information systems with numerous users require solutions for transaction-level security.

After identifying the requirements, examination and comparison of products is needed. Wheeler (2010) suggests the following steps in selecting FOS software: (1) identification of candidates; (2) reading existing reviews; (3) comparison of the leading programs' attributes according to specific needs and (4) analysis of the top candidates. These steps are denoted as "IRCA" (identify, read reviews, compare, and analyze).

The simplest examination is to read the product documentation (user's guide) and inspect: (1) whether it discusses how to make and keep the program secure; (2) does the project have a process for reporting security vulnerabilities and (3) does the project have cryptographic signatures for its current release? Examining available reports of security vulnerabilities can be useful, but it should be noted that some of the most secure products might have more reported weaknesses because of more extensive testing.

"Common Criteria" (CC) is the internationally recognized IT security evaluation criteria standard for IT products and systems (International Organization for Standardization [ISO], 2005). CC is intended to software consumers, developers and evaluators. CC evaluation is performed in authorized laboratories and it encompasses testing of different features, such as the development environment, security functionality, the handling of security vulnerabilities, and security related documentation. If a product is CC certified, its "Security Target" will be made available to the public. Security Target is a document that contains report about security threats, objectives, requirements, and summary specification of security functions and assurance measures. However, CC certification is too expensive for most of the open source software developers. For example, the Linux operating system has undergone a number of CC evaluations. If the product under consideration has been CC certified and the Security Target describes a configuration that is similar to the user's configuration, environment and requirements, the user can consider the evaluation results for security assurance.

The Open Web Application Security Project (OWASP) was formed to help companies and developers with the challenging task of securing Web applications. The OWASP Enterprise Application Security Project (OWASP-EAS) exists to provide guidance to people involved in the procurement, design, implementation or sign-off of enterprise applications (OWASP, 2009). This project includes several subprojects concerning with enterprise business application security vulnerabilities, implementation assessment guide, vulnerability testing guide and development of free tools for enterprise business applications assessment.

It is arguable whether FOS ERP solutions are generally more vulnerable than the commercial ones. The potential advantages of FOS ERP systems concerning security are:

- Transparency and availability in the public domain enables also a quick notice about security failures.
- Potential vulnerabilities are identified and fixed much more quickly and easily.

Thus, Thoke (2009) claims that most of the commercial ERP systems are tested to a decent extent, but still suffer from security flaws, traps, pitfalls and loop holes (except a very few products that are the best and the most expensive). The author also states that the open source ERP packages are thoroughly tested and 99% of the bugs are reported by the open source users in the process of development; hence they are very hard to break through, in terms of security loop holes.

On the contrary, the study, carried out by Fortify Software, evaluated 11 open source software packages and clearly indicated that the open source community failed to adhere to minimal security best practices (Messmer, 2008).

Obviously, security problems may pose limitations to the applicability area of FOS ERP. Although open source solutions may appear more cost-effective than the commercial ones, the problem of maintenance must be examined very carefully.

There is a strong need to perform a comprehensive information security risk analysis. However, this task is complex and expensive. Identifying all relevant threats and estimating the probability of occurrences is very difficult or even impossible. Consequently, estimating costs related to various types of security failures may be ambiguous or inaccurate. The problem is particularly expressed in SMEs, which typically do not employ IT experts and cannot afford a proper outsourcing expertise (Beachboard, Cole, Mellor, Hernandez, Aytes, & Massad, 2008).

Security risk analysis can be either qualitative or quantitative (Tsiakis, 2010). Qualitative analysis assumes methods that consider loss in a subjective measurement (e.g., low, medium or high risk). Quantitative analysis relies on an appropriate mathematical approach (numeric analysis and statistical methods) to express risk as a numerical value (e.g., monetary terms and threats frequency).

Rane (2010) proposes the tree key mitigation strategies that can help the SaaS providers to ensure the security and integrity of their application and data. The first strategy refers to secure deployment, concerning applications as well as network services and infrastructure. The second strategy proposes involvement of the trusted third party in order to validate the security and integrity of the SaaS application and its deployment. The third strategy proposes Governance and Regulatory Compliance (GRC) audits that validate conformance to government regulations and industry standards.

## SECURING THE NETWORK INFRASTRUCTURE

Traditionally, ERP security focused on the internal mechanisms that intend to control user rights while enterprises rely on network solutions (firewalls, virtual private networks, intrusion detection systems) to prevent outsiders from accessing their ERP systems.

An evident progress achieved in the area of information assurance is based on the following three components: firewalls, intrusion detection systems and cryptographic techniques. Firewalls should control access rights and filter information flows that enter the network or its particular segments. Intrusion detection systems perform network monitoring and detect attacks by means of different techniques. Cryptographic techniques enable authentication, confidentiality and data integrity.

However, there is a real possibility that the network infrastructure (routers, servers, gateways) be jeopardized by internal or external attacks. External attacker usually masquerades to some network element and then distributes constructed, delayed or false control information. Internal attacks are performed by network elements that have been compromised by malicious adversaries.

IP security (IPsec) protocols represent a set of open IETF standards that provide cryptographic-based protection mechanisms for IP packets (Kent & Seo, 2005). IPsec provides confidentiality, data integrity, authentication, and replay protection by two security protocols: Encapsulating Security Payload (ESP) and Authentication Header (AH). ESP can provide all four protections, whereas AH can provide only three: integrity protection, origin authentication, and replay protection. Both protocols can operate in two modes, transport mode and tunnel mode. Transport mode protects upper-layer protocols only, while tunnel mode protects the entire IP packet. IPsec also specifies the protocol for dynamic establishment of cryptographic keys – Internet Key Exchange (IKE).

Today, the most widespread application for IPsec is in virtual private networks (VPN). VPN represents a service that enables restricted communication between a set of sites, making use of a backbone that is shared with other traffic not belonging to that communication. In the past few years, IP-based VPNs, in several forms and based on different network technologies, have become a leading solution for a wide range of corporate network services (Carugi & De Clercq, 2004; Mohapatra, Metz & Cui, 2007; Stojanovic & Acimovic-Raspopovic, 2008). In a VPN, IPsec provides protection for IP traffic between geographically disparate sites of a corporation, and for IP traffic between a mobile user and a corporate site.

Chakrabarti and Manimaran (2002) proposed a taxonomy of attacks to the Internet infrastructure and possible solutions, with four basic categories: (1) Domain Name System (DNS) hacking; (2)

routing table poisoning; (3) packet mistreatment and (4) Denial of Service (DoS) attacks.

We will further address DoS in more details, because this type of attack attempts to make a computer resource unavailable to its intended users. In a typical DoS attack, the attacker spoofs its IP address and uses a number of intermediate nodes to forward large amounts of traffic towards the target destination. The aim is to put out of use important servers, which serve large amount of end users, for a certain period. It can also be used to disrupt the services of intermediate routers. The effect of attack is multiplied if distributed attacker agents are used (distributed DoS, DDoS). They simultaneously attack the target, which can completely disable user's access to the network.

In QoS-enabled networks, the intention of a DoS attack can be complete blocking of certain higher-level services. Denial of service also appears because of attacks to routing and signaling protocols, as well as packet mistreatment.

Possible security solutions can generally be divided to preventive and reactive. Preventive techniques rely on some preliminary information, which may help in preventing attacks and/or perform packet filtering.

An important step is preventing the attacker to identify operating systems of hosts and network devices ("fingerprinting"), which usually precedes attacks. For example, Nmap (Network mapper) is a free and open source utility for network exploration and security auditing (Lyon, 2010). Nmap uses a database with more than 500 TCP/IP "fingerprints" on different hardware and software platforms in free or commercial operating systems, routers and other devices.

The aim of reactive techniques is identifying the source of the attacks. Since attackers spoof their addresses, special techniques are needed to trace back to the source of the attack. This task is particularly challenging in the case of DDos attack. Possible solutions encompass different intrusion detection techniques, including link testing in reverse direction, IP traceback, etc.

In the most cases, implementation of QoS architectures and mechanisms significantly increases operational security risks. For that reason directions of the Internet Engineering Task Force (IETF) regarding Internet research include a recommendation that "any new research on QoS mechanisms or architectures ought to specifically discuss the potential security issues associated with the new proposal(s) and how to mitigate those security issues" (Atkinson & Floyd, 2004, p.18).

Securing services that are provided through a heterogeneous multi-domain network is a very complex task. Distributed access control managed by different organizations requires a high degree of adaptability to security management, concerning both specification of particular actions and change of management policies in the presence of network threats.

## The Role of Service Level Agreements

Service negotiation between the customer and the provider results in a service level agreement (SLA), which is a contract that defines all technical, financial and legal aspects related to a particular service. Regardless of the applied QoS model, SLA should consist of two parts: the technical part and the administrative part. The technical part encompasses set of descriptors and associated attributes that describe the particular service class and the traffic profile. Administrative part covers financial and legal aspects: information about pricing, charging, billing and payment, penalties for both the user and the provider in the case of contract violation, etc.

SLA represents a starting point for provisioning of QoS and security services in the NGN environment. Service management is performed by means of a per-domain software agent (bandwidth broker, VPN broker, QoS manager) that is responsible for monitoring and management of the service specified in SLA, admission control and network resource management (Zeng & Ansari, 2003; Stojanovic & Acimovic-Raspopovic, 2008; Stojanovic, Bostjancic Rakas & Acimovic-Raspopovic, 2010).

The ITU-T has provided guidelines for the definition of SLA representation templates, independently of the applied QoS model (ITU-T, 2006). Technical part of the SLA is divided into the service, technology and QoS report parts. Service part describes the detailed information about the service provided to the customer. It includes the negotiated service contents and the agreed service level. Technology part gives the detailed information about QoS parameters, metrics set, and some technical supporting infrastructure, such as supporting equipments and system design information, etc. QoS report includes the information provided to the customer in order to evaluate service level negotiated in the SLA.

Service providers can make use of electronic SLAs to promote and offer their services while customers are able to formalize their service level requirements through SLAs (Hasselmeyer, Mersch, Koller, Quyen, Schubert & Wieder, 2007; Stojanovic, Bostjancic Rakas & Acimovic-Raspopovic, 2010). Service provider may simply offer an electronic SLA form to customers, e.g. through an appropriate Web interface. Customer should complete the form, thus expressing his or her requirements for a particular service. After processing the requirement, customer should be informed about the offered service.

Considering that different users and environments often pose different security requirements, we point out that security services should also be negotiated and, consequently, specified through the SLA. A simple example of the security descriptor for IPsec is illustrated in Figure 1. Consider an administrative domain that provides $n$ different service classes and let us observe class $p$ ($1 \leq p \leq n$). By default, security services are not included in description of the class $p$. However, service offer can be enriched by the definition of class

extension ($p+$), which encompasses security descriptor with specification of IPsec services and the associated mechanisms.

IPsec descriptor contains the following parameters: identification of the IPsec protocol (AH or ESP), mode (transport or tunnel), algorithm for data confidentiality (only in ESP), configurable parameters for IKE (exchange mode, cipher algorithm, hash algorithm, etc.) and the information whether protection against replay is applicable.

IP VPN service may be offered to the users according to following principles: separate VPN per application type, multiple application types per VPN or multiple VPNs per application type. Consequently, a specification of VPN service level should consist of: (1) the generic part, which describes IP service for individual traffic flow and (2) the VPN-specific part, which describes VPN tunnels, mutual reachability of the VPN service users, network address translation and security mechanisms (Stojanovic & Acimovic-Raspopovic, 2008).

## Security Management Systems

We claim that a properly defined SLA represents the basis for securing NGN services, which are offered to end users/applications. Certainly, this is very true for FOS ERP systems, including SaaS FOS ERP. Since different users and environments may pose different security requirements, the NGN provider and the user (either enterprise or SaaS provider) should precisely agree upon security

*Figure 1. Example of IPsec descriptor in service level specification*

```
Service class: p+
IPsec:
- Protocol: <AH> <ESP>
- Mode: <transport> <tunnel>
- Confidentiality: <algorithm> <not relevant>
- IKE: <parameter 1> … <parameter m>
- Protection against replay: <Yes> <No>
```

services to be provided and compensation for those services. The NGN provider then selects the most appropriate security policy that should be applied to fulfill the negotiated contract.

The NGN provider should usually keep track on a very large number of SLAs. Implementation of different security policies practically means that a multitude of parameters should be configured in each network element. For example, only IPsec protocols require several tenths of configurable parameters in each network element (Li, 2003). Under such circumstances, manual network configuration is inefficient or even unfeasible.

Automation of security management process is one of the key challenges for network and service providers in the NGN environment. Development of automated systems that implement

sets of abstractly defined rules – policies (Policy Based Management, PBM) seems to be a promising approach for fulfilling such requirement (Verma, 2002).

A proposal of security management architecture is considered in a wider context of quality of service PBM oriented system (Figure 2). We assume a central QoS management entity in each administrative domain. It encompasses the following functional sub-entities:

- Service level agreement manager;
- Policy selector;
- Network resource manager;
- Configuration manager;
- Security manager.

*Figure 2. A proposal of security management architecture*

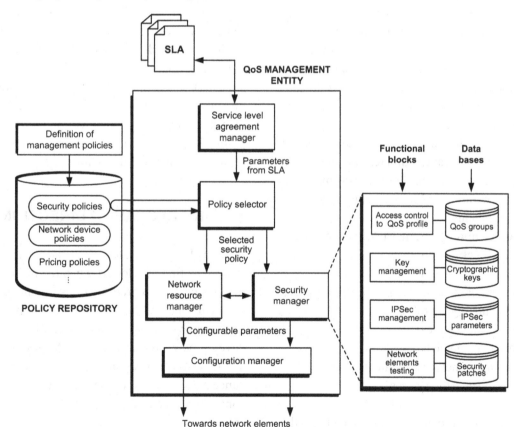

**Service level agreement manager** encompasses the following functions:

- Dynamic service negotiating for novel traffic flows, e.g. by means of an appropriate signaling protocol (Sarangan & Chen, 2006; Stojanovic & Acimovic-Raspopovic, 2009).
- Comparison of technical requirements for QoS with profiles of service classes supported by the network and selection of the appropriate class.
- Selection of the appropriate pricing model.

The inputs to the **Policy selector** are relevant SLA parameters obtained from the Service level agreement manager. Figure 2 illustrates how Policy selector, based on these inputs, fetches the appropriate security policy from the policy repository. It further forwards the policy to Network resource manager and Security manager.

**Network resource manager** implements the admission control procedure. It decides whether SLA request is accepted, denied or renegotiation is suggested. Chao and Guo (2002) provide a taxonomy and comprehensive overview of admission control procedures.

**Configuration manager** is responsible for configuring of relevant parameters, obtained from Network resource manager and Security manager, as well as forwarding of those parameters towards network elements.

**Security manager** consists of the following functional blocks:

- Access control of the new traffic flow to a particular QoS profile;
- IPsec management;
- Key management;
- Testing of network elements and distribution of security patches.

The appropriate database is associated with the each aforementioned functional block.

Access control policy should be implemented using different options of operating systems and communication devices by assigning user names and the associated passwords to all users. Besides, administrator can assign rights and obligations to users, concerning system maintaining, administration, and restrictions in access to particular services.

Application of the set of IPsec protocols assumes implementation of the appropriate security policy in network elements, which support IPsec.

Key management refers to dynamic establishment of cryptographic keys that are used in the IPsec (IKE), as well as in different security mechanisms that can be applied to control protocols (routing, signaling).

Testing of network elements includes different control functions that aim to detect and correct errors in operating systems, which may be misused by malicious users, as well as updating of anti-virus programs and their associated data bases. These complex tasks require testing of network equipment on a daily basis and permanent tracking of information about new forms of external attacks. For example, an efficient prevention of operating system fingerprinting can be performed by automatic testing and detection of vulnerable points. Depending on test results, distribution of security patches should be initiated.

## FUTURE RESEARCH DIRECTIONS

Securing FOS ERP systems is still an open research topic. The first problem is when the information or system is considered secure, while the second problem concerns the price for it (Tsiakis, 2010). An intensive research work is still needed to develop new, efficient methods for security risk analysis. Another research topic affects maintenance of FOS ERP solutions (including security), concerning need for the expertise and its estimated cost.

System developers should design and implement security solutions that conform to proved practical experiences (Messmer, 2008). Enterprise should first identify its own security requirements, and then select the most appropriate product. In the NGN environment, relevant security requirements should be a part of the service level agreement.

Requirements for end-to-end QoS provisioning, network reliability and dependability stipulate new approaches to design and development of network management systems. The following aspects are essential: definition of novel architectures; development of new methods and tools for management automation; development of hardware and software platforms that enable efficient implementation of fault, configuration, accounting, performance and security management functions (Pras, Schönwälder, Burgess, et al., 2007).

PBM system is a promising solution for implementing flexible and scalable management platform.

Unification of service level specification formats is an important prerequisite for management automation, and for achieving interoperability between service providers. From the provider's perspective, the most important open issues encompass: (1) structure and extent of management functions that should be integrated and (2) degree of measurement and collection of management information.

Another active research area is development of real-time techniques that should prevent disclosure of device operating systems and/or eliminate possible ambiguities in application and communication software implementation. Besides, essential prerequisites for efficient prevention from cyber attacks are automated testing, detection of vulnerable network points and reporting the security management system.

One of the main problems in securing the NGN infrastructure is the lack of uniform security models that should be consistently applied in all involved domains. Besides, the security

mechanisms must be sufficiently powerful to prevent attackers from injecting malicious agents or modifying ("poisoning") the existing ones (Dearle, 2007; Stojanovic, Bostjancic Rakas, & Acimovic-Raspopovic, 2010).

## CONCLUSION

FOS ERP systems are cost-effective solutions, particularly intended for small and medium enterprises, as well as organizations that need continuous adaptation of the software to changing processes and requirements. However, security problems may pose limitations to the applicability area of FOS ERP.

Evaluating security of a particular product is not straightforward, because different users and environments often pose different security requirements. Assessment of FOS ERP system security should start from the definition of enterprise's security requirements. After identifying the requirements, analysis and comparison of available products is needed. If the product is CC certified, the public "Security Target" document contains report about security testing for particular configuration and environment. It is highly desirable to carry out an information security risk analysis (qualitative or quantitative); however, a proper expertise is a complex and expensive task.

Traditionally, ERP security focused on the internal mechanisms that intended to control user rights, while enterprises implicitly supposed reliable and trustworthy network infrastructure. However, in the "all-IP" NGN environment, significant research efforts are focused to securing the network infrastructure. This is particularly important for FOS ERP SaaS providers who deploy their software on a third party cloud computing infrastructure service.

Properly defined SLA represents a starting point for provisioning of secure services with the required QoS level. We propose a PBM oriented security management architecture, with the following functions: access control to a particular QoS profile, IPsec management, cryptographic key management, testing of network elements and distribution of security patches. Possible network security solutions include automatic scanning of network vulnerable points to prevent fingerprinting and reporting to network management system on a regular basis. Preventive techniques require a permanent analysis of increasing number and types of attacks, as well as the appropriate upgrade of security mechanisms.

## REFERENCES

Atem de Carvalho, R., & Johansson, B. (2010). Enterprise resource planning systems for small and medium-sized enterprises. In Ramachandran, M., & Atem de Carvalho, R. (Eds.), *Handbook of Research on Software Engineering and Productivity Technologies: Implications of Globalization* (pp. 373–381). New York: Information Science Reference.

Atkinson, R., & Floyd, S. (2004). IAB concerns and recommendations regarding Internet research and evolution. *IETF RFC 3869 (Informational)*. Retrieved April 15, 2008 from http://www.rfc-editor.org/rfcsearch.html

Beachboard, J., Cole, A., Mellor, M., Hernandez, S., Aytes, K., & Massad, N. (2008). Improving information security risk analysis practices for small- and medium-sized enterprises: a research agenda. *Issues in Informing Science and Information Technology, 5*, 73–85.

Carugi, M., & De Clercq, J. (2004). Virtual private network services: scenarios, requirements and architectural constructs from a standardization perspective. *IEEE Communications Magazine, 42*(6), 116–122. doi:10.1109/MCOM.2004.1304246

Cereola, S. (2008). *The performance effects of latent factors on assimilation of commercial open-source ERP software on small-medium enterprises*. Ph. D. dissertation. Virginia Commonwealth University, Richmond, Virginia. Retrieved October 08, 2010, from http://hdl.handle.net/10156/2295.

Chakrabarti, A., & Manimaran, G. (2002). Internet infrastructure security. *IEEE Network, 16*(6), 13–21. doi:10.1109/MNET.2002.1081761

Chao, H. J., & Guo, X. (2002). *Quality of service control in high-speed networks*. New York: John Wiley & Sons.

De Búrca, S., & Fynes, B. (2003, September). *Relationships and technology: combining ERP and Internet technologies*. Paper presented at the 19th IMP Conference, Lugano, Switzerland. Retrieved September 01, 2010, from http://www.impgroup.org.

Dearle, A. (2007). Software deployment, past, present and future. In *Proceedings of the International Conference on Software Engineering: 2007 Future of Software Engineering* (pp. 269-284). Washington, DC: IEEE Computer Society.

Hasselmeyer, P., Mersch, H., Koller, B., Quyen, H. N., Schubert, L., & Wieder, P. (2007). Implementing an SLA negotiation framework. In *Proceedings of the eChallenges e-2007 Conference*, Hague, Netherlands.

Hendrawirawan, D., Tanriverdi, H., Zetterlund, C., Hakam, H., Kim, H. H., Paik, H., & Yoon, Y. (2007). ERP security and segregation duties audit: a framework solution. *ISACA Journal 2007*, vol. 2. Retrieved October 01, 2010, from http://www.isaca.org/Journal/Past-Issues/2007/Volume-2/Pages/default.aspx.

Hertenberger, M. P. (2005). *A reference framework for security in enterprise resource planning (ERP) systems*. Ph. D. dissertation. University of Johannesburg, South Africa. Retrieved October 01, 2010, from http://ujdigispace.uj.ac.za:8080/dspace/bitstream/10210/496/1/AReference-Framework.pdf.

International Organization for Standardization (ISO). (2005). Information technology - Security techniques - Evaluation criteria for IT security. *Standard ISO/IEC 15408:2005.*

International Telecommunication Union – Telecommunication Standardization Sector (ITU-T). (2004). General overview of NGN. *ITU-T recommendation Y.2001*. Geneva, ITU-T.

International Telecommunication Union – Telecommunication Standardization Sector (ITU-T). (2006). *Guidelines for the definition of SLA representation templates. ITU-T Recommendation M.3342*. Geneva ITU-T.

Iskanius, P. (2009). Experiences of ERP Risk Management in SMEs. *In Proceedings of the CENTERIS 2009 Conference on ENTERprise Information Systems – CENTERIS* (pp. 269-282). Ofir, Portugal.

Kent, S., & Seo, K. (2005). Security architecture for the Internet protocol. *IETF RFC 3869 (Standards Track)*. Retrieved April 16, 2008 from http://www.rfc-editor.org/rfcsearch.html.

Li, M. (2003). Policy-based IPsec management. *IEEE Network*, *17*(6), 36–43. doi:10.1109/MNET.2003.1248659

Lion, G. F. (2010). *NMAP Network Scanning*. Retrieved September 15, 2010, from http://nmap.org.book/toc.html.

Marnewick, C., & Labuschagne, L. (2005, June). *A security framework for an ERP system*. Paper presented at the ISSA 2005 New Knowledge Today Conference, Sandton, South Africa. Retrieved September 01, 2010, from http://icsa.cs.up.ac.za/issa/2005/Proceedings/Full/009_Article.pdf.

Messmer, E. (2008). *Open source software a security risk*. Retrieved August 29, 2010, from http://www.cio.com/article/438728/Open_Source_Software_a_Security_Risk.

Mohapatra, P., Metz, C., & Cui, Y. (2007). Layer 3 VPN services over IPv6 backbone networks: requirements, technology, and standardization efforts. *IEEE Communications Magazine*, *45*(4), 32–37. doi:10.1109/MCOM.2007.343609

Mordelet, N., Festraets, E., & Wang, M. (2006). The enterprise: a high-value market for broadband services. *Alcatel Telecommunications Review* (3rd Quarter 2006). Retrieved September 5, 2008 from http://www.alcatel-lucent.com.

Open Web Application Security Project (OWASP). (2009). *OWASP Enterprise Application Security Project*. Retrieved, February 08, 2011, from http://www.owasp.org/index.php/OWASP_Enterprise_Application_Security_Project.

Pras, A., Schönwälder, J., Burgess, M., Festor, O., Martínez Pérez, G., Stadler, R., & Stiller, B. (2007). Key research challenges in network management. *IEEE Communications Magazine*, *45*(10), 104–110. doi:10.1109/MCOM.2007.4342832

Rane, P. (2010). *Enterprise applications in the cloud: a SaaS security perspective*. Retrieved, January 20, 2011, from http://esj.com/articles/2010/02/09/cloud-saas-security.aspx.

Russell, R. S. (2006, March). *A framework for analyzing ERP security threats*. Paper presented at the Euro-Atlantic Symposium on Critical Information Infrastructure Assurance, Switzerland. Retrieved, October 01, 2010, from http://www.cimap.vt.edu/CIIA/Papers/Session1-4-Russell.pdf

Sarangan, V., & Chen, J.-C. (2006). Comparative study of protocols for dynamic service negotiation in the next-generation internet. *IEEE Communications Magazine, 44*(3), 151–156. doi:10.1109/MCOM.2006.1607879

Somers, T. M., & Nelson, K. G. (2004). A taxonomy of players and activities across the ERP project life cycle. *Information & Management, 41*, 257–278. doi:10.1016/S0378-7206(03)00023-5

Stojanovic, M., & Acimovic-Raspopovic, V. (2008). QoS provisioning framework in IP-based VPN. In Putnik, G., & Cruz-Cunha, M. (Eds.), *Encyclopedia of Networked and Virtual Organizations* (Vol. III, pp. 1317–1324). Hershey, New York: Information Science Reference. doi:10.4018/978-1-59904-885-7.ch173

Stojanovic, M., & Acimovic-Raspopovic, V. (2009). Communication issues for small and medium enterprises: provider and customer perspectives. In Cruz-Cuncha, M. (Ed.), *Enterprise Information Systems for Bussiness Integration in SMEs: Technological, Organizational, and Social Dimensions* (pp. 230–251). Hershey, New York: Information Science Reference. doi:10.4018/978-1-60566-892-5.ch013

Stojanovic, M., Bostjancic Rakas, S., & Acimovic-Raspopovic, V. (2010). End-to-end quality of service specification and mapping: the third party approach. *Computer Communications, 33*(11), 1354–1368. doi:10.1016/j.comcom.2010.03.024

Thoke, O. (2009). How do open source ERP packages score over custom ERP solutions. Retrieved, January 15, 2011, from http://www.brighthub.com/computing/linux/articles/53581.aspx.

Tsiakis, T. (2010). Information security expenditures: a techno-economic analysis. *IJCSNS International Journal of Computer Science and Network Security, 10*(4), 7–11.

Vadalasetty, S. R. (2003). Security concerns in using open source software for enterprise requirements. SANS Institute, white paper. Retrieved October 10, 2010, from http://www.sans.org/reading_room/whitepapers/awareness/security-concerns-open-source-software-enterprise-requirements_1305

Van Holsbeck, M., & Johnson, J. Z. (2004). *Security in an ERP world.* Retrieved, July 15, 2010, from http://www.net-security.org.

Verma, D. C. (2002). Simplifying network administration using policy-based management. *IEEE Network, 16*(2), 20–26. doi:10.1109/65.993219

Wheeler, D. A. (2010). *How to evaluate open source software / free software (OSS/FS) programs.* Retrieved July 10, 2010, from http://www.dwheeler.com/oss_fs_eval.html.

Zeng, J., & Ansari, N. (2003). Toward IP virtual private network quality of service: a service provider perspective. *IEEE Communications Magazine, 41*(4), 113–119. doi:10.1109/MCOM.2003.1193984

Zou, C. C., Duffield, N., Towsley, D., & Gong, W. (2006). Adaptive defense against various network attacks. *IEEE Selected Areas in Communications, 24*(10), 1877–1888. doi:10.1109/JSAC.2006.877137

Zunnurhain, K., & Vrbsky, S. V. (2010, November-December). *Security attacks and solutions in clouds.* Paper presented at the 2nd IEEE International Conference on Cloud Computing Technology and Science (CloudCom 2010), Indianapolis, IN. Retrieved January 20, 2011, from http://salsahpc.indiana.edu/CloudCom20101/Poster/cloudcom2010_submission_98.pdf.

## ADDITIONAL READING

Acimovic-Raspopovic, V., & Stojanovic, M. (2008). Pricing quality of service in DiffServ IP networks. In Putnik, G., & Cruz-Cuncha, M. (Eds.), *Encyclopedia of Networked and Virtual Organizations* (*Vol. II*, pp. 1245–1251). Hershey, New York: Information Science Reference. doi:10.4018/978-1-59904-885-7.ch164

Aizuddin, A. (2001). *The Common Criteria ISO/IEC 15408 – the insight, some thoughts, questions and issues*. SANS Institute, white paper. Retrieved October 10, 2010, from http://www.sans.org/reading_room/whitepapers/standards/common-criteria-iso-iec-15408-insight-thoughts-questions-issues_545.

Anderson, R., & Moore, T. (2006). The economics of information security. *Science Magazine*, *314*, 610–613.

Androulidakis, G., Chatzigiannakis, V., & Papavassiliou, S. (2009). Network anomaly detection and classification via opportunistic sampling. *IEEE Network*, *23*(1), 6–13. doi:10.1109/MNET.2009.4804318

Ángeles Callejo-Rodriguez, M., & Enriquez-Gabeiras, J. (2008). Bridging the standardization gap to provide QoS in current NGN architectures. *IEEE Communications Magazine*, *46*(10), 132–137. doi:10.1109/MCOM.2008.4644130

Castelucio, A., Ziviani, A., & Salles, R. M. (2009). An AS-level overlay network for IP Traceback. *IEEE Network*, *23*(1), 36–41. doi:10.1109/MNET.2009.4804322

Davis, A. (2005). Return on security investment – proving it's worth it. *Network Security*, *11*, 8–10. doi:10.1016/S1353-4858(05)70301-9

De Búrca, S., Fynes, B., & Marshall, D. (2005). Strategic technology adoption: extending ERP across the supply chain. *Journal of Enterprise Information Management*, *18*(4), 427–440. doi:10.1108/17410390510609581

De Pablos Heredero, C., & De Pablos Heredero, M. (2009). Elements that can explain the degree of success of ERP systems implementation. In Cruz-Cuncha, M. (Ed.), *Enterprise Information Systems for Bussiness Integration in SMEs: Technological, Organizational, and Social Dimensions* (pp. 468–498). Hershey, New York: Information Science Reference. doi:10.4018/978-1-60566-892-5.ch026

Gibson, T. (2002). Securing large-scale military networks: homogeneous protection for disparate environments. *IEEE Network*, *16*(6), 8–12. doi:10.1109/MNET.2002.1081760

Huang, D., Qing, H., & Ravi, B. (2008). An economic analysis of the optimal information security investment in the case of a risk-averse firm. *International Journal of Production Economics*, *114*(2), 793–804. doi:10.1016/j.ijpe.2008.04.002

International Telecommunication Union – Telecommunication Standardization Sector (ITU-T). (2004). General principles and general reference model for next generation networks. *ITU-T recommendation* [Geneva, ITU-T.]. *Y (Dayton, Ohio)*, 2011.

International Telecommunication Union – Telecommunication Standardization Sector (ITU-T). (2006). Converged services framework functional requirements and architecture. *ITU-T recommendation Y.2013*. Geneva, ITU-T.

Jacobs, P., & Davie, B. (2005). Technical challenges in the delivery of interprovider QoS. *IEEE Communications Magazine*, *43*(6), 112–118. doi:10.1109/MCOM.2005.1452839

Kaufman, C., Hoffman, P., Nir, Y., & Eronen, P. (2010). Internet Key Exchange protocol version 2 (IKEv2). *IETF RFC 5996 (Standards Track)*. Retrieved October 15, 2010 from http://www. rfc-editor.org/rfcsearch.html

Kent, S. (2005). IP Authentication Header. *IETF RFC 4302 (Standards Track)*. Retrieved October 15, 2010 from http://www.rfc-editor.org/rfcsearch. html

Kent, S. (2005). IP Encapsulating Security Payload (ESP). *IETF RFC 4303 (Standards Track)*. Retrieved October 15, 2010 from http://www. rfc-editor.org/rfcsearch.html

Knight, P., & Lewis, K. (2004). Layer 2 and 3 virtual private networks: taxonomy, technology and standardization efforts. *IEEE Communications Magazine, 42*(6), 124–131. doi:10.1109/ MCOM.2004.1304248

Meddeb, A. (2010). Internet QoS: pieces of the puzzle. *IEEE Communications Magazine, 48*(1), 86–94. doi:10.1109/MCOM.2010.5394035

Møller, C. (2005). ERP II: a conceptual framework for next-generation enterprise systems? *Journal of Enterprise Information Management, 18*(4), 483–497. doi:10.1108/17410390510609626

Papadimitratos, P., & Haas, Z. J. (2002). Securing the Internet routing infrastructure. *IEEE Communications Magazine, 40*(10), 60–68. doi:10.1109/ MCOM.2002.1039858

Rao, N. (2008). *Unified communications – communication enabled business process (CEBP)*. Wipro Technologies white paper. Retrieved July 07, 2010, from http://www.wipro.com.

Röhrig, S., & Knorr, K. (2004). Security analysis of electronic business processes. *Electronic Commerce Research, 4*(1-2), 59–81. doi:10.1023/ B:ELEC.0000009282.06809.c5

Stallings, W. (2003). *Cryptography and Network Security: Principles and Practice* (3rd ed.). New Jersey: Prentice-Hall.

Sutton, R. J. (2002). *Secure communications*. New York: John Wiley & Sons.

Tschofenig, H., & Fu, X. (2006). Securing the next steps in signaling (NSIS) protocol suite. *International Journal of Internet Protocol Technology, 1*(4), 271–282.

Wang, C., Wang, G., Wang, H., Chen, A., & Santiago, R. (2007). Quality of service contract specification, establishment, and monitoring for service level management. *Journal of Object Technology, 6*(11), 25–44. doi:10.5381/jot.2007.6.11.a2

Watson, D., Smart, M., Malan, G. R., & Jahanian, F. (2004). Protocol scrubbing: network security through transparent flow modification. *IEEE/ACM Transactions on Networking, 12*(2), 261–273. doi:10.1109/TNET.2003.822645

Yaar, A., Perrig, A., & Song, D. (2006). Stack-Pi: new packet marking and filtering mechanisms for DDoS and IP spoofing defense. *IEEE Selected Areas in Communications, 24*(10), 1853–1863. doi:10.1109/JSAC.2006.877138

## KEY TERMS AND DEFINITIONS

**Authentication:** Assurance that the received data origin from the claimed source.

**Confidentiality:** Assurance that the information is not exposed or available to unauthorized persons, entities or processes.

**Data integrity:** Assurance that the data are not altered or destroyed during transmission over the network.

**Denial of Service (DoS):** A cyber attack, which attempts to make a computer resource unavailable to its intended users.

**Next Generation Network (NGN):** An architectural concept of future telecommunication core and access networks, which assumes transport of all information and services over a common network, typically built around the IP.

**Policy Based Management (PBM):** IETF framework that encompasses conceptual, functional and informational models for development of highly automated management systems that implement sets of abstractly defined rules – policies.

**Protection Against Replay:** Assurance that the information is not captured by some network element and resent later.

**Service Level Agreement (SLA):** A contract between the service provider and the customer, which defines QoS guarantees, performance metrics, measurement methods, tariffs and billing principles, and penalties for the customer and the provider in the case of contract violation.

## ENDNOTE

[1]   A comprehensive list of FOS ERPs is available at: http://open-source-erp-site.com/list-of-open-source-erps.html.

# Related References

To continue our tradition of advancing information science and technology research, we have compiled a list of recommended IGI Global readings. These references will provide additional information and guidance to further enrich your knowledge and assist you with your own research and future publications.

## REFERENCES

Adams, P. J., & Capiluppi, A. (2011). Bridging the gap between agile and free software approaches: The Impact of sprinting . In Koch, S. (Ed.), *Multi-disciplinary advancement in open source software and processes* (pp. 54–66).

Adamson, G. (2010). Challenges in researching portals and the Internet . *International Journal of Web Portals (IJWP)*, *2*(2), 26–37. doi:.doi:10.4018/jwp.2010040103

Alnoukari, M. (2012). ASD-BI: A knowledge discovery process modeling based on adaptive software development agile methodology . In El Sheikh, R., & Alnoukari, M. (Eds.), *Business intelligence and agile methodologies for knowledge-based organizations: Cross-disciplinary applications* (pp. 183–207).

Alzoabi, Z. (2012). Agile software: Body of knowledge . In El Sheikh, R., & Alnoukari, M. (Eds.), *Business intelligence and agile methodologies for knowledge-based organizations: Cross-disciplinary applications* (pp. 14–34).

Akabawi, M. (2011). ERP post-implementation adoption success dynamics: A cultural perspective . In Abdallah, S., & Albadri, F. A. (Eds.), *ICT acceptance, investment and organization: Cultural practices and values in the Arab world* (pp. 88–113).

Allyn, M. R., & Misra, R. B. (2009). Motivation of open source developers: Do license type and status hierarchy matter? *International Journal of Open Source Software and Processes (IJOSSP)*, *1*(4), 65–81. doi:.doi:10.4018/jossp.2009100104

Altarawneh, H., Alamaro, S., & El Sheikh, A. (2012). Web engineering and business intelligence: Agile Web engineering development and practice . In El Sheikh, R., & Alnoukari, M. (Eds.), *Business intelligence and agile methodologies for knowledge-based organizations: Cross-disciplinary applications* (pp. 313–344).

Alwabel, S. A., Zairi, M., & Gunasekaran, A. (2006). The evolution of ERP and its relationship with e-business. *International Journal of Enterprise Information Systems (IJEIS)*, *2*(4), 58–76. doi:.doi:10.4018/jeis.2006100104

Andersson, P., Sweet, S., & Rosenqvist, C. (2012). ICTs for business enterprise mobility: Mobile communications, mobility and the creation of sustainable value. In IR Management Association, USA (Ed.), *Wireless technologies: Concepts, methodologies, tools and applications.* (pp. 1909-1926). doi:10.4018/978-1-61350-101-6.ch712

Anttiroiko, A. (2012). Innovation 2.0: Business networks in the global innovation ecology . In Cruz-Cunha, M. M., Gonçalves, P., Lopes, N., Miranda, E. M., & Putnik, G. D. (Eds.), *Handbook of research on business social networking: Organizational, managerial, and technological dimensions* (pp. 583–602).

Argyropoulou, M., Ioannou, G., Koufopoulos, D. N., & Motwani, J. (2009). Measuring the impact of an ERP project at SMEs: A framework and empirical investigation. *International Journal of Enterprise Information Systems (IJEIS)*, *5*(3), 1–13. doi:.doi:10.4018/jeis.2009070101

Asnina, E., & Osis, J. (2011). Topological functioning model as a CIM-business model . In Osis, J., & Asnina, E. (Eds.), *Model-driven domain analysis and software development: Architectures and functions* (pp. 40–64).

Atieh, K., & Farzali, E. (2012). Towards a business intelligence governance framework within e-government system . In Rahman El Sheikh, A. A., & Alnoukari, M. (Eds.), *Business intelligence and agile methodologies for knowledge-based organizations: Cross-disciplinary applications* (pp. 268–284).

Austin, W. W., Brennan, L. L., & Hunt, J. L. (2011). Legal truth and consequences for a failed ERP implementation. *Journal of Cases on Information Technology (JCIT)*, *13*(1), 37–56. doi:.doi:10.4018/jcit.2011010103

Averweg, U. (2007). Portal technologies and executive information systems implementation . In Tatnall, A. (Ed.), *Encyclopedia of portal technologies and applications* (pp. 763–768).

Baker, C. R. (2007). Enterprise information systems and B2B e-commerce: Enhancing secure transactions using XM . In Gunasekaran, A. (Ed.), *Modelling and analysis of enterprise information systems* (pp. 150–166).

Balzli, C. E., & Fragnière, E. (2012). How ERP systems are centralizing and standardizing the accounting function in public organizations for better and worse . In Chhabra, S., & Kumar, M. (Eds.), *Strategic enterprise resource planning models for e-government: Applications and methodologies* (pp. 55–72).

Barjis, J., & Barjis, I. (2007). Business process modeling as a blueprint for enterprise architecture . In Saha, P. (Ed.), *Handbook of enterprise systems architecture in practice* (pp. 114–128).

Barretto, S. F., Piazalunga, R., Martins, D., & Prado, C. (2007). Digital culture and sharing: Theory and practice of a Brazilian cultural public policy . In Law, W. K. (Ed.), *Information resources management: global challenges* (pp. 146–160).

Berzosa, D. L., Lorenzo, M., de Pablos Heredero, C., & Camarillo, G. (2012). Practising open innovation in the mobile industry. In de Pablos Heredero, C., & López, D. (Eds.), *Open innovation in firms and public administrations: Technologies for value creation.* (pp. 209-220). doi:10.4018/978-1-61350-341-6.ch012

Bibikas, D., Paraskakis, I., Psychogios, A. G., & Vasconcelos, A. C. (2009). The potential of enterprise social software in integrating exploitative and explorative knowledge strategies . In Hatzipanagos, S., & Warburton, S. (Eds.), *Handbook of research on social software and developing community ontologies* (pp. 285–297).

Boateng, B. A., & Boateng, K. (2007). Issues to consider when choosing open source content management systems (CMSs) . In St.Amant, K., & Still, B. (Eds.), *Handbook of research on open source software: Technological, economic, and social perspectives* (pp. 255–268).

Bogers, M. (2012). Knowledge sharing in open innovation: An overview of theoretical perspectives on collaborative innovation. In de Pablos Heredero, C., & López, D. (Eds.), *Open innovation in firms and public administrations: Technologies for value creation.* (pp. 1-14). doi:10.4018/978-1-61350-341-6.ch001

Bossinger, S. M. (2009). Open source software use in local governments . In Reddick, C. (Ed.), *Handbook of research on strategies for local e-government adoption and implementation: Comparative studies* (pp. 516–534).

Boughzala, I. (2012). Collaboration 2.0 through the new organization (2.0) transformation . In Boughzala, I., & Dudezert, A. (Eds.), *Knowledge management 2.0: Organizational models and enterprise strategies* (pp. 1–16).

Bradley, J. (2009). Enterprise resource planning system risks and rewards . In Gupta, J. N., Sharma, S., & Rashid, M. A. (Eds.), *Handbook of research on enterprise systems* (pp. 83–95).

Brainin, E. (2008). Experiences of cultures in global ERP implementation . In Ferran, C., & Salim, R. (Eds.), *Enterprise resource planning for global economies: Managerial issues and challenges* (pp. 167–188).

Brydon, M., & Vining, A. R. (2010). A dynamic model of adoption and improvement for open source business applications . In Siau, K., & Erickson, J. (Eds.), *Principle advancements in database management technologies: New applications and frameworks* (pp. 225–249).

Brydon, M., & Vining, A. R. (2008). Adoption, improvement, and disruption: Predicting the impact of open source applications in enterprise software markets. *Journal of Database Management (JDM),* *19*(2), 73–94. doi:.doi:10.4018/jdm.2008040104

Bughin, J. (2010). The power laws of enterprise 2.0 . In Lee, I. (Ed.), *Encyclopedia of e-business development and management in the global economy* (pp. 23–35).

Burns, J. R., Jung, D. G., & Hoffman, J. J. (2009). Capturing and comprehending the behavioral/dynamical interactions within an ERP implementation. *Journal of Organizational and End User Computing (JOEUC),* *21*(2), 67–89. doi:.doi:10.4018/joeuc.2009040104

Butler, T., Feller, J., Pope, A., & Murphy, C. (2007). Making knowledge management systems open: A case study of the role of open source software . In Lytras, M. D., & Naeve, A. (Eds.), *Open source for knowledge and learning management: Strategies beyond tools* (pp. 150–174).

Caudill, J. G. (2010). Helping to bridge the digital divide with free software and services . In Reddick, C. (Ed.), *Politics, democracy and e-government: Participation and service delivery* (pp. 315–331).

Çetin, G., & Gokturk, M. (2010). Collaboration in open source domains: A perspective on usability . In Rummler, S., & Ng, K. B. (Eds.), *Collaborative technologies and applications for interactive information design: Emerging trends in user experiences* (pp. 167–178).

Carillo, K., & Okoli, C. (2006). Open source software communities . In Dasgupta, S. (Ed.), *Encyclopedia of virtual communities and technologies* (pp. 363–367).

Carton, F., & Adam, F. (2008). Integrated manufacturing applications and management decision making: Putting the P back into ERP . In Laha, D., & Mandal, P. (Eds.), *Handbook of computational intelligence in manufacturing and production management* (pp. 263–280).

Cassell, M. (2009). When local governments choose open source technology . In Reddick, C. (Ed.), *Handbook of research on strategies for local e-government adoption and implementation: Comparative studies* (pp. 535–553).

Chan, J. O. (2012). An enterprise model for customer-centric knowledge management and knowledge-oriented customer relationship management . In Al-Shammari, M. (Ed.), *Customer-centric knowledge management: Concepts and applications* (pp. 203–222).

Chang, H., Yin, C., & Chou, H. (2008). Diffusion of enterprise resource planning systems in Taiwan: Influence sources and the Y2K effect. *International Journal of Enterprise Information Systems (IJEIS)*, *4*(1), 34–47. doi:.doi:10.4018/jeis.2008010103

Cheng, C. (2009). Integrated research and training in enterprise Information Systems . In Gunasekaran, A. (Ed.), *Global implications of modern enterprise Information Systems: Technologies and applications* (pp. 195–208).

Chew, E. K., & Gottschalk, P. (2009). Enterprise and technology architectures . In Chew, E., & Gottschalk, P. (Eds.), *Information Technology strategy and management: Best practices* (pp. 167–221).

Choudhury, I., de Cesare, S., & Di Florido, E. (2008). An object-oriented abstraction mechanism for generic enterprise modeling. *International Journal of Enterprise Information Systems (IJEIS)*, *4*(1), 48–62. doi:.doi:10.4018/jeis.2008010104

Christou, I. T., & Ponis, S. (2008). Enhancing traditional ATP functionality in open source ERP systems: A case study from the food & beverages industry. *International Journal of Enterprise Information Systems (IJEIS)*, *4*(1), 18–33. doi:.doi:10.4018/jeis.2008010102

Comino, S., & Manenti, F. M. (2007). On the role of public policies supporting free/open source software . In St.Amant, K., & Still, B. (Eds.), *Handbook of research on open source software: Technological, economic, and social perspectives* (pp. 412–427).

Conklin, M. (2007). Motives and methods for quantitative FLOSS research . In St.Amant, K., & Still, B. (Eds.), *Handbook of research on open source software: Technological, economic, and social perspectives* (pp. 282–293).

Corso, M., Martini, A., & Crespi, F. (2012). The social network and community approach for enterprise 2.0: Drivers and barriers in marketing . In Cruz-Cunha, M. M., Gonçalves, P., Lopes, N., Miranda, E. M., & Putnik, G. D. (Eds.), *Handbook of research on business social networking: Organizational, managerial, and technological dimensions* (pp. 662–685).

Costa, L., Loughran, N., & Grønmo, R. (2012). Model-driven engineering, services and interactive real-time applications . In Kyriazis, D., Varvarigou, T., & Konstanteli, K. G. (Eds.), *Achieving Real-time in distributed computing: From grids to clouds* (pp. 16–40).

Costin, Y. (2012). Adopting ICT in the mompreneurs business: A strategy for growth? In Romm Livermore, C. (Ed.), *Gender and social computing: Interactions, differences and relationships* (pp. 17–34).

Coulson, T., Olfman, L., Ryan, T., & Shayo, C. (2010). Enterprise systems training strategies: Knowledge Levels and user understanding. *Journal of Organizational and End User Computing (JOEUC)*, *22*(3), 22–39. doi:.doi:10.4018/joeuc

Cucinotta, T., & Gogouvitis, S. V. (2012). Real-time attributes in operating systems . In Kyriazis, D., Varvarigou, T., & Konstanteli, K. G. (Eds.), *Achieving real-time in distributed computing: From grids to clouds* (pp. 275–287).

Cui, L., Zhang, C., Zhang, C., & Huang, L. (2008). Exploring IT adoption process in Shanghai firms: An empirical study. *Journal of Global Information Management (JGIM)*, *16*(2), 1–17. doi:.doi:10.4018/jgim.2008040101

Cunha, M. M., Putnik, G. D., & Ávila, P. S. (2008). Market of resources for virtual enterprise integration . In Putnik, G. D., & Cruz-Cunha, M. M. (Eds.), *Encyclopedia of networked and virtual organizations* (pp. 918–925).

Dai, V., Daloukas, V., Rigou, M., & Sirmakessis, S. (2011). Context-free educational games: Open-source and flexible . In Felicia, P. (Ed.), *Handbook of research on improving learning and motivation through educational games: Multidisciplinary approaches* (pp. 1064–1085).

Daneva, M. (2010). Engineering the coordination requirements in cross-organizational ERP projects: A package of good practices . In Parthasarathy, S. (Ed.), *Enterprise Information Systems and implementing IT infrastructures: Challenges and issues* (pp. 1–19).

Daneva, M., & Ahituv, N. (2011). What practitioners think of inter-organizational ERP requirements engineering practices: Focus group results. *International Journal of Information System Modeling and Design (IJISMD)*, *2*(3), 49–74. doi:.doi:10.4018/jismd.2011070103

da Rimini, F. (2007). Social technologies and the digital commons . In St.Amant, K., & Still, B. (Eds.), *Handbook of research on open source software: Technological, economic, and social perspectives* (pp. 47–67).

Davis, A. (2008). Enterprise resource planning under open source software . In Ferran, C., & Salim, R. (Eds.), *Enterprise resource planning for global economies: Managerial issues and challenges* (pp. 56–76).

de Carvalho, R. A. (2009). Free and open source enterprise resources planning . In Gupta, J. N., Sharma, S., & Rashid, M. A. (Eds.), *Handbook of research on enterprise systems* (pp. 32–44).

Demetriou, N. (2007). The development of the open ACS community . In Lytras, M. D., & Naeve, A. (Eds.), *Open source for knowledge and learning management: Strategies beyond tools* (pp. 298–318).

de Souza, C. A., & Zwicker, R. (2005). Life cycle of ERP systems . In Khosrow-Pour, M. (Ed.), *Encyclopedia of information science and technology* (pp. 1844–1849).

Dewever, F. (2006). Opportunities for open source elearning. *International Journal of Web-Based Learning and Teaching Technologies (IJWLTT)*, *1*(2), 50–61. doi:.doi:10.4018/jwltt.2006040104

Di Cerbo, F., Scotto, M., Sillitti, A., Succi, G., & Vernazza, T. (2007). Toward a GNU/Linux distribution for corporate environments . In Sowe, S. K., Stamelos, I. G., & Samoladas, I. (Eds.), *Emerging free and open source software practices* (pp. 215–236).

du Preez, J. A. (2007). Novell's open source evolution . In St.Amant, K., & Still, B. (Eds.), *Handbook of research on open source software: Technological, economic, and social perspectives* (pp. 590–608).

Dyer, A. (2009). Measuring the benefits of enterprise architecture: Knowledge management maturity . In Saha, P. (Ed.), *Advances in government enterprise architecture* (pp. 106–127).

Edwards, H. M., & Humphries, L. P. (2006). Change management of people & technology in an ERP implementation . In Khosrow-Pour, M. (Ed.), *Cases on Information Technology: Lessons learned* (*Vol. 7*, pp. 537–553).

Egyedi, T. M., & Joode, R. V. (2006). Standardization and other coordination mechanisms in open source software . In Jakobs, K. (Ed.), *Advanced Topics in Information Technology standards and standardization research* (*Vol. 1*, pp. 71–90).

Elpern, J., & Dascalu, S. (2009). A framework for understanding the open source revolution . In Tiako, P. (Ed.), *Designing software-intensive systems: Methods and principles* (pp. 439–454).

Elsammani, Z. (2006). SMEs ECT reality: From ad-hoc implementation to strategic planning . In Al-Qirim, N. (Ed.), *Global electronic business research: Opportunities and directions* (pp. 63–87).

Encinar, M., Herrarte, A., & Muñoz, F. (2012). Firms' connections and open innovation: The case of innovative Spanish firms. In de Pablos Heredero, C., & López, D. (Eds.), *Open innovation in firms and public administrations: Technologies for value creation.* (pp. 155-174). doi:10.4018/978-1-61350-341-6.ch009

Equey, C., & Fragnière, E. (2008). Elements of perception regarding the implementation of ERP Systems in Swiss SMEs. *International Journal of Enterprise Information Systems (IJEIS)*, *4*(3), 1–8. doi:.doi:10.4018/jeis.2008070101

Escobar-Pérez, B., Escobar-Rodríguez, T., & Monge-Lozano, P. (2010). ERP systems in hospitals: A case study. *Journal of Information Technology Research (JITR)*, *3*(4), 34–50. doi:.doi:10.4018/jitr.2010100103

Evdoridis, T. (2007). A generalized comparison of open source and commercial database management systems . In St.Amant, K., & Still, B. (Eds.), *Handbook of research on open source software: Technological, economic, and social perspectives* (pp. 294–308).

Favier, L., & Mekhantar, J. (2007). Use of OSS by local e-administration: The French situation . In St.Amant, K., & Still, B. (Eds.), *Handbook of research on open source software: Technological, economic, and social perspectives* (pp. 428–444).

Feindt, S., Jeffcoate, J., & Chappell, C. (2006). E-commerce links for SMEs within the industry value chain . In Al-Qirim, N. (Ed.), *Global electronic business research: Opportunities and directions* (pp. 133–157).

Feng, X. (2007). A generic model of an enterprise portal . In Tatnall, A. (Ed.), *Encyclopedia of portal technologies and applications* (pp. 419–424).

Ferreira, M. P. (2011). SMEs and e-business: Implementation, strategies and policy . In Cruz-Cunha, M. M., & Varajão, J. (Eds.), *E-business managerial aspects, solutions and case studies* (pp. 1–22).

Feuerlicht, G. (2009). The impact of new trends in the delivery and utilization of enterprise ICT on supplier and user organizations . In Al-Hakim, L., & Memmola, M. (Eds.), *Business Web strategy: Design, alignment, and application* (pp. 46–60).

Fitzgerald, B. (2009). Open source software adoption: Anatomy of success and failure. *International Journal of Open Source Software and Processes (IJOSSP)*, *1*(1), 1–23. doi:.doi:10.4018/jossp.2009010101

Fortino, G., & Palau, C. E. (2007). An open streaming content distribution network . In Tatnall, A. (Ed.), *Encyclopedia of portal technologies and applications* (pp. 677–683).

Franquesa, J., & Brandyberry, A. (2011). Organizational slack and information technology innovation adoption in SMEs . In Lee, I. (Ed.), *E-Business applications for product development and competitive growth: Emerging technologies* (pp. 25–48).

Fui-Hoon Nah, F., Islam, Z., & Tan, M. (2009). Empirical assessment of factors influencing success of enterprise resource planning implementations . In Hunter, M. (Ed.), *Selected readings on strategic Information Systems* (pp. 276–299).

Gagalis, D., Tahinakis, P., Protogeros, N., & Ginoglou, D. (2010). Challenges and trends towards an effective application of ERP and SCM systems in SMEs . In Cruz-Cunha, M. M. (Ed.), *Enterprise Information Systems for business integration in SMEs: Technological, organizational, and social dimensions* (pp. 376–399).

Gaudeul, A. (2009). Consumer welfare and market structure in a model of competition between open source and proprietary software. *International Journal of Open Source Software and Processes (IJOSSP)*, *1*(2), 43–65. doi:.doi:10.4018/jossp.2009040104

Gómez, J. M., & Lübke, D. (2008). Automatic creation of GUI's for Web-Based ERP systems . In Brandon, D. M. (Ed.), *Software engineering for modern Web applications: Methodologies and technologies* (pp. 179–190).

Grant, D., & Tu, Q. (2007). An investigation of the existence of levels of enterprise integration . In Gunasekaran, A. (Ed.), *Modelling and analysis of enterprise information systems* (pp. 311–338).

Guilloux, V., & Kalika, M. (2009). An activity theory view of E-HR and open source . In Torres-Coronas, T., & Arias-Oliva, M. (Eds.), *Encyclopedia of human resources Information Systems: Challenges in e-HRM* (pp. 7–11).

Haab, M. J., & Cramer, S. F. (2011). Enterprise resource planning systems in higher education . In Surry, D. W., Gray, R. M. Jr, & Stefurak, J. R. (Eds.), *Technology integration in higher education: Social and organizational aspects* (pp. 236–252).

Hahsler, M. (2005). A quantitative study of the adoption of design patterns by open source software developers . In Koch, S. (Ed.), *Free/open source software development* (pp. 103–124).

Hammami, S., & Alkhaldi, F. M. (2012). Enhancing BI systems application through the integration of IT governance and knowledge capabilities of the organization . In Rahman El Sheikh, A. A., & Alnoukari, M. (Eds.), *Business intelligence and agile methodologies for knowledge-based organizations: Cross-disciplinary applications* (pp. 161–182).

Hanafizadeh, P., Gholami, R., Dadbin, S., & Standage, N. (2010). The core critical success factors in implementation of enterprise resource planning systems. *International Journal of Enterprise Information Systems (IJEIS)*, *6*(2), 82–111. doi:.doi:10.4018/jeis.2010040105

Hassan, A., & Hietnen, H. (2006). Open content distribution management in virtual organizations . In Khosrow-Pour, M. (Ed.), *Encyclopedia of e-commerce, e-government, and mobile commerce* (pp. 878–883).

Hawking, P. (2008). Enterprise resource planning systems in a global environment . In Ferran, C., & Salim, R. (Eds.), *Enterprise resource planning for global economies: Managerial issues and challenges* (pp. 23–36).

Hinds, D., & Lee, R. M. (2009). Communication network characteristics of open source communities. *International Journal of Open Source Software and Processes (IJOSSP)*, *1*(4), 26–48. doi:.doi:10.4018/jossp.2009100102

Stam, W., & van Wendel de Joode, R. (2007). Analyzing firm participation in open source communities. In St.Amant, K., & Still, B. (Eds.), *Handbook of research on open source software: Technological, economic, and social perspectives* (pp. 495–509).

Huett, J. B., Sharp, J. H., & Huett, K. C. (2010). What's all the FOSS?: How freedom and openness are changing the face of our educational landscape. *International Journal of Open Source Software and Processes (IJOSSP)*, *2*(1), 1–14. doi:.doi:10.4018/jossp.2010010101

Jacobsson, A., & Davidsson, P. (2009). A formal analysis of virtual enterprise creation and operation . In Król, D., & Nguyen, N. (Eds.), *Intelligence integration in distributed knowledge management* (pp. 48–62).

Jakupovic, A., Pavlic, M., & Vrcek, N. (2010). A proposition for classification of business sectors by ERP solutions support. *International Journal of Enterprise Information Systems (IJEIS)*, *6*(3), 59–86. doi:.doi:10.4018/jeis.2010070105

Janev, V., Dudukovic, J., & Vraneš, S. (2010). Semantic Web based integration of knowledge resources for expertise finding . In Cruz-Cunha, M. M. (Ed.), *Social, managerial, and organizational dimensions of enterprise Information Systems* (pp. 496–514).

Janssens, G., Kusters, R., & Heemstra, F. (2008). Sizing ERP implementation projects: An activity-based approach. *International Journal of Enterprise Information Systems (IJEIS)*, *4*(3), 25–47. doi:. doi:10.4018/jeis.2008070103

Jensen, S. S. (2012). User-driven content creation in Second Life a source of innovation? Three case studies of business and public service . In Zagalo, N., Morgado, L., & Boa-Ventura, A. (Eds.), *Virtual worlds and metaverse platforms: New communication and identity paradigms* (pp. 1–15).

Jewels, T., Al-Rawshdi, A., Abusharekh, R. N., & Shamisi, A. S. (2012). Organisational culture and its effects on innovation within ERP systems. In de Pablos Heredero, C., & López, D. (Eds.), *Open innovation in firms and public administrations: Technologies for value creation.* (pp. 126-138). doi:10.4018/978-1-61350-341-6.ch007

Jha, M., & Kumar, S. (2010). Implementation of ERP systems: A seven stage adoption model . In Parthasarathy, S. (Ed.), *Enterprise Information Systems and implementing IT infrastructures: Challenges and issues* (pp. 76–90).

Jin, L., Robey, D., & Boudreau, M. (2007). Beyond development: A research agenda for investigating open source software user communities. *Information Resources Management Journal (IRMJ)*, *20*(1), 68–80. doi:.doi:10.4018/irmj.2007010105

Jones, P., Packham, G., Pickernell, D., & Beynon-Davies, P. (2010). E-commerce trading patterns within the SME sector: An opportunity missed? In Thomas, B., & Simmons, G. (Eds.), *E-commerce adoption and small business in the global marketplace: Tools for optimization* (pp. 23–46).

Kalliamvakou, E. (2007). Open source software basics: An overview of a revolutionary research context . In Lytras, M. D., & Naeve, A. (Eds.), *Open source for knowledge and learning management: Strategies beyond tools* (pp. 1–15).

Kamhawi, E. M. (2010). Factors influencing the use of decision support tools of enterprise resource planning systems . In Khosrow-Pour, M. (Ed.), *Global, social, and organizational implications of emerging information resources management: Concepts and applications* (pp. 205–224).

Kamhawi, E. M. (2009). Examining the factors affecting project and business success of ERP implementation . In Gunasekaran, A. (Ed.), *Global implications of modern enterprise Information Systems: Technologies and applications* (pp. 1–16).

Kamthan, P. (2007). A perspective on software engineering education with open source software . In St.Amant, K., & Still, B. (Eds.), *Handbook of research on open source software: Technological, economic, and social perspectives* (pp. 690–702).

Kask, S. (2012). Modes of open innovation in service industries and process innovation: A comparative analysis. In de Pablos Heredero, C., & López, D. (Eds.), *Open innovation in firms and public administrations: Technologies for value creation.* (pp. 15-36). doi:10.4018/978-1-61350-341-6.ch002

Katsamakas, E., Janamanchi, B., Raghupathi, W., & Gao, W. (2009). A classification analysis of the success of open source health Information Technology projects. *International Journal of Healthcare Information Systems and Informatics (IJHISI)*, *4*(4), 19–36. doi:.doi:10.4018/jhisi.2009071002

Kelsey, S. (2007). Open source software and the corporate world . In St.Amant, K., & Still, B. (Eds.), *Handbook of research on open source software: Technological, economic, and social perspectives* (pp. 570–577).

Kerr, D. (2008). Feral systems and other factors influencing the success of global ERP implementations . In Ferran, C., & Salim, R. (Eds.), *Enterprise resource planning for global economies: Managerial issues and challenges* (pp. 147–165).

Kim, T., Lee, S., Lee, J., & Kim, K. (2007). Enterprise architecture framework for agile and interoperable virtual enterprises . In Saha, P. (Ed.), *Handbook of enterprise systems architecture in practice* (pp. 62–84).

Koch, S., & Neumann, C. (2008). Exploring the effects of process characteristics on products quality in open source software development. *Journal of Database Management (JDM)*, *19*(2), 31–57. doi:. doi:10.4018/jdm.2008040102

Kohlhase, A., & Müller, N. (2008). Added-value: Getting people into semantic work environments . In Rech, J., Decker, B., & Ras, E. (Eds.), *Emerging technologies for semantic work environments: Techniques, methods, and applications* (pp. 181–201).

Kourtesis, D., & Paraskakis, I. (2010). Supporting semantically enhanced Web service discovery for enterprise application integration . In Mentzas, G., & Friesen, A. (Eds.), *Semantic enterprise application integration for business processes: Service-oriented frameworks* (pp. 105–130).

Koyuncugil, A. S. (2009). Early warning system for SMEs as a financial risk detector . In Rahman, H. (Ed.), *Data mining applications for empowering knowledge societies* (pp. 220–238).

Krechmer, K. (2007). Open systems in digital convergence . In Park, S. (Ed.), *Strategies and policies in digital convergence* (pp. 115–134).

Kumar, M., Sareen, M., & Chhabra, S. (2011). Technology related trust issues in SME B2B E-Commerce. *International Journal of Information Communication Technologies and Human Development (IJICTHD)*, *3*(4), 31–46. doi:.doi:10.4018/jicthd.2011100103

Kung, M. T., & Zhang, J. Y. (2010). Implementation and modeling of enterprise Web services: A framework with strategic work flows . In Lee, I. (Ed.), *Transforming e-business practices and applications: Emerging technologies and concepts* (pp. 407–430).

Kurshan, B., Schreiber, A., & Levy, P. (2011). Open and shared educational resources – A Collaborative strategy for advancing e-learning communities: A case exemplified by Curriki . In Czerkawski, B. Ö. (Ed.), *Free and open source software for e-learning: Issues, successes and challenges* (pp. 75–91).

Lai, I. K. (2008). The critical success factors across ERP implementation processes . In Gunasekaran, A. (Ed.), *Techniques and tools for the design and implementation of enterprise information systems* (pp. 57–85).

Lakka, S., Stamati, T., Michalakelis, C., & Martakos, D. (2011). The ontology of the OSS business model: An exploratory study. *International Journal of Open Source Software and Processes (IJOSSP)*, *3*(1), 39–59. doi:.doi:10.4018/jossp.2011010103

Laszlo, G. (2007). Issues and aspects of open source software usage and adoption in the public sector . In St.Amant, K., & Still, B. (Eds.), *Handbook of research on open source software: Technological, economic, and social perspectives* (pp. 445–459).

Lawrence, C. (2007). Architecture-driven business transformation . In Saha, P. (Ed.), *Handbook of enterprise systems architecture in practice* (pp. 207–220).

Lawrence, J. E. (2011). The growth of e-commerce in developing countries: An exploratory study of opportunities and challenges for SMEs. *International Journal of ICT Research and Development in Africa (IJICTRDA)*, *2*(1), 15–28. doi:.doi:10.4018/jictrda.2011010102

Leahy, M. G., & Hall, G. B. (2010). Using open source software components to implement a modular Web 2.0 design for map-based discussions. *International Journal of Open Source Software and Processes (IJOSSP)*, *2*(3), 30–47. doi:.doi:10.4018/jossp.2010070102

Lee, C. (2009). Introduction to open source products . In Chao, L. (Ed.), *Utilizing open source tools for online teaching and learning: Applying Linux technologies* (pp. 1–27).

Lee, H., Davis, R. A., & Chi, Y. (2011). Integrating XML technologies and open source software for personalization in e-learning . In Ng, E., Karacapilidis, N., & Raisinghani, M. (Eds.), *Dynamic advancements in teaching and learning based technologies: New concepts* (pp. 216–231).

Lee, J. (2008). Ontologies for model-driven business transformation . In Rittgen, P. (Ed.), *Handbook of ontologies for business interaction* (pp. 237–253).

Le Texier, T., & Versailles, D. W. (2009). Open source software governance serving technological agility: The case of open source software within the DoD. *International Journal of Open Source Software and Processes (IJOSSP)*, *1*(2), 14–27. doi:.doi:10.4018/jossp.2009040102

Li, Y. (2010). Managing enterprise service level agreement. *International Journal of Applied Logistics (IJAL)*, *1*(3), 18–43. doi:.doi:10.4018/jal.2010070102

Lin, F., & Liu, L. (2007). Enterprise architecture and enterprise information architecture: What is it and how to teach it . In Targowski, A., & Tarn, J. (Eds.), *Enterprise systems education in the 21st century* (pp. 213–229).

Lin, Y., & Krogstie, J. (2012). Semantic annotation of process models for facilitating process knowledge management. In Management Association, USA, I. (Ed.), *Organizational learning and knowledge: Concepts, methodologies, tools and applications.* (pp. 733-754). doi:10.4018/978-1-60960-783-8.ch219

Loukis, E., Sapounas, I., & Aivalis, K. (2009). Enterprise systems strategic alignment and business value . In Gupta, J. N., Sharma, S., & Rashid, M. A. (Eds.), *Handbook of research on enterprise systems* (pp. 152–168).

Lowenthal, P. R., & White, J. W. (2009). Enterprise model . In Rogers, P. L., Berg, G. A., Boettcher, J. V., Howard, C., Justice, L., & Schenk, K. D. (Eds.), *Encyclopedia of distance learning* (2nd ed., pp. 932–936).

Luthiger, B., & Jungwirth, C. (2007). The chase for OSS quality: The meaning of member roles, motivations, and business models . In Sowe, S. K., Stamelos, I. G., & Samoladas, I. (Eds.), *Emerging free and open source software practices* (pp. 147–168).

Ma, D. (2007). Enterprise integration architecture for harmonized messaging . In Saha, P. (Ed.), *Handbook of enterprise systems architecture in practice* (pp. 434–454).

Macías, E., Suarez, A., & Espino, F. (2012). Multi-platform video streaming implementation on mobile terminals . In Sarmiento, A., & Lopez, E. (Eds.), *Multimedia services and streaming for mobile devices: Challenges and innovations* (pp. 288–314).

Mahapatra, R., & Perumal, S. (2007). Enterprise architecture as an enabler for e-governance: An Indian perspective . In Saha, P. (Ed.), *Handbook of Enterprise Systems Architecture in Practice* (pp. 272–289).

Mallach, E. G. (2009). Information System conversion strategies: A unified view. *International Journal of Enterprise Information Systems (IJEIS)*, *5*(1), 44–54. doi:.doi:10.4018/jeis.2009010104

Márquez-García, A. M., Garrido-Álvarez, M. T., & del Carmen Moreno-Martos, M. (2008). FON: A social collaborative technological entrepreneurship . In Medina-Garrido, J., Martínez-Fierro, S., & Ruiz-Navarro, J. (Eds.), *Cases on Information Technology entrepreneurship* (pp. 1–35).

Martens, B. V., & Hawamdeh, S. (2010). The professionalization of knowledge management . In Pankl, E., Theiss-White, D., & Bushing, M. C. (Eds.), *Recruitment, development, and retention of information professionals: Trends in human resources and knowledge management* (pp. 139–156).

Matei, S. A., & Bruno, R. J. (2012). Individualist motivators and community functional constraints in social media: The case of Wikis and Wikipedia . In Comunello, F. (Ed.), *Networked sociability and individualism: Technology for personal and professional relationships* (pp. 1–23).

Mathrani, S., Rashid, M. A., & Viehland, D. (2009). Enterprise systems in small and medium-sized enterprises . In Gupta, J. N., Sharma, S., & Rashid, M. A. (Eds.), *Handbook of research on enterprise systems* (pp. 170–184).

McGrath, O. (2010). Data mining user activity in free and open source software (FOSS)/ open learning management systems. *International Journal of Open Source Software and Processes (IJOSSP)*, *2*(1), 65–75. doi:.doi:10.4018/jossp.2010010105

McKeachie, I. (2007). Dynamic enterprise modeling for knowledge worker industries . In Cruz-Cunha, M. M., Conceicao Cortes, B., & Putnik, G. D. (Eds.), *Adaptive technologies and business integration: Social, managerial and organizational dimensions* (pp. 59–81).

Mejía, R., Peñaranda, N., Molina, A., & Augenbroe, G. (2008). Supporting collaborative processes in virtual organizations . In Kock, N. (Ed.), *Encyclopedia of e-collaboration* (pp. 589–595).

Mendoza, R. A., & Ravichandran, T. (2010). An empirical evaluation of the assimilation of industry-specific data standards using firm-level and community-level constructs. *International Journal of Enterprise Information Systems (IJEIS)*, *6*(2), 58–81. doi:.doi:10.4018/jeis.2010040104

Messica, A. (2010). Open source – Collaborative innovation . In Kollmann, T., Kuckertz, A., & Stöckmann, C. (Eds.), *E-entrepreneurship and ICT ventures: Strategy, organization and technology* (pp. 213–234).

Meza, J., & Zhu, Q. (2009). Mix, match, rediscovery: A mashup experiment of knowledge organization in an enterprise environment. *International Journal of Enterprise Information Systems (IJEIS)*, *5*(2), 37–48. doi:.doi:10.4018/jeis.2009040103

Misic, V. B., & Zhao, J. L. (2007). E-business reference models . In Fettke, P., & Loos, P. (Eds.), *Reference modeling for business systems analysis* (pp. 241–265).

Misra, H. (2012). ICT mediated value chain for managing weavers' livelihoods: A case of Jaipur Rugs Company . In Rahman, H., & Ramos, I. (Eds.), *Cases on SMEs and open innovation: Applications and investigations* (pp. 126–162).

Mo, J., & Nemes, L. (2009). Architecture based engineering of enterprises with government involvement . In Saha, P. (Ed.), *Advances in government enterprise architecture* (pp. 371–391).

Molhanec, M., & Merunka, V. (2012). BORM: Agile modelling for business intelligence . In Rahman El Sheikh, A. A., & Alnoukari, M. (Eds.), *Business intelligence and agile methodologies for knowledge-based organizations: Cross-disciplinary applications* (pp. 120–131).

Moyle, K. (2007). Selecting open source software for use in schools . In St.Amant, K., & Still, B. (Eds.), *Handbook of research on open source software: Technological, economic, and social perspectives* (pp. 624–637).

Mu, Z., Wenli, L., Jing, L., Xiang, Y., Congying, R., & Chengjuan, W. (2010). Research on the innovation mechanism and model of logistics enterprise: A Chinese perspective . In Luo, Z. (Ed.), *Service science and logistics informatics: Innovative perspectives* (pp. 21–45).

Mukerji, B., & Palanisamy, R. (2012). Review of open source software (OSS): Advantages and issues related with its adoption in e-government . In Shareef, M., Archer, N., & Dutta, S. (Eds.), *E-government service maturity and development: Cultural, organizational and technological perspectives* (pp. 198–212).

Muscatello, J. R., & Parente, D. H. (2008). A post-implementation case study and review of enterprise resource planning (ERP) implementations . In Khosrow-Pour, M. (Ed.), *Innovative technologies for information resources management* (pp. 1–20).

Narasimhamurthy, S., Muggeridge, M., Waldschmidt, S., Checconi, F., & Cucinotta, T. (2012). Data storage in cloud based real-time environments . In Kyriazis, D., Varvarigou, T., & Konstanteli, K. G. (Eds.), *Achieving real-time in distributed computing: From grids to clouds* (pp. 236–258).

Negash, S. (2010). Accessing ICT enabled content in low-income countries: Think big, start small, and scale up. *International Journal of Information and Communication Technology Education (IJICTE)*, *6*(4), 49–60. doi:.doi:10.4018/jicte.2010100105

Nuvolari, A., & Rullani, F. (2007). Curious exceptions? Open source software and "open" technology . In St.Amant, K., & Still, B. (Eds.), *Handbook of research on open source software: Technological, economic, and social perspectives* (pp. 227–239).

O'Donnell, C. (2007). The labor politics of scratching an itch . In St.Amant, K., & Still, B. (Eds.), *Handbook of research on open source software: Technological, economic, and social perspectives* (pp. 460–467).

Okoli, C., & Carillo, K. (2006). Intellectual property rights in open source software communities . In Dasgupta, S. (Ed.), *Encyclopedia of virtual communities and technologies* (pp. 285–290).

Olla, P. (2007). Open source e-learning systems: Evaluation of features and functionality . In St.Amant, K., & Still, B. (Eds.), *Handbook of research on open source software: Technological, economic, and social perspectives* (pp. 638–648).

Olla, P., & Crider, R. (2007). Open-source online knowledge portals for education . In Tatnall, A. (Ed.), *Encyclopedia of portal technologies and applications* (pp. 684–688).

O'Neill, T., Denford, M., Leaney, J., & Dunsire, K. (2007). Managing enterprise architecture change . In Saha, P. (Ed.), *Handbook of enterprise systems architecture in practice* (pp. 192–205).

Pang, N. (2008). Cultivating communities through the knowledge commons: The case of open content licenses . In Sasaki, H. (Ed.), *Intellectual property protection for multimedia Information Technology* (pp. 260–277).

Papajorgji, P., & Pardalos, P. M. (2010). Towards a model-centric approach for developing enterprise Information Systems . In Parthasarathy, S. (Ed.), *Enterprise Information Systems and implementing IT infrastructures: Challenges and issues* (pp. 140–158).

Papastergiou, S., & Polemi, D. (2009). A secure and trustful e-ordering architecture (TOES) for small and medium size enterprises (SMEs). *International Journal of Enterprise Information Systems (IJEIS)*, 5(2), 1–17. doi:.doi:10.4018/jeis.2009040101

Parthasarathy, S. (2010). Directed basic research in enterprise resource planning (ERP) . In Ramachandran, M., & de Carvalho, R. (Eds.), *Handbook of research on software engineering and productivity technologies: Implications of globalization* (pp. 382–395).

Pataricza, A., Balogh, A., & Gonczy, L. (2007). Verification and validation of nonfunctional aspects in enterprise modeling . In Rittgen, P. (Ed.), *Enterprise modeling and computing with UML* (pp. 257–298).

Peizer, J. (2007). Open source technology and ideology in the nonprofit context . In St.Amant, K., & Still, B. (Eds.), *Handbook of research on open source software: Technological, economic, and social perspectives* (pp. 468–479).

Peslak, A. R., & Boyle, T. A. (2010). An exploratory study of the key skills for entry-level ERP employees. *International Journal of Enterprise Information Systems (IJEIS)*, 6(2), 1–14. doi:.doi:10.4018/jeis.2010040101

Polovina, S., & Hill, R. (2009). A transactions pattern for structuring unstructured corporate information in enterprise applications. *International Journal of Intelligent Information Technologies (IJIIT)*, 5(2), 33–47. doi:.doi:10.4018/jiit.2009040103

Portougal, V. (2006). Enterprise systems implementation phases . In Portougal, V., & Sundaram, D. (Eds.), *Business processes: Operational solutions for SAP implementation* (pp. 89–127).

Potosky, D., & Olshan, B. (2008). The secret success of a global ERP champion: Everything changed and nothing happened . In Ferran, C., & Salim, R. (Eds.), *Enterprise resource planning for global economies: Managerial issues and challenges* (pp. 94–107).

Pscheidt, M., & van der Weide, T. (2010). Bridging the digital divide by open source: A theoretical model of best practice. *International Journal of Innovation in the Digital Economy (IJIDE)*, *1*(2), 44–60. doi:. doi:10.4018/jide.2010040103

Pucihar, A., Lenart, G., & Sudzina, F. (2010). ERP system selection criteria: SMEs' perceptions . In Bharati, P., Lee, I., & Chaudhury, A. (Eds.), *Global perspectives on small and medium enterprises and strategic Information Systems: International approaches* (pp. 57–80).

Qiu, R. G. (2007). Information Technology as a service . In Qiu, R. (Ed.), *Enterprise service computing: From concept to deployment* (pp. 1–24).

Qureshil, S., Kamal, M., & Wolcott, P. (2009). Information Technology interventions for growth and competitiveness in micro-enterprises. *International Journal of Enterprise Information Systems (IJEIS)*, *5*(2), 71–95. doi:.doi:10.4018/jeis.2009040105

Radtke, N. P., Janssen, M. A., & Collofello, J. S. (2009). What makes free/libre open source software (FLOSS) projects successful? An agent-based model of FLOSS projects. *International Journal of Open Source Software and Processes (IJOSSP)*, *1*(2), 1–13. doi:.doi:10.4018/jossp.2009040101

Rainey, D. L. (2012). A model for improving the adoption of sustainability in the context of globalization and innovation . In Nobre, F. S., Walker, D., & Harris, R. J. (Eds.), *Technological, managerial and organizational core competencies: Dynamic innovation and sustainable development* (pp. 18–39).

Rajala, R., & Nissilä, J. (2007). Revenue models in the open source software business . In St.Amant, K., & Still, B. (Eds.), *Handbook of research on open source software: Technological, economic, and social perspectives* (pp. 541–554).

Ramanathan, J., & Ramnath, R. (2009). Co-engineering IT services for lean operations . In Ramanathan, J., & Ramnath, R. (Eds.), *Co-engineering applications and adaptive business technologies in practice: Enterprise service ontologies, models, and frameworks* (pp. 271–298).

Ranjan, R., & Buyya, R. (2010). Decentralized overlay for federation of enterprise clouds . In Li, K., Hsu, C., Yang, L., Dongarra, J., & Zima, H. (Eds.), *Handbook of research on scalable computing technologies* (pp. 191–217).

Raza, A., Capretz, L. F., & Ahmed, F. (2011). An empirical study of open source software usability: The industrial perspective. *International Journal of Open Source Software and Processes (IJOSSP)*, *3*(1), 1–16. doi:.doi:10.4018/jossp.2011010101

Razi, M. A. (2007). Teaching ERP with Microsoft Business Solutions - Great Plains . In Targowski, A., & Tarn, J. (Eds.), *Enterprise systems education in the 21st century* (pp. 230–245).

Remus, U. (2007). Success factors for the implementation of enterprise portals . In Tatnall, A. (Ed.), *Encyclopedia of portal technologies and applications* (pp. 985–991).

Rennard, J. (2006). Producing and sharing free advanced scientific and technological knowledge using the Internet. In Marshall, S., Taylor, W., & Yu, X. (Eds.), *Encyclopedia of developing regional communities with information and communication technology.* (pp. 587–592). doi:10.4018/978-1-59140-575-7.ch104

Robinson, P., & Gout, F. (2007). Extreme architecture framework: A minimalist framework for modern times . In Saha, P. (Ed.), *Handbook of enterprise systems architecture in practice* (pp. 18–38).

Rooney, D., Ferrier, E., Graham, P., & Jones, A. (2007). Cultural knowledge management and broadband content in development: Open content platforms, copyright and archives . In Rahman, H. (Ed.), *Information and communication technologies for economic and regional developments* (pp. 148–165).

Rosenberg, F., Michlmayr, A., Nagl, C., & Dustdar, S. (2009). Distributed business rules within service-centric systems . In Giurca, A., Gasevic, D., & Taveter, K. (Eds.), *Handbook of research on emerging rule-based languages and technologies: Open solutions and approaches* (pp. 448–470).

Rosu, S. M., & Dragoi, G. (2012). Virtual enterprise network solutions and monitoring as support for geographically dispersed business . In Cruz-Cunha, M. M., Gonçalves, P., Lopes, N., Miranda, E. M., & Putnik, G. D. (Eds.), *Handbook of research on business social networking: Organizational, managerial, and technological dimensions* (pp. 34–62).

Russo, B., Scotto, M., Sillitti, A., & Succi, G. (2010). Open source assessment methodologies . In Russo, B., Scotto, M., Sillitti, A., & Succi, G. (Eds.), *Agile technologies in open source development* (pp. 302–310).

Russo, B., & Succi, G. (2009). A cost model of open source software adoption. *International Journal of Open Source Software and Processes (IJOSSP)*, *1*(3), 60–82. doi:.doi:10.4018/jossp.2009070105

Saha, P. (2007). A synergistic assessment of the federal enterprise architecture framework against GERAM (ISO15704: 2000) . In Saha, P. (Ed.), *Handbook of enterprise systems architecture in practice* (pp. 1–17).

Sankar, C., & Rau, K. (2006). Technical issues in implementing ERP systems . In Sankar, C., & Rau, K. (Eds.), *Implementation strategies for SAP R/3 in a multinational organization: Lessons from a real-world case study* (pp. 105–137).

Scacchi, W. (2007). Understanding the development of free e-commerce/e-business software: A resource-based view . In Sowe, S. K., Stamelos, I. G., & Samoladas, I. (Eds.), *Emerging Free and open source software practices* (pp. 170–190).

Schnackenberg, H. L., & Vega, E. S. (2010). Open source and bridging the digital divide: A case study . In Luppicini, R., & Haghi, A. (Eds.), *Cases on digital technologies in higher education: Issues and challenges* (pp. 24–33).

Schoenherr, T., Hilpert, D., Soni, A. K., Venkataramanan, M., & Mabert, V. A. (2009). Enterprise system in the German manufacturing Mittelstand . In Gupta, J. N., Sharma, S., & Rashid, M. A. (Eds.), *Handbook of research on enterprise systems* (pp. 201–217).

Sedera, D. (2009). Size matters! Enterprise system success in medium and large organizations . In Gupta, J. N., Sharma, S., & Rashid, M. A. (Eds.), *Handbook of research on enterprise systems* (pp. 218–231).

Segall, R. S. (2009). Comparing FOUR-SELECTED DATA MINING SOFTWARE . In Wang, J. (Ed.), *Encyclopedia of data warehousing and mining* (2nd ed., pp. 269–277).

Shakir, M. (2008). ERP trends, opportunities, and challenges: A focus on the Gulf region in the Middle East . In Ferran, C., & Salim, R. (Eds.), *Enterprise resource planning for global economies: Managerial issues and challenges* (pp. 309–327).

Shakir, M., & Viehland, D. (2006). The selection of the IT platform: Enterprise system implementation in the NZ Health Board . In Khosrow-Pour, M. (Ed.), *Cases on Information Technology and business process reengineering* (pp. 21–32).

Sharma, S. (2012). The didactic approach to manage strategic inconsistencies in ERP: An e-initiative . In Chhabra, S., & Kumar, M. (Eds.), *Strategic enterprise resource planning models for e-government: Applications and methodologies* (pp. 73–89).

Sharma, S. K., & Gupta, J. N. (2005). Designing e-commerce portal for an enterprise- A framework . In Tatnall, A. (Ed.), *Web portals: The new gateways to internet information and services* (pp. 99–118).

Simmons, D. B., Lively, W., & Nelson, C. (2007). Rapid insertion of leading edge industrial strength software into university classrooms . In St.Amant, K., & Still, B. (Eds.), *Handbook of research on open source software: Technological, economic, and social perspectives* (pp. 670–680).

Singla, A. R. (2010). Challenges in enterprise information systems implementation: An empirical study . In Parthasarathy, S. (Ed.), *Enterprise Information Systems and implementing IT infrastructures: Challenges and issues* (pp. 195–209).

Skidmore, D. (2007). FLOSS legal and engineering terms and a license taxonomy . In St.Amant, K., & Still, B. (Eds.), *Handbook of research on open source software: Technological, economic, and social perspectives* (pp. 394–410).

Sliman, L., Biennier, F., & Badr, Y. (2009). Collaborative business and enterprise urbanization: Towards a production-oriented urbanization strategy. *International Journal of Enterprise Information Systems (IJEIS)*, *5*(1), 9–31. doi:.doi:10.4018/jeis.2009010102

Smolander, K., & Rossi, M. (2009). Conflicts, compromises, and political decisions: Methodological challenges of enterprise-wide e-business architecture creation. *International Journal of Enterprise Information Systems (IJEIS)*, *5*(2), 49–70. doi:.doi:10.4018/jeis.2009040104

Soriano, J., Frutos, S., & Jiménez, M. (2008). Collaborative development within open source communities . In Putnik, G. D., & Cruz-Cunha, M. M. (Eds.), *Encyclopedia of networked and virtual organizations* (pp. 232–236).

Soriano, J., Lizcano, D., Reyes, M., & Alonso, F. (2009). Enterprise 2.0: Collaboration and knowledge emergence as a business Web strategy enabler . In Al-Hakim, L., & Memmola, M. (Eds.), *Business Web strategy: Design, alignment, and application* (pp. 61–93).

Sousa, P., Caetano, A., Vasconcelos, A., Pereira, C., & Tribolet, J. (2007). Enterprise architecture modeling with the unified modeling language . In Rittgen, P. (Ed.), *Enterprise modeling and computing with UML* (pp. 67–94).

Squire, M. (2009). Integrating projects from multiple open source code forges. *International Journal of Open Source Software and Processes (IJOSSP)*, *1*(1), 46–57. doi:.doi:10.4018/jossp.2009010103

Srinivasan, M. (2010). E-business and ERP: A conceptual framework toward the business transformation to an integrated e-supply chain. *International Journal of Enterprise Information Systems (IJEIS)*, *6*(4), 1–19. doi:.doi:10.4018/jeis.2010100101

Stam, W., & van Wendel de Joode, R. (2007). Analyzing firm participation in open source communities . In St.Amant, K., & Still, B. (Eds.), *Handbook of research on open source software: Technological, economic, and social perspectives* (pp. 495–509).

Stamelos, I. G. (2011). Teaching software engineering with free/libre open source projects . In Koch, S. (Ed.), *Multi-disciplinary advancement in open source software and processes* (pp. 67–85).

Stephens, R. T. (2007). Governance and the open source repository . In St.Amant, K., & Still, B. (Eds.), *Handbook of research on open source software: Technological, economic, and social perspectives* (pp. 480–493).

Stephenson, S. V., & Sage, A. P. (2007). Information and knowledge perspectives in systems engineering and management for innovation and productivity through enterprise resource planning. *Information Resources Management Journal (IRMJ)*, *20*(2), 44–73. doi:.doi:10.4018/irmj.2007040104

Sticklen, D. J., & Issa, T. (2011). An initial examination of free and proprietary software-selection in organizations. *International Journal of Web Portals (IJWP)*, *3*(4), 27–43. doi:.doi:10.4018/jwp.2011100103

Tang, L., Dong, J., & Zhao, Y. (2012). SLA-aware enterprise service computing. In Cardellini, V., Casalicchio, E., Castelo Branco, K. L., Estrella, J. C., & Monaco, F. J. (Eds.), *Performance and dependability in service computing: Concepts, techniques and research directions.* (pp. 26-52). doi:10.4018/978-1-60960-794-4.ch002

Taranovych, Y. (2007). A coaching portal for IT PROJECT MANAGEMENT . In Tatnall, A. (Ed.), *Encyclopedia of portal technologies and applications* (pp. 126–133).

Tawileh, A., Rana, O., Ivins, W., & McIntosh, S. (2007). Evidence-based assurance to support process quality in the F/OSS community . In Sowe, S. K., Stamelos, I. G., & Samoladas, I. (Eds.), *Emerging free and open source software practices* (pp. 120–146).

Tektonidis, D., & Bokma, A. (2008). The utilization of Semantic Web for integrating enterprise systems . In Protogeros, N. (Ed.), *Agent and Web service technologies in virtual enterprises* (pp. 97–114).

Terán, O., Alvarez, J., Abraham, B., & Aguilar, J. (2008). An incremental functionality-oriented free software development methodology . In Oktaba, H., & Piattini, M. (Eds.), *Software process improvement for small and medium enterprises: Techniques and case studies* (pp. 242–257).

Thomsen, C., & Pedersen, T. B. (2009). A survey of open source tools for business intelligence. *International Journal of Data Warehousing and Mining (IJDWM)*, *5*(3), 56–75. doi:.doi:10.4018/jdwm.2009070103

Thomson, J. (2011). Mapping and data base modeling for public sector strategic enterprise resource planning . In Al Ajeeli, A. T., & Al-Bastaki, Y. A. (Eds.), *Handbook of research on e-services in the public sector: E-government strategies and advancements* (pp. 312–325).

Thomson, J. D. (2010). Enterprise resource planning: An e-entrepreneurial challenge . In Kollmann, T., Kuckertz, A., & Stöckmann, C. (Eds.), *E-entrepreneurship and ICT ventures: Strategy, organization and technology* (pp. 235–250).

Tribunella, T., & Baroody, J. (2007). Open source for accounting and enterprise systems . In St.Amant, K., & Still, B. (Eds.), *Handbook of research on open source software: Technological, economic, and social perspectives* (pp. 555–569).

Tsourakakis, C. E. (2012). Large scale graph mining with MapReduce: Counting triangles in large real networks . In Sakr, S., & Pardede, E. (Eds.), *Graph data management: Techniques and applications* (pp. 299–314).

Ueno, K., & Tatsubori, M. (2012). Early capacity testing of an enterprise service bus . In Jie-Zhang, L. (Ed.), *Innovations, standards and practices of Web services: Emerging research topics* (pp. 288–305).

Uzoka, F. E., Abiola, R. O., & Nyangeresi, R. (2008). Influence of product and organizational constructs on ERP acquisition using an extended technology acceptance model. *International Journal of Enterprise Information Systems (IJEIS)*, *4*(2), 67–83. doi:.doi:10.4018/jeis.2008040105

Vaidyanathan, G. (2009). Enterprise resource systems software implementation . In Gupta, J. N., Sharma, S., & Rashid, M. A. (Eds.), *Handbook of research on enterprise systems* (pp. 245–261).

Vambenepe, W., Thompson, C., Talwar, V., Rafaeli, S., Murray, B., & Milojicic, D. (2007). Dealing with scale and adaptation of global Web services management. *International Journal of Web Services Research (IJWSR)*, *4*(3), 65–84. doi:.doi:10.4018/jwsr.2007070104

van Wendel de Joode, R., de Bruijn, H., & van Eeten, M. (2007). Software development and coordination tools in open source communities . In Sowe, S. K., Stamelos, I. G., & Samoladas, I. (Eds.), *Emerging free and open source software practices* (pp. 96–119).

van Wendel de Joode, R., & Spaeth, S. (2008). Key concepts and definitions of open source communities . In Putnik, G. D., & Cruz-Cunha, M. M. (Eds.), *Encyclopedia of networked and virtual organizations* (pp. 753–760).

Vassiliadis, B. (2011). The Grid as a virtual enterprise enabler . In Wang, J. (Ed.), *Information Systems and new applications in the service sector: Models and methods* (pp. 76–89).

Ven, K., & De Bruyn, P. (2011). Factors affecting the development of absorptive capacity in the adoption of open source software. *International Journal of Open Source Software and Processes (IJOSSP)*, *3*(1), 17–38. doi:.doi:10.4018/jossp.2011010102

Ven, K., Van Nuffel, D., & Verelst, J. (2007). The migration of public administrations towards open source desktop software: Recommendations from research and validation through a case study . In Sowe, S. K., Stamelos, I. G., & Samoladas, I. (Eds.), *Emerging free and open source software practices* (pp. 191–214).

Ven, K., & Verelst, J. (2008). The impact of ideology on the organizational adoption of open source software. *Journal of Database Management (JDM)*, *19*(2), 58–72. doi:.doi:10.4018/jdm.2008040103

Vinck, D., Rivera-Gonzales, I., & Penz, B. (2010). Enterprise resource planning (ERP) embedding: Building of software/ enterprise integration . In Cruz-Cunha, M. M. (Ed.), *Enterprise Information Systems for business integration in SMEs: Technological, organizational, and social dimensions* (pp. 432–453).

von Kortzfleisch, H., Schaarschmidt, M., & Magin, P. (2010). Open scientific entrepreneurship: How the open source paradigm can foster entrepreneurial activities in scientific institutions. *International Journal of Open Source Software and Processes (IJOSSP)*, *2*(4), 48–66. doi:.doi:10.4018/IJOSSP.2010100104

Wang, B., & Paper, D. (2006). A case of an IT-enabled organizational change intervention: The missing pieces . In Khosrow-Pour, M. (Ed.), *Cases on Information Technology and business process reengineering* (pp. 1–20).

Wang, J., Hu, X., Hollister, K., & Zhu, D. (2008). A comparison and scenario analysis of leading data mining software. *International Journal of Knowledge Management (IJKM)*, *4*(2), 17–34. doi:.doi:10.4018/jkm.2008040102

Weiss, M., & Moroiu, G. (2007). Ecology and dynamics of open source communities . In Sowe, S. K., Stamelos, I. G., & Samoladas, I. (Eds.), *Emerging free and open source software practices* (pp. 46–67).

Weng, T., Lin, Y., & Stu, J. (2012). Case study on SOA implementation framework and applications . In Lee, J., Ma, S., & Liu, A. (Eds.), *Service life cycle tools and technologies: Methods, trends and advances* (pp. 272–302).

Wenrich, K., & Ahmad, N. (2009). Lessons learned during a decade of ERP experience: A case study. *International Journal of Enterprise Information Systems (IJEIS)*, *5*(1), 55–73. doi:.doi:10.4018/jeis.2009010105

Werth, D., & Makuch, P. (2009). Mobile technologies extending ERP systems. In Unhelkar, B. (Ed.), *Handbook of research in mobile business, second edition: Technical, methodological and social perspectives.* (pp. 440-444). doi:10.4018/978-1-60566-156-8.ch041

Wickramasinghe, N., & Von Lubitz, D. (2007). The KM business infrastructure . In Wickramasinghe, N., & von Lubitz, D. (Eds.), *Knowledge-based enterprise: Theories and fundamentals* (pp. 65–95).

Williams van Rooij, S. (2010). Higher education and FOSS for e-learning: The role of organizational sub-cultures in enterprise-wide adoption. *International Journal of Open Source Software and Processes (IJOSSP)*, *2*(1), 15–31. doi:.doi:10.4018/jossp.2010010102

Wognum, N., & Ip-Shing, F. (2007). Maturity of IT-business alignment: An assessment tool . In Saha, P. (Ed.), *Handbook of enterprise systems architecture in practice* (pp. 221–236).

Wu, D., & Zhao, F. (2008). Performance measurement in the SMEs in the information industry . In Zhao, F. (Ed.), *Information Technology entrepreneurship and innovation* (pp. 79–99).

Wynn, D. Jr. (2007). Assessing the health of an open source ecosystem . In Sowe, S. K., Stamelos, I. G., & Samoladas, I. (Eds.), *Emerging free and open source software practices* (pp. 238–258).

Xu, L., de Vrieze, P., Bouguettaya, A., Liang, P., Phalp, K., & Jeary, S. (2012). Service-oriented collaborative business processes. In Cardellini, V., Casalicchio, E., Castelo Branco, K. L., Estrella, J. C., & Monaco, F. J. (Eds.), *Performance and dependability in service computing: Concepts, techniques and research directions.* (pp. 116-132). doi:10.4018/978-1-60960-794-4.ch005

Xu, M., Rohatgi, R., & Duan, Y. (2008). Engaging SMEs in e-business: Insights from an empirical study . In Lee, I. (Ed.), *E-business models, services and communications* (pp. 119–137).

Yan, Y., & Klein, M. (2007). Web services vs. ebXML: An evaluation of Web services and ebXML for e-business applications . In Qiu, R. (Ed.), *Enterprise service computing: From concept to deployment* (pp. 242–260).

Yeats, D. (2007). Morality and pragmatism in free software and open source . In St.Amant, K., & Still, B. (Eds.), *Handbook of research on open source software: Technological, economic, and social perspectives* (pp. 23–33).

Zhao, L., Deek, F. P., & McHugh, J. A. (2009). Strategies for improving open source software usability: An exploratory learning framework and a Web-based inspection tool. *International Journal of Open Source Software and Processes (IJOSSP), 1*(4), 49–64. doi:.doi:10.4018/jossp.2009100103

Zhao, W., Moser, L. E., & Melliar-Smith, P. M. (2006). High availability and data consistency for three-tier enterprise applications . In Khosrow-Pour, M. (Ed.), *Encyclopedia of E-commerce, e-government, and mobile commerce* (pp. 552–558).

Zutshi, A., Zutshi, S., & Sohal, A. (2006). How e-entrepreneurs operate in the context of open source software . In Zhao, F. (Ed.), *Entrepreneurship and innovations in e-business: An integrative perspective* (pp. 62–88).

# Compilation of References

Abboud, L. (2007). *SAP's New Model: Think Smaller*. The Wall Street Journal On Line, USA: 2007, available at http://online.wsj.com/article/SB119016383913731920. html, Retrieved in 2009, July.

Adam, F., & O'Doherty, P. (2000). Lessons from enterprise resource planning implementations in Ireland - towards smaller and shorter ERP projects. *Journal of Information Technology, 15*, 305–316. doi:10.1080/02683960010008953

Agerfalk, P., & Fitzgerald, B. (2008). Outsourcing to an Unknown Workforce: Exploring Opensourcing as a Global Sourcing Strategy. *Management Information Systems Quarterly, 32*(2), 385–409.

Agerfalk, P., Fitzgerald, B., & Slaughter, S. (2009). Flexible and Distributed Information Systems Development: State of the Art and Research Challenges. *Information Systems Research, 20*(3), 317–328. doi:10.1287/isre.1090.0244

Ågerfalk, P. J., & Fitzgerald, B. (2008). Outsourcing to an Unknown Workforce: Exploring Opensourcing as a Global Sourcing Strategy. *Management Information Systems Quarterly, 32*(2), 385–409.

Ahmed, O. (2005). *Migrating from proprietary to Open Source: Learning Content Management Systems*. Doctoral Dissertation, Department of Systems and Computer Engineering, Carleton University, Ottawa, Ontario, Canada.

Ajila, S. A., & Wu, D. (2007). Empirical study of the effects of open source adoption on software development economics. *Journal of Systems and Software, 80*, 1517–1529. doi:10.1016/j.jss.2007.01.011

Al-Mashari, M., Al-Mudimigh, A., & Zairi, M. (2003). Enterprise resource planning: A taxonomy of critical factors. *European Journal of Operational Research, 146*, 352–364. doi:10.1016/S0377-2217(02)00554-4

Alshawi, S., Themistocleous, M., Almadani, R. (2004). Integrating diverse ERP systems: a case study. *The Journal of Enterprise Information Management*, Volume 17, Number 6,. Emerald Group Publishing Limited, pp.454-462.

Anand, S. & Ganesh, J. (2006) Towards Enterprise Agility Through Effective Decision Making. *SETLabs Briefings, 4* (1).

Arima, K. (2009). *O ERP Agora é Open Source. Info Exame Magazine, 2009* (pp. 94–95). June, Brazil: Editora Abril. (in Portuguese)

Atem de Carvalho, R., & Johansson, B. (2010). Enterprise resource planning systems for small and medium-sized enterprises . In Ramachandran, M., & Atem de Carvalho, R. (Eds.), *Handbook of Research on Software Engineering and Productivity Technologies: Implications of Globalization* (pp. 373–381). New York: Information Science Reference.

Atkinson, R., & Floyd, S. (2004). IAB concerns and recommendations regarding Internet research and evolution. *IETF RFC 3869 (Informational)*. Retrieved April 15, 2008 from http://www.rfc-editor.org/rfcsearch.html

Baki, B., & Cakar, K. (2005). Determining the ERP package-selecting criteria: the case of Turkish manufacturing companies. *Business Process Management Journal, 11*(1), 75–86. doi:10.1108/14637150510578746

Baskerville, R., & Wood-Harper, A. T. (1998). Diversity in information systems action research methods. *European Journal of Information Systems*, 7, 90–107. doi:10.1057/palgrave.ejis.3000298

Beachboard, J., Cole, A., Mellor, M., Hernandez, S., Aytes, K., & Massad, N. (2008). Improving information security risk analysis practices for small- and medium-sized enterprises: a research agenda. *Issues in Informing Science and Information Technology*, 5, 73–85.

Benlian, A., & Hess, T. (2010). Comparing the relative importance of evaluation criteria in proprietary and open-source enterprise application software selection: a conjoint study of ERP and office systems. *Information Systems Journal*. (Early view)

Bernroider, E., & Koch, S. (2001). ERP selection process in mid-size and large organizations. *Business Process Management Journal*, 7(3), 251–257. doi:10.1108/14637150110392746

Berry, D. M. (2008). *Copy, rip, Burn: the Politics of Copyleft and Open Source*. London: Pluto Press.

Bigaton, A. L. W. (2005). *Gestão Estratégica da Informação nas Pequenas Empresas: Estudo Comparativo de Casos em Empresas do Setor Industrial de São José do Rio Preto – SP*. Unpublished Master Degree Dissertation, University of São Paulo, São Carlos, Brazil, 2005. (in Portuguese)

Bitzer, J. (2004). Commercial versus open source software: the role of product heterogeneity in competition. *Economic Systems*, 28, 369–381. doi:10.1016/j.ecosys.2005.01.001

Bitzer, J., Schrettl, W., & Schöder, P. (2007). Intrinsic motivation in open source software development. *Journal of Comparative Economics*, 35, 160–169. doi:10.1016/j.jce.2006.10.001

Bitzer, J. (2005). The impact of entry and competition by Open Source Software on Innovation Activity. *Industrial Organization 051201*, EconWPA.

Bonaccorsi, A., Giannangeli, S., & Rossi, C. (2006). Entry Strategies Under Competing Standards: Hybrid Business Models in the Open Source Software Industry. *Management Science*, 52(7), 1085–1098. doi:10.1287/mnsc.1060.0547

Bonaccorsi, A., & Rossi, C. (2003). Why Open Source software can succeed. *Research Policy*, 32, 1243–1258. doi:10.1016/S0048-7333(03)00051-9

Boyer, M., & Robert, J. (2006). *The Economics of Free and Open Source Software: Contributions to a Government Policy on Open Source Software*. Montreal: CIRANO.

Bravo, E. & Santana, M. (2010). El impacto de la implantación de los Sistemas de Planeamiento de Recursos Empresariales ERP en el desempeño individual. *AMCIS Proceedings*, paper 265.

Brehm, L., Heinzl, A., & Markus, M. L. (2001). Tailoring ERP systems: A spectrum of choices and their implications. In *Proceedings of the 34th Annual Hawaii International Conference on System Sciences, Maui, Hawaii*. New York: Institute of Electrical and Electronics Engineers.

Brocke., J. vom, Schenk, B. & Sonnenberg C. 2009. Organizational Implications of Implementing Service Oriented ERP Systems: An Analysis Based on New Institutional Economics. In: Abramowicz, W. (Ed.). *BIS 2009, LNBIP 21*, 252–263, 2009, Springer-Verlag Berlin Heidelberg.

Bruce, G., Robson, P., & Spaven, R. (2006). OSS opportunities in open source software — CRM and OSS standards. *BT Technology Journal*, 24(1), 127–140. doi:10.1007/s10550-006-0028-9

Brydon, M., & Vinning, A. R. (2008). Adoption, improvement, and disruption: Predicting the impact of open source applications in enterprise software markets. *Journal of Database Management*, 19(2), 73–94. doi:10.4018/jdm.2008040104

Bueno, S., & Gallego, M. D. (2010). Evaluating acceptance of OSS-ERP based on user perceptions . In Sobh, T. (Ed.), *Innovations and Advances in Computer Sciences and Engineering, Springer Science+Business Media B. V.* doi:10.1007/978-90-481-3658-2_10

Buonanno, G., Faverio, P., Pigni, F., Ravarini, A., Sciuto, D., & Tagliavini, M. (2005). Factors affecting ERP system adoption. *Journal of Enterprise Information Management*, 18(4), 384–426. doi:10.1108/17410390510609572

Caldeira, M. M., & Ward, J. M. (2002). Understanding the successful adoption and use of IS/IT in SME's: an explanation from Portuguese manufacturing industries. *Information Systems Journal*, *12*(2), 121–152. doi:10.1046/j.1365-2575.2002.00119.x

Campbell-Kelly, M., & Garcia-Swartz, D. D. (2009). Pragmatism, not ideology: Historical perspectives on IBM's adoption of open-source software. *Information Economics and Policy*, *21*, 229–244. doi:10.1016/j.infoecopol.2009.03.006

Carugi, M., & De Clercq, J. (2004). Virtual private network services: scenarios, requirements and architectural constructs from a standardization perspective. *IEEE Communications Magazine*, *42*(6), 116–122. doi:10.1109/MCOM.2004.1304246

Carvalho, R. A. (2006). *Issues on Evaluating Free/Open Source ERP Systems. Research and Practical Issues of Enterprise Information Systems* (pp. 667–676). Springer-Verlag. doi:10.1007/0-387-34456-X_72

Carvalho, R. A. (2008). *(Org.). Handbook of Research on Enterprise Systems. Information Science Reference* (pp. 32–44). Hershey, USA: Free and Open Source Enterprise Resources Planning. In Jatinder N. D. Gupta, Mohammad Abdur Rashid, Sushil K. Sharma.

Carvalho, R. A., & Johansson, B. (2010). *ERP Licensing Perspectives on Adoption of ERPs in Small and Medium-sized Enterprises*. In The Fourth IFIP International Conference on Research and Practical Issues of Enterprise Information Systems, Natal, Brazil.

Casacubierta, D. (2003). *Collective creation*. Barcelona: Gedisa.

Castillo, J. J. (2009). *Convenience Sampling*. Retrieved March 17, 2010 from Experiment Resources.com, http://www.experiment-resources.com/convenience-sampling.html.

Caulliraux, H. M. Proença, A. & Prado, C. A. S. (2000). ERP Systems from a Strategic Perspective. *Sixth International Conference on Industrial Engineering and Operations Management*, Niteroi, Brazil.

Cereola, S. (2008). *The performance effects of latent factors on assimilation of commercial open-source ERP software on small-medium enterprises*. Ph. D. dissertation. Virginia Commonwealth University, Richmond, Virginia. Retrieved October 08, 2010, from http://hdl.handle.net/10156/2295.

Chakrabarti, A., & Manimaran, G. (2002). Internet infrastructure security. *IEEE Network*, *16*(6), 13–21. doi:10.1109/MNET.2002.1081761

Chao, H. J., & Guo, X. (2002). *Quality of service control in high-speed networks*. New York: John Wiley & Sons.

Chau, P. Y. K. (1995). Factors used in the selection of packaged software in small business: views of owners and managers. *Information & Management*, *29*, 71–78. doi:10.1016/0378-7206(95)00016-P

Church, Z. (2008) SAP ERP on-demand challenge lofty, but not impossible. p. Available from: http://searchcio-midmarket.techtarget.com/news/article/0,289142,sid183_gci1301840,00.html.

Ciborra, C. (2000). *From Control to Drift: The Dynamics of Corporate Information Infrastructures*. Oxford.

Compiere (2008). *Seven Years and Still Growing with Compiere Open Source ERP*. Retrieved from http://www.compiere.com/downloads/success-stories/compiere-erp-ss-pharmanord.pdf

Contini, F., & Lanzara, G. (2009). *ICT and innovation in the Public Sector*. New York: Palgrave MacMillan.

Copyright, Designs and Patents Act 1988.

Cornish, W., & Llewelyn, D. (2010). *Intellectual Property: Patents, Copyright, Trade Marks and Allied Rights* (7th ed.). Sweet and Maxwell.

Crowston, K., & Howison, J. (2006). Assessing the Health of Open Source Communities. *IEEE Computer*, May, pp. 89-91.

Cummings, M. (2004). Work groups, structural diversity, and knowledge sharing in a global organization. *Management Science*, *50*(3), 123–156. doi:10.1287/mnsc.1030.0134

Cunningham, S. J., & Jones, M. (2005). *Autoethnography: a tool for practice and education*. In CHINZ; Vol. 94 Proc. of the 6th ACM SIGCHI conf. on Computer-human interaction: making CHI natural.

Dahlander, L., & Magnusson, M. G. (2005). Relationships between open source software companies and communities: Observations from Nordic firms. *Research Policy, 34*, 481–493.

Dalle, J. M., David, P. A., den Besten, M., & Steinmueller, W. E. (2008). Empirical issues in open source software. *Information Economics and Policy, 20*, 301–304. doi:10.1016/j.infoecopol.2008.09.001

Datanews. (2006, September). *Erp & accountancy guide.* Appendix to number 32.

Davenport, T. (1998). Putting the enterprise into the enterprise system. *Harvard Business Review*, (June): 98–123.

Davenport, T., & Prusak, E. (1998). *Working knowledge, how organizations manage what they know*. Boston: Harvard Business Review School Press.

David, P. A., & Shapiro, J. S. (2008). Community-based production of open-source software: What do we know about the developers who participate? *Information Economics and Policy, 20*, 364–398. doi:10.1016/j.infoecopol.2008.10.001

David, P.& Steinmueller, E. (1994). Information Economics and Policy. *Special Issue on The Economics of Standards, 6*(3-4), December.

Davis, A. (2008). Enterprise resource planning under open source software . In Ferran, C., & Salim, R. K. (Eds.), *Enterprise resource planning for global economies: Managerial issues and challenges* (pp. 56–76). Hershey, PA: Information Science Reference. doi:10.4018/978-1-59904-531-3.ch004

De Búrca, S., & Fynes, B. (2003, September). *Relationships and technology: combining ERP and Internet technologies*. Paper presented at the 19th IMP Conference, Lugano, Switzerland. Retrieved September 01, 2010, from http://www.impgroup.org.

de Campos, R., de Carvalho, R. A., & Rodrigues, J. S. (2007, May). *Enterprise modeling for development processes of open-source ERP*. Paper presented at the 18th Production and Operation Management Society Conference, Dallas, TX.

De Carvalho, R. A. (2006). Issues on Evaluating Free/Open Source ERP Systems . In *Research and Practical Issues of Enterprise Information Systems* (pp. 667–676). Springer-Verlag. doi:10.1007/0-387-34456-X_72

De Carvalho, R. A. (2009). Free/Open Source Enterprise Resources Planning . In Gupta, J. N. D., Rashid, M. A., & Sharma, S. K. (Eds.), *Handbook of Research on Enterprise Systems* (pp. 32–44). Hershey, PA: Information Science Reference. doi:10.4018/978-1-59904-859-8.ch003

de Carvalho, R. A., & Monnerat, R. (2007). ERP5: designing for maximum adaptability . In Oram, A., & Wilson, G. (Eds.), *Beautiful code* (pp. 339–351). Sebastopol, CA: O'Reilly Media.

de Carvalho, R. A., & Johansson, B. (2009). Enterprise Resource Planning Systems for Small and Medium Enterprises . In Ramachandran, M., & de Carvalho, R. A. (Eds.), *Handbook of Research on Software Engineering and Productivity Technologies: Implications of Globalisation* (pp. 373–381). Hershey, PA: IGI Global. doi:10.4018/978-1-60566-731-7.ch024

De Carvalho, R. A., & de Campos, R. (2006). A Development Process Proposal for the ERP5 System. *IEEE International Conference on Systems, Man, and Cybernetics,* October 8-11, 2006, Taipei, Taiwan, 4703-4708.

De Carvalho, R. A., & Monnerat, R. M. (2008). Development support tools for Enterprise Resource Planning. *IEEE,* Computer.org/ITPro

De La Rosa, G., & Valentín, M. Fernandez.Renedo, C.; López, D.; De Pablos, C & De la Puerta, E. (2010). Productivity models in knowledge intensive service activities. *Grand Challenge in service week*, University of Cambridge, 22nd September 2010, UK.

De Pablos, C. (2004). *Ilustraciones de la aplicación de Tecnologías de información en la empresa española*. Madrid: ESIC.

De Pablos, C., & López, D. (2010). The implementation of free software in firms: an empirical analysis. *The International Journal of Digital Accounting Research, 10*(3), 45–67.

De Pablos, C., & De Pablos, M. (2008). Elements that can explain the degree of success of ERP systems implementation . In Cruz-Cunha, M. M. (Ed.), *Social, Managerial and Organizational Dimensions of Enterprise Information Systems*. Hershey, PA: IGI Publishing.

Dearle, A. (2007). Software deployment, past, present and future. In *Proceedings of the International Conference on Software Engineering: 2007 Future of Software Engineering* (pp. 269-284). Washington, DC: IEEE Computer Society.

Deep, A., Guttridge, P., Dani, S., & Burns, N. (2008). Investigating factors affecting ERP selection in made-to-order SME sector. *Journal of Manufacturing Technology Management, 19*(4), 430–446. doi:10.1108/17410380810869905

Dreiling, A. Klaus, H. Rosemann, M. & Wyssusek, B. (2005). Open Source Enterprise Systems: Towards a Viable Alternative. *38th Annual Hawaii International Conference on System Sciences*, Hawaii.

Dynaway (2010). *About Dynaway*. Retrieved from http://www.dynaway.com/en-GB/aboutdynaway/Pages/Default.aspx

Economides, N., & Katsamakas, E. (2006). Two-Sided Competition of Proprietary vs. Open Source Technology Platforms and the Implications for the Software Industry. *Management Science, 52*, 1057–1071. doi:10.1287/mnsc.1060.0549

Eisenhardt, K. M. (1989). Building theories from case study research. *Academy of Management Review, 14*(4), 532–550.

Enquist, H., & Skielse, G. J. (2010). Value Propositions in Service Oriented Business Models for ERP: Case Studies, in W. Abramowicz and R. Tolksdorf (Eds.) *BIS 2010, LNBIP 47*, 268–279, Springer-Verlag Berlin Heidelberg.

European Commission. (2009b). *SBA fact sheet*. Belgium.

European Commission. (2003). *Commission recommendation of 6 may 2003 concerning the definition of micro, small and medium-sized enterprises (2003/362/ec)* (Vol. 46) (No. L124/36).

European Commission. (2009a). *European SMEs under pressure: Annual report on EU small and medium-sized enterprises 2009.*

Everdingen, Y., Hillegersberg, J., & Waarts, E. (2000). ERP adoption by European midsize companies. *Communications of the ACM, 43*, 27–31. doi:10.1145/332051.332064

Falkowski, G., Pedigo, P., Smith, B., & Swamson, D. (1998). A recipe for ERP success. Beyond Computing. *International Journal of Human-Computer Interaction, 16*(1), 5–22.

Farhoomand, A. (2007). Opening up of the Software Industry: The Case of SAP. *Communications of the Association for Information Systems, 20*(49).

FIESP. (2004). *Perfil da Empresa Digital 2003/2004.* Sao Paulo State Federation of Industries, Retrieved from http://www.idigital.fea.usp.br/iDigital/Repositorio/0/Documentos/iDigital2004.pdf, Retrieved in 2009, July. (in Portuguese)

Finney, S., & Corbett, M. (2007). ERP implementation: a compilation and analysis of critical success factors. *Business Process Management Journal, 13*(3), 329–347. doi:10.1108/14637150710752272

Fitzgerald, B. (2006). The Transformation of Open Source Software. *Management Information Systems Quarterly, 30*(2), 587–598.

Fitzgerald, B. (2005). Has open source software a future? In Feller, J., Fitzgerald, B., Hissam, S. A., & Lakhani, K. R. (Eds.), *Perspectives on free and open source software* (pp. 93–106). Cambridge, MA: MIT Press.

Ford, D., et al. (2003). *Managing Business Relationships 2ed.* London: Wiley.

Fosser, E., Leister, O. H., Moe, C. E., & Newman, M. (2008). Organisations and vanilla software: What do we know about ERP systems and competitive advantage? *16th European Conference on Information Systems*. Galway, Ireland.

Fowler, M. (2002). *Patterns of Enterprise Application Architecture*. Boston: The Addison-Wesley.

García Bravo, D. (2000). *Sistemas de información en la empresa. Conceptos y aplicaciones*. Madrid: Pirámide.

Giuri, P., Rullani, F., & Torrisi, S. (2008). Explaining leadership in virtual teams: The case of open source software. *Information Economics and Policy*, *20*, 305–315. doi:10.1016/j.infoecopol.2008.06.002

Goode, S. (2005). Something for nothing: management rejection of open source software in Australia's top firms. *Information & Management*, *42*, 669–681. doi:10.1016/j.im.2004.01.011

Gorny, B., Nowak, Ł., & Perrin, J. (2008, March 28). *How to use property sheets*. Nexedi & ERP5 Community. Retrieved July 7, 2010, from http://www.erp5.org/HowToUsePropertySheets

Goth, G. (2005). Open Source Business Models: Ready for Prime Time. *IEEE Software*, (November/December): 98–100. doi:10.1109/MS.2005.157

Graham, I., & Koch, C. (2001). Tailor or configure? – Challenges in designing IT for support of Business Processes. In *Proceedings of WMSCI 2001*.

Gräning, A., Wendler, R., Leyh, C., & Strahringer, S. (2010). Rigorous Selection of Input Artifacts in Design Science Research – TAVIAS. In *AMCIS 2010 Proceedings*. Paper 51.

Grant, D., Hall, R., Wailes, N., & Wright, C. (2006). The false promise of technological determinism: the case of enterprise resource planning systems. *New Technology, Work and Employment*, *21*(1). doi:10.1111/j.1468-005X.2006.00159.x

Gruman, G. (2007). *Is Open Source The Answer to ERP? CIO.COM*, February 15, 2007. Retrieved from http://www.cio.com/article/28812/Is_Open_Source_The_Answer_to_ERP_ [Accessed 20.03.2010]

Gruman, G. (2007). More Midmarket firms choose open-source ERP. *Computerworld*

Gwebu, K. L., & Wang, J. (2010). Seeing eye to eye? An exploratory study of free open source software users' perceptions. *Journal of Systems and Software*, *83*(11), 2287–2296. doi:10.1016/j.jss.2010.07.011

Hajjar, D., & Moura, R. (2009).*Acabaram as fusões no mercado de ERP?* Reseller Web, 2009, Retrieved from http://www.resellerweb.com.br/noticias/index.asp?cod=58588, Retrieved in 2009, May. (in Portuguese)

Hallikainen, P., Kivijrvi, H., Rossi, M., Sarpola, S., & Talvinen, J. (2002). Evaluating IT investments: Selection of ERP software in finnish SME's. In *Proceedings of the 13th Australian conference on information systems (ACIS 2002)*.

Hammer. 1994. *Reengineering the corporation: A manifesto for business revolution*. Boston: HarperBusiness.

Hansen, K. M., Jónasson, K., & Neukirchen, H. (2009). *An Empirical Study of Open Source Software Architectures' Effect on Product Quality*. Engineering Research Institute, University of Iceland, Technical report VHI-01-2009, July 2009

Harison, E., & Koski, H. (2009). Applying open innovation in business strategies: Evidence from Finnish software firms. *Research Policy*, *39*, 351–359. doi:10.1016/j.respol.2010.01.008

Harmon, T. (November, 01, 2010). *Forrester Research: Making IT work in small and mid sized firms*. Available from: http://www.computerweekly.com/Articles/2010/11/01/243612/Forrester-Research-Making-IT-work-in-small-and-mid-sized.htm

Hars, A., & Qu, S. (2002). Working for Free? Motivations for Participating in Open-Source Projects. *International Journal of Electronic Commerce*, *6*, 25.

Hasselmeyer, P., Mersch, H., Koller, B., Quyen, H. N., Schubert, L., & Wieder, P. (2007). Implementing an SLA negotiation framework. In *Proceedings of the eChallenges e-2007 Conference*, Hague, Netherlands.

Hauge, Ø., Ayala, C., & Conradi, R. (2010). Adoption of open source software in software-intensive organizations – A systematic literature review. *Information and Software Technology*, *52*, 1133–1154. doi:10.1016/j.infsof.2010.05.008

Hedman, J., & Kalling, T. (2003). The Business Model Concept: Theoretical Underpinnings and Empirical Illustrations. *European Journal of Information Systems*, *12*, 49–59. doi:10.1057/palgrave.ejis.3000446

Hendrawirawan, D., Tanriverdi, H., Zetterlund, C., Hakam, H., Kim, H. H., Paik, H., & Yoon, Y. (2007). ERP security and segregation duties audit: a framework solution. *ISACA Journal 2007*, vol. 2. Retrieved October 01, 2010, from http://www.isaca.org/Journal/Past-Issues/2007/Volume-2/Pages/default.aspx.

Hendricks, K. B., Singhal, V. R., & Stratman, J. K. (2007). The impact of enterprise systems on corporate performance: A study of ERP, SCM, and CRM system implementations. *Journal of Operations Management, 25*(1), 65–82. doi:10.1016/j.jom.2006.02.002

Hertenberger, M. P. (2005). *A reference framework for security in enterprise resource planning (ERP) systems.* Ph. D. dissertation. University of Johannesburg, South Africa. Retrieved October 01, 2010, from http://ujdigispace.uj.ac.za:8080/dspace/bitstream/10210/496/1/AReferenceFramework.pdf.

Herzog, T. (2006). *A Comparison of Open Source ERP Systems*. Master thesis, Vienna University of Economics and Business Administration, Vienna, Austria.

Hevner, A. R., March, S. T., & Park, J. (2004). Design science in information systems research. *Management Information Systems Quarterly, 28*(1), 75–105.

Hicks, C., & Pachamanova, D. (2007). Back-propagation of user innovations: The open source compatibility edge. *Business Horizons, 50*, 315–324. doi:10.1016/j.bushor.2007.01.006

Hippel, E. v., & Krogh, G. v. (2003). Open Source Software and the "Private-Collective" Innovation Model: Issues for Organization Science. *Organization Science, 14*(2), 209–223. doi:10.1287/orsc.14.2.209.14992

Hippern, L., & Krogh, S. (2003). Open source software and the private-collective innovation model: Issues for organization science. *Organization Science, 14*(2), 241–248.

Hofmann, P. (2008, July–August). ERP is dead, long live ERP. *Internet Computing, IEEE, 12*(4), 84–88. doi:10.1109/MIC.2008.78

Holland, C. P., & Light, B. (1999). A critical success factors model for ERP implementation. *IEEE Software*, (May/June): 30–36. doi:10.1109/52.765784

Hong, K. K., & Kim, Y. G. (2002). The Critical Success Factors for ERP Implementation: an Organizational Fit Perspective. *Information & Management, 40*(1), 25–40. doi:10.1016/S0378-7206(01)00134-3

Hunter, H. (2006). *Open Source Data Base Driven Web Development*. Oxford, UK: Chandos.

IFIP – IFAC Task Force on Architectures for Enterprise Integration. (1999). GERAM: Generalized Enterprise Reference Architecture and Methodology, 31p.

International Organization for Standardization (ISO). (2005). Information technology - Security techniques - Evaluation criteria for IT security. *Standard ISO/IEC 15408:2005.*

International Telecommunication Union – Telecommunication Standardization Sector (ITU-T). (2004). General overview of NGN. *ITU-T recommendation* [Geneva, ITU-T.]. *Y (Dayton, Ohio)*, 2001.

International Telecommunication Union – Telecommunication Standardization Sector (ITU-T). (2006). *Guidelines for the definition of SLA representation templates. ITU-T Recommendation M.3342*. Geneva ITU-T.

Iskanius, P. (2009). Experiences of ERP Risk Management in SMEs. *In Proceedings of the CENTERIS 2009 Conference on ENTERprise Information Systems – CENTERIS* (pp. 269-282). Ofir, Portugal.

Ives, B., & Olson, M. (1983). The measurement of User Information Satisfaction. *Management of Computing, 26*(10), 519–529.

James, P. (2003) Open Source Software: An Australian Perspective. In Fitzgerald, B. & Bassett, G (Ed), *Legal Issues Relating To Free and Open Source Software* (pp. 63-88). Essays in Technology Policy and Law Volume 1, Queensland University of Technology School of Law.

Janssens, G., Kusters, R. J., & Heemstra, F. (2007, June). Clustering ERP implementation project activities: A foundation for project size definition. In S. Sadiq, M. Reichert, K. Schulz, J. Trienekens, C. Moller, & R. J. Kusters (Eds.), *Proceedings of the 1st international joint workshop on Technologies for Collaborative Business Processes and Management of Enterprise Information Systems, Funchal, Portugal* (pp. 23–32). Portugal: Institute for Systems and Technologies of Information.

Johansson, B., & Newman, M. (2010). Competitive advantage in the ERP system's value-chain and its influence on future development. *Enterprise Information Systems*, *4*(1), 79–93. doi:10.1080/17517570903040196

Johansson, B., & Sudzina, F. (2008). ERP systems and open source: an initial review and some implications for SMEs. *Journal of Enterprise Information Management*, *21*(6), 1741–0398. doi:10.1108/17410390810911230

Johansson, B. (2008). Knowledge Diffusion in ERP Development: The Case Of Open Source Erp Downloads. *IFIP International Federation for Information Processing*. In León, G., Bernardos, A., Casar, J., Kautz, K., & DeGross, J. (Eds.), *Open IT-Based Innovation: Moving Towards Cooperative IT Transfer and Knowledge Diffusion* (*Vol. 287*, pp. 247–259). Boston: Springer. doi:10.1007/978-0-387-87503-3_14

Johansson, B., & de Carvalho, R. A. (2009). Management of requirements in ERP development: A comparison between proprietary and open source ERP. In *Proceedings of the 24th annual ACM symposium on applied computing, Honolulu, Hawaii, March 9–12, 2009* (pp. 1605–1609). New York: ACM.

Johansson, B., & Sudzina, F. (2009). Choosing open source ERP systems: What reasons are there for doing so? In C. Boldyreff, K. Crowston, B. Lundell, & A. I. Wasserman (Eds.), *Open source ecosystems: Diverse communities interacting, proceedings of the 5th IFIP WG 2.13 international conference on open source systems (OSS 2009), Skövde, Sweden, June 3–6, 2009* (Vol. 299, pp. 143–155). Berlin: Springer.

Joode, R.v.W.d, & Egyedi, T.M. (2005). Handling variety: the tension between adaptability and interoperability of open source software. *Computer Standards & Interfaces*, *28*, 109–121. doi:10.1016/j.csi.2004.12.004

Jutras, C. (2009). SaaS ERP: Trends and observations. *An Aberdeen Report*

Kavanagh, P. (2004). *Open Source Software – Implementation and Management*. New York: Elsevier.

Keil, M., & Tiwana, A. (2006). Relative importance of evaluation criteria for enterprise systems: a conjoint study. *Information Systems Journal*, *16*, 237–262. doi:10.1111/j.1365-2575.2006.00218.x

Kent, S., & Seo, K. (2005). Security architecture for the Internet protocol. *IETF RFC 3869 (Standards Track)*. Retrieved April 16, 2008 from http://www.rfc-editor.org/rfcsearch.html.

Kerr, D.V., Houghton, L., Burgess, K. (2007) Power Relationships that Lead to the Development of Feral Systems. *Australasian Journal of Information Systems, 14* (2).

Kim, H., & Boldyreff, C. (2005). Open source ERP for SMEs. In *Proceedings of the 3rd international conference on manufacturing research (ICMR 2005)*, Cranfield, UK, September 6–8, 2005. Cranfield, U.K.: Cranfield University.

Kimberling, E. (November, 15, 2010). *Top Ten ERP Software Predictions for 2011*. Available from: http://panorama-consulting.com/top-ten-erp-software-predictions-for-2011

King, S. (2010). Implementing Open Source Software . In Simon, P. (Ed.), *The Next Wave of Technologies; Opportunities from Chaos*. New York: John Wiley & Sons.

Kinni, T. B. (1995). Process improvement, part 2. *Industry Week*, *244*(4), 45.

Klein, H. K., & Myers, M. (1999). A Set of Principles for Conducting and Evaluating Interpretive Field Studies in Information Systems . *Management Information Systems Quarterly*, *23*(1), 67–97. doi:10.2307/249410

Koch, C. (2007). ERP – a moving target. *International Journal of Business Information Systems*, *2*(4), 426–443. doi:10.1504/IJBIS.2007.012544

Koch, S. (2008). Effort modeling and programmer participation in open source software projects. *Information Economics and Policy*, *20*, 345–355. doi:10.1016/j.infoecopol.2008.06.004

Koch, C. (2001). *ERP-systemer, erfaringer, ressourcer, forandringer.* (In Danish: ERP systems – experiences, resources, change.) Copenhagen: Ingeniøren-bøger.

Koch, C., Olsen, M., & Tambo, T. (2010) How little do we need to know about Enterprise Resource Planning (ERP)? - A critical review of information systems research on ERP. *Proceedings of the 33rd Information Systems Research Seminar in Scandinavia*

Kock, N. (Ed.). (2007). Information Systems Action Research – An Applied View on Emerging Concepts and Methods. *Integrated Series on Information Systems 13.*

Koh, S. C. L., & Simpson, M. (2007). Could enterprise resource planning create a competitive advantage for small businesses? *Benchmarking: An International Journal, 14*(1), 59–76. doi:10.1108/14635770710730937

Korn, N., Oppenheim, C., & Picciotto, S. (2007). *IPR Issues and Software: A Briefing Document.* In collaboration with JISC Legal and OSS Watch. Retrieved 15 October 2010: http://www.jisc.ac.uk/media/documents/projects/iprissuesrelatingtosoftwarefinal.pdf

Krishnamurthy, S., & Tripathi, A. K. (2009). Monetary donations to an open source software platform. *Research Policy, 38,* 404–414. doi:10.1016/j.respol.2008.11.004

Krivoruchko, J. (2007). The Use of Open Source Software in Enterprise Distributed Computing Environments. *IFIP, Vol.24: Open source development, adoption and innovation.*

Krogh, G. v. (2003). Community, joining, and specialization in open source software innovation: a case study. *Research Policy, 32,* 1217–1241. doi:10.1016/S0048-7333(03)00050-7

la Rovere, R. L. (2001). *Perspectivas das micro, pequenas e médias empresas no Brasil. Journal of Contemporary Economy, Special Edition Economy Institute.* Brazil: UFRJ. (in Portuguese)

Lakhan, R., & Jhunjhunwala, V. (2008). Open Source in Education. *EDUCAUSE Quarterly, 31*(2), 32–40.

LeClaire, J. (December 30, 2006). *Open Source, BI and ERP: The Perfect Match?*http://www.linuxinsider.com/story/LjdZlB0x0j04cM/Open-Source-BI-and-ERP-The-Perfect-Match.xhtml

Lee, A. S. (2009). A Scientific Methodology for MIS Case Studies. *Management Information Systems Quarterly, 13*(1), 33–50. doi:10.2307/248698

Lemos, R. (2008). Open-source ERP grows up. [Accessed 20.03.2010]. *InfoWorld,* (april): 22. Retrieved from http://www.infoworld.com/t/applications/open-source-erp-grows-615?page=0,1.

Lerner, J., & Tirole, J. (2005). The Economics of Technology Sharing: Open Source and Beyond. *The Journal of Economic Perspectives, 19*(2), 99–120. doi:10.1257/0895330054048678

Lerner, J., & Tirole, J. (2002). Some Simple Economics of Open Source. *The Journal of Industrial Economics, 50*(2), 197–234. doi:10.1111/1467-6451.00174

Lerner, J., & Tirole, J. (2005). The Scope of Open Source Licensing. *Journal of Law Economics and Organization, 21,* 20–56. doi:10.1093/jleo/ewi002

Li, M. (2003). Policy-based IPsec management. *IEEE Network, 17*(6), 36–43. doi:10.1109/MNET.2003.1248659

Lilly, N. (November, 03, 2010). *Not Sweet.* Available from: http://www.erpgraveyard.com/2010/11/not-sweet.html

Lin, L. (2008). Impact of user skills and network effects on the competition between open source and proprietary software. *Electronic Commerce Research and Applications, 7,* 68–81. doi:10.1016/j.elerap.2007.01.003

Lion, G. F. (2010). *NMAP Network Scanning.* Retrieved September 15, 2010, from http://nmap.org.book/toc.html.

Loh, T. C., & Koh, S. C. L. (2004). Critical elements for a successful enterprise resource planning implementation in small-and medium-sized enterprises. *International Journal of Production Research, 42*(17), 3433–3455. doi:10.1080/00207540410001671679

Longenecker, J. G., Moore, C. W., & Petty, J. W. (1997). *Administração de Pequenas Empresas: Ênfase na Gerência Empresarial.* São Paulo, CA: Makron Books.

López, D., & De Pablos, C. (2010). Profiling F/OSS Adoption Modes: An Interpretive Approach. *IFIP Advances in Information and Communication Technology, 319,* 354-360. Springer, Boston.

Mabert, V., Soni, A., & Venkatamara, M. (2003). Enterprise Resource Planning: managing implementation process. *European Journal of Operational Research, 146*(2), 302–314. doi:10.1016/S0377-2217(02)00551-9

Mabert, V. A., Soni, A., & Venkataramanan, M. A. (2003). The impact of organisation size on enterprise resource planning (ERP) implementations in the US manufacturing sector. *Omega, 31*(3), 235–246. doi:10.1016/S0305-0483(03)00022-7

Madsen, M. (2009). The role of open source in data integration. *Third nature Technology Report.*

Mahadevan, B. (2000). Business Models for Internet-Based E-Commerce: An Anatomy. *California Management Review*, *42*(4), 55–69.

Markus, M. L., & Tanis, C. (2000). The Enterprise System Experience ● From Adoption to Success . In Zmud, R. W., & Price, M. F. (Eds.), *Framing the domains of IT management: projecting the future through the past* (pp. 173–207). Cincinatti, OH: Pinnaflex.

Marnewick, C., & Labuschagne, L. (2005, June). *A security framework for an ERP system.* Paper presented at the ISSA 2005 New Knowledge Today Conference, Sandton, South Africa. Retrieved September 01, 2010, from http://icsa.cs.up.ac.za/issa/2005/Proceedings/Full/009_Article.pdf.

Mata, F. J., Fuerst, W. L., & Barney, J. B. (1995). Information technology and sustained competitive advantage: A resource-based analysis. *Management Information Systems Quarterly*, *19*(4), 487–505. doi:10.2307/249630

Mathiassen, L. & Nielsen, P.A., (2008). Engaged Scholarship in IS Research. *Scandinavian Journal of Information Systems.*

McLeod, R. (2000). *Management Information Systems.* D.F., Mexico: Prentice Hall.

Messmer, E. (2008). *Open source software a security risk.* Retrieved August 29, 2010, from http://www.cio.com/article/438728/Open_Source_Software_a_Security_Risk.

Microsoft. (2010). *Microsoft Dynamics.* Retrieved from http://community.dynamics.com

Mohapatra, P., Metz, C., & Cui, Y. (2007). Layer 3 VPN services over IPv6 backbone networks: requirements, technology, and standardization efforts. *IEEE Communications Magazine*, *45*(4), 32–37. doi:10.1109/MCOM.2007.343609

Monforte Moreno, M. (1995). *Sistemas de Información para la Dirección.* Madrid: Pirámide.

Monnerat, R. M., de Carvalho, R. A., & de Campos, R. (2008). Enterprise systems modeling: the ERP5 development process. In *Proceedings of the 2008 ACM symposium on Applied Computing* (pp. 1062–1068). New York, NY: ACM.

Monsores, M. (2009). *Software Livre e Sistemas ERP: Levantamento Analítico e Proposta de Metodologia de Pré-Implantação.* Unpublished Master Degree Dissertation, Federal University of the Rio de Janeiro State, Rio de Janeiro, 2009. (in Portuguese)

Morabito, V., Pace, S., & Previtali, P. (2005). ERP marketing and Italian SMEs. *European Management Journal*, *23*(5), 590–598. doi:10.1016/j.emj.2005.09.014

Mordelet, N., Festraets, E., & Wang, M. (2006). The enterprise: a high-value market for broadband services. *Alcatel Telecommunications Review* (3rd Quarter 2006). Retrieved September 5, 2008 from http://www.alcatel-lucent.com.

Morris, M., Schindehutteb, M., & Al, J. (2005). The Entrepreneur's Business Model: Toward a Unified Perspective. *Journal of Business Research*, *58*, 726–735. doi:10.1016/j.jbusres.2003.11.001

Motwani, J., Mirchandani, M., & Gunasekaran, A. (2002). Successful implementation of ERP Projects: evidence from two case studies. *International Journal of Production Economics*, *75*, 83–96. doi:10.1016/S0925-5273(01)00183-9

Motwani, j., Subramanian, R. & Gopalakrishna, P. (2005). Critical factors for successful ERP implementation: Exploratory findings from four case studies. *Computers in Industry*, *56*, 529–544.

Myers, M. D. (1997). Qualitative Research in Information Systems. *Management Information Systems Quarterly*, (Jun): 97, 241–242.

Nah, F. F. H., Lau, J. L. S., & Kuang, J. (2001). Critical factors for successful implementation of enterprise systems. *Business Process Management Journal*, *7*(3), 285–296. doi:10.1108/14637150110392782

Nexedi, S. A. (n.d.). *Nexedi opensource on demand.* Retrieved May 10, 2010, from http://www.nexedi.com

O'Brien, J. A., & Marakas, G. (2008). *Management Information Systems.* McGraw-Hill.

Offermann, P., Levina, O., Schönherr, M., & Bub, U. (2009). Outline of a design science research process. In *Proceedings of the 4th International Conference on Design Science Research in Information Systems and Technology, Philadelphia, PA.* New York, NY: Association for Computing Machinery.

Open Web Application Security Project (OWASP). (2009). *OWASP Enterprise Application Security Project.* Retrieved, February 08, 2011, from http://www.owasp.org/index.php/OWASP_Enterprise_Application_Security_Project.

Openbravo. (2010). *Global Partner Program.* Retrieved April 2, 2010, from Openbravo Web Site: http://www.openbravo.com/partners/become-partner/global-partner-program/

Openbravo. (2010). *Openbravo Services.* Retrieved April 2, 2010, from Openbravo Web site: http://www.openbravo.com/services/

Openbravo. (2010, January). *Openbravo Backgrounder.* Retrieved March 30, 2010, from Openbravo Web Site: http://www.openbravo.com/docs/openbravo-backgrounder_January2010.pdf

Oracle (2010). *Oracle E-Business Suite Knowledge Zone.* Retrieved from http://www.oracle.com/partners/en/knowledge-zone/applications/021473.htm

Osterloh & Rota. (2007). Open source software development, just another case of collective invention. *Research Policy, 36*(2), 157–171. doi:10.1016/j.respol.2006.10.004

Ouédraogo, L.-D. (2005). *Policies of United Nations System Organizations Towards the Use of Open Source Software (OSS) in the Secretariats.* Geneva, 43p.

Paepcke, A. (1993). *Object-Oriented Programming: The CLOS Perspective.* Cambridge, MA: MIT Press.

Panorama Consulting Group. (2008). *2008 ERP Report,* USA, Denver, 2009.

Parr, A. N., & Dr. Shanks, G. (2000). Taxonomy of ERP Implementation Approaches. *Proceedings of the 33rd Hawaii International Conference on System Sciences.*

Polkinghorne, D. E. (2005). Language and Meaning: Data Collection in Qualitative Research. *Journal of Counseling Psychology, 52*(2), 137–145. doi:10.1037/0022-0167.52.2.137

Pollock, N., & Williams, R. (2009). *Software and Organisations: The biography of the enterprise-wide system or how SAP conquered the world.* Oxon: Routledge.

Porter, M. E. (1996). What is strategy? *Harvard Business Review,* (Nov-Dec): 1996.

Pras, A., Schönwälder, J., Burgess, M., Festor, O., Martínez Pérez, G., Stadler, R., & Stiller, B. (2007). Key research challenges in network management. *IEEE Communications Magazine, 45*(10), 104–110. doi:10.1109/MCOM.2007.4342832

Rajala, R., & Westerlund, M. (2007). Business Models - a new Perspective on Firms' Assets and Capabilities. Observations from the Finnish Software Industry. *International Journal of Entrepreneurship and Innovation, 8,* 115–125. doi:10.5367/000000007780808039

Rajala, R., Rossi, M., & Tuunainen, V. (2003). A Framework for Analyzing Software Business Models. *Proceedings of the European Conference on Information Systems 2003, Conference on Information Systems - New Paradigms in Organizations, Markets and Society,* June 18-22, 2003, Naples, Italy

Ramdani, B., Kawalek, P., & Lorenzo, O. (2009). Predicting SMEs' adoption of enterprise systems. *Journal of Enterprise Information Management, 22*(1/2), 10–24. doi:10.1108/17410390910922796

Rane, P. (2010). *Enterprise applications in the cloud: a SaaS security perspective.* Retrieved, January 20, 2011, from http://esj.com/articles/2010/02/09/cloud-saas-security.aspx.

Rao, S. S. (2000). Enterprise resource planning: business needs and technologies. *Industrial Management & Data Systems,* 81–88. doi:10.1108/02635570010286078

Raymond, E. (1999). The Cathedral and the bazaar. *Knowledge . Technology and Policy, 12*(3), 23–49. doi:10.1007/s12130-999-1026-0

Riehle, D. (2007). The economic motivation of open source: stakeholders perspectives. *Computer, IEE . Computers & Society, 40*(4), 25–32.

Robb, D. (January, 26, 2011). *Ten More ERP Trends: Open Source and Pricing Pressures.* Available from: http://www.ecrmguide.com/article.php/3922361/ten-more-erp-trends-open-source-and-pricing-pressures.htm

Robert Jacobsen v (1) Matthew Katzer (2) Kamind Associates Inc., 13 August 2008.

Rosemann, M., & Recker, J. (2006). Context-aware process design: Exploring the extrinsic drivers for process flexibility. In *Latour, T., Petit, M. (eds.): The 18th International Conference on Advanced Information Systems Engineering. Proceedings of Workshops and Doctoral Consortium* (pp. 149–158). Namur University Press, Luxembourg, Grand-Duchy of Luxembourg

Rossi, C. (2009). Software Innovativeness: a comparison between proprietary and free/open source solutions offered by Italian SMEs. *R & D Management, 39*(2), 153–169. doi:10.1111/j.1467-9310.2009.00547.x

Rossi, D. (2006). Decoding the green open source software puzzle: A survey of theoretical and empirical contributions. *The Economics of Open Source Software Development, 22nd* IEEE International Parallel and Distributed Processing Symposium, New York.

Russell, R. S. (2006, March). *A framework for analyzing ERP security threats*. Paper presented at the Euro-Atlantic Symposium on Critical Information Infrastructure Assurance, Switzerland. Retrieved, October 01, 2010, from http://www.cimap.vt.edu/CIIA/Papers/Session1-4-Russell.pdf

Sadagopan, S. (2004). Enterprise Resource Planning. *Encyclopedia of Information Systems*, 169-184.

SAP. (2010). *SAP Ecosystem and Partners Sharing Best Practices with Sap Communities*. Retrieved from http://www.sap.com/ecosystem/communities/index.epx

Sarangan, V., & Chen, J.-C. (2006). Comparative study of protocols for dynamic service negotiation in the next-generation internet. *IEEE Communications Magazine, 44*(3), 151–156. doi:10.1109/MCOM.2006.1607879

Sarkis, J., & Sundarraj, R. P. (2003). Evaluating Componentized Enterprise Information Technologies: A Multiattribute Modeling Approac. [Boston: Kluwer Academic Publishers.]. *Information Systems Frontiers, 5*(3), 303–319. doi:10.1023/A:1025605529006

Scheer, A. (1997). *Wirtschaftsinformatik: Referenzmodelle für industrielle Geschäftsprozesse (7., durchges. Aufl.)*. Berlin: Springer.

Sebastiani, F. (2002). Machine learning in automated text categorization. *ACM Computing Surveys, 34*(1), 1–47. doi:10.1145/505282.505283

SEBRAE. (2007). *Relatório de Gestão Estratégica do Sistema SEBRAE. Brazilian Service of Micro and Small Enterprises Supporting*. Brazil: SEBRAE. (in Portuguese)

Seethamraju, R., & Seethamraju, J. (2008). Adoption of ERPs in a Medium-sized Enterprise - A Case Study. *19th Australasian Conference on Information Systems*, pp.887-896.

Sen, R., Subramaniam, C., & Nelson, M. L. (2008). Determinants of the Choice of Open Source\ Software License. *Journal of Management Information Systems, 25*(3), 207–239. doi:10.2753/MIS0742-1222250306

Sen, R. (2007). Waiting For Usable Open Source Software? Don't Hold Your Breath! *Communications of the Association for Information Systems, 20*, 382–392.

Serrano, N. S., & Sarriegi, J. M. (2006). Open Source Software ERPs: A New Alternative for an Old Need. *IEEE Software, 23*(3), 94–97. doi:10.1109/MS.2006.78

Sharif, A. M. (2010). It's written in the cloud: the hype and promise of cloud computing. *Invited Viewpoint in Journal of Enterprise Information Management, 23*(2), 131–134.

Shiff, T. (2002). The Economics of Open Source Software: a survey of the early literature. *Review of Network Economics, 1*(1), 66–74.

Sia, C. L. (2008). Impact of Organisational Resources on implementaion of ERP by an SME Firm: An Exploratory Study. *PACIS 2008 Proceedings*. Paper 111.

Silverman, M. G. (2008). *Compliance management for public, private and nonprofit organizations*. New York: McGraw-Hill.

Singh, I., Stearns, B., & Johnson, M.Enterprise Team. (2002). *Designing Enterprise Applications with the J2EETM Platform* (2nd ed.). Reading, MA: Addison-Wesley.

Singh, P. V., & Phelps, C. C. (2009) Determinants of Open Source Software License Choice: A Social Influence Perspective. Available at SSRN: http://ssrn.com/abstract=1436153

Sivadas, E., & Dwyer, F. R. (2000). An Examination of Organizational Factors Influencing new Product Success in Internal and Alliance-based Processes. *Journal of Marketing, 64*(1), 31–49. doi:10.1509/jmkg.64.1.31.17985

Smets, J.-P. (2008, March). *ERP5 industries overview*. Nexedi SA. Retrieved May 11, 2010, from https://www.myerp5.com/kb/web page module/233

Smets, J.-P. (n.d.). *ERP5 implementation*. Nexedi SA. Retrieved October 10, 2009, from https://www.myerp5.com/kb/documentation section/consultant/consultant-Front.Page/consultant-Implementation.Process/view (Restricted)

Smets-Solanes, J., & Carvalho, R. Atem de. (2003, July–August). ERP5: a next-generation, open-source ERP architecture. *IT Professional*, *5*(4), 38–44. doi:10.1109/MITP.2003.1216231

Smets-Solanes, J. (2002). ERP5: *a technical introduction*. Paper presented at Linux Tag, Karlsruhe, Germany. Available from http://cps.erp5.org/sections/free/erp/linuxtag.pdf/view

Smets-Solanes, J.-P., & De Carvalho, R. A. (2002). An Abstract Model for an Open Source ERP System: The ERP5 Proposal. *8th International Conference on Industrial Engineering and Operations Management*, Curitiba, Brazil.

Snider, B., Da Silveira, G., & Balakrishnan, J. (2009). ERP implementation at SMEs: analysis of five Canadian cases. *International Journal of Operations & Production Management*, *29*(1), 4–29. doi:10.1108/01443570910925343

Soh, C., Kien, S. S., & Tay-Yap, J. (2000). Cultural fits and misfits: is ERP a universal solution? *Communications of the ACM*, *43*(4), 47–51. doi:10.1145/332051.332070

Somers, T. M., & Nelson, K. G. (2004). A taxonomy of players and activities across the ERP project life cycle. *Information & Management*, *41*, 257–278. doi:10.1016/S0378-7206(03)00023-5

Somers, T. M., & Nelson, K. (2001). The impact of critical success factors across the stages of enterprise resource planning implementation. *34th Hawaii International Conference on System Sciences,* Mavis, HI, pp 2936-45.

Sowe, S. K., Stamelos, I., & Angelis, L. (2008). Understanding knowledge sharing activities in free/open source software projects: An empirical study. *Journal of Systems and Software*, *81*, 431–446. doi:10.1016/j.jss.2007.03.086

Spinellis, D. (2006). Open Source and Professional Advancement. *IEEE Software*, (September/October): 70–71. doi:10.1109/MS.2006.136

Stam, W. (2009). When does community participation enhance the performance of open source software companies? *Research Policy*, *38*, 1288–1299. doi:10.1016/j.respol.2009.06.004

Stefanou, C. J. (2001). A framework for the ex-ante evaluation of ERP software. *European Journal of Information Systems*, *10*(4), 204–215. doi:10.1057/palgrave.ejis.3000407

Stefanou, C. J. (2001). A Framework for the Evaluation and Selection of ERP Systems. *European Journal of Information Systems . Special Issue on IT Evaluation*, *10*, 204–215.

Stojanovic, M., Bostjancic Rakas, S., & Acimovic-Raspopovic, V. (2010). End-to-end quality of service specification and mapping: the third party approach. *Computer Communications*, *33*(11), 1354–1368. doi:10.1016/j.comcom.2010.03.024

Stojanovic, M., & Acimovic-Raspopovic, V. (2009). Communication issues for small and medium enterprises: provider and customer perspectives . In Cruz-Cuncha, M. (Ed.), *Enterprise Information Systems for Bussiness Integration in SMEs: Technological, Organizational, and Social Dimensions* (pp. 230–251). Hershey, New York: Information Science Reference. doi:10.4018/978-1-60566-892-5.ch013

Stojanovic, M., & Acimovic-Raspopovic, V. (2008). QoS provisioning framework in IP-based VPN . In Putnik, G., & Cruz-Cunha, M. (Eds.), *Encyclopedia of Networked and Virtual Organizations* (Vol. III, pp. 1317–1324). Hershey, New York: Information Science Reference. doi:10.4018/978-1-59904-885-7.ch173

Subramaniam, C., Sen, R., & Nelson, M. L. (2009). Determinants of open source software project success: A longitudinal study. *Decision Support Systems*, *46*, 576–585. doi:10.1016/j.dss.2008.10.005

Tambo, T. (2010) Bespoke ERP - A Systems View On Enterprise Management. In Hosni et al. (eds), *Proceedings of the 19th Conference of the International Association for Management of Technology.* Maimi: IAMOT.

Targowski, M. (2009). *The enterprise systems approach. social, managerial, and organizational dimensions of enterprise information systems. The Enterprise Systems Approach. Social, Managerial, and.* Organizational Dimensions of Enterprise Information Systems.

Tawileh, A., Rana, O., Ivins, W., & McIntosh, S. (2006). Managing Quality in the Free and Open Source Software Community. *Twelfth Americas Conference on Information Systems,* Acapulco, Mexico.

Teixeira, S., Jr. (2006). *A Busca Pelos Pequenos.* Available at http://portalexame.abril.com.br/revista/exame/edicoes/0859/negocios/m0080278.html, Retrieved in 2009, August. (in Portuguese)

Teltumbde, A. (2000). A framework for evaluating ERP projects. *International Journal of Production Research, 38*(17), 4507–4520. doi:10.1080/00207540050205262

Thoke, O. (2009). How do open source ERP packages score over custom ERP solutions. Retrieved, January 15, 2011, from http://www.brighthub.com/computing/linux/articles/53581.aspx.

Timbrell, G., & Gable, G. (2002). The SAP ecosystem: a knowledge perspective. In *Proceedings of the Information Resources Management Association international conference* (pp. 1115–1118). Hershey, PA: Information Resources Management Association.

Tomaschek, N. (2010). *Einführung Eines Open Source CRM ERP System in einem mittelständisches unternehmen.* Saarbrücken: VDM Verlag.

Treasury, H. M. (2006). *Gowers Review of Intellectual Property.* Norwich, CT: The Stationery Office.

Tsiakis, T. (2010). Information security expenditures: a techno-economic analysis. *IJCSNS International Journal of Computer Science and Network Security, 10*(4), 7–11.

UOC (2009) UOC Report. *The use of open source in Public Administrations in Spain,* Universitat Oberta de Calalunya, Report.

Vadalasetty, S. R. (2003). Security concerns in using open source software for enterprise requirements. SANS Institute, white paper. Retrieved October 10, 2010, from http://www.sans.org/reading_room/whitepapers/awareness/security-concerns-open-source-software-enterprise-requirements_1305

Valkov, S. (2008). Innovative concept of open source Enterprise Resource Planning (ERP) system. *International Conference on Computer Systems and Technologies - CompSysTech'08.*

van Everdingen, Y., Van Hillegersberg, J., & Waarts, E. (2000). ERP adoption by European midsize companies. *Communications of the ACM, 43*(4), 27–31. doi:10.1145/332051.332064

Van Holsbeck, M., & Johnson, J. Z. (2004). *Security in an ERP world.* Retrieved, July 15, 2010, from http://www.net-security.org.

Van Nuffel, D., & De Backer, C. (2007). Ook kleine ondernemingen hebben een ERP-pakket nodig. *Informatie, 49*(1), 35–39.

Van Nuffel, D., & De Backer, C. (2010). *ERP acquisition within SMEs: A holistic study.* (Working paper)

Ven, K., Van Nuffel, D., & Verelst, J. (2007). The migration of public administrations towards open source desktop software: Recommendations from research and validation through a case study . In Sowe, S. K., Stamelos, I., & Samoladas, I. (Eds.), *Emerging free and open source software practices* (pp. 191–214). Hershey, PA: IGI Publishing. doi:10.4018/978-1-59904-210-7.ch009

Ven, K. (2008). *The organizational adoption of open source server software: An information systems innovation perspective.* Unpublished PhD dissertation, Universiteit Antwerpen, Antwerp, Belgium.

Verma, D. C. (2002). Simplifying network administration using policy-based management. *IEEE Network, 16*(2), 20–26. doi:10.1109/65.993219

Vidyaranya, B. G., & Cydnee, B. (2005). Success and failure factors of adopting SAP in ERP system implementation. *Business Process Management Journal, 11*(5), 501–517. doi:10.1108/14637150510619858

Von Hippel, E. (1986). Lead Users: A Source of Novel Product Concepts. *Management Science, 32*(7), 791–805. doi:10.1287/mnsc.32.7.791

Von Hippel. (2005). *Democratizing Innovation.* Cambridge, MA: MIT Press, April 2005.

von Krogh, G., & Spaeth, S. (2007). The Open Source Software Phenomenon: Characteristics that Promote Research. *The Journal of Strategic Information Systems, 16*(3), 236–253. doi:10.1016/j.jsis.2007.06.001

von Krogh, G., & von Hippel, E. (2006). The Promise of Research on Open Source Software. *Management Science, 52*(7), 975–983. doi:10.1287/mnsc.1060.0560

Wang, L., Tao, J., Kunze, M., Castellanos, A. C., Kramer, D., & Karl, W. (2008). *Scientific cloud computing: early definition and experience. In 10ᵗʰ IEEE international conference on High Performance Computing and Communications* (pp. 825–830). New York, N.Y: Institute of Electrical and Electronics Engineers.

Wang, F.-R. He, D. & Chen, J. (2005). Motivations of Individuals and Firms Participating in Open Source Communities. *Fourth International Conference on Machine Learning and Cybernetics*, p309-314.

Waring, T., & Maddocks, P. (2005). Open Source Software implementation in the UK public sector: Evidence from the field and implications for the future. *International Journal of Information Management, 25*, 411–428.

Wei, C.-C., Chein, C.-F., & Wang, M.-J. (2005, April 18). J. (2005). An AHP-based approach to ERP system selection. *International Journal of Production Economics, 96*(1), 47–62. doi:10.1016/j.ijpe.2004.03.004

West, J., & Mace, M. (2010). Browsing as the killer app: Explaining the rapid success of Apple's iPhone. *Telecommunications Policy, 4*(34), 241–267.

West, J., & O'Mahony, S. (2005). Contrasting Community Building in Sponsored and Community Founded Open Source Projects. *38th Annual Hawaii International Conference on System Sciences*, Hawaii.

Wheeler, D. A. (2010). *How to evaluate open source software/free software (OSS/FS) programs.* Retrieved July 10, 2010, from http://www.dwheeler.com/oss_fs_eval.html.

WinterGreen Research. (2009). Worldwide Cloud Computing -- Markets Reach $160.2 Billion by 2015. *Press Release*, Lexington, Massachusetts (July 24, 2009).

Wohl, A. (2010). Software as a Service . In Simon, P. (Ed.), *The Next Wave of Technologies; Opportunities from Chaos* (p. 105). New York: John Wiley & Sons.

Wu, H. & Cao, L. (2009). Harnessing Web 2.0 for ERP Implementations. *IEEE Software*.

Xu, N. (2003). An Exploratory Study of Open Source Software Based on Public Archives. Master Thesis, John Molson School of Business, Concordia University, Montreal, Canada.

Yin, R. K. (2003). *Case study research: Design and methods* (3rd ed.). Newbury Park, CA: Sage Publications.

Yu, L. (2008). Self-organization process in open-source software: An empirical study. *Information and Software Technology, 50*, 361–374. doi:10.1016/j.infsof.2007.02.018

Zeng, J., & Ansari, N. (2003). Toward IP virtual private network quality of service: a service provider perspective. *IEEE Communications Magazine, 41*(4), 113–119. doi:10.1109/MCOM.2003.1193984

Zhao, L., & Elbaum, S. (2003). Quality assurance under the open source development model. *Journal of Systems and Software, 66*, 65–75.

Zott, C., & Amit, R. (2008). The Fit between Product Market Strategy and Business Model: Implications for Firm Performance. *Strategic Management Journal, 29*(1), 1–26. doi:10.1002/smj.642

Zou, C. C., Duffield, N., Towsley, D., & Gong, W. (2006). Adaptive defense against various network attacks. *IEEE Selected Areas in Communications, 24*(10), 1877–1888. doi:10.1109/JSAC.2006.877137

Zunnurhain, K., & Vrbsky, S. V. (2010, November-December). *Security attacks and solutions in clouds.* Paper presented at the 2ⁿᵈ IEEE International Conference on Cloud Computing Technology and Science (CloudCom 2010), Indianapolis, IN. Retrieved January 20, 2011, from http://salsahpc.indiana.edu/CloudCom20101/Poster/cloudcom2010_submission_98.pdf.

# About the Contributors

**Rogerio Atem de Carvalho** holds a B.Sc. in Computer Science and M.Sc. and D.Sc. in Industrial Engineering. He is a teacher and researcher at the Instituto Federal Fluminense (Federal Fluminense Institute) - IFF, Campos, Brazil, where he coordinates Nucleo de Pesquisa em Sistemas de Informaçao (NSI - Information Systems Research Group), which has been producing innovative software in partnership with government and private sectors since 2002. He is also a teacher and researcher with the Production Engineering Graduation programs at Universidade Federal Fluminense and Universidade Estadual do Norte Fluminense. His research on FOS-ERP was awarded by IFIP in 2006 and jointly by IFIP and IEEE in 2007. He is a consultant for government and private sectors and authored many book chapters and research papers on ERP, ECM, Software Engineering, Project Management, and Decision Support Systems.

**Björn Johansson** holds a PhD and a Licentiate degree in Information Systems Development from the Department of Management & Engineering at Linköping University and a Bachelor degree in Business Informatics from Jönköping International Business School. He defended his doctoral thesis "Deciding on Sourcing Option for Hosting of Software Applications in Organisations" in 2007. Currently he works as an Associate Senior Lecturer at the Department of Informatics at School of Economics and Management, Lund University. Before that he had a Post Doc position for three years at Center for Applied ICT at Copenhagen Business School, within the 3gERP project (http://www.3gERP.org). He is a member of the IFIP Working Group on Diffusion, Adoption and Implementation of Information and Communication Technologies (IFIP TC8 WG8.6), the IFIP Working Group on Enterprise Information Systems (IFIP TC8 WG8.9) and the research networks: VITS Work practice development, IT usage, Coordination and Cooperation and KiO Knowledge in Organizations.

*\*\*\**

**Vladanka S. Acimovic-Raspopovic** received her B.Sc. (1976), M.Sc. (1984) and Ph.D. (1995) degrees in electrical engineering, all from the University of Belgrade, Serbia. She is professor at the University of Belgrade, Faculty of Transport and Traffic Engineering – Department for telecommunication traffic and networks. Dr. Acimovic-Raspopovic managed or participated in a large number of research projects and studies concerning radio and optical transmission systems and telecommunication networks design and implementation, as well as pricing and economic aspects of networks. Her scientific, research and professional work encompasses the field of telecommunication traffic and networking (planning, resource control, security management, quality of service implementation in NGN, pricing communication networks). She also deals with communication systems and infrastructure in intelligent transportation systems. As author or coauthor, she published more than 130 papers in national and international journals, books and conferences.

**Swanand Deodhar** is a research scholar in the area of Information Management at Management Development Institute, Gurgaon. He has worked in the field of web development as well as business intelligence. He holds a Master of Business Administration from Symbiosis International University, Pune. His research interests include open source software, open innovation, and software business models. He also invests time in understanding the emergence of organizational practice in the field of management research.

**Rajen K. Gupta** has a first degree in Electrical Engineering from Indian Institute of Technology, Kanpur and is a Fellow of Indian Institute of Management, Ahmedabad. He is a Professor in the area of Human Behavior and Organizational Development at Management Development Institute, Gurgaon, India. He has worked in the State Bank of India and Jyoti Ltd. before moving to Indian Institute of Management, Lucknow as a faculty member. His research interests include organizational culture and design, organizational learning, and spirituality.

**Carmen de Pablos Heredero** is a Professor in the Business Administration Area at the Rey Juan Carlos University in Madrid, Spain from 1994. She is responsible for the PhD in Business Administration. She is specialised in the impact of information technologies over organisational systems where she develops main research. She has chaired Doctoral Dissertations and Projects on the impact of information and communication technologies in organisational performance. She has presented communications in different international venues and has published in specialised journals. She has also worked as a consultant in the area of IS management at Primma Consulting. She is the Academic Director for the Master's Degree and Doctoral program in Business Administration and Entrepreneurship at the Rey Juan Carlos University.

**Andrés Seco Hernández** is CIO at Cajasol, a savings bank in Sevilla, Spain from 1992. It comes from Caja de Guadalajara, joined with Cajasol recently at 2010. He is responsible in IT governance and IT project management. He is open source software developer and has presented communications in different congress related with open source software. He is Master in Service Science, Management and Enginiering at the Alcala University.

**Nasimul Huq** is now working in a software company as an intern. He holds a Master of Science in Information Technology and Management with a major in Informatics from Jönköping International Business School (JIBS). Before started at JIBS, Nasimul completed his Bachelor of Science in Computer Science and Engineering from International Islamic University Chittagong (IIUC), Bangladesh. He intends to build his career as a researcher in the area of Information Systems and Enterprise Modelling.

**Christian Koch**, PhD, MSc, is a Professor of technology based business development at Aarhus University, Institute for Business and Technology. He is center manager of centre for innovation and business development. He have researched, consulted and taught Enterprise Resource Planning for a number of years. Sectors studied include manufacturing, professional services and consulting. Articles, and conference papers on ERP are published widely. Research is done in a multidisciplinary manner and approaches include organisation and management theory, innovation theory, information systems research, science, technology and society studies.

**David López** holds a PhD in Telematic Engineering by the Technical University of Madrid and a MBA by the I.E Business School. His research interests are related to operations and knowledge management with special emphasis in healthcare and telecommunications.At present time he is a visiting researcher at Rey Juan Carlos University and adjunct professor at I.E Business School.

**Daniela Mihailescu** is lecturer in informatics at Jönköping International Business School (JIBS). She holds a Licentiate in Technology from Linköping University and since 2000, when she started at JIBS, Daniela has been Program Manager for two external programs. Currently, she's teaching focuses on enterprise systems. Daniela's research focuses on two areas Information Systems Design and Enterprise Systems. She has published in European Journal of Information Systems Evaluation and she served as a reviewer and presented her research in several academic conferences such as European Conference on Information Systems, Americas Conference on Information Systems, and the European and the International Conferences on Information Management and Evaluation.

**Marcelo Monsores** is a System Analyst with 15 years of experience in the IT Industry. Currently he works in the SAP team at Petrobras in Brazil and owns an IT company which provides Free/Open Source software solutions. As a researcher, Marcelo is a former student from UNIRIO (Federal University of the State of Rio de Janeiro), where he obtained his M.Sc in Information Systems with his studies focused in an implementation methodology for Free/Open Source ERP Systems.

**Dieter Van Nuffel** is a PhD candidate and Research and Teaching assistant of Management Information Systems at the University of Antwerp (Belgium). His research interests include business process management, enterprise architecture, enterprise computing, and open source adoption. He currently works on a PhD in the field of business process design, aimed at designing modular and evolvable business processes. He has already published in international journals such as International Journal on Advances in Software, and presented his research at key international refereed conferences, such as the International Conference on Design Science Research in Information Systems and Technology (DESRIST) and the International Conference on Advanced Information Systems (CAiSE).

**David L. Olson** is the James & H.K. Stuart Professor in MIS and Chancellor's Professor at the University of Nebraska. He has published research in over 100 refereed journal articles, primarily on the topic of multiple objective decision-making and information technology. He has authored 17 books, is associate editor of Service Business and co-editor in chief of International Journal of Services Sciences. He has made over 100 presentations at international and national conferences on research topics. He is a member of the Decision Sciences Institute, the Institute for Operations Research and Management Sciences, the Association for Information Systems, and the Multiple Criteria Decision Making Society. He was a Lowry Mays endowed Professor at Texas A&M University from 1999 to 2001. He was named the Raymond E. Miles Distinguished Scholar award for 2002, and was a James C. and Rhonda Seacrest Fellow from 2005 to 2006. He was named Best Enterprise Information Systems Educator by IFIP in 2006. He is a Fellow of the Decision Sciences Institute.

**Slavica V. Bostjancic Rakas** received her B.Sc. (2004) and M.Sc. (2007) degrees in traffic engineering and her Ph.D. degree (2011) in technical sciences, all from the University of Belgrade, Serbia. She joined Mihailo Pupin Institute in Belgrade in 2005, where she is currently research associate in telecommunications networking. She has participated in several research projects and studies concerning NGN design, quality of service and network management systems. As author or coauthor, she published more than 20 papers at national and international journals, books and conferences. Her research interests include security solutions, QoS routing and network management in next generation networks.

**Mikko Ruohonen** is the professor of business & information systems at the University of Tampere. Mikko Ruohonen has worked in the field of information resources strategy and organization development since 1984. He holds a D.Sc (Economics) from Turku School of Economics, Finland. He has over forty years of experience in academics, research and consulting. He has published over 100 articles, reports and columns, four textbooks, and large research reports. He also serves as a special consultant and newsletter editor for Technical Committee 3 (Education) of the International Federation of Information Processing (IFIP). He has also served as member of the advisory boards for Finnish companies. In addition he served as the president of Executive Board for Association of Information Systems (AIS) Scandinavian Chapter 2006-2007. IFIP granted him IFIP Silver Core Award year 2007.

**Kulbhushan C. Saxena** is an expert on business process innovation/management, business process outsourcing strategies, e-governance, and knowledge management. Currently he is a senior Professor in the Information Systems and Management area at Fortune Institute of International Business (FIIB), New Delhi, India. He has more than 40 years of academic and diversified industrial experience in information systems management, business process management and strategic information management, including 14 years of teaching, research and consulting experience at Erasmus University, Rotterdam, the Netherlands and Hong Kong Polytechnic University, Hong Kong. He has also been a visiting faculty at Delft University of Technology, Delft, Netherlands and University of Tampere, Finland.

**Syed Mushtaq Ali Shah** is a student of Master of Science in Information Engineering and Management at Jönköping School of Engineering (JTH), Jönköping University. He holds a Master of Science in Information Technology and Management with a major in Informatics from Jönköping International Business School (JIBS). Before started at JIBS, Syed completed his Bachelor of Science in Information Technology from University of Peshawar, Pakistan. Syed Mushtaq Ali shah is interested in further research studies. Knowledge Modelling and Knowledge Management is his areas of interest.

**Sam De Silva** is a Partner and the Head of Technology and Outsourcing Law at leading UK law firm, Manches LLP. Prior to joining Manches, Sam has worked for leading law firms in London, Sydney, Australia and Auckland, New Zealand. His main areas of practice are technology and business process outsourcing and technology projects, such as software licensing and support, system development and systems integration. He has been published widely, speaks regularly on outsourcing and technology law topics and is on the Law Society's Technology and Law Committee. Sam is also a Council Representative for the Chartered Institute of Purchasing and Supply. In addition to his LLB and Masters in Business Law, Sam has post-graduate degrees in information technology and business administration so is well aware of the commercial, business and technical issues facing both users and suppliers of technology. Sam is also one of very few UK solicitors who is a Member of the Chartered Institute of Purchasing and Supply (MCIPS), Fellow of the British Computer Society (FBCS) and a Chartered IT Professional (CITP). Sam also has in-house industry legal experience having been seconded to Accenture UK as a senior legal counsel. Dr De Silva is a Barrister and Solicitor of the High Court of New Zealand, a Solicitor of the Supreme Court of England and Wales and a Solicitor of the Supreme Court of New South Wales, Australia. Sam is also a Society of Computers and Law IT Law Accredited member.

**Jean-Paul Smets** is the founder of Nexedi SA and the initial author of ERP5. He is currently in charge of Nexedi international development, investment relations and technology partnerships. Jean-Paul graduated from Ecole Normale Supérieure with a PhD in computer science and from Ecole des Mines de Paris with a Master in Public Administration. He gained industrial experience in Apparel Industry, Oil industry, Non Profit Organizations and Lorraine Region Public Administration. He is an active member of Free Software associations and has played in key role in the Eurolinux campaign which succeeded in protecting innovation from software patents.

**Constantinos J. Stefanou** is Professor of Business Information Systems and the Director of the Laboratory of Enterprise Resources, which he established in 2004, of the Alexander Technological Educational Institute (ATEI) of Thessaloniki, Greece. Dr Stefanou teaches Enterprise Resource Planning and has supervised a large number of students' theses at both undergraduate and postgraduate levels as well as several PhD dissertations. He publishes, speaks at conferences and seminars and co-edited special issue journals in the area of ERP and Business Software. He has authored four books on Business Software Applications, ERP (SAP R/3) Systems, Enterprise Systems, and Financial Analysis using Excel. He has been on the editorial boards of international journals and currently joins the editorial board of the International Journal of Accounting Information Systems. He is the chair of the Organizing Committee of the International Conference on Enterprise Systems, Accounting and Logistics (ICESAL) (www.icesal.org).

**Mirjana D. Stojanovic** received her B.Sc. (1985) and M.Sc. (1993) degrees in Electrical Engineering and her Ph.D. degree (2005) in technical sciences, all from the University of Belgrade, Serbia. Dr. Stojanovic has been with the Mihailo Pupin Institute in Belgrade from 1985 to 2010, where she managed or participated in development of a number of communication devices and systems for data and voice transmission and network management, which were successfully applied in major Serbian corporate systems. As author or coauthor, she published more than 85 papers in national and international journals, books and conferences. She is currently assistant professor in networking at the University of Belgrade, Faculty of Transport and Traffic Engineering and Faculty of Electrical Engineering. Her research interests include security solutions, QoS and traffic engineering in NGN, as well as service and network management.

**Torben Tambo,** MSc, GDBA, is Associate Professor of Aarhus University, Institute of Business and Technology, and has previously worked 17 years worked with management and information technology in manufacturing, supply chain and retailing enterprises. His research interests include information technology, supply chain management, fashion, retailing, e-commerce, and business – technology inter-relationships. Research has been published in Journal of Enterprise Architecture, Journal of Economic Dynamics and Control, International Association for Management of Technology, International Conference of Information Systems – Logistics – Supply Chain. Torben Tambo is a graduate in IT and organisation from Technical University of Denmark (1989).

**Asterio Tanaka** is Professor of Database and Information Systems in the School of Applied Informatics at UNIRIO (Federal University of the State of Rio de Janeiro). He is also the Director of Planning at UNIRIO, where he currently works on IT Governance and Strategic Planning. He has worked in the IT industry as a consultant while teaching in the academy for over 30 years. As a researcher, he has collaborated in international projects with European, Asian, North American and Latin American partners, and published two books and more than forty refereed articles. He currently participates in a research group on Distributed Information Integration in Brazil, with more than twenty researchers. He received his BS in Civil Engineering and MS in Systems Engineering from the Military Institute of Engineering, in Brazil, and his PhD in Computer and Information Sciences from the Georgia Institute of Technology, in the USA.

**Kris Ven** received his Ph.D. in Applied Economics from the Faculty of Applied Economics of the University of Antwerp, Belgium, in 2008. He is currently a postdoctoral researcher at the Department of Management Information Systems of the University of Antwerp. His research interests include the organizational adoption of IT and the link between innovation in organizations and the use of information technology. He has performed several studies on the organizational adoption of open source software. He has authored and presented several papers at international conferences on open source software, and has published in several academic journals, including the Journal of Database Management, Communications of the Association for Information Systems, IEEE Software and Information and Software Technology.

**Klaus Wölfel** is a PhD student at Technische Universität Dresden, Department of Business Management and Economics, Chair of Business Informatics, esp. Information Systems in Manufacturing and Commerce. He is currently writing his thesis about automating ERP package configuration and training based ERP self implementation.

# Index